SLEEPY PRINCESS IN THE DEMON CASTLE

• • • • • •

15

STORY & ART BY
KAGIJI KUMANOMATA

NIGHTS

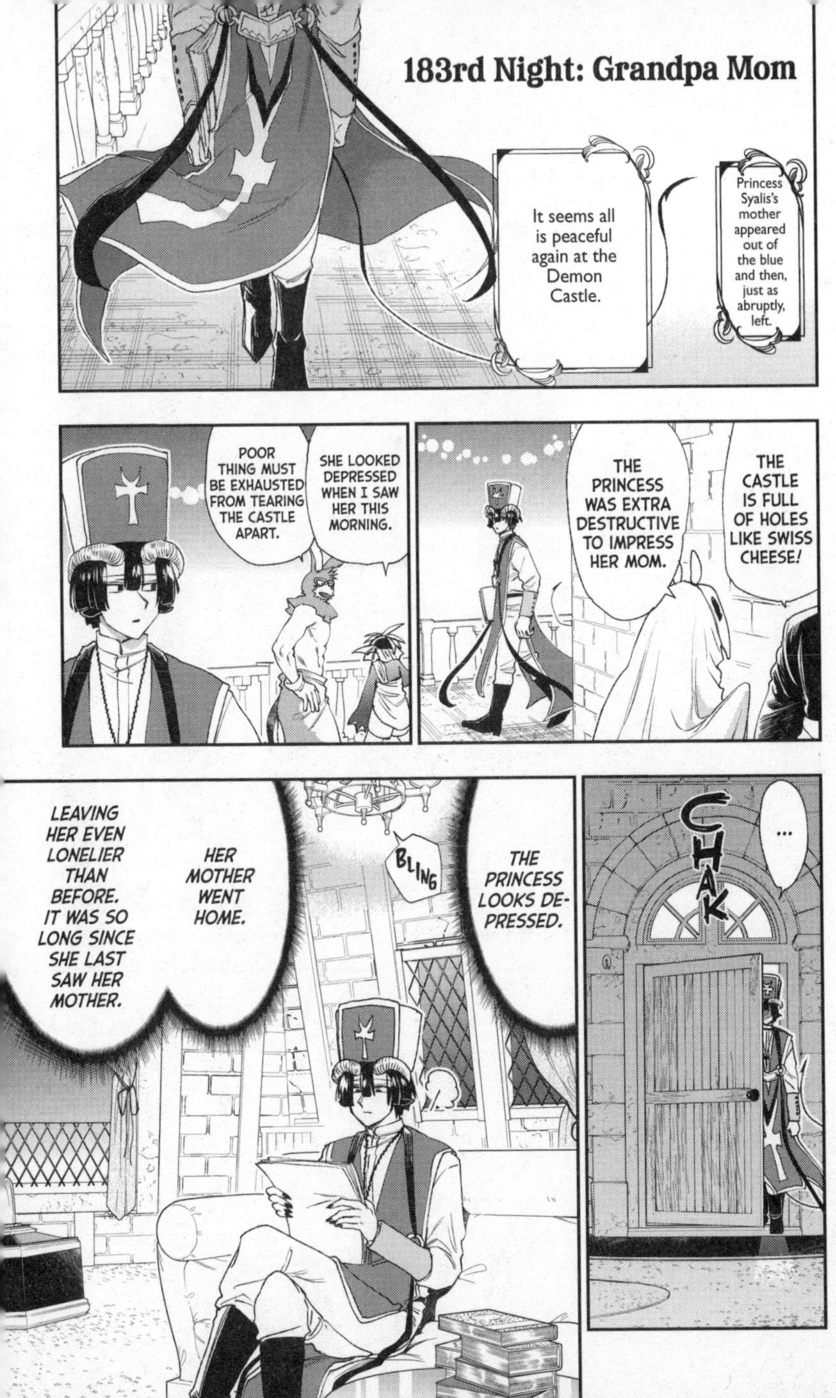
183rd Night: Grandpa Mom
Princess Syalis's mother appeared out of the blue and then, just as abruptly, left.
It seems all is peaceful again at the Demon Castle.
THE CASTLE IS FULL OF HOLES LIKE SWISS CHEESE!
THE PRINCESS WAS EXTRA DESTRUCTIVE TO IMPRESS HER MOM.
SHE LOOKED DEPRESSED WHEN I SAW HER THIS MORNING.
POOR THING MUST BE EXHAUSTED FROM TEARING THE CASTLE APART.
...
CHAK
THE PRINCESS LOOKS DE-PRESSED.
BLING
HER MOTHER WENT HOME.
LEAVING HER EVEN LONELIER THAN BEFORE. IT WAS SO LONG SINCE SHE LAST SAW HER MOTHER.

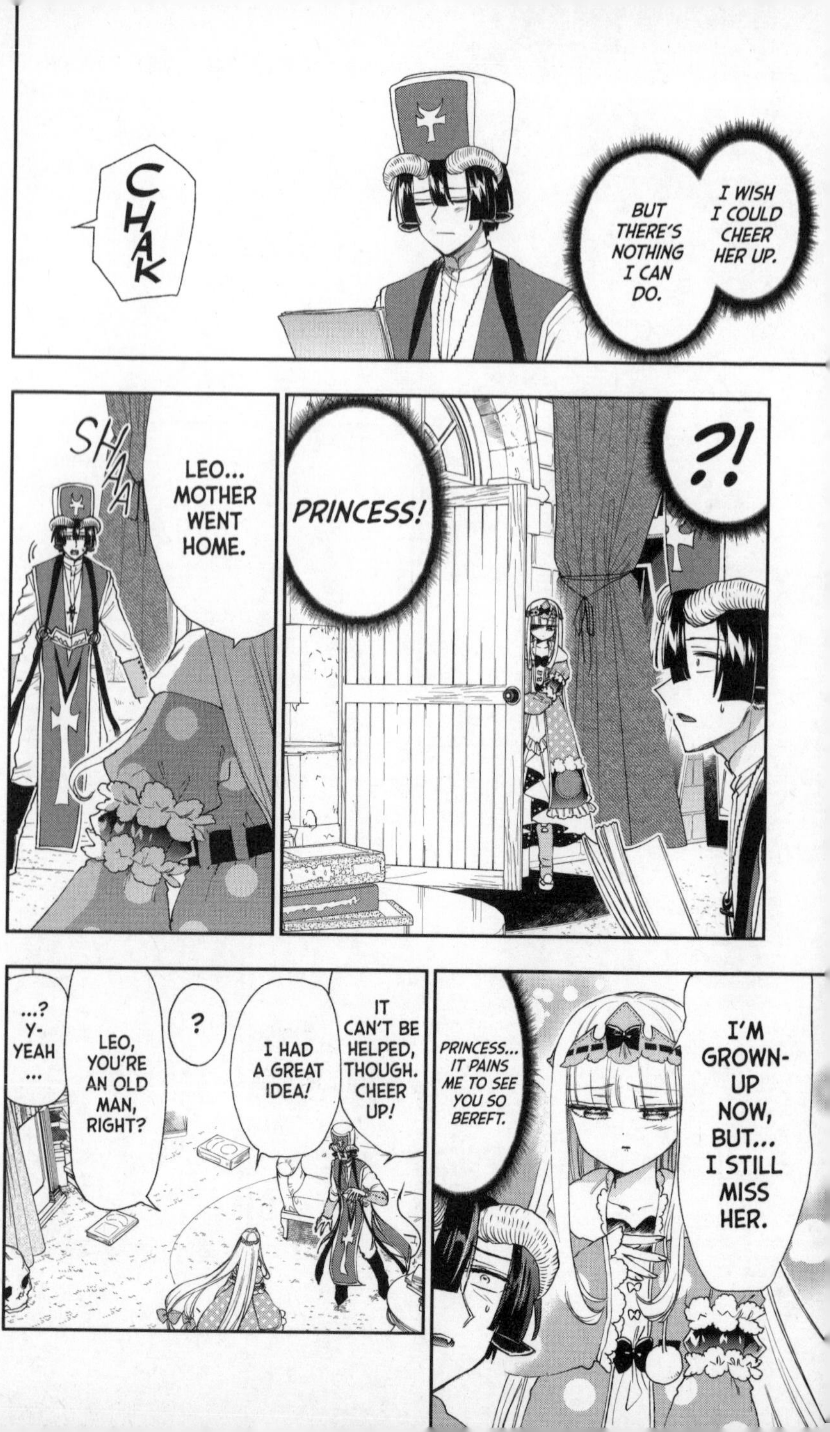
I WISH I COULD CHEER HER UP.
BUT THERE'S NOTHING I CAN DO.
CHAK
?!
PRINCESS!
SHAA
LEO... MOTHER WENT HOME.
I'M GROWN-UP NOW, BUT... I STILL MISS HER.
PRINCESS... IT PAINS ME TO SEE YOU SO BEREFT.
IT CAN'T BE HELPED, THOUGH. CHEER UP!
I HAD A GREAT IDEA!
?
LEO, YOU'RE AN OLD MAN, RIGHT?
...? Y-YEAH ...

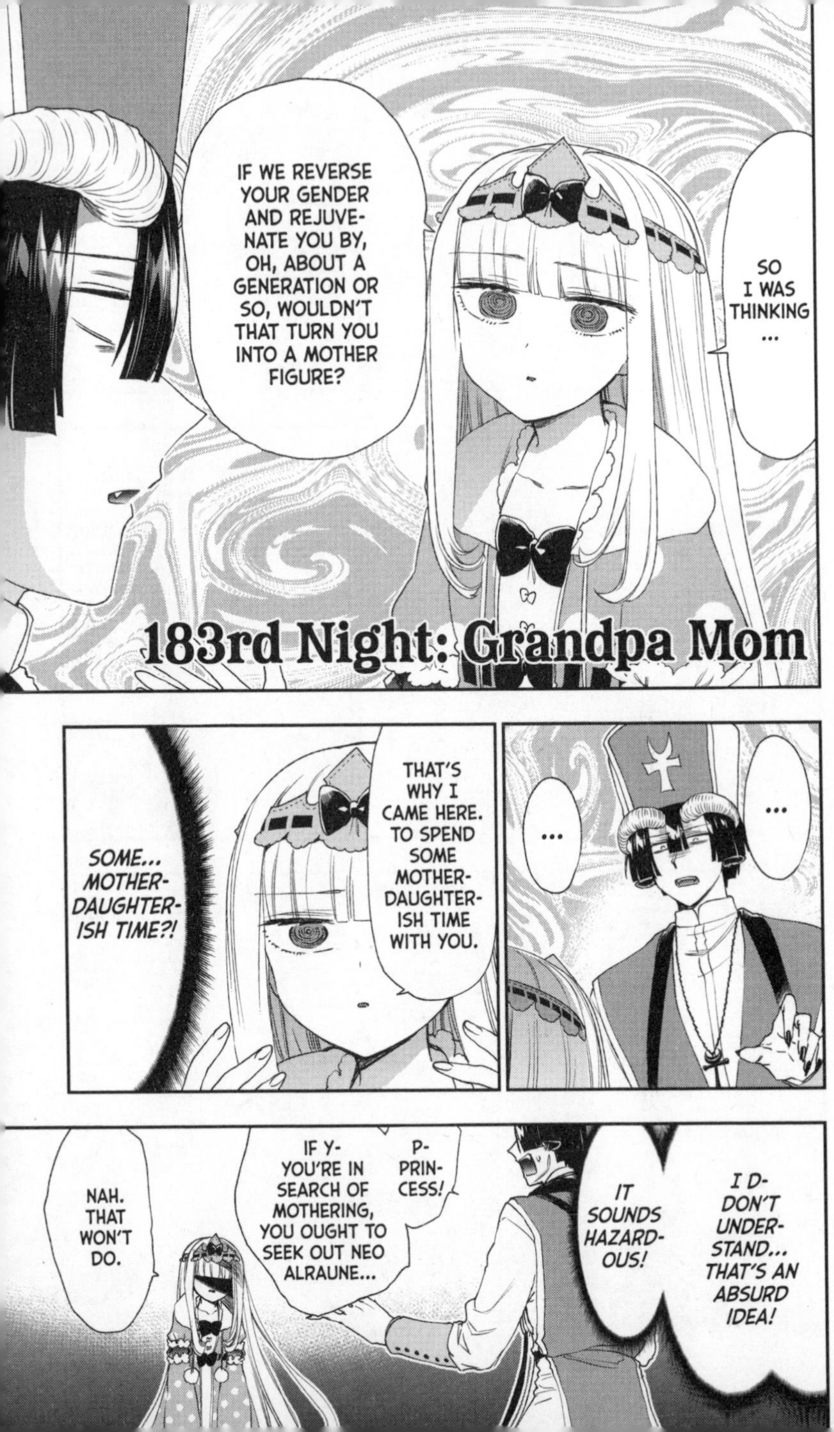
SO I WAS THINKING...
IF WE REVERSE YOUR GENDER AND REJUVENATE YOU BY, OH, ABOUT A GENERATION OR SO, WOULDN'T THAT TURN YOU INTO A MOTHER FIGURE?
183rd Night: Grandpa Mom
...
...
THAT'S WHY I CAME HERE. TO SPEND SOME MOTHER-DAUGHTER-ISH TIME WITH YOU.
SOME... MOTHER-DAUGHTER-ISH TIME?!
I D-DON'T UNDERSTAND... THAT'S AN ABSURD IDEA!
IT SOUNDS HAZARDOUS!
P-PRINCESS!
IF Y-YOU'RE IN SEARCH OF MOTHERING, YOU OUGHT TO SEEK OUT NEO ALRAUNE...
NAH. THAT WON'T DO.

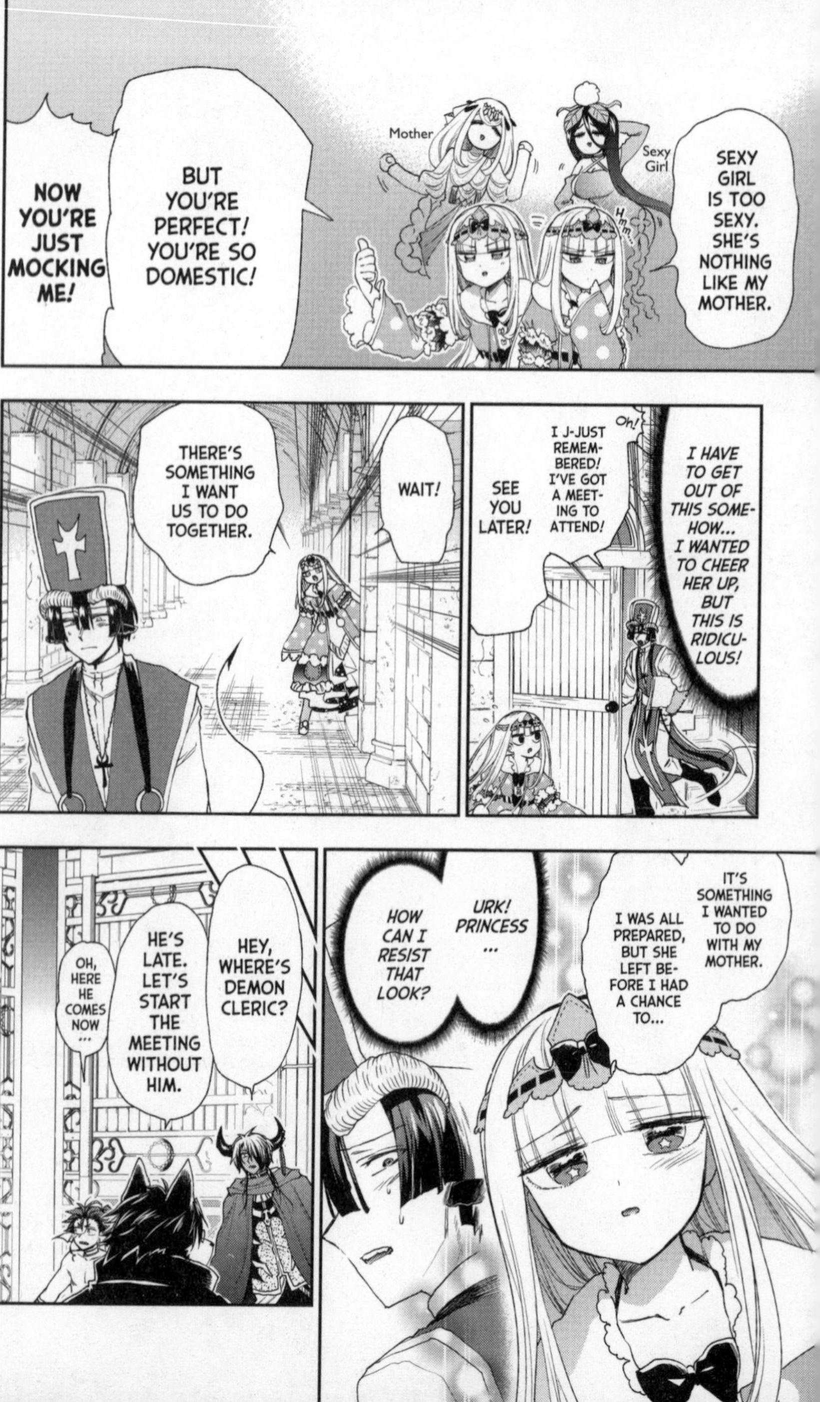
SEXY GIRL IS TOO SEXY. SHE'S NOTHING LIKE MY MOTHER.
Sexy Girl
Hmm...
Mother
BUT YOU'RE PERFECT! YOU'RE SO DOMESTIC!
NOW YOU'RE JUST MOCKING ME!
I HAVE TO GET OUT OF THIS SOMEHOW... I WANTED TO CHEER HER UP, BUT THIS IS RIDICULOUS!
Oh!
I J-JUST REMEMBERED! I'VE GOT A MEETING TO ATTEND!
SEE YOU LATER!
WAIT!
THERE'S SOMETHING I WANT US TO DO TOGETHER.
IT'S SOMETHING I WANTED TO DO WITH MY MOTHER.
I WAS ALL PREPARED, BUT SHE LEFT BEFORE I HAD A CHANCE TO...
URK! PRINCESS...
HOW CAN I RESIST THAT LOOK?
HEY, WHERE'S DEMON CLERIC?
HE'S LATE. LET'S START THE MEETING WITHOUT HIM.
OH, HERE HE COMES NOW...

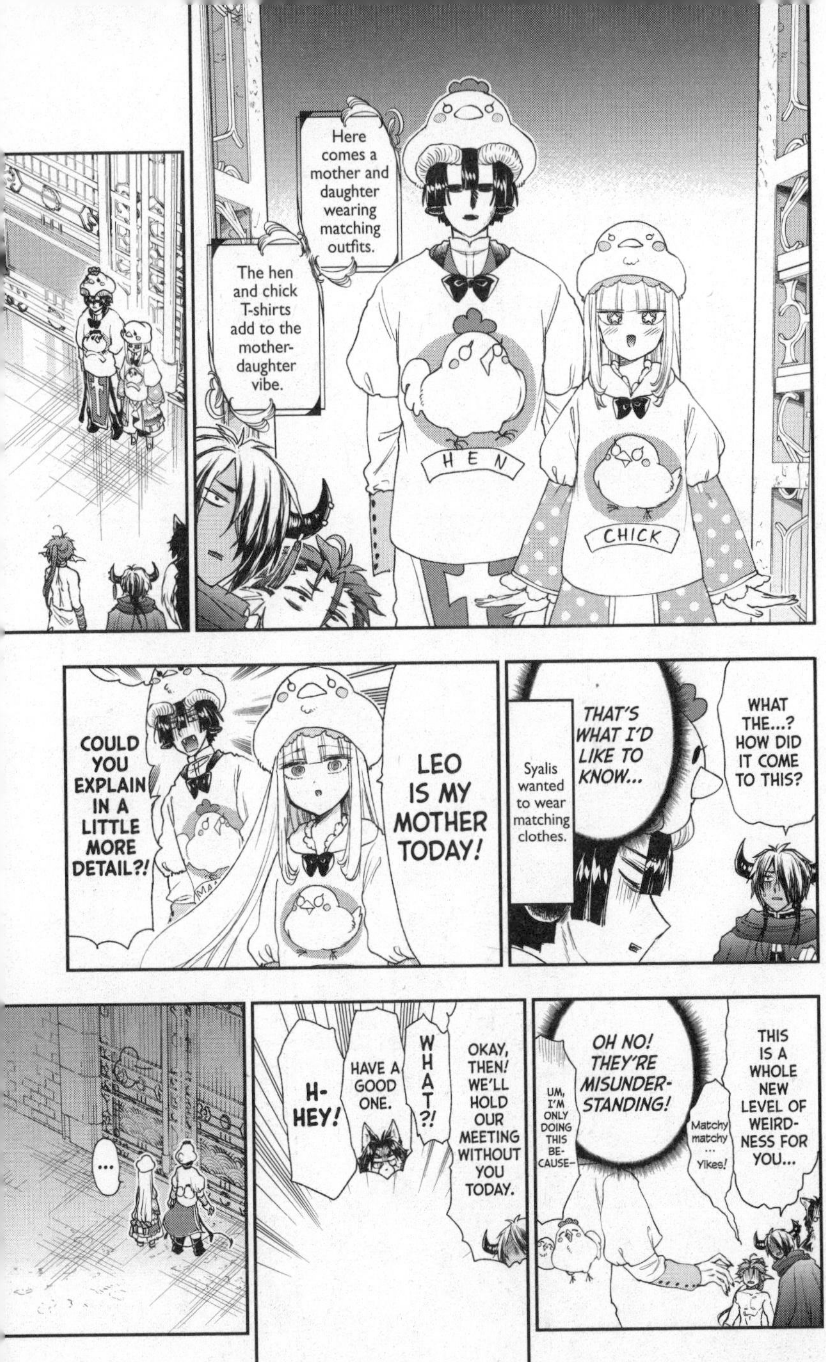
Here comes a mother and daughter wearing matching outfits.
The hen and chick T-shirts add to the mother-daughter vibe.
HEN
CHICK
WHAT THE...? HOW DID IT COME TO THIS?
THAT'S WHAT I'D LIKE TO KNOW...
Syalis wanted to wear matching clothes.
LEO IS MY MOTHER TODAY!
COULD YOU EXPLAIN IN A LITTLE MORE DETAIL?!
THIS IS A WHOLE NEW LEVEL OF WEIRDNESS FOR YOU...
Matchy matchy... Yikes!
OH NO! THEY'RE MISUNDERSTANDING!
UM, I'M ONLY DOING THIS BECAUSE—
OKAY, THEN! WE'LL HOLD OUR MEETING WITHOUT YOU TODAY.
WHAT?!
HAVE A GOOD ONE.
H-HEY!
...

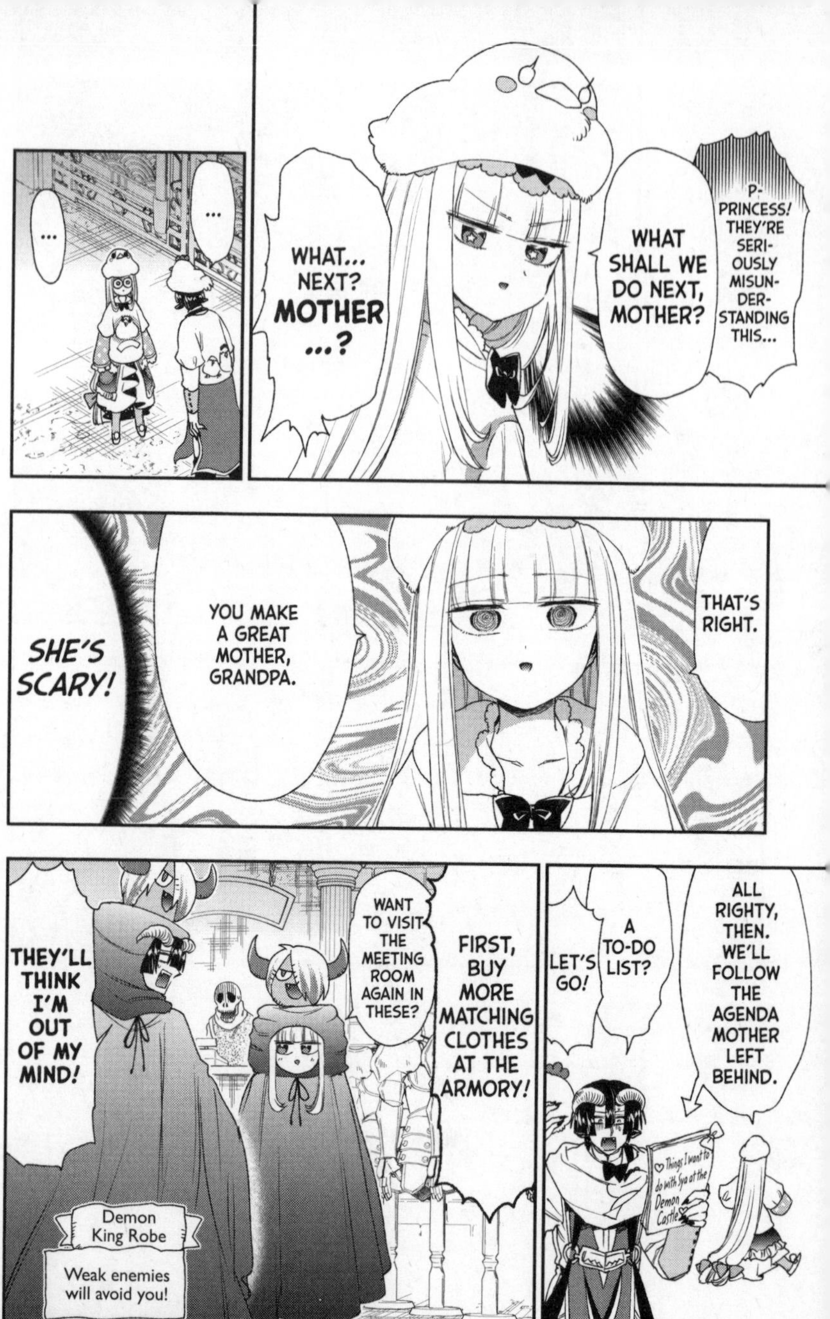
P-PRINCESS! THEY'RE SERIOUSLY MISUNDERSTANDING THIS...
WHAT SHALL WE DO NEXT, MOTHER?
WHAT... NEXT? MOTHER ...?
...
...
THAT'S RIGHT.
YOU MAKE A GREAT MOTHER, GRANDPA.
SHE'S SCARY!
ALL RIGHTY, THEN. WE'LL FOLLOW THE AGENDA MOTHER LEFT BEHIND.
A TO-DO LIST?
LET'S GO!
Things I want to do with Sya at the Demon Castle
FIRST, BUY MORE MATCHING CLOTHES AT THE ARMORY!
WANT TO VISIT THE MEETING ROOM AGAIN IN THESE?
THEY'LL THINK I'M OUT OF MY MIND!
Demon King Robe
Weak enemies will avoid you!

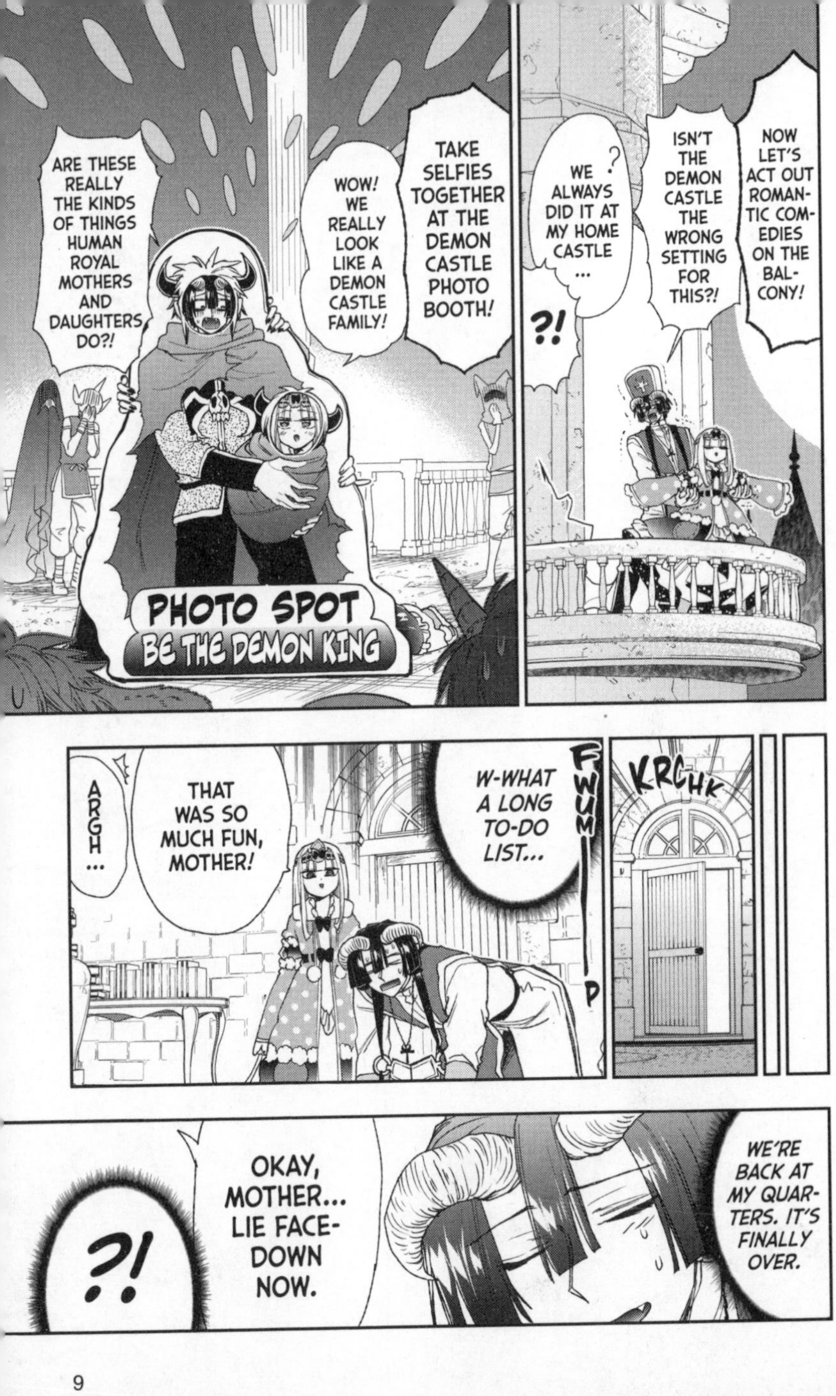
NOW LET'S ACT OUT ROMANTIC COMEDIES ON THE BALCONY!
ISN'T THE DEMON CASTLE THE WRONG SETTING FOR THIS?!
WE ALWAYS DID IT AT MY HOME CASTLE ...
?!
TAKE SELFIES TOGETHER AT THE DEMON CASTLE PHOTO BOOTH!
WOW! WE REALLY LOOK LIKE A DEMON CASTLE FAMILY!
ARE THESE REALLY THE KINDS OF THINGS HUMAN ROYAL MOTHERS AND DAUGHTERS DO?!
PHOTO SPOT
BE THE DEMON KING
KRCHK
FWUMP
W-WHAT A LONG TO-DO LIST...
THAT WAS SO MUCH FUN, MOTHER!
ARGH...
WE'RE BACK AT MY QUARTERS. IT'S FINALLY OVER.
OKAY, MOTHER... LIE FACE-DOWN NOW.
?!

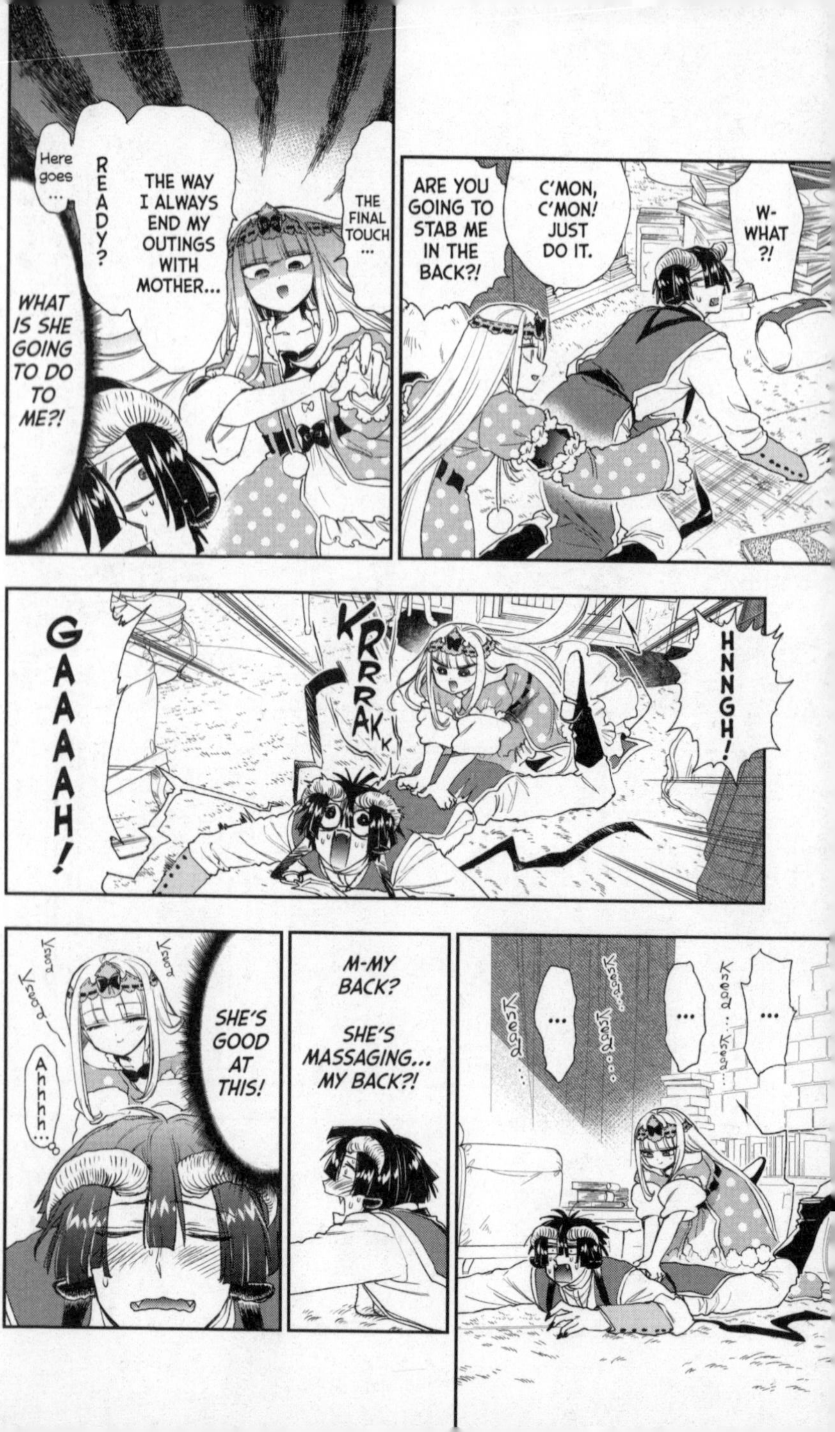
W-WHAT?!
C'MON, C'MON! JUST DO IT.
ARE YOU GOING TO STAB ME IN THE BACK?!
THE FINAL TOUCH...
THE WAY I ALWAYS END MY OUTINGS WITH MOTHER...
READY?
Here goes...
WHAT IS SHE GOING TO DO TO ME?!
HNNGH!
KRRRAKK
GAAAAAH!
...
Knead... Knead...
...
Knead... Knead...
...
Knead...
M-MY BACK?
SHE'S MASSAGING... MY BACK?!
Knead
SHE'S GOOD AT THIS!
Knead
Ahhhh...

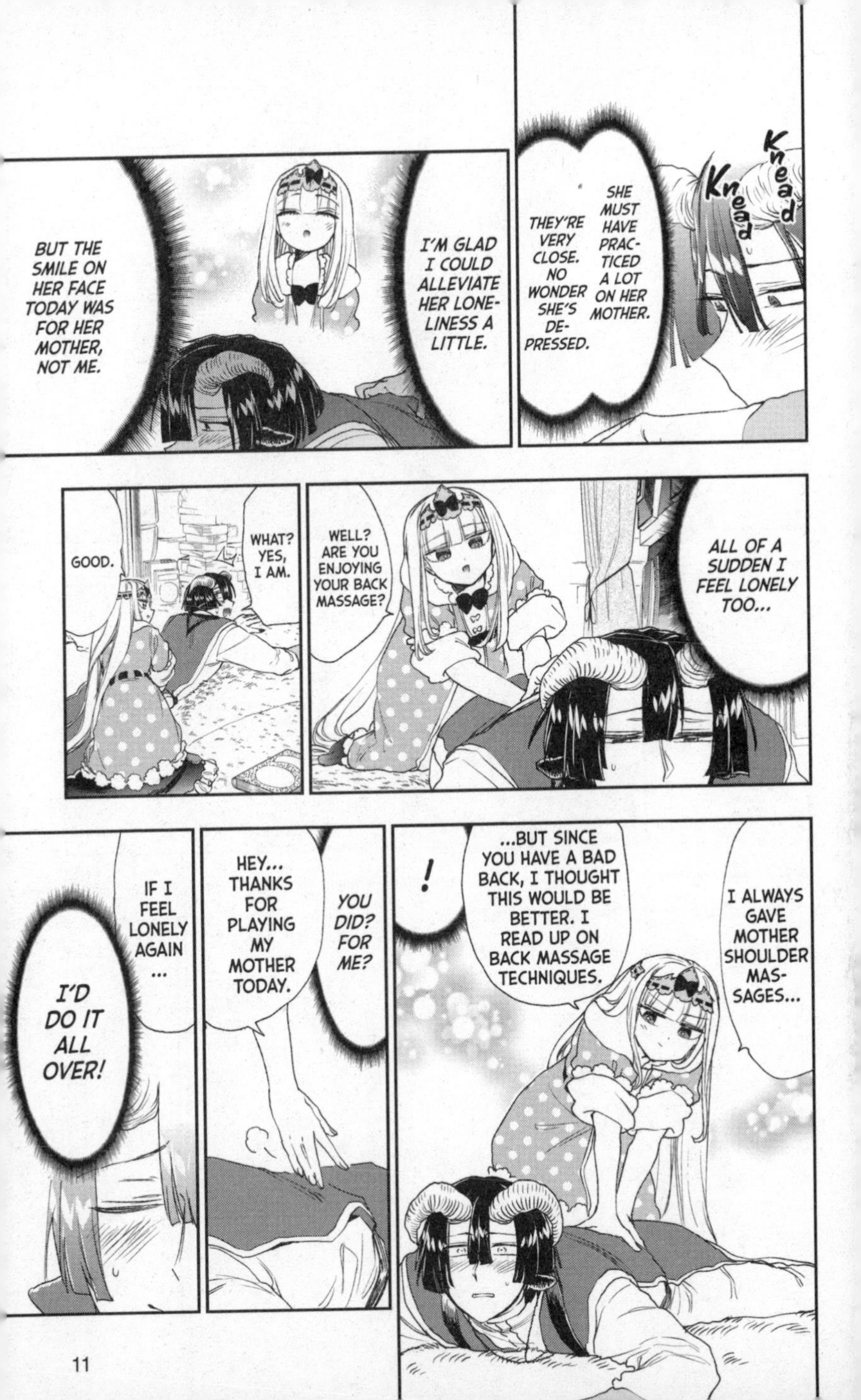
Knead Knead
SHE MUST HAVE PRAC-TICED A LOT ON HER MOTHER.
THEY'RE VERY CLOSE. NO WONDER SHE'S DE-PRESSED.
I'M GLAD I COULD ALLEVIATE HER LONE-LINESS A LITTLE.
BUT THE SMILE ON HER FACE TODAY WAS FOR HER MOTHER, NOT ME.
ALL OF A SUDDEN I FEEL LONELY TOO...
WELL? ARE YOU ENJOYING YOUR BACK MASSAGE?
WHAT? YES, I AM.
GOOD.
I ALWAYS GAVE MOTHER SHOULDER MAS-SAGES...
...BUT SINCE YOU HAVE A BAD BACK, I THOUGHT THIS WOULD BE BETTER. I READ UP ON BACK MASSAGE TECHNIQUES.
!
YOU DID? FOR ME?
HEY... THANKS FOR PLAYING MY MOTHER TODAY.
IF I FEEL LONELY AGAIN ...
I'D DO IT ALL OVER!

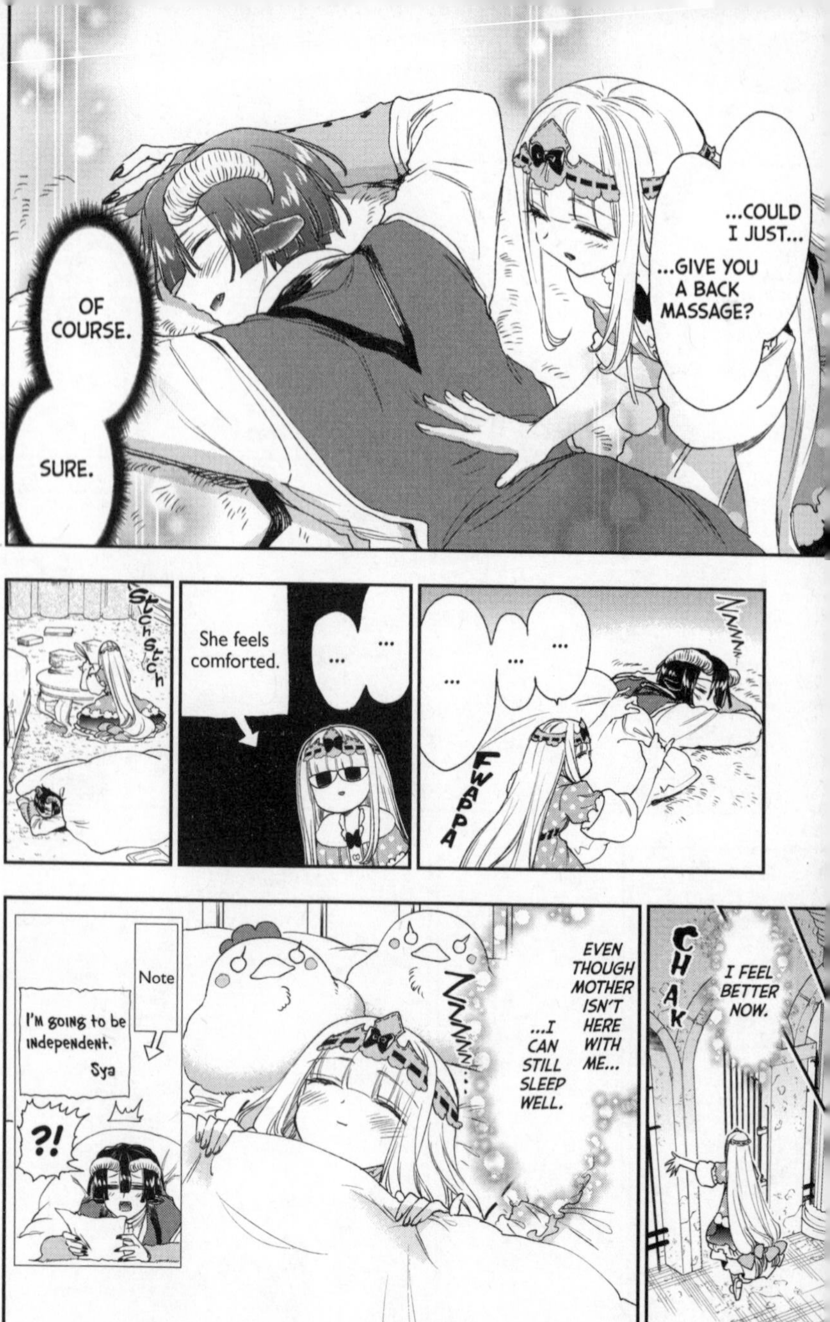
...COULD I JUST...
...GIVE YOU A BACK MASSAGE?
OF COURSE.
SURE.
ZZZZ...
...
...
...
FWAPPA
...
...
She feels comforted.
STCHSTCH
CHAK
I FEEL BETTER NOW.
EVEN THOUGH MOTHER ISN'T HERE WITH ME...
...I CAN STILL SLEEP WELL.
ZZZZZ...
Note
I'm going to be independent.
Sya
?!

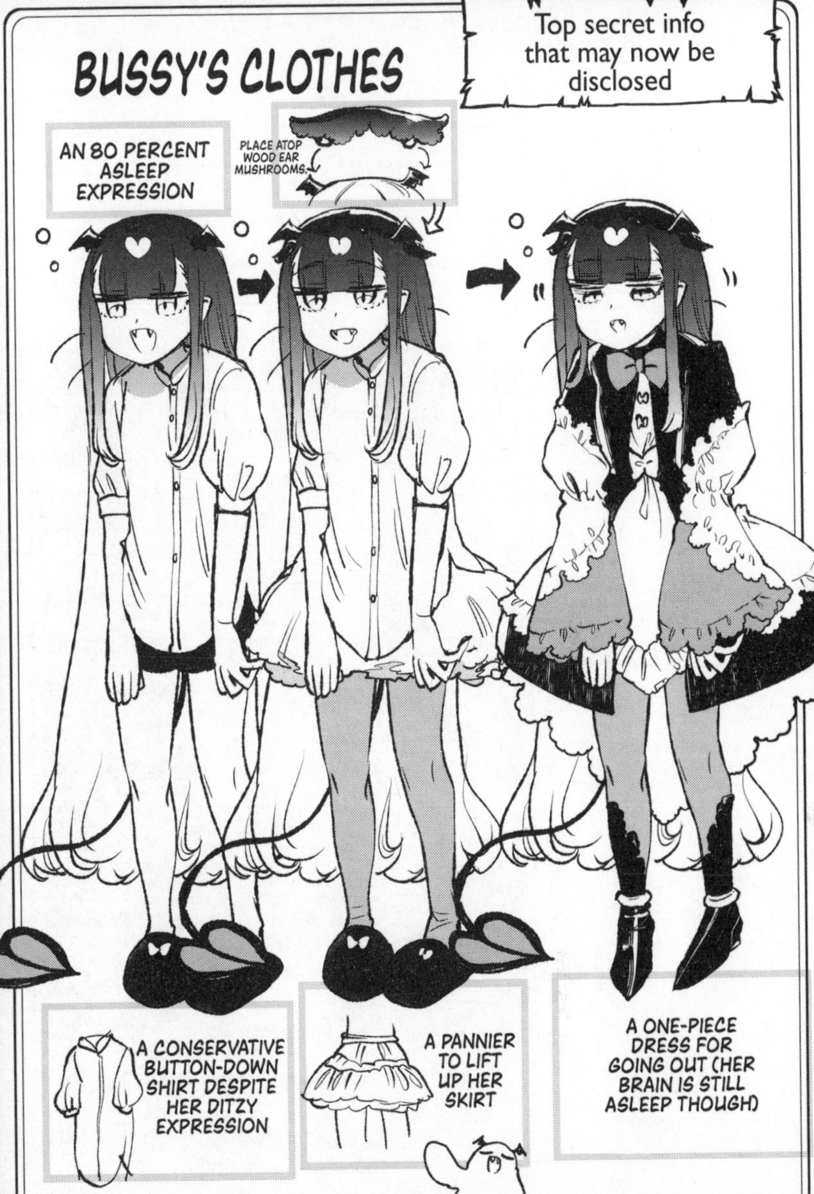
Top secret info that may now be disclosed
BUSSY'S CLOTHES
AN 80 PERCENT ASLEEP EXPRESSION
PLACE ATOP WOOD EAR MUSHROOMS.
A CONSERVATIVE BUTTON-DOWN SHIRT DESPITE HER DITZY EXPRESSION
A PANNIER TO LIFT UP HER SKIRT
A ONE-PIECE DRESS FOR GOING OUT (HER BRAIN IS STILL ASLEEP THOUGH)

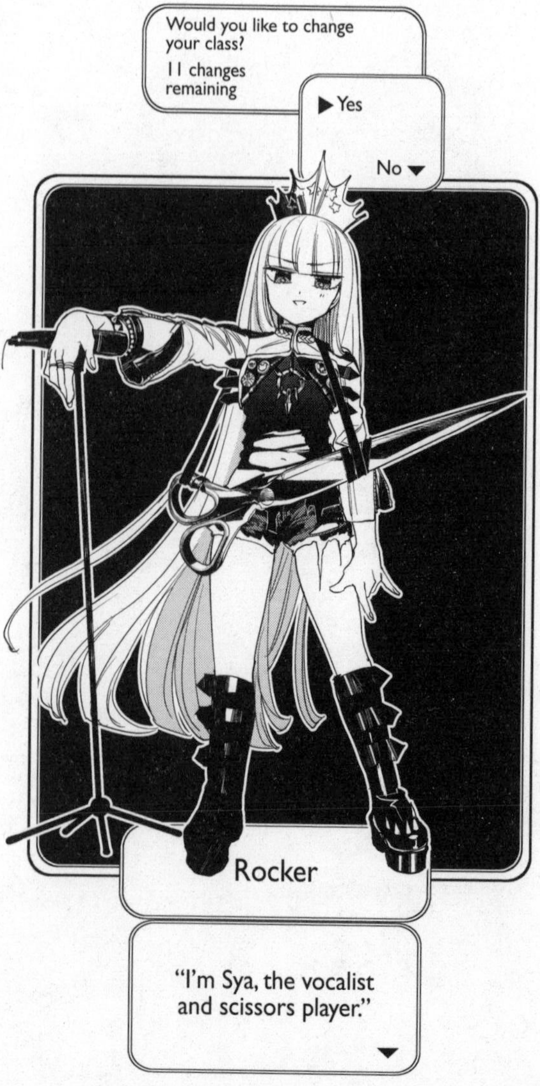
Would you like to change your class?
11 changes remaining
▶Yes
No
Rocker
"I'm Sya, the vocalist and scissors player."

184th Night: Even the Darkest Night Comes to an End

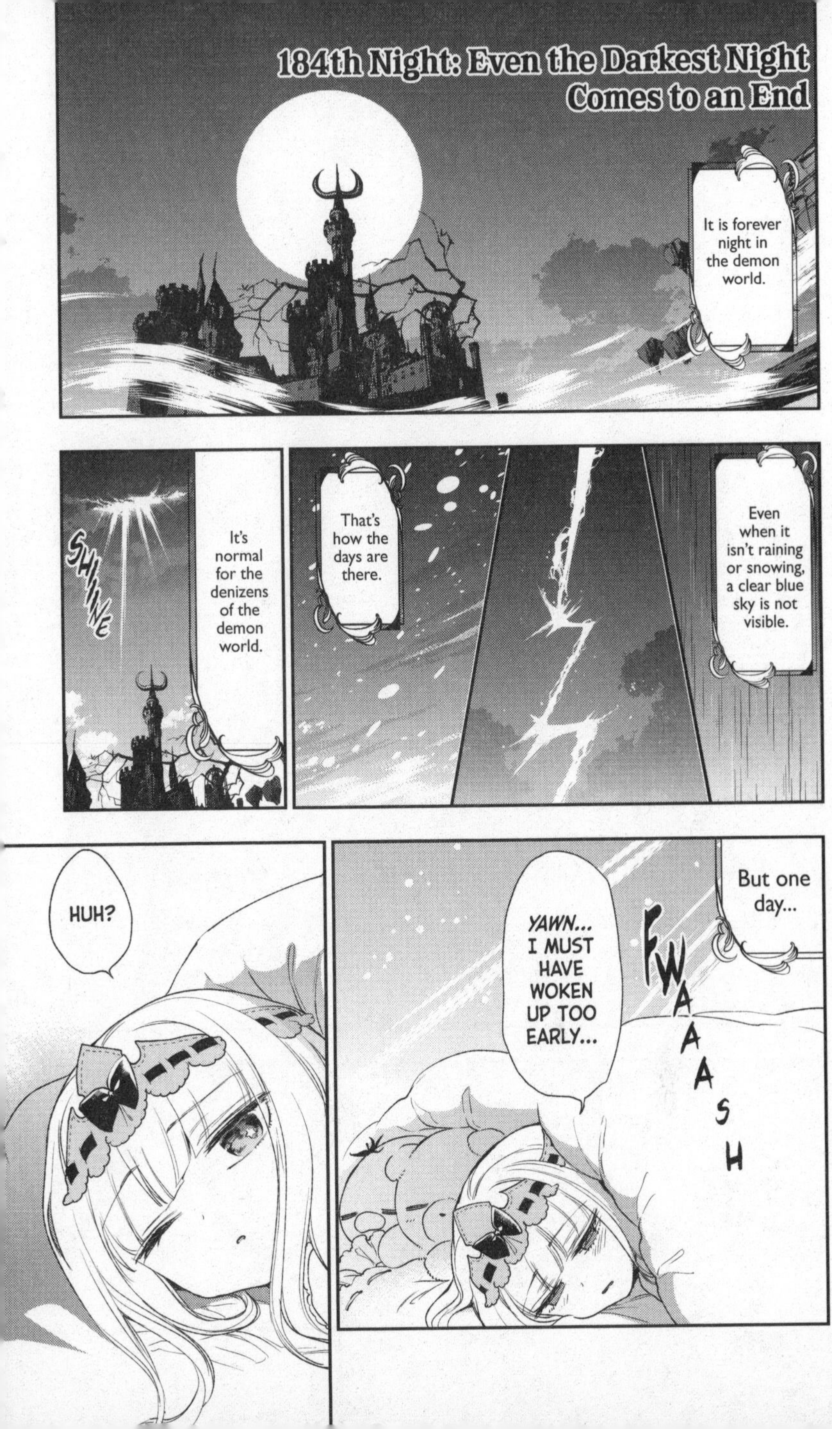
It is forever night in the demon world.
Even when it isn't raining or snowing, a clear blue sky is not visible.
That's how the days are there.
It's normal for the denizens of the demon world.
SHINE
But one day...
FWAAASH
YAWN... I MUST HAVE WOKEN UP TOO EARLY...
HUH?

184th Night: Even the Darkest Night Comes to an End

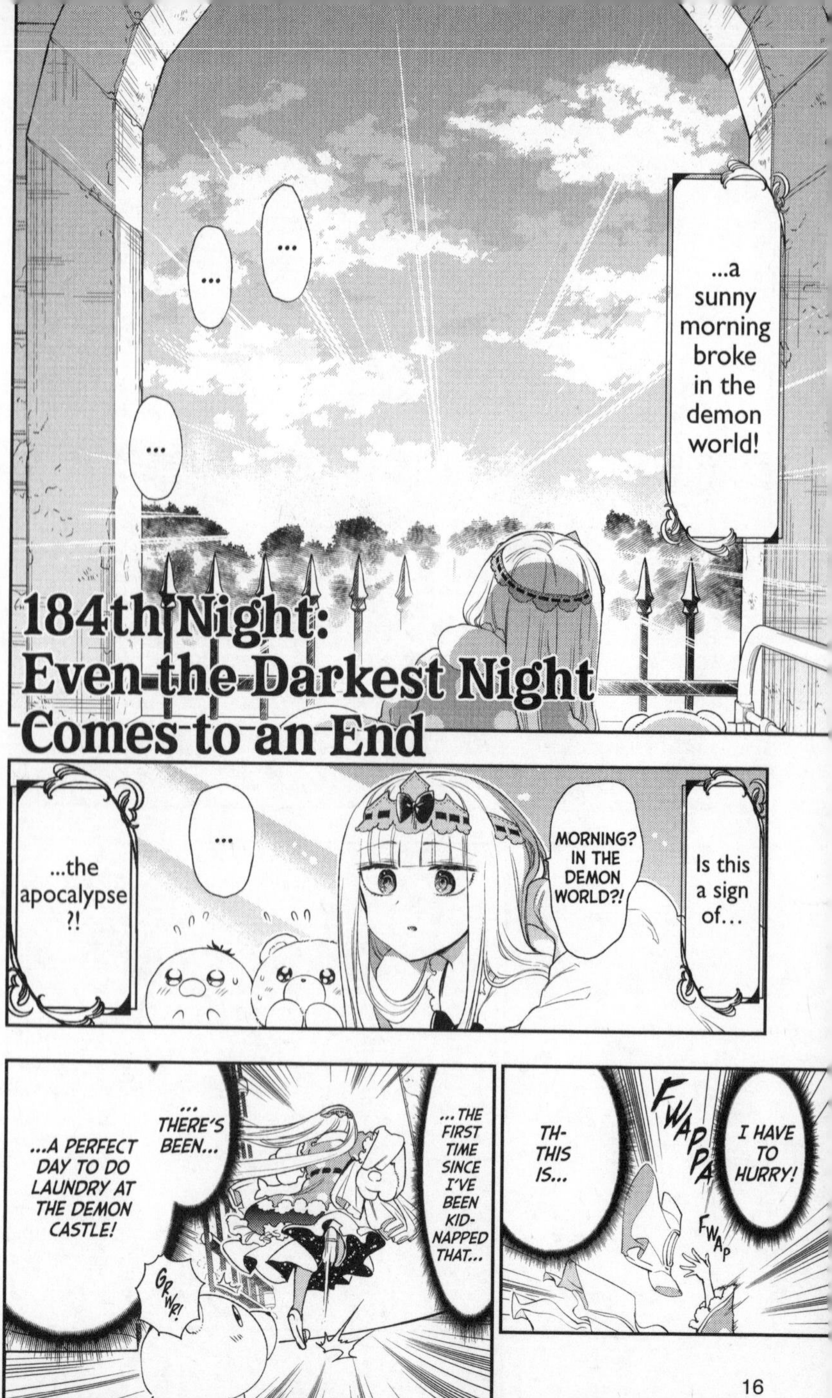
...a sunny morning broke in the demon world!
...
...
...
Is this a sign of…
MORNING? IN THE DEMON WORLD?!
...
...the apocalypse ?!
I HAVE TO HURRY!
FWAPPA
TH-THIS IS...
FWAP
...THE FIRST TIME SINCE I'VE BEEN KID-NAPPED THAT...
...THERE'S BEEN...
...A PERFECT DAY TO DO LAUNDRY AT THE DEMON CASTLE!
GRWR!

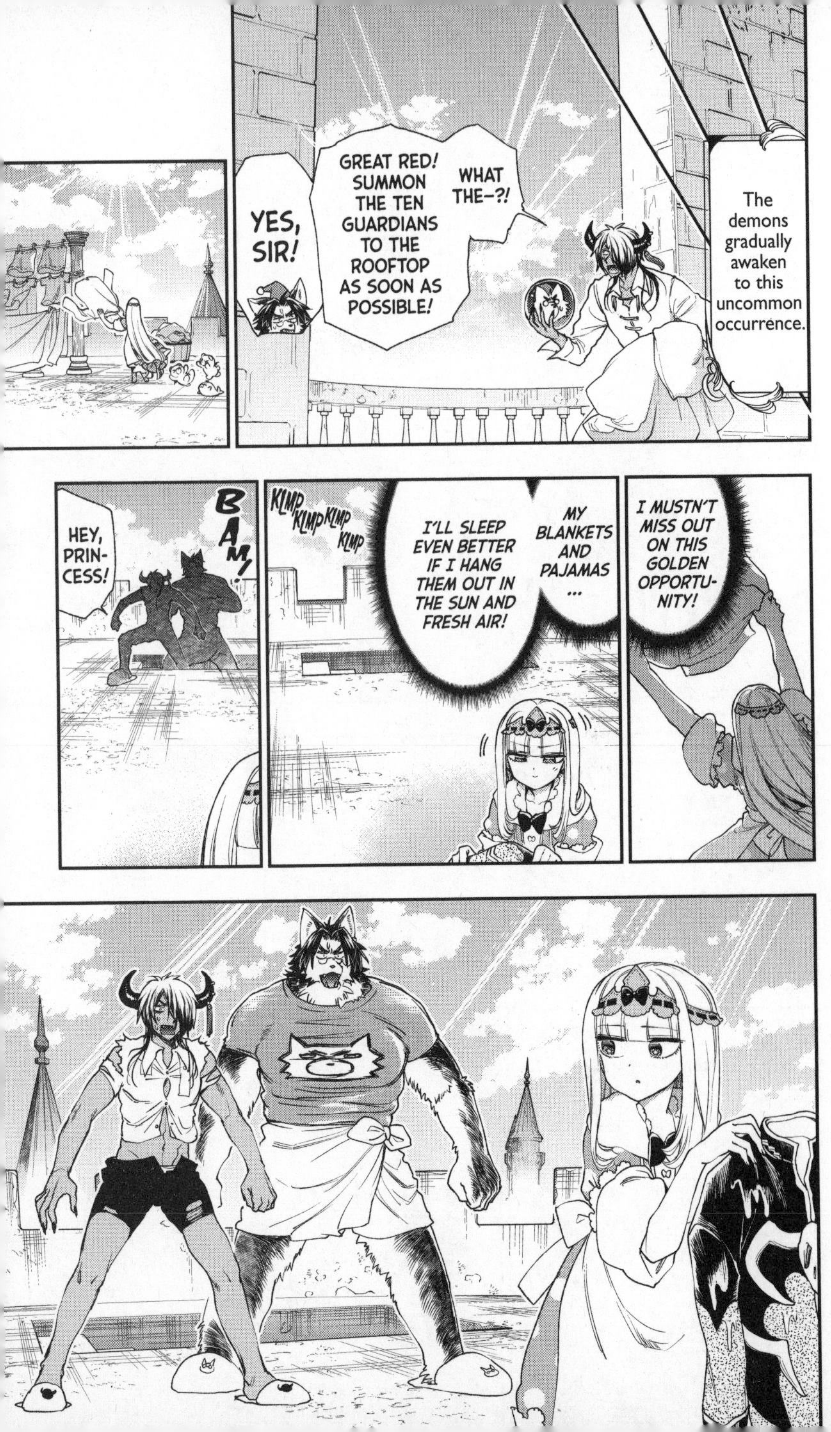
The demons gradually awaken to this uncommon occurrence.
WHAT THE–?!
GREAT RED! SUMMON THE TEN GUARDIANS TO THE ROOFTOP AS SOON AS POSSIBLE!
YES, SIR!
I MUSTN'T MISS OUT ON THIS GOLDEN OPPORTU-NITY!
MY BLANKETS AND PAJAMAS ...
I'LL SLEEP EVEN BETTER IF I HANG THEM OUT IN THE SUN AND FRESH AIR!
KLMP KLMP KLMP KLMP
BAM!
HEY, PRINCESS!

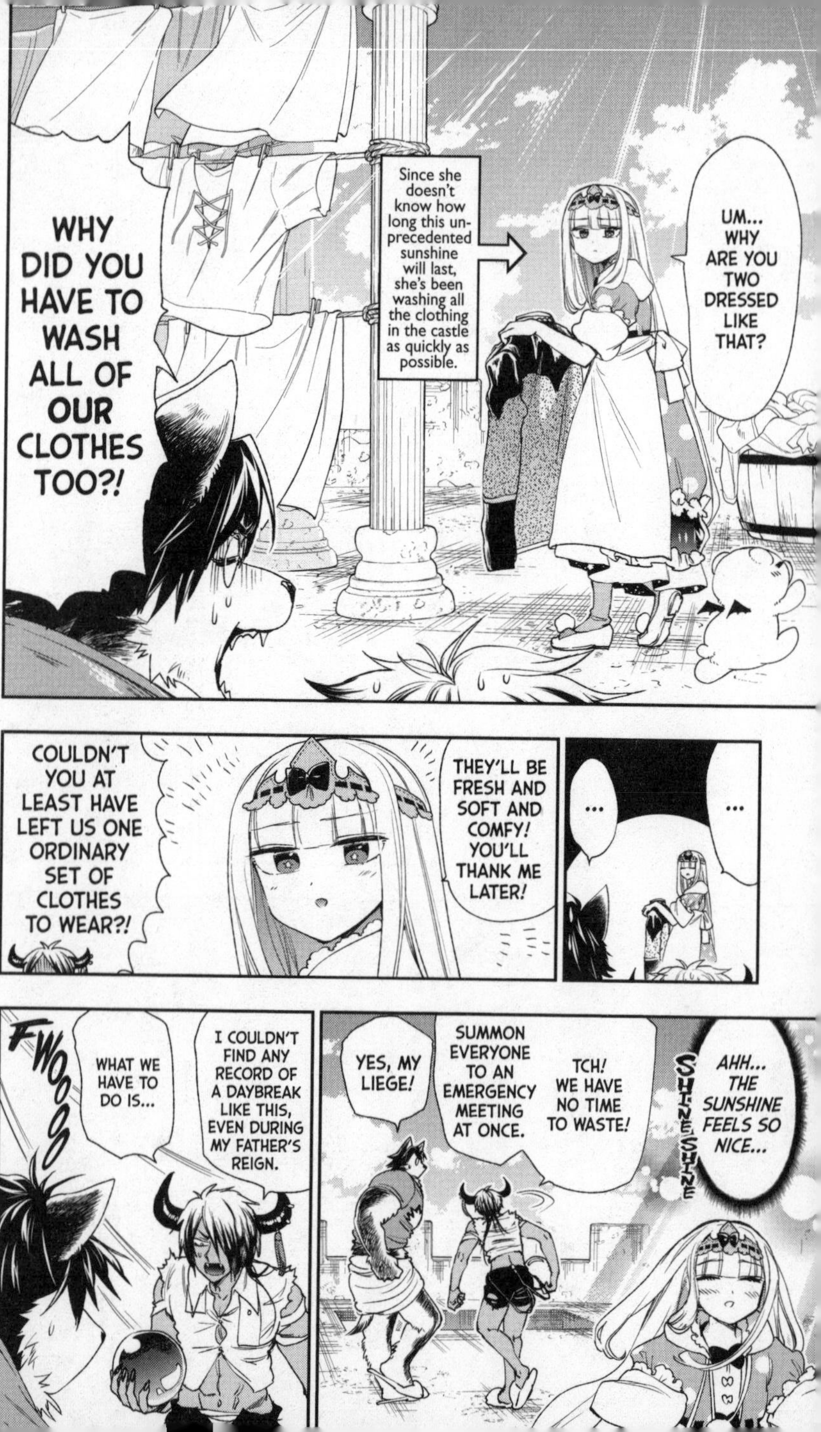
UM... WHY ARE YOU TWO DRESSED LIKE THAT?
Since she doesn't know how long this unprecedented sunshine will last, she's been washing all the clothing in the castle as quickly as possible.
WHY DID YOU HAVE TO WASH ALL OF OUR CLOTHES TOO?!
...
...
THEY'LL BE FRESH AND SOFT AND COMFY! YOU'LL THANK ME LATER!
COULDN'T YOU AT LEAST HAVE LEFT US ONE ORDINARY SET OF CLOTHES TO WEAR?!
AHH... THE SUNSHINE FEELS SO NICE...
SHINE SHINE
TCH! WE HAVE NO TIME TO WASTE!
SUMMON EVERYONE TO AN EMERGENCY MEETING AT ONCE.
YES, MY LIEGE!
I COULDN'T FIND ANY RECORD OF A DAYBREAK LIKE THIS, EVEN DURING MY FATHER'S REIGN.
WHAT WE HAVE TO DO IS...
FWOOOO

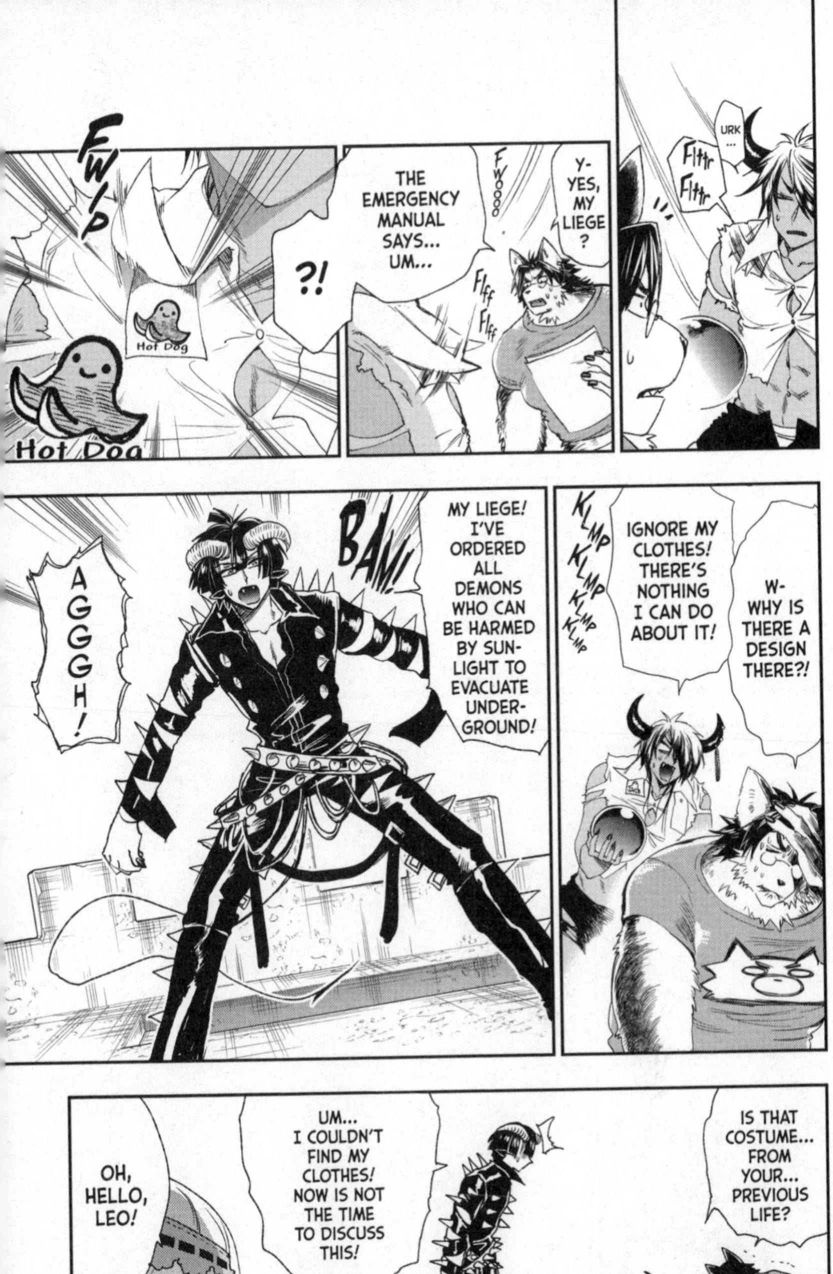
URK...
Flttr Flttr
Y- YES, MY LIEGE?
FWOOOO
THE EMERGENCY MANUAL SAYS... UM...
?!
Flff Flff
FWIP
Hot Dog
Hot Dog
W- WHY IS THERE A DESIGN THERE?!
IGNORE MY CLOTHES! THERE'S NOTHING I CAN DO ABOUT IT!
KLMP KLMP KLMP KLMP KLMP
MY LIEGE! I'VE ORDERED ALL DEMONS WHO CAN BE HARMED BY SUN-LIGHT TO EVACUATE UNDER-GROUND!
BAM!
AGGGH!
IS THAT COSTUME... FROM YOUR... PREVIOUS LIFE?
UM... I COULDN'T FIND MY CLOTHES! NOW IS NOT THE TIME TO DISCUSS THIS!
OH, HELLO, LEO!

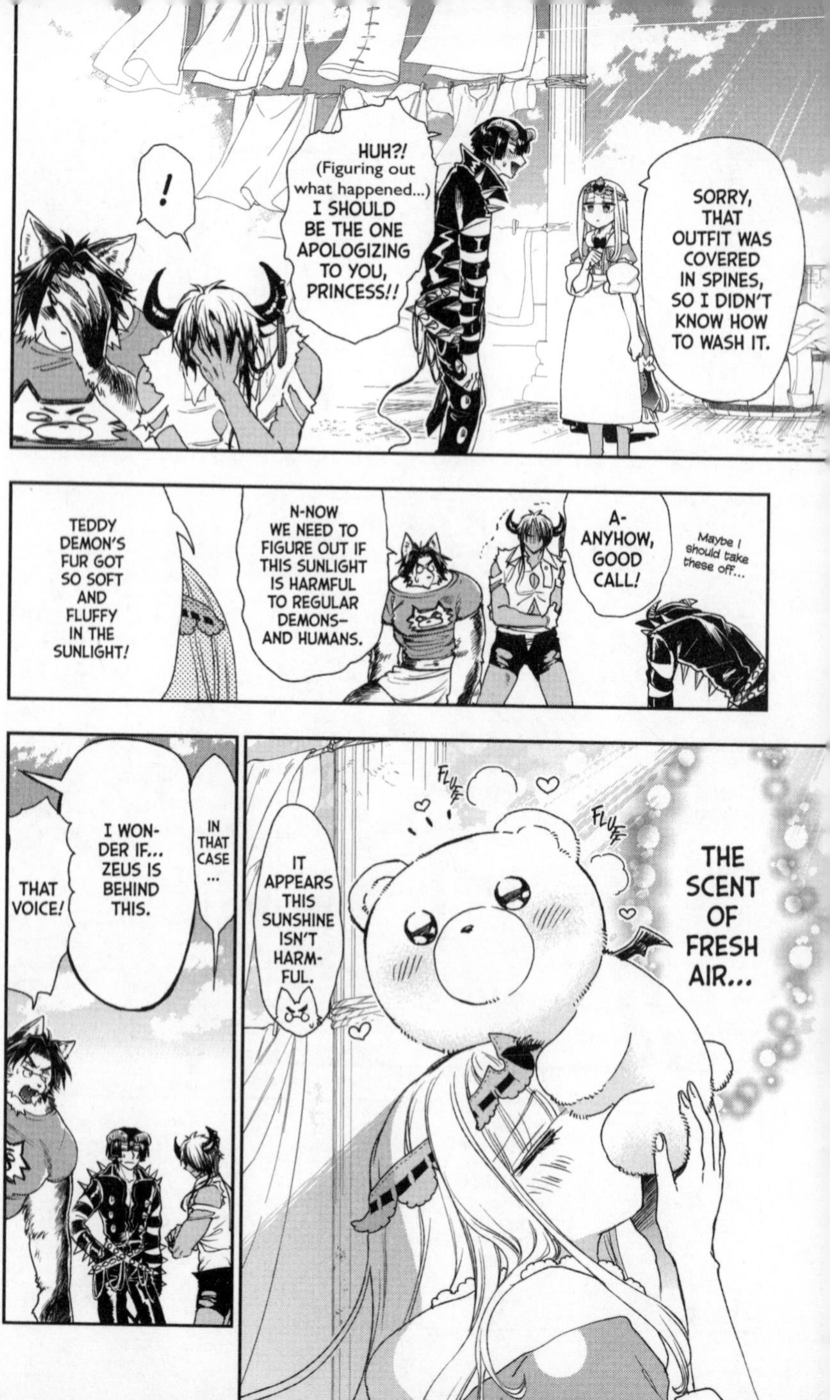
SORRY, THAT OUTFIT WAS COVERED IN SPINES, SO I DIDN'T KNOW HOW TO WASH IT.
HUH?! (Figuring out what happened...) I SHOULD BE THE ONE APOLOGIZING TO YOU, PRINCESS!!
!
Maybe I should take these off...
A-ANYHOW, GOOD CALL!
N-NOW WE NEED TO FIGURE OUT IF THIS SUNLIGHT IS HARMFUL TO REGULAR DEMONS—AND HUMANS.
TEDDY DEMON'S FUR GOT SO SOFT AND FLUFFY IN THE SUNLIGHT!
THE SCENT OF FRESH AIR...
FLUFF
FLUFF
IT APPEARS THIS SUNSHINE ISN'T HARMFUL.
IN THAT CASE...
I WONDER IF... ZEUS IS BEHIND THIS.
THAT VOICE!

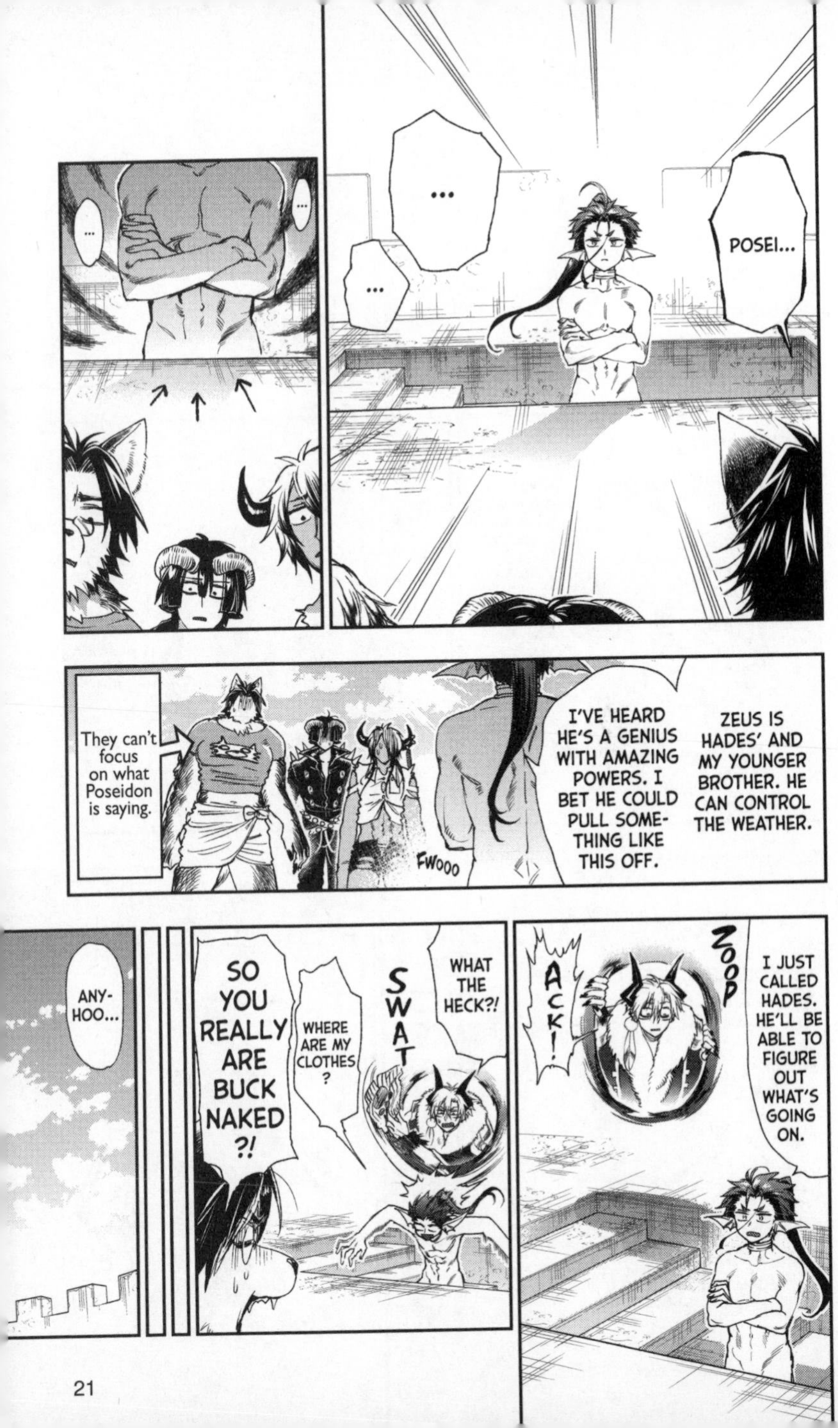
POSEI...
...
...
...
...
ZEUS IS HADES' AND MY YOUNGER BROTHER. HE CAN CONTROL THE WEATHER.
I'VE HEARD HE'S A GENIUS WITH AMAZING POWERS. I BET HE COULD PULL SOMETHING LIKE THIS OFF.
FWOOO
They can't focus on what Poseidon is saying.
I JUST CALLED HADES. HE'LL BE ABLE TO FIGURE OUT WHAT'S GOING ON.
ZOOP
ACK!
WHAT THE HECK?!
SWAT
WHERE ARE MY CLOTHES?
SO YOU REALLY ARE BUCK NAKED?!
ANY-HOO...

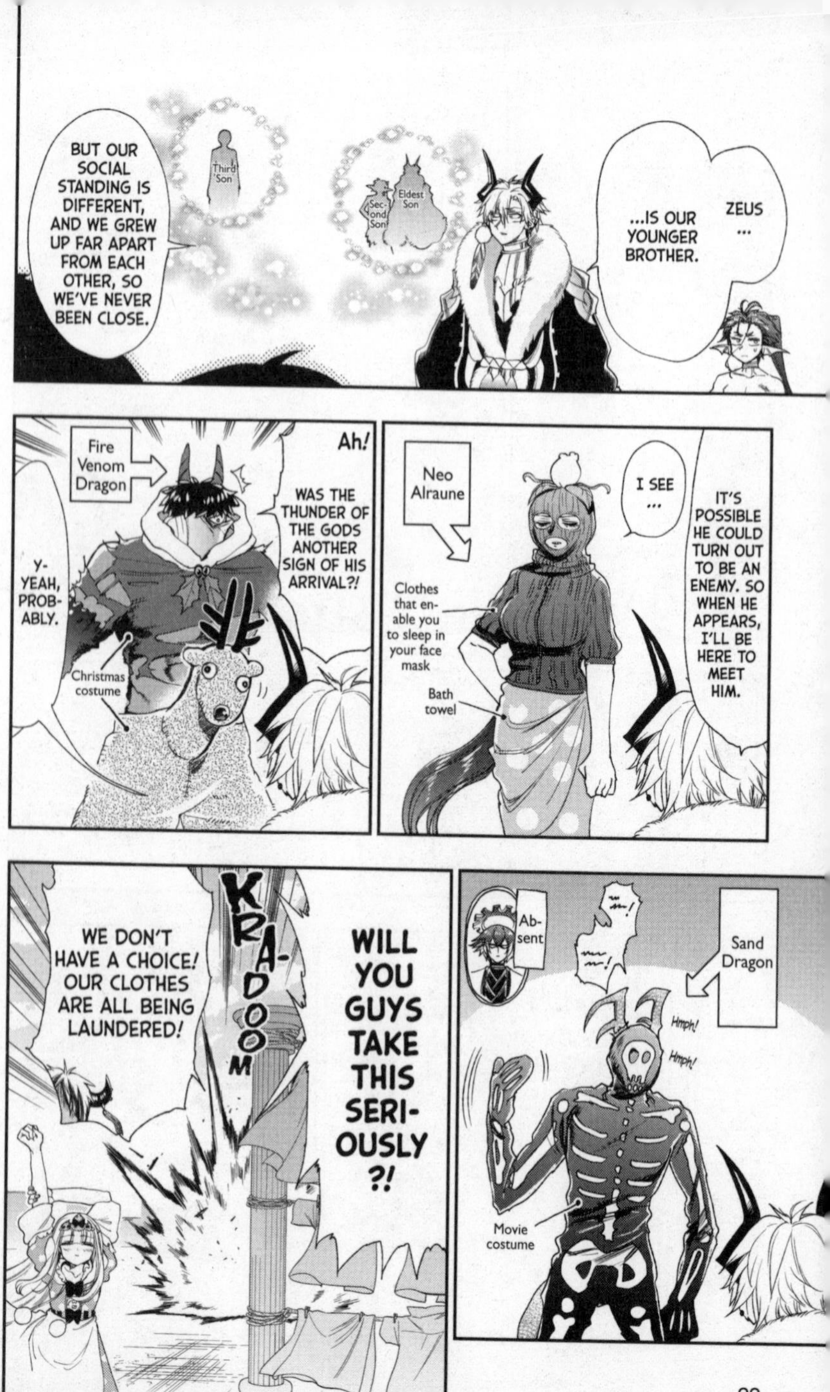
ZEUS ...
...IS OUR YOUNGER BROTHER.
Eldest Son
Sec-ond Son
Third Son
BUT OUR SOCIAL STANDING IS DIFFERENT, AND WE GREW UP FAR APART FROM EACH OTHER, SO WE'VE NEVER BEEN CLOSE.
Neo Alraune
IT'S POSSIBLE HE COULD TURN OUT TO BE AN ENEMY. SO WHEN HE APPEARS, I'LL BE HERE TO MEET HIM.
I SEE ...
Clothes that en-able you to sleep in your face mask
Bath towel
Ah!
WAS THE THUNDER OF THE GODS ANOTHER SIGN OF HIS ARRIVAL?!
Fire Venom Dragon
Y-YEAH, PROB-ABLY.
Christmas costume
Sand Dragon
Ab-sent
Hmph!
Hmph!
Movie costume
KRA-DOOOM
WILL YOU GUYS TAKE THIS SERI-OUSLY ?!
WE DON'T HAVE A CHOICE! OUR CLOTHES ARE ALL BEING LAUNDERED!

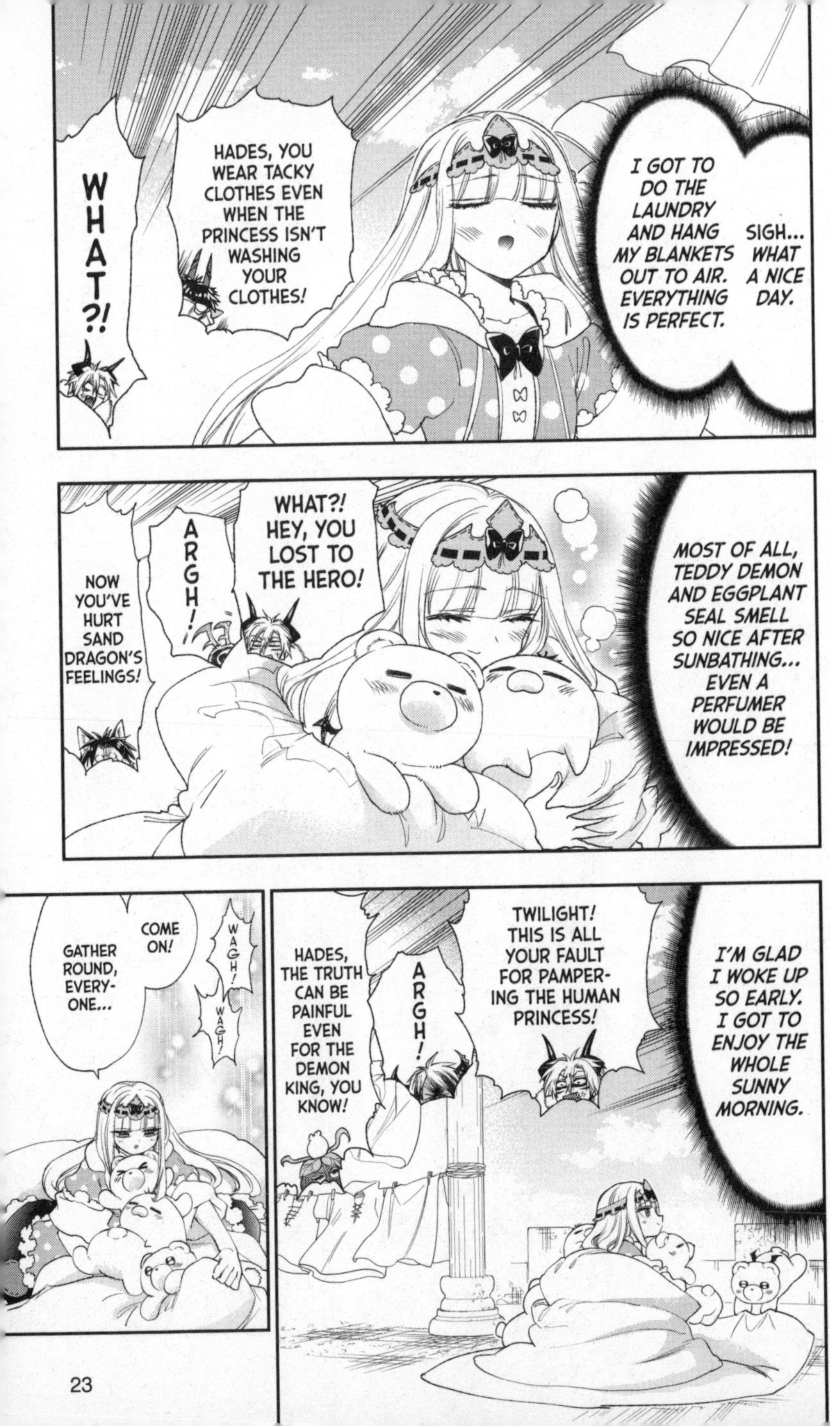

SIGH... WHAT A NICE DAY.
I GOT TO DO THE LAUNDRY AND HANG MY BLANKETS OUT TO AIR. EVERYTHING IS PERFECT.
HADES, YOU WEAR TACKY CLOTHES EVEN WHEN THE PRINCESS ISN'T WASHING YOUR CLOTHES!
WHAT?!
MOST OF ALL, TEDDY DEMON AND EGGPLANT SEAL SMELL SO NICE AFTER SUNBATHING... EVEN A PERFUMER WOULD BE IMPRESSED!
WHAT?! HEY, YOU LOST TO THE HERO!
ARGH!
NOW YOU'VE HURT SAND DRAGON'S FEELINGS!
I'M GLAD I WOKE UP SO EARLY. I GOT TO ENJOY THE WHOLE SUNNY MORNING.
TWILIGHT! THIS IS ALL YOUR FAULT FOR PAMPERING THE HUMAN PRINCESS!
ARGH!
HADES, THE TRUTH CAN BE PAINFUL EVEN FOR THE DEMON KING, YOU KNOW!
WAGH!
WAGH!
COME ON!
GATHER ROUND, EVERYONE...

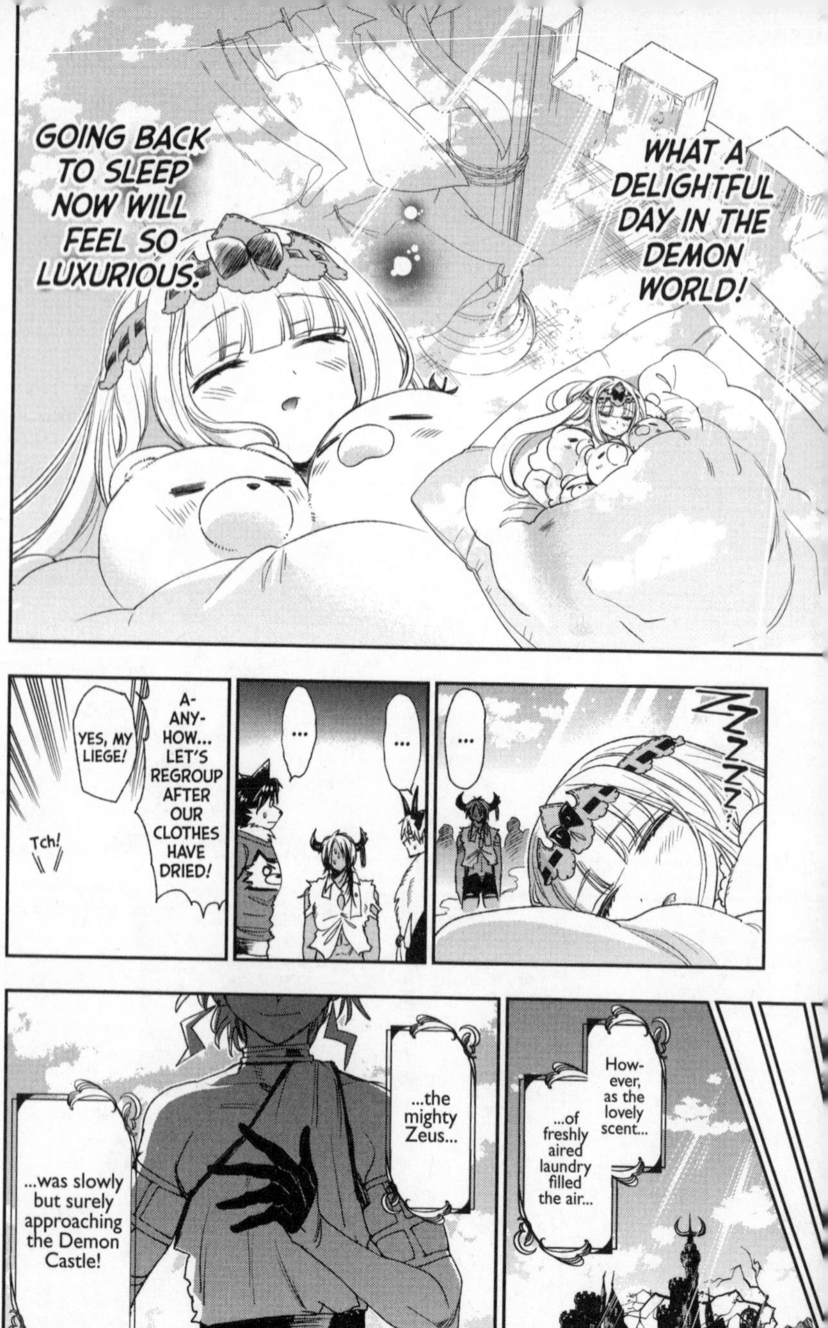
WHAT A DELIGHTFUL DAY IN THE DEMON WORLD!
GOING BACK TO SLEEP NOW WILL FEEL SO LUXURIOUS.
...
ZZZZZ
...
...
...
A-ANYHOW... LET'S REGROUP AFTER OUR CLOTHES HAVE DRIED!
YES, MY LIEGE!
Tch!
However, as the lovely scent...
...of freshly aired laundry filled the air...
...the mighty Zeus...
...was slowly but surely approaching the Demon Castle!

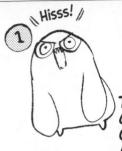

Demon Castle Question Corner

1
Hisss!

THIS IS A HAPPY-GO-LUCKY CORNER WHERE I ANSWER QUESTIONS FROM TWITTER AND LETTERS.

Q I would like to learn the real names of Minotaur and the others.

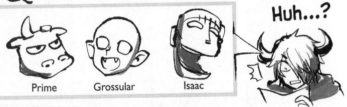

Prime
Grossular
Isaac
Huh...?

Q Can the demons at the Demon Castle cook?
I want to learn how to make their specialties.

Demon King: As good a cook as any of the rookies in their first year living alone. His specialty is sweet omelets. (And they're not that good.)

Demon Cleric: Veteran chef. His specialty is seasoned rice.

Great Red: Pooch. Basically a smart dog. He can make tea and coffee, though!

Poseidon: Good with seafood. He's scared of deep-frying, so he asks his brother to do it for him.

Hades: Especially good at deep-frying. He cooks for his dogs every day.

Alraune: She can manage, somehow, as long as she has a recipe to go on. But she's bad with fire and even manages to burn pancakes.

Fire Venom Dragon: He likes to eat by himself, so he's good at making hearty dishes. For some reason, he's also good at congee.

Sand Dragon: Can cook well enough to survive on a desert island.

M.O.T.H.E.R.: Considers cooking to be a form of scientific experiment, so he's good at baking and confectionaries.

Quilly: Makes ramen every now and then. It's extra greasy.

Harpy: Not a bad cook. Likes to use fruits and chicken a lot.

Midnight: Abysmal. His cooking gives those who eat it PTSD.

Vampire: Literally a bloodbath. Only his kin are capable of eating his dishes.

Teddy Demon & Eggplant Seal: They can melt DIY candies for kids. ♡ How cute. ♡

GRWR ♥
Stir
Stir

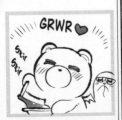

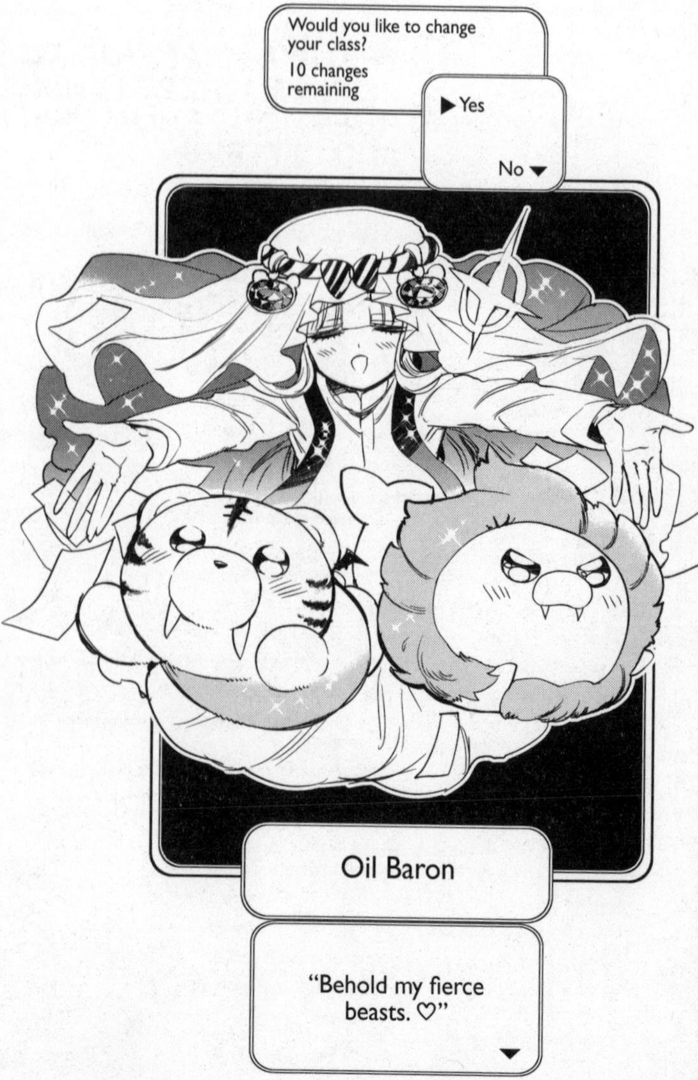
Would you like to change your class?
10 changes remaining
▶Yes
No
Oil Baron
"Behold my fierce beasts. ♡"

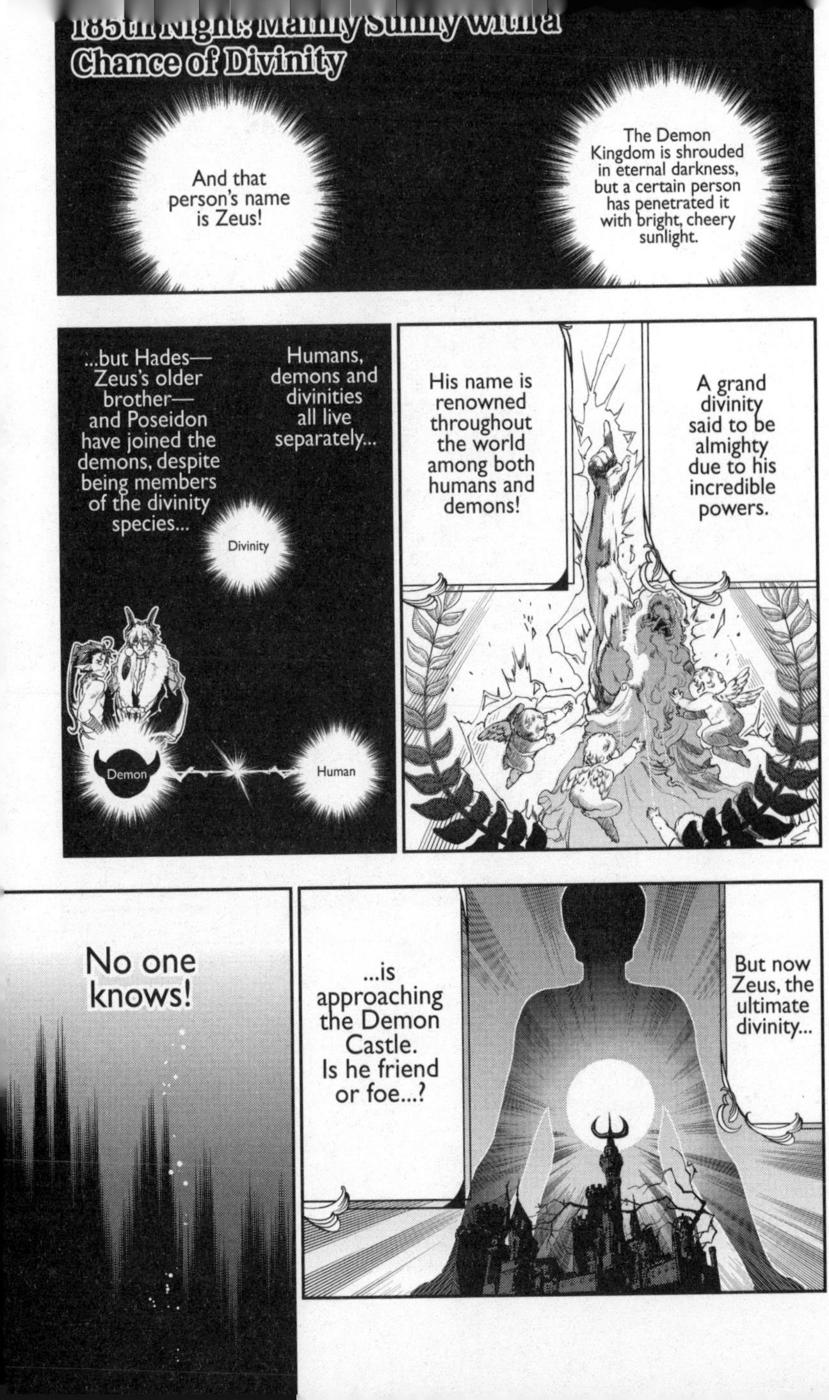
185th Night: Mainly Sunny with a Chance of Divinity
The Demon Kingdom is shrouded in eternal darkness, but a certain person has penetrated it with bright, cheery sunlight.
And that person's name is Zeus!
A grand divinity said to be almighty due to his incredible powers.
His name is renowned throughout the world among both humans and demons!
Humans, demons and divinities all live separately...
...but Hades—Zeus's older brother—and Poseidon have joined the demons, despite being members of the divinity species...
Divinity
Demon
Human
But now Zeus, the ultimate divinity...
...is approaching the Demon Castle. Is he friend or foe...?
No one knows!

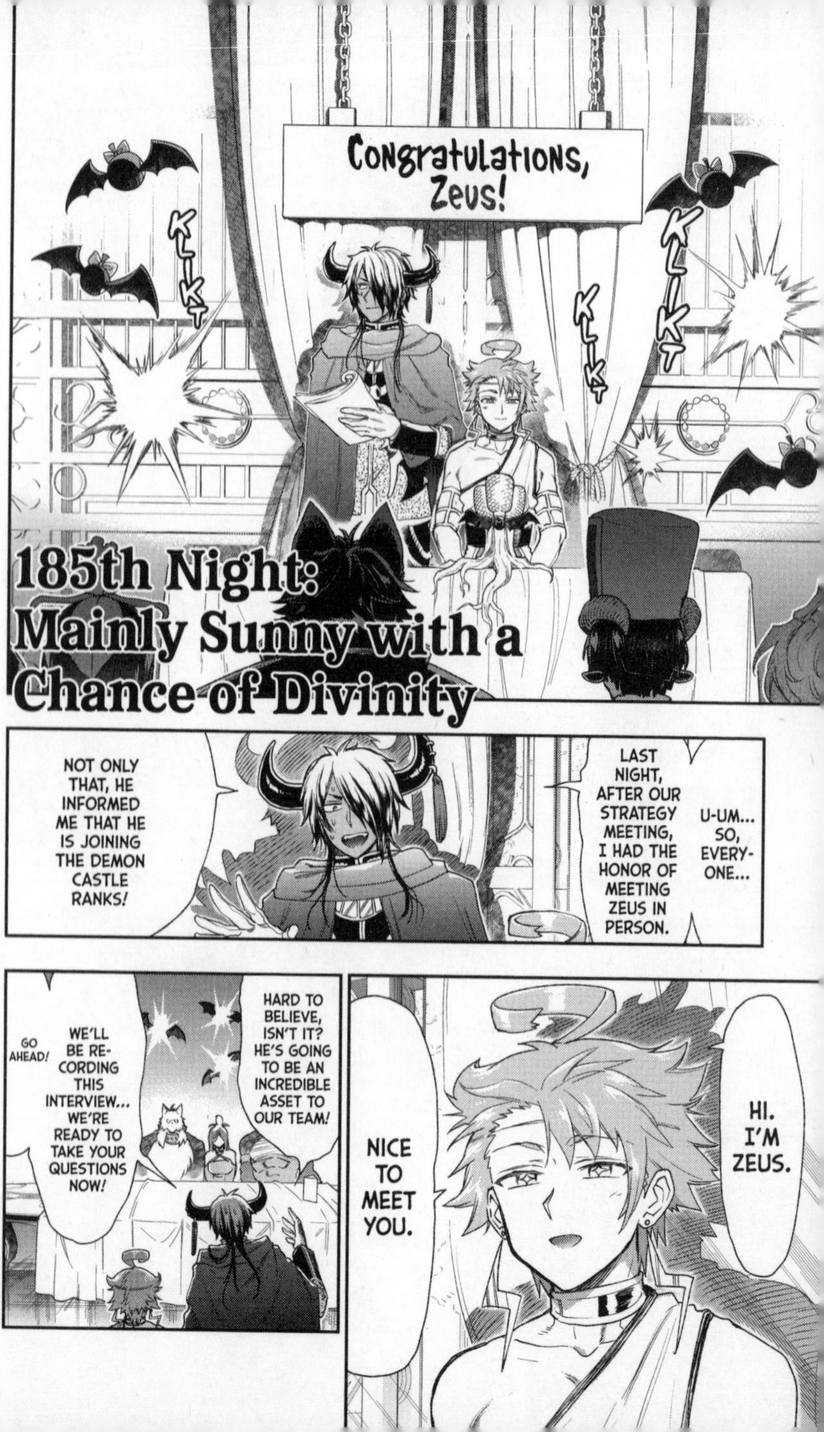
Congratulations, Zeus!
KLIKT
KLIKT
KLIKT
KLIKT
185th Night: Mainly Sunny with a Chance of Divinity
U-UM... SO, EVERY-ONE...
LAST NIGHT, AFTER OUR STRATEGY MEETING, I HAD THE HONOR OF MEETING ZEUS IN PERSON.
NOT ONLY THAT, HE INFORMED ME THAT HE IS JOINING THE DEMON CASTLE RANKS!
HI. I'M ZEUS.
NICE TO MEET YOU.
HARD TO BELIEVE, ISN'T IT? HE'S GOING TO BE AN INCREDIBLE ASSET TO OUR TEAM!
WE'LL BE RE-CORDING THIS INTERVIEW... WE'RE READY TO TAKE YOUR QUESTIONS NOW!
GO AHEAD!

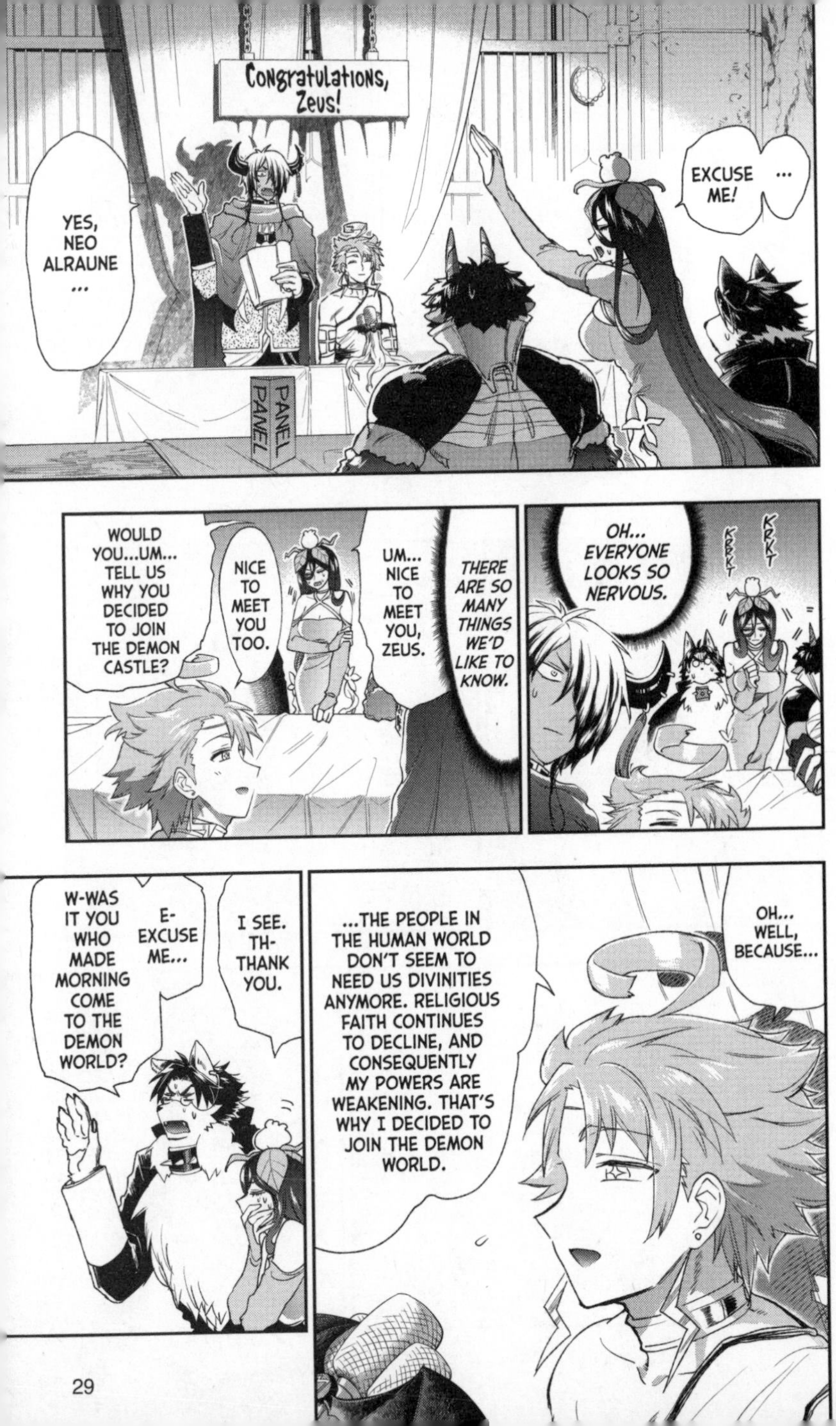
Congratulations, Zeus!
EXCUSE ME! ...
YES, NEO ALRAUNE ...
PANEL
PANEL
OH... EVERYONE LOOKS SO NERVOUS.
KRKT
KRKT
THERE ARE SO MANY THINGS WE'D LIKE TO KNOW.
UM... NICE TO MEET YOU, ZEUS.
NICE TO MEET YOU TOO.
WOULD YOU...UM... TELL US WHY YOU DECIDED TO JOIN THE DEMON CASTLE?
OH... WELL, BECAUSE...
...THE PEOPLE IN THE HUMAN WORLD DON'T SEEM TO NEED US DIVINITIES ANYMORE. RELIGIOUS FAITH CONTINUES TO DECLINE, AND CONSEQUENTLY MY POWERS ARE WEAKENING. THAT'S WHY I DECIDED TO JOIN THE DEMON WORLD.
I SEE. TH-THANK YOU.
E-EXCUSE ME...
W-WAS IT YOU WHO MADE MORNING COME TO THE DEMON WORLD?

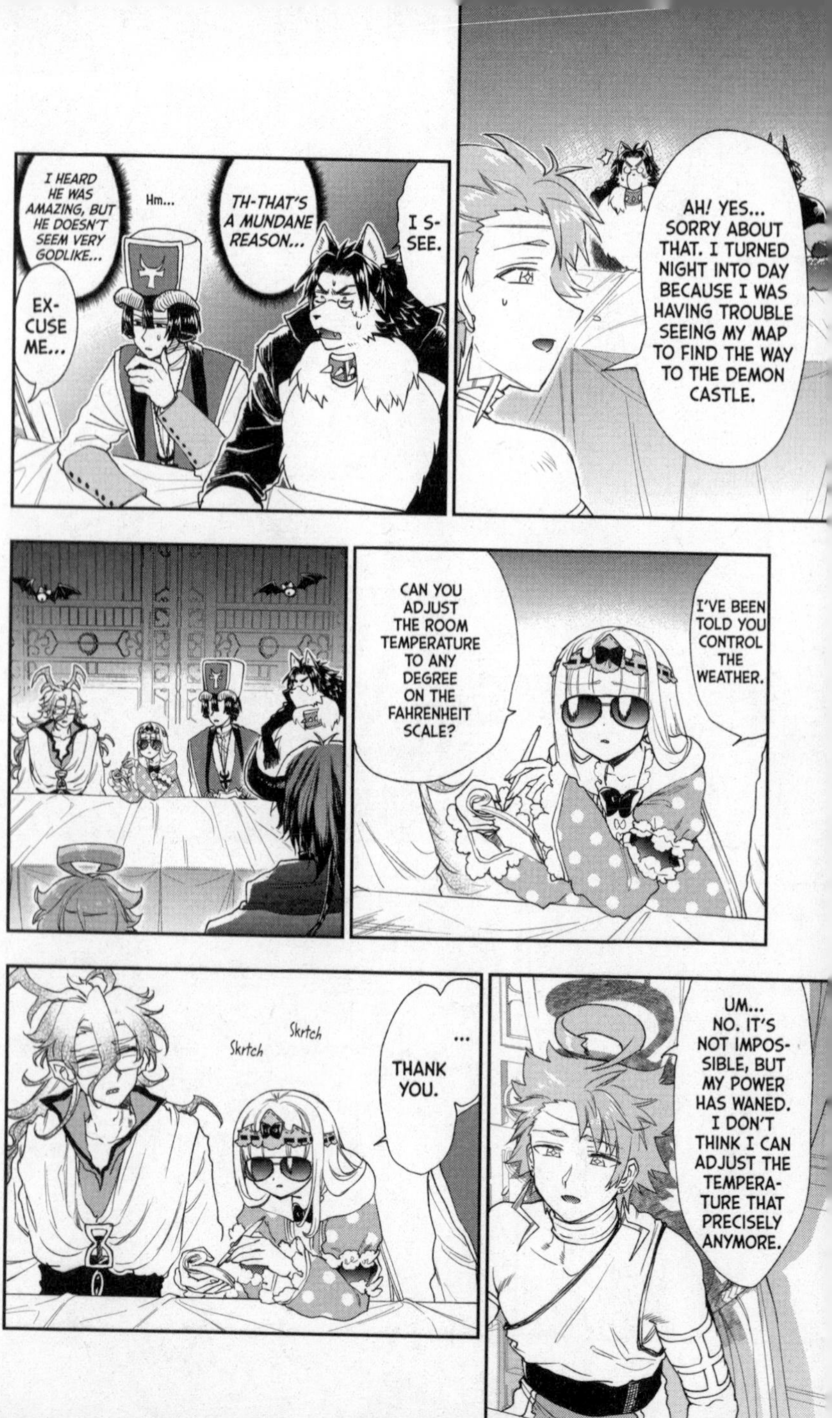
AH! YES... SORRY ABOUT THAT. I TURNED NIGHT INTO DAY BECAUSE I WAS HAVING TROUBLE SEEING MY MAP TO FIND THE WAY TO THE DEMON CASTLE.
I S-SEE.
TH-THAT'S A MUNDANE REASON...
Hm...
I HEARD HE WAS AMAZING, BUT HE DOESN'T SEEM VERY GODLIKE...
EX-CUSE ME...
I'VE BEEN TOLD YOU CONTROL THE WEATHER.
CAN YOU ADJUST THE ROOM TEMPERATURE TO ANY DEGREE ON THE FAHRENHEIT SCALE?
UM... NO. IT'S NOT IMPOS-SIBLE, BUT MY POWER HAS WANED. I DON'T THINK I CAN ADJUST THE TEMPERA-TURE THAT PRECISELY ANYMORE.
... THANK YOU.
Skrtch
Skrtch

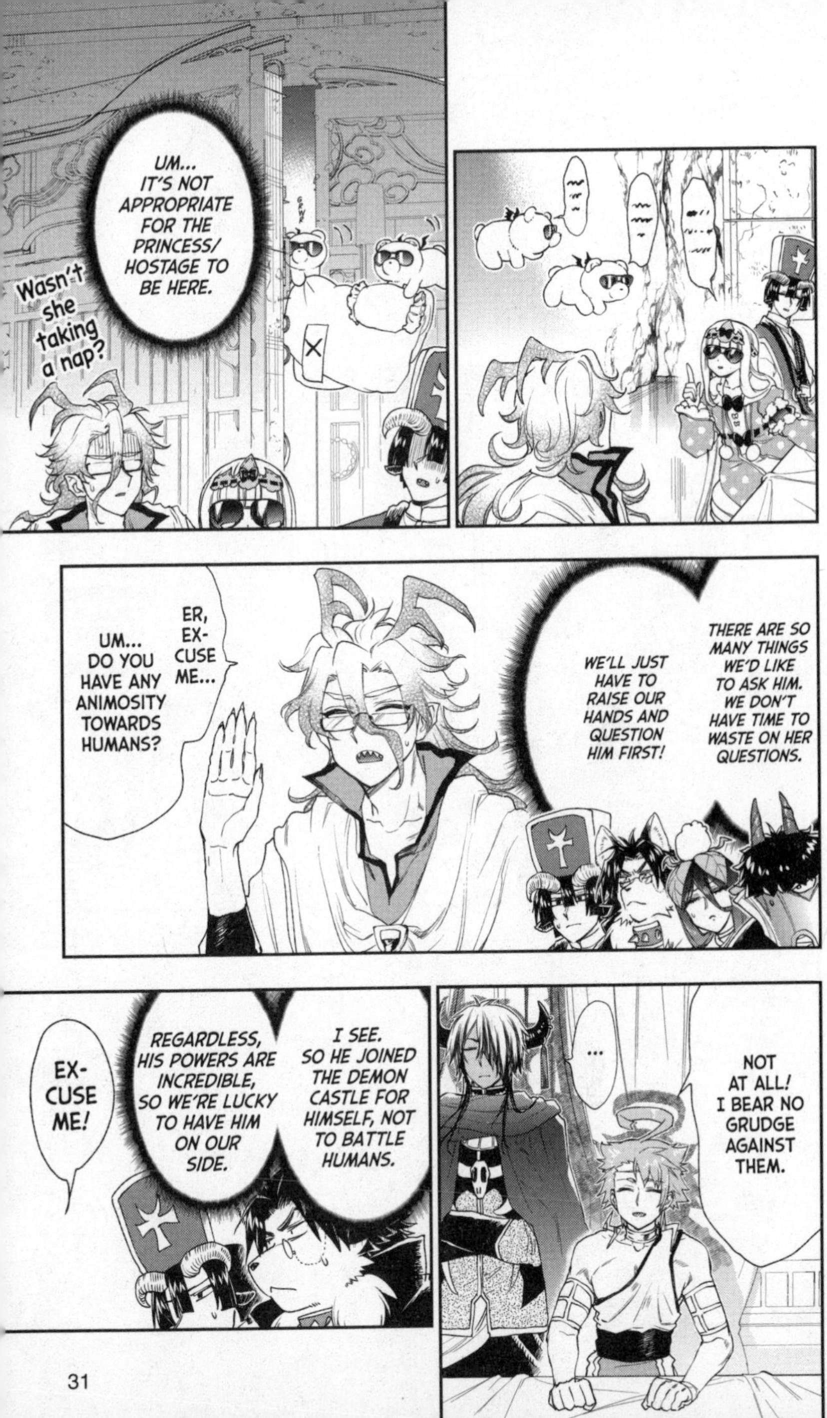
UM... IT'S NOT APPROPRIATE FOR THE PRINCESS/ HOSTAGE TO BE HERE.
Wasn't she taking a nap?
THERE ARE SO MANY THINGS WE'D LIKE TO ASK HIM. WE DON'T HAVE TIME TO WASTE ON HER QUESTIONS.
WE'LL JUST HAVE TO RAISE OUR HANDS AND QUESTION HIM FIRST!
ER, EX-CUSE ME...
UM... DO YOU HAVE ANY ANIMOSITY TOWARDS HUMANS?
NOT AT ALL! I BEAR NO GRUDGE AGAINST THEM.
...
I SEE. SO HE JOINED THE DEMON CASTLE FOR HIMSELF, NOT TO BATTLE HUMANS.
REGARDLESS, HIS POWERS ARE INCREDIBLE, SO WE'RE LUCKY TO HAVE HIM ON OUR SIDE.
EX-CUSE ME!

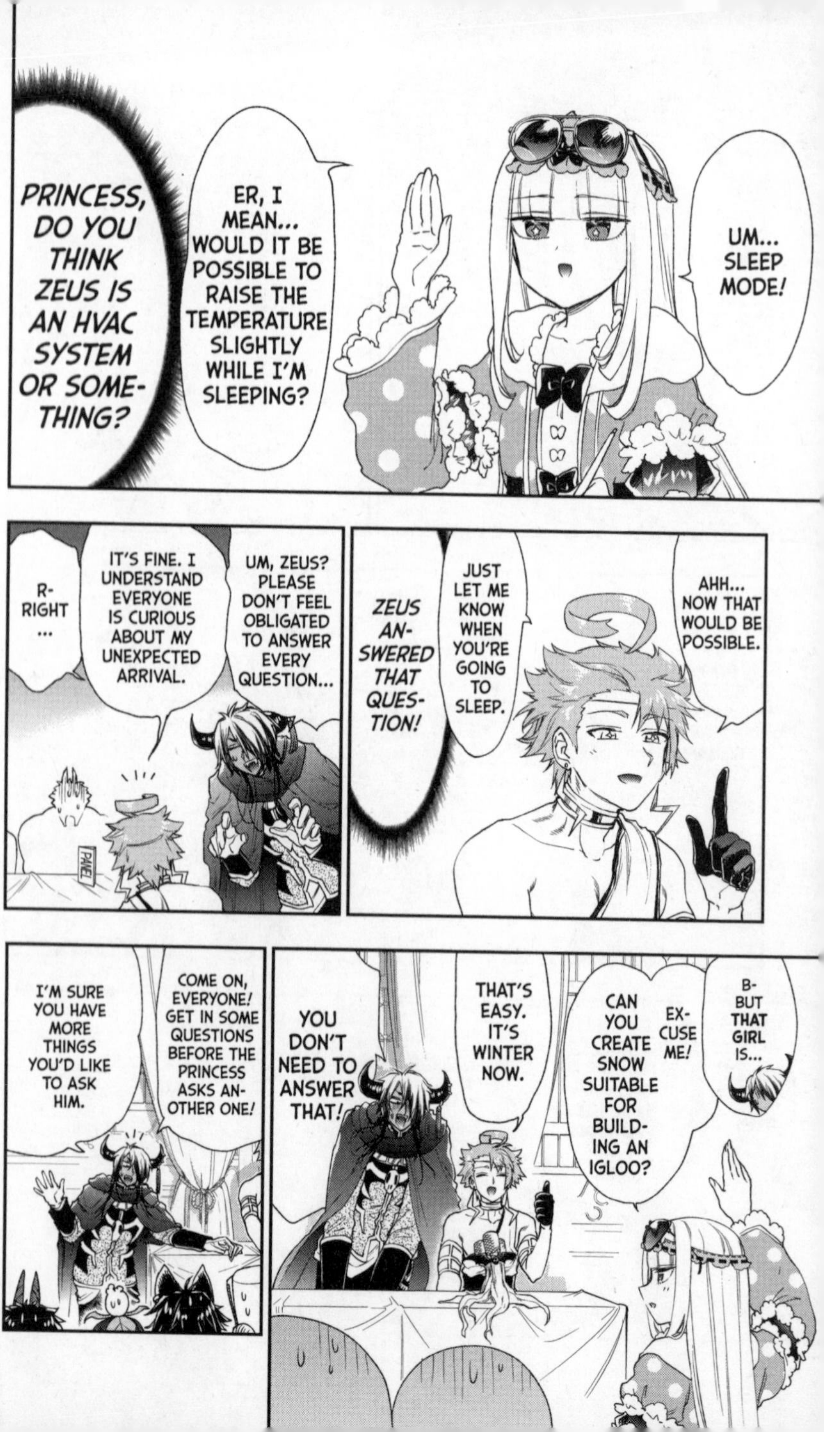
UM... SLEEP MODE!
ER, I MEAN... WOULD IT BE POSSIBLE TO RAISE THE TEMPERATURE SLIGHTLY WHILE I'M SLEEPING?
PRINCESS, DO YOU THINK ZEUS IS AN HVAC SYSTEM OR SOME-THING?
AHH... NOW THAT WOULD BE POSSIBLE.
JUST LET ME KNOW WHEN YOU'RE GOING TO SLEEP.
ZEUS AN-SWERED THAT QUES-TION!
UM, ZEUS? PLEASE DON'T FEEL OBLIGATED TO ANSWER EVERY QUESTION...
IT'S FINE. I UNDERSTAND EVERYONE IS CURIOUS ABOUT MY UNEXPECTED ARRIVAL.
R-RIGHT...
PANEL
B-BUT THAT GIRL IS...
EX-CUSE ME!
CAN YOU CREATE SNOW SUITABLE FOR BUILD-ING AN IGLOO?
THAT'S EASY. IT'S WINTER NOW.
YOU DON'T NEED TO ANSWER THAT!
COME ON, EVERYONE! GET IN SOME QUESTIONS BEFORE THE PRINCESS ASKS AN-OTHER ONE!
I'M SURE YOU HAVE MORE THINGS YOU'D LIKE TO ASK HIM.

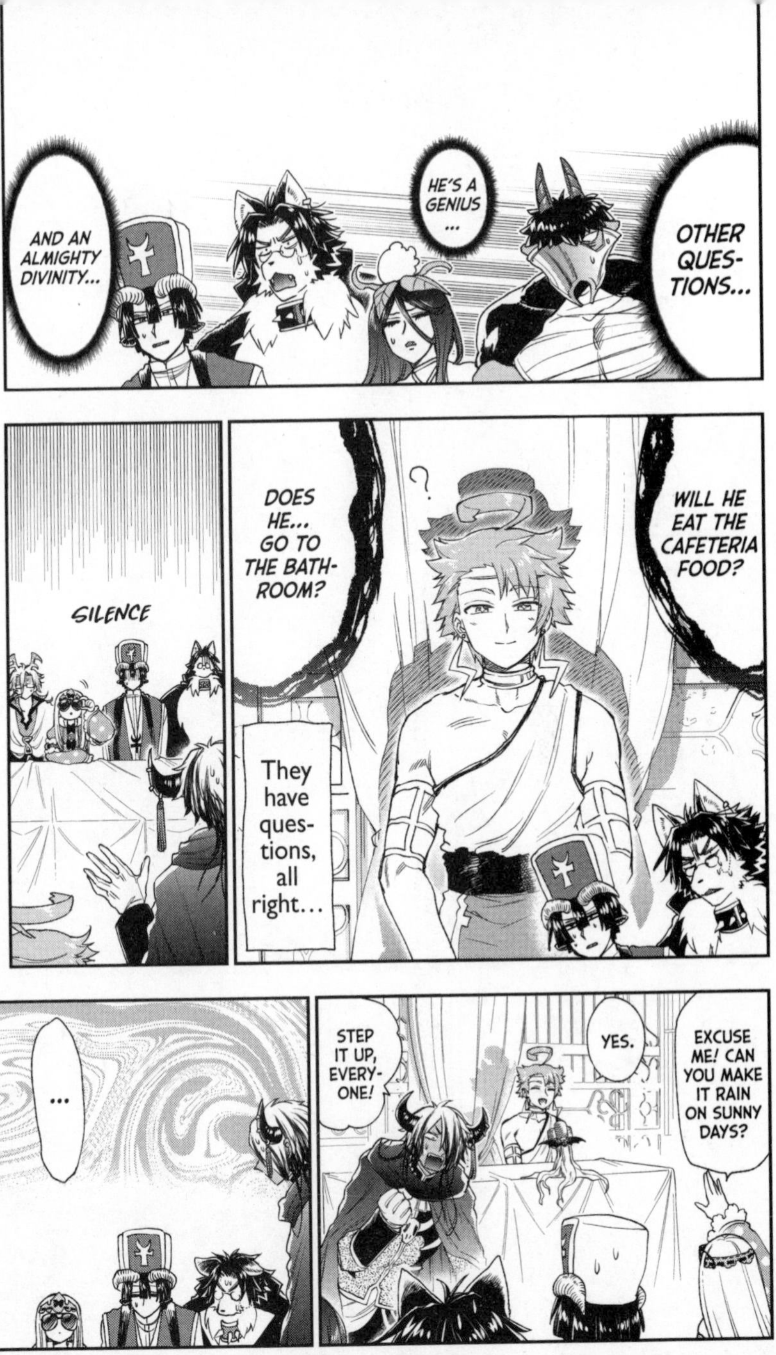
OTHER QUESTIONS...
HE'S A GENIUS ...
AND AN ALMIGHTY DIVINITY...
WILL HE EAT THE CAFETERIA FOOD?
?
DOES HE... GO TO THE BATHROOM?
They have questions, all right...
SILENCE
EXCUSE ME! CAN YOU MAKE IT RAIN ON SUNNY DAYS?
YES.
STEP IT UP, EVERYONE!
...

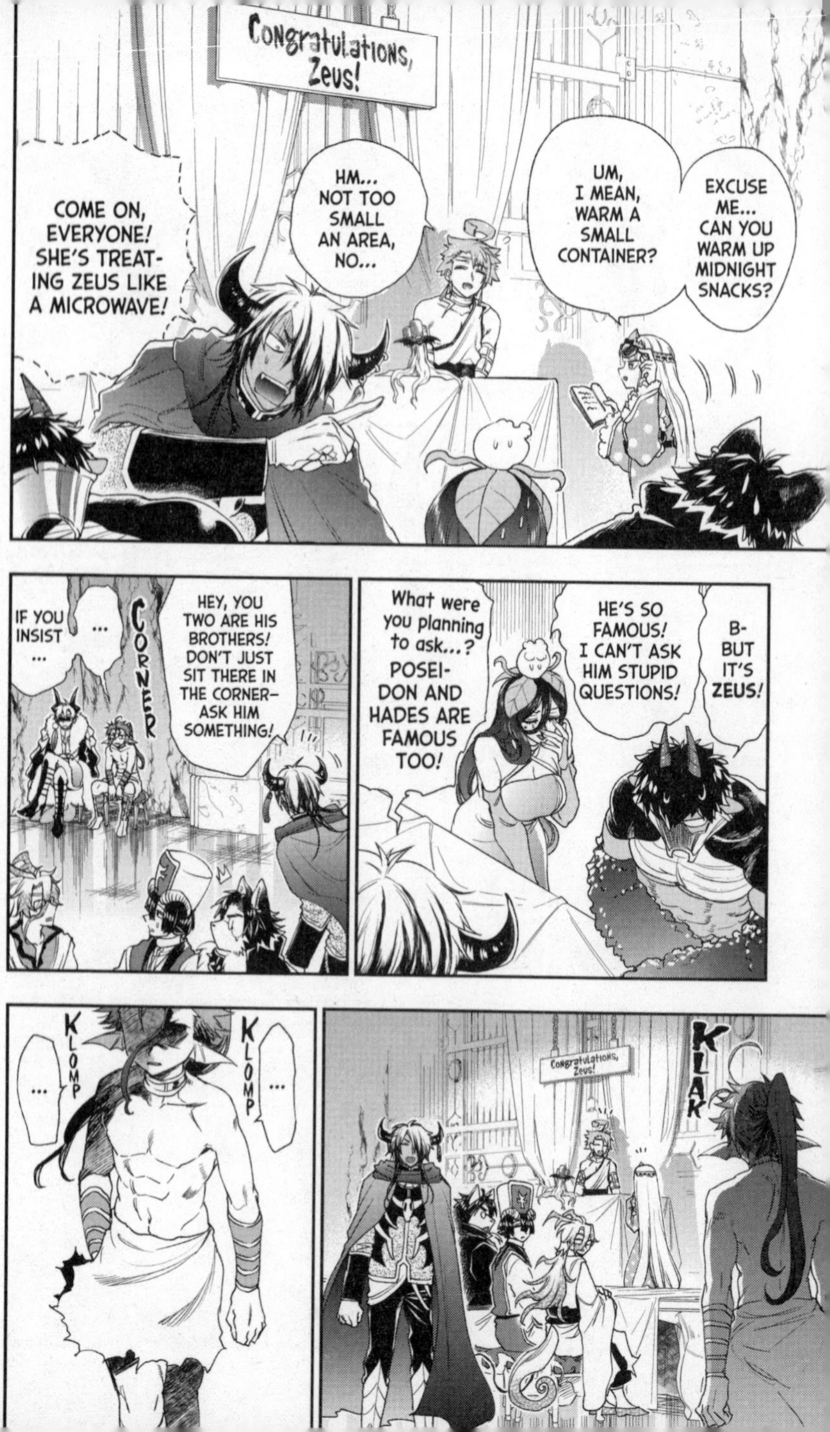
Congratulations, Zeus!
EXCUSE ME... CAN YOU WARM UP MIDNIGHT SNACKS?
UM, I MEAN, WARM A SMALL CONTAINER?
HM... NOT TOO SMALL AN AREA, NO...
COME ON, EVERYONE! SHE'S TREAT-ING ZEUS LIKE A MICROWAVE!
B- BUT IT'S ZEUS!
HE'S SO FAMOUS! I CAN'T ASK HIM STUPID QUESTIONS!
What were you planning to ask...?
POSEI-DON AND HADES ARE FAMOUS TOO!
HEY, YOU TWO ARE HIS BROTHERS! DON'T JUST SIT THERE IN THE CORNER—ASK HIM SOMETHING!
CORNER
...
IF YOU INSIST ...
KLAK
Congratulations, Zeus!
KLOMP
...
KLOMP
...

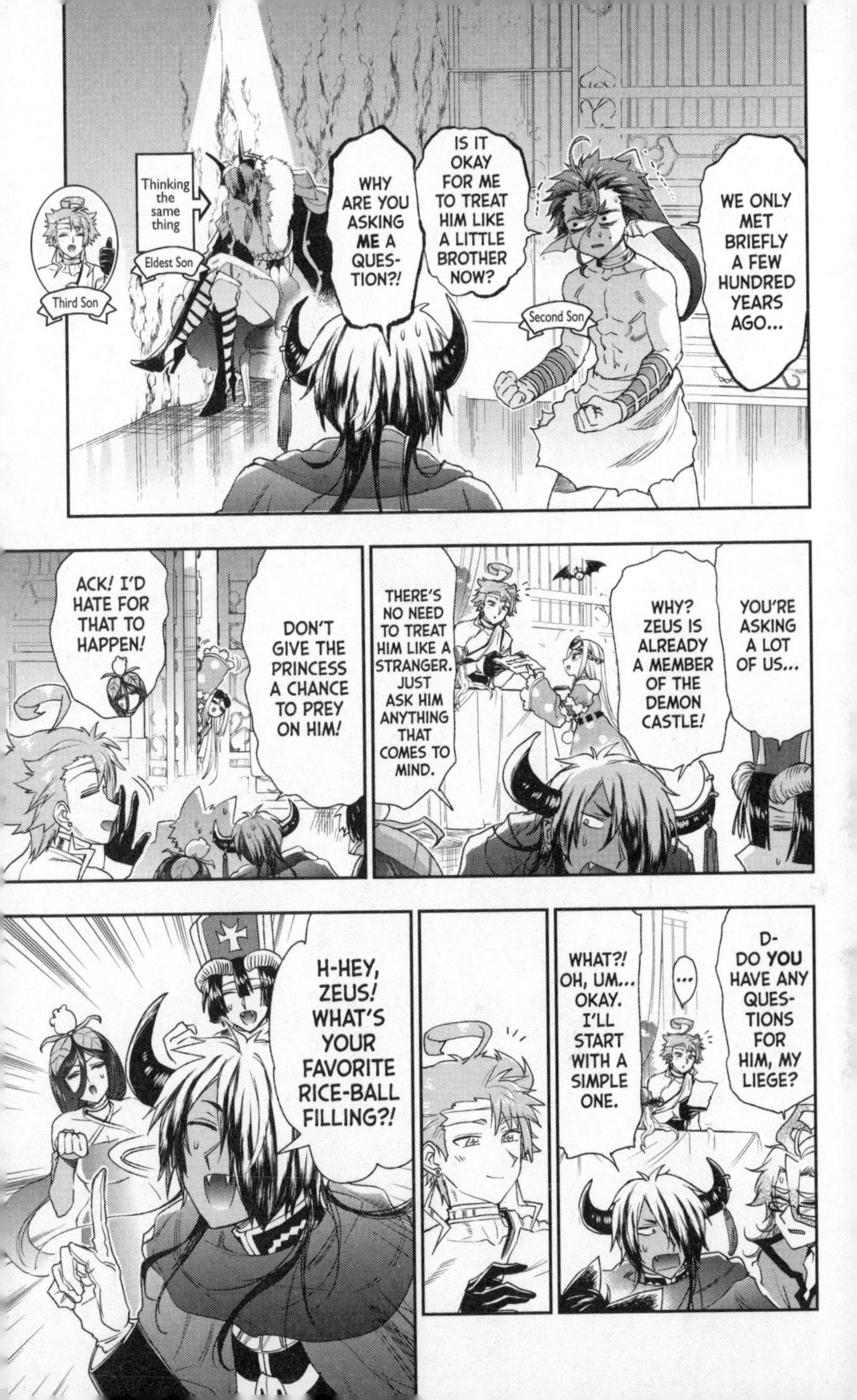
WE ONLY MET BRIEFLY A FEW HUNDRED YEARS AGO...
Second Son
IS IT OKAY FOR ME TO TREAT HIM LIKE A LITTLE BROTHER NOW?
WHY ARE YOU ASKING ME A QUESTION?!
Eldest Son
Thinking the same thing
Third Son
YOU'RE ASKING A LOT OF US...
WHY? ZEUS IS ALREADY A MEMBER OF THE DEMON CASTLE!
THERE'S NO NEED TO TREAT HIM LIKE A STRANGER. JUST ASK HIM ANYTHING THAT COMES TO MIND.
DON'T GIVE THE PRINCESS A CHANCE TO PREY ON HIM!
ACK! I'D HATE FOR THAT TO HAPPEN!
D-DO YOU HAVE ANY QUESTIONS FOR HIM, MY LIEGE?
...
WHAT?! OH, UM... OKAY. I'LL START WITH A SIMPLE ONE.
H-HEY, ZEUS! WHAT'S YOUR FAVORITE RICE-BALL FILLING?!

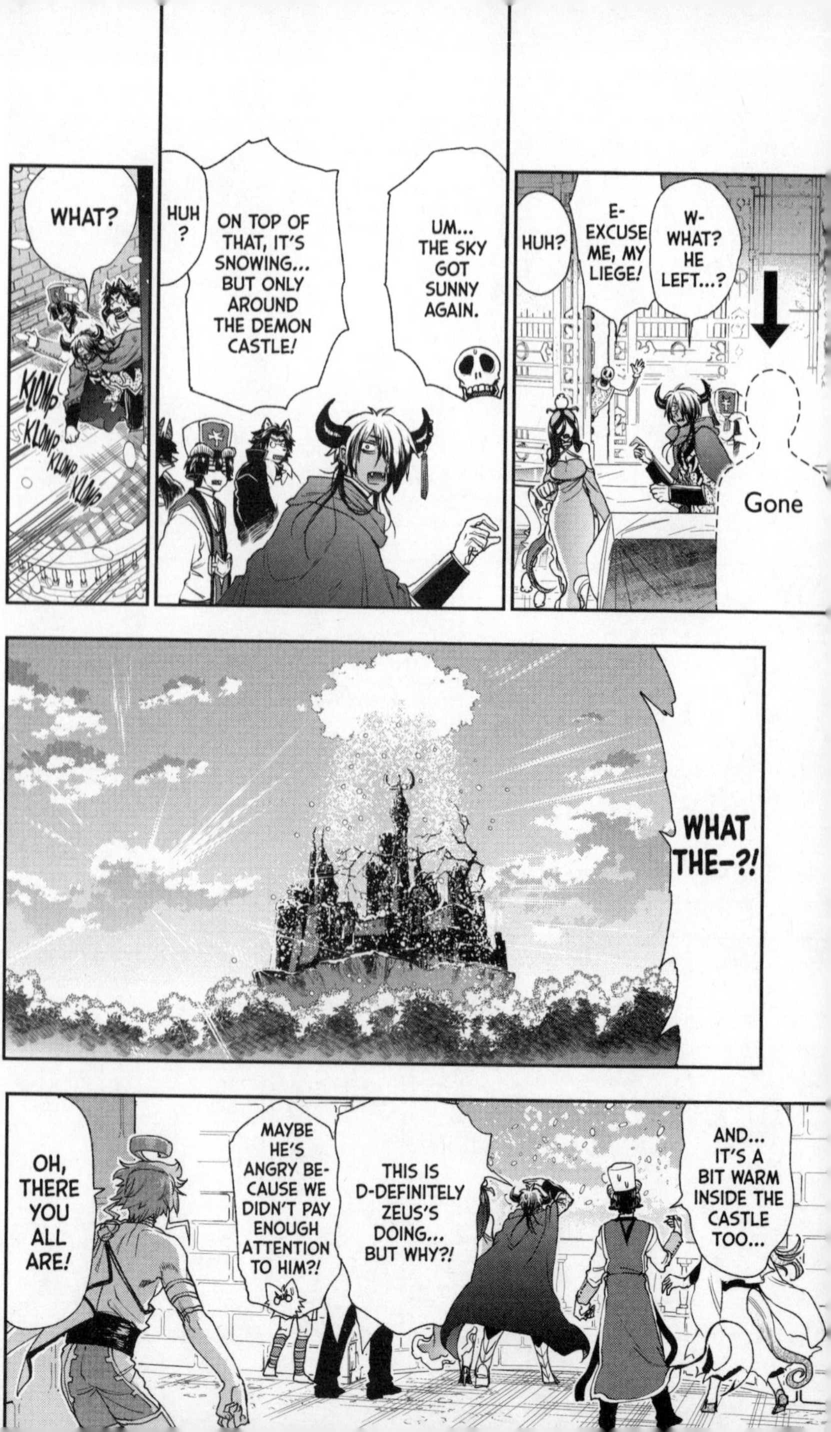

W-WHAT? HE LEFT...?
E-EXCUSE ME, MY LIEGE!
HUH?
Gone
UM... THE SKY GOT SUNNY AGAIN.
ON TOP OF THAT, IT'S SNOWING... BUT ONLY AROUND THE DEMON CASTLE!
HUH?
WHAT?
KLOMP KLOMP KLOMP KLOMP
WHAT THE-?!
AND... IT'S A BIT WARM INSIDE THE CASTLE TOO...
THIS IS D-DEFINITELY ZEUS'S DOING... BUT WHY?!
MAYBE HE'S ANGRY BE-CAUSE WE DIDN'T PAY ENOUGH ATTENTION TO HIM?!
OH, THERE YOU ALL ARE!

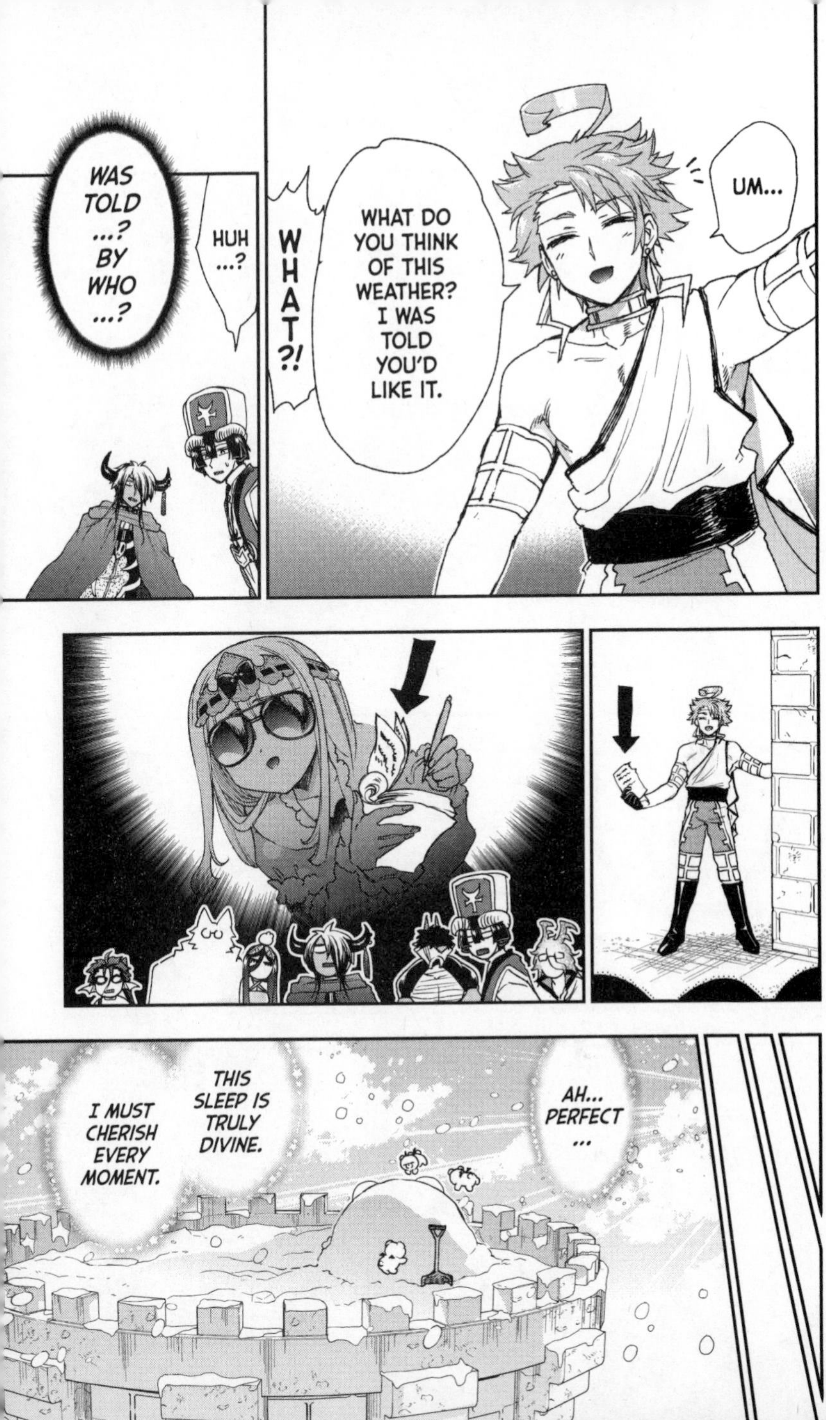
UM...
WHAT DO YOU THINK OF THIS WEATHER? I WAS TOLD YOU'D LIKE IT.
WHAT?!
HUH ...?
WAS TOLD ...? BY WHO ...?
AH... PERFECT ...
THIS SLEEP IS TRULY DIVINE.
I MUST CHERISH EVERY MOMENT.

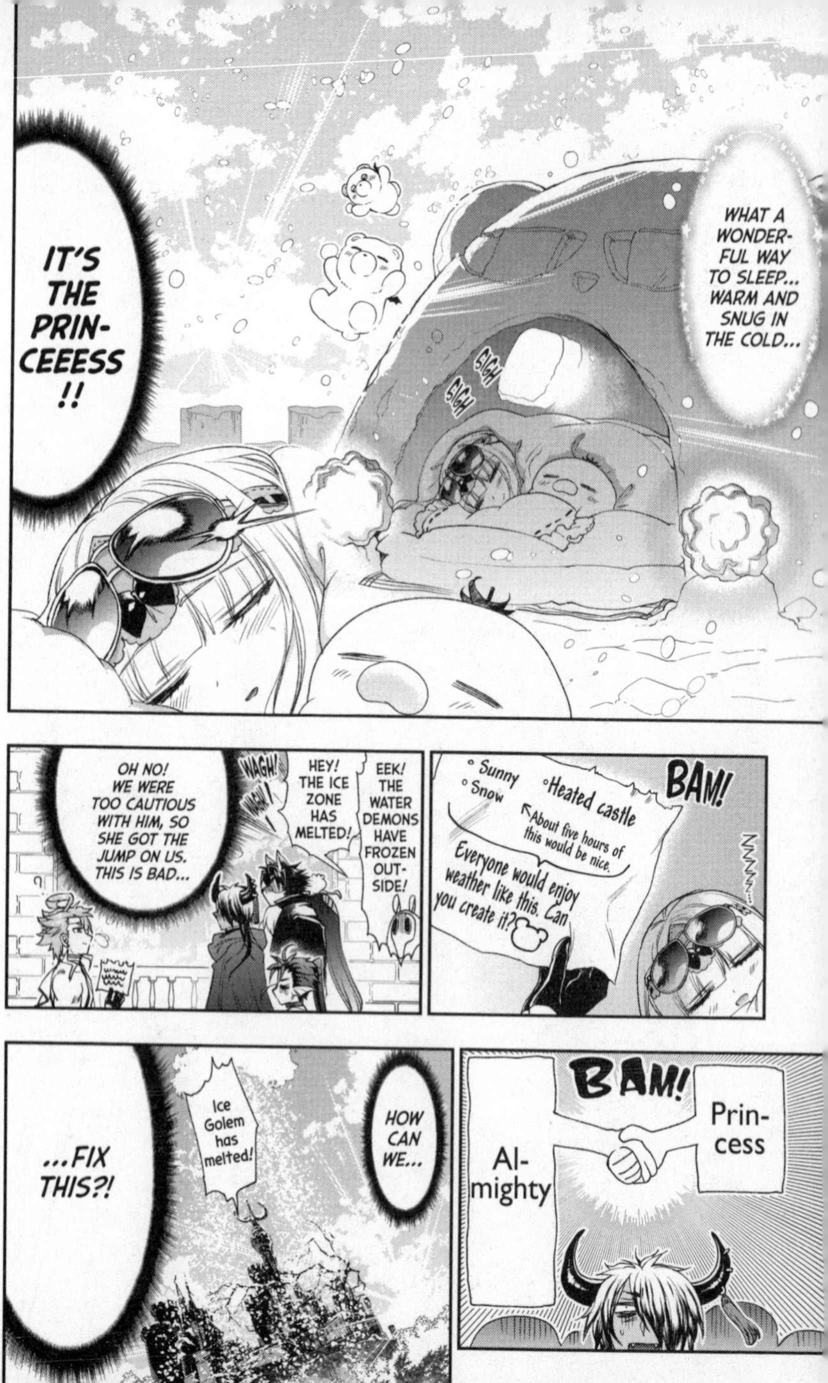
WHAT A WONDER-FUL WAY TO SLEEP... WARM AND SNUG IN THE COLD...
SIGH
SIGH
IT'S THE PRIN-CEEESS!!
BAM!
◦ Sunny
◦ Snow
◦ Heated castle
About five hours of this would be nice.
Everyone would enjoy weather like this. Can you create it?
ZZZZZ...
EEK! THE WATER DEMONS HAVE FROZEN OUT-SIDE!
HEY! THE ICE ZONE HAS MELTED!
WAGH!
WAGH!
OH NO! WE WERE TOO CAUTIOUS WITH HIM, SO SHE GOT THE JUMP ON US. THIS IS BAD...
BAM!
Prin-cess
Al-mighty
HOW CAN WE...
Ice Golem has melted!
...FIX THIS?!

Demon Castle Question Corner

2
Ooh, ahh.

Q I'd love to know who gave Princess Syalis which present back in Vol. 14, 172th Night.

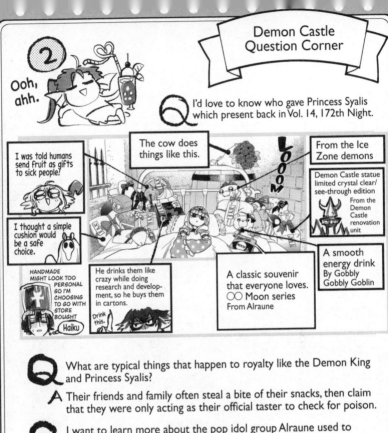

I was told humans send fruit as gifts to sick people!
The cow does things like this.
LOOOOOM
From the Ice Zone demons
Demon Castle statue limited crystal clear/see-through edition
From the Demon Castle renovation unit
I thought a simple cushion would be a safe choice.
HANDMADE MIGHT LOOK TOO PERSONAL SO I'M CHOOSING TO GO WITH STORE BOUGHT
Haiku
He drinks them like crazy while doing research and development, so he buys them in cartons.
Drink this.
A classic souvenir that everyone loves.
○○ Moon series
From Alraune
A smooth energy drink
By Gobbly Gobbly Goblin

Q What are typical things that happen to royalty like the Demon King and Princess Syalis?

A Their friends and family often steal a bite of their snacks, then claim that they were only acting as their official taster to check for poison.

Q I want to learn more about the pop idol group Alraune used to be a fan of!

A It was a female group with five or six members, each of whom had a signature color.

Q What does the lower half of Alazif's body look like!

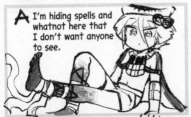

A I'm hiding spells and whatnot here that I don't want anyone to see.

Q I'd love to hear what the Demon King, Lord Midnight and Hades have to say about their beloved dogs.

A Demon King Twilight: "He's big and cute."

Former Demon King Midnight: "He's small and cute."

Hades: "They're small and noisy."

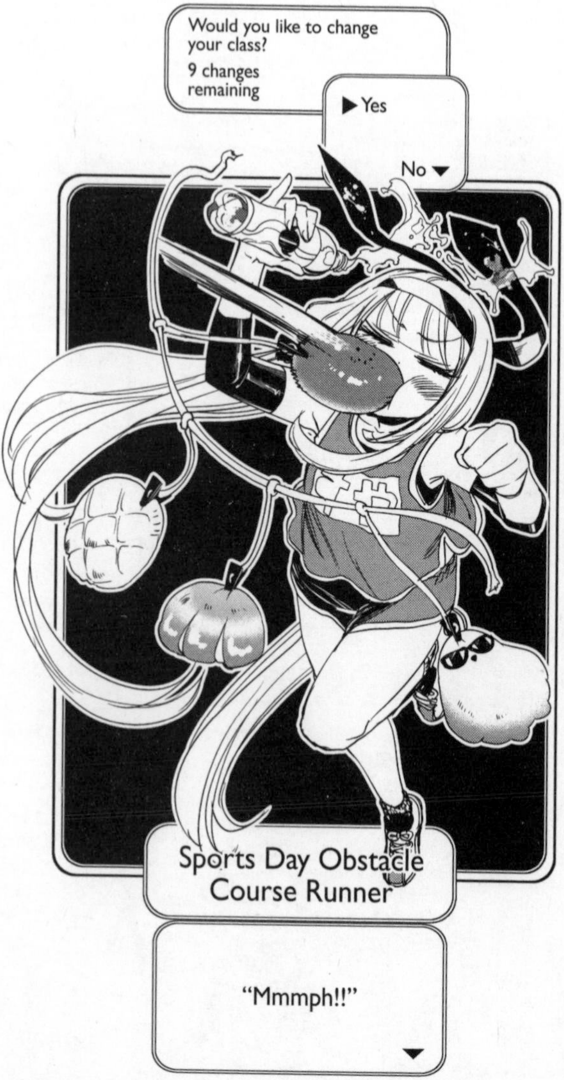
Would you like to change your class?
9 changes remaining
▶Yes
No
Sports Day Obstacle Course Runner
"Mmmph!!"

186th Night: Be My Big Brother

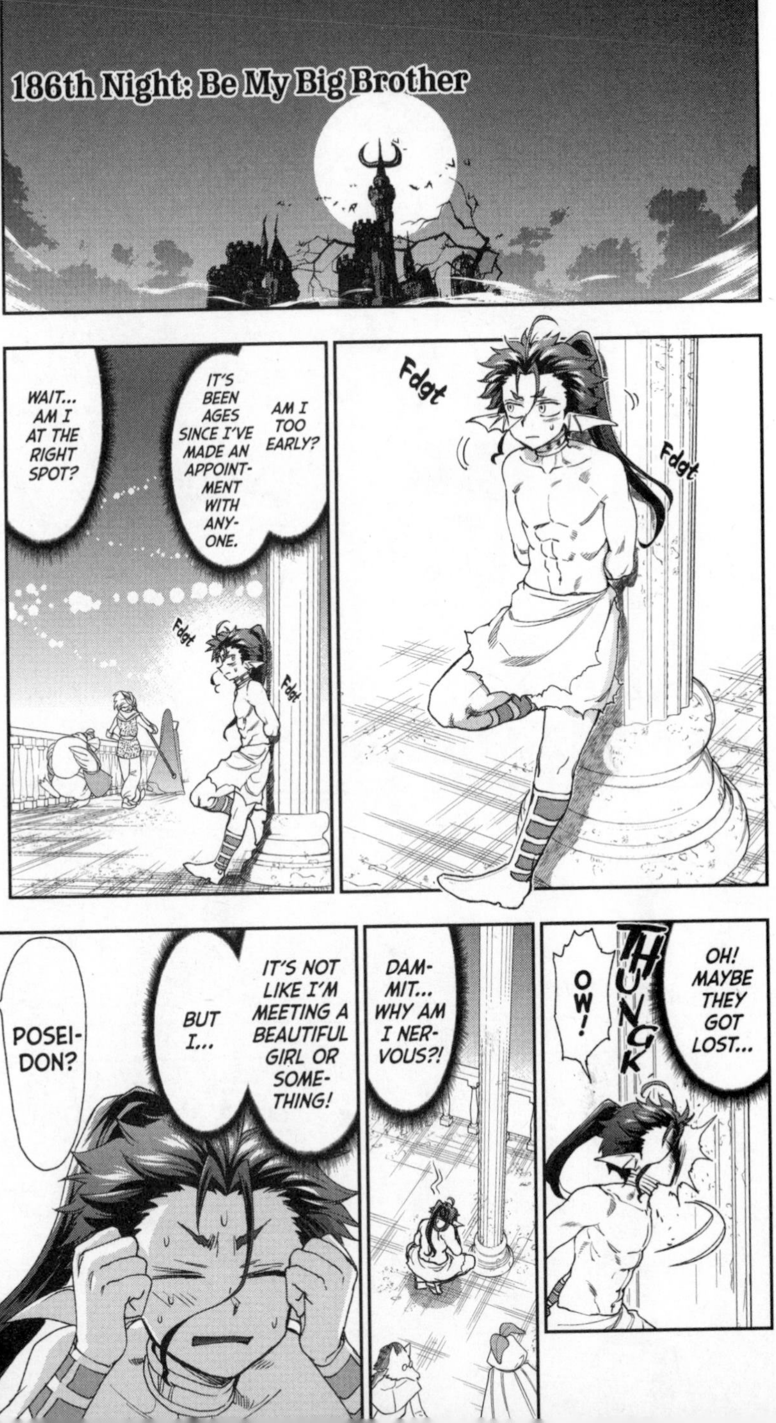
Fdgt
Fdgt
AM I TOO EARLY?
IT'S BEEN AGES SINCE I'VE MADE AN APPOINTMENT WITH ANYONE.
WAIT... AM I AT THE RIGHT SPOT?
Fdgt
Fdgt
OH! MAYBE THEY GOT LOST...
THUNK
OW!
DAMMIT... WHY AM I NERVOUS?!
IT'S NOT LIKE I'M MEETING A BEAUTIFUL GIRL OR SOMETHING!
BUT I...
POSEIDON?

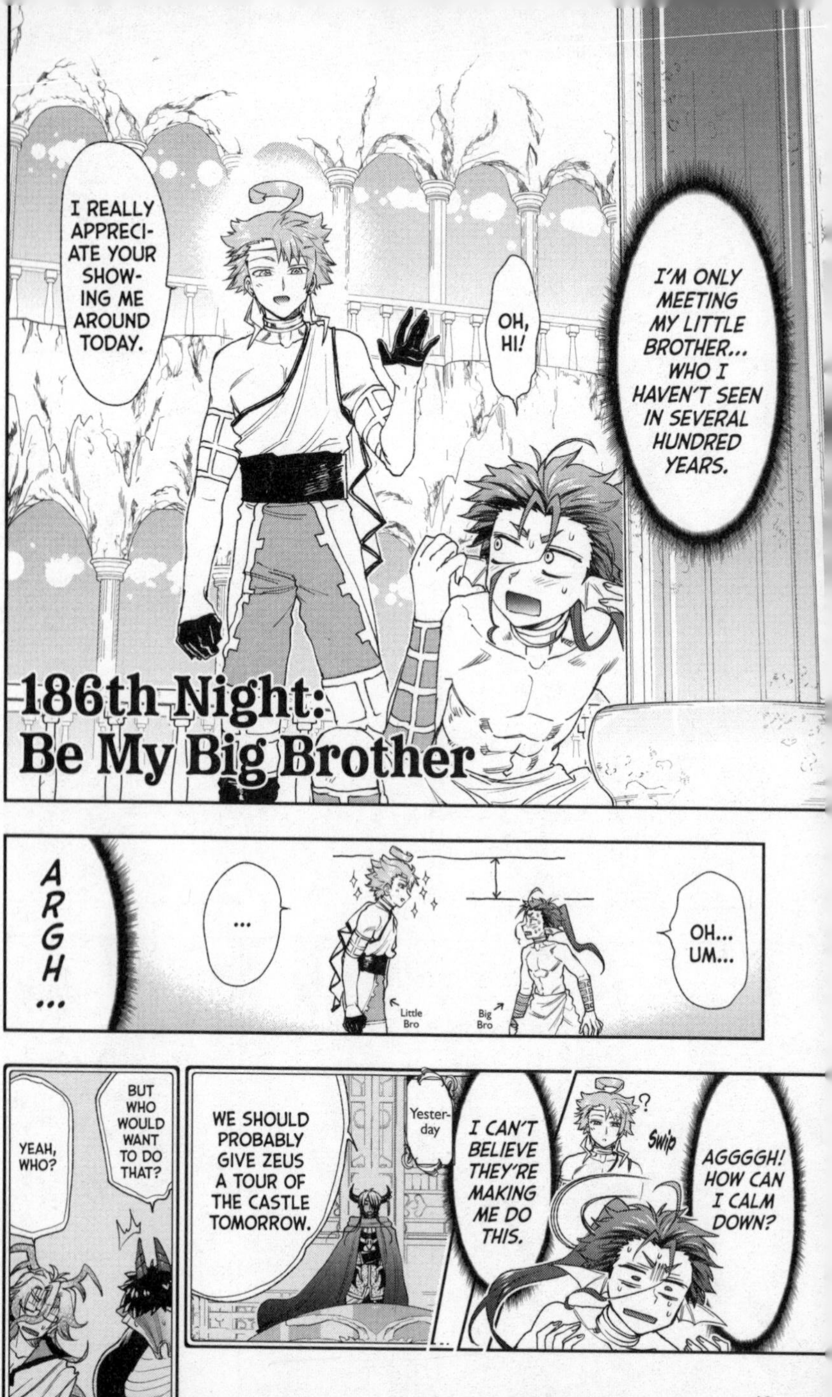
I'M ONLY MEETING MY LITTLE BROTHER... WHO I HAVEN'T SEEN IN SEVERAL HUNDRED YEARS.
OH, HI!
I REALLY APPRECIATE YOUR SHOWING ME AROUND TODAY.
186th Night: Be My Big Brother
OH... UM...
Big Bro
Little Bro
...
ARGH...
AGGGGH! HOW CAN I CALM DOWN?
Swip
I CAN'T BELIEVE THEY'RE MAKING ME DO THIS.
Yesterday
WE SHOULD PROBABLY GIVE ZEUS A TOUR OF THE CASTLE TOMORROW.
BUT WHO WOULD WANT TO DO THAT?
YEAH, WHO?

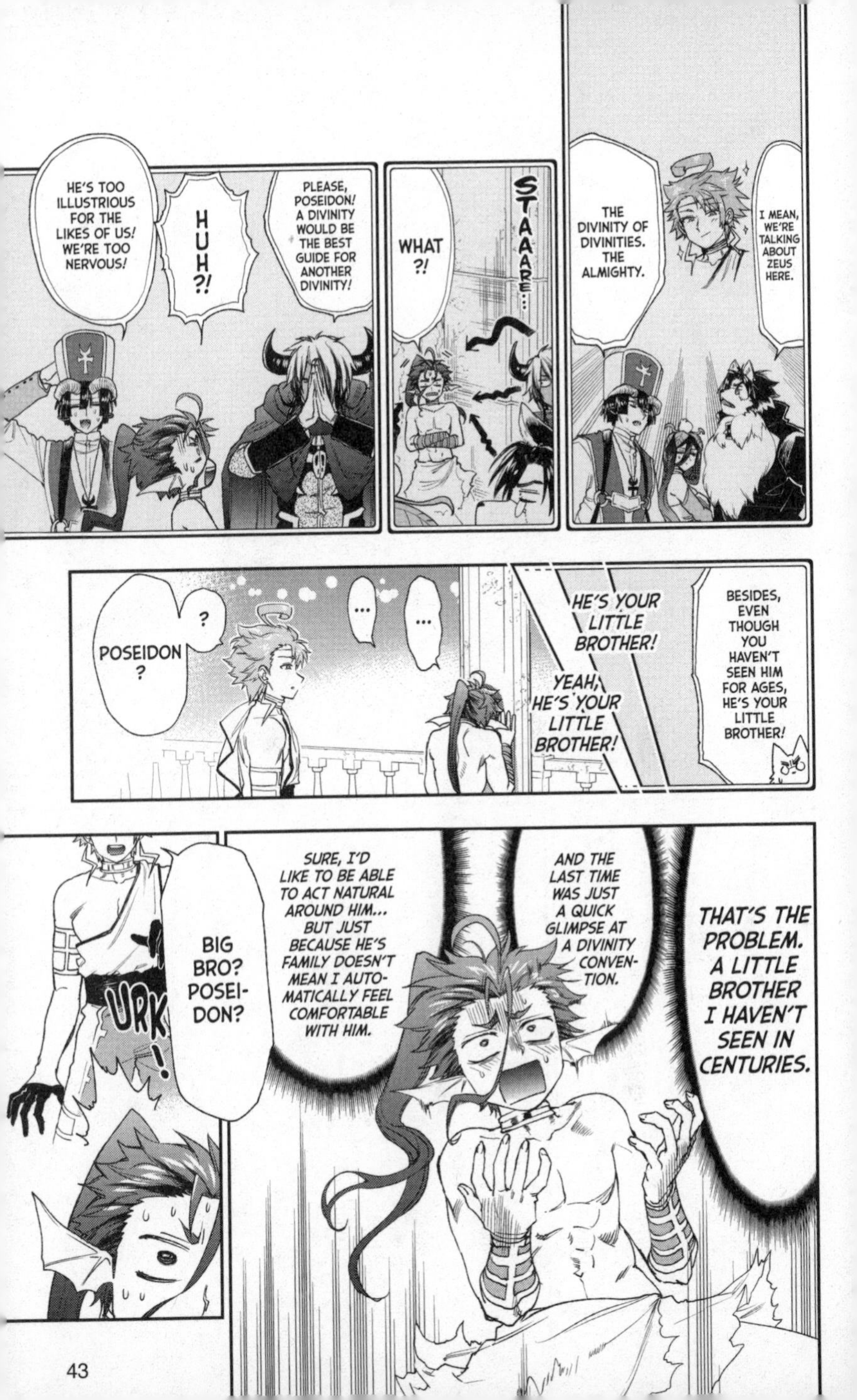
I MEAN, WE'RE TALKING ABOUT ZEUS HERE.
THE DIVINITY OF DIVINITIES. THE ALMIGHTY.
STAAAARE...
WHAT ?!
PLEASE, POSEIDON! A DIVINITY WOULD BE THE BEST GUIDE FOR ANOTHER DIVINITY!
HUH ?!
HE'S TOO ILLUSTRIOUS FOR THE LIKES OF US! WE'RE TOO NERVOUS!
BESIDES, EVEN THOUGH YOU HAVEN'T SEEN HIM FOR AGES, HE'S YOUR LITTLE BROTHER!
HE'S YOUR LITTLE BROTHER!
YEAH, HE'S YOUR LITTLE BROTHER!
...
...
?
POSEIDON ?
THAT'S THE PROBLEM. A LITTLE BROTHER I HAVEN'T SEEN IN CENTURIES.
AND THE LAST TIME WAS JUST A QUICK GLIMPSE AT A DIVINITY CONVEN-TION.
SURE, I'D LIKE TO BE ABLE TO ACT NATURAL AROUND HIM... BUT JUST BECAUSE HE'S FAMILY DOESN'T MEAN I AUTO-MATICALLY FEEL COMFORTABLE WITH HIM.
BIG BRO? POSEI-DON?
URK !

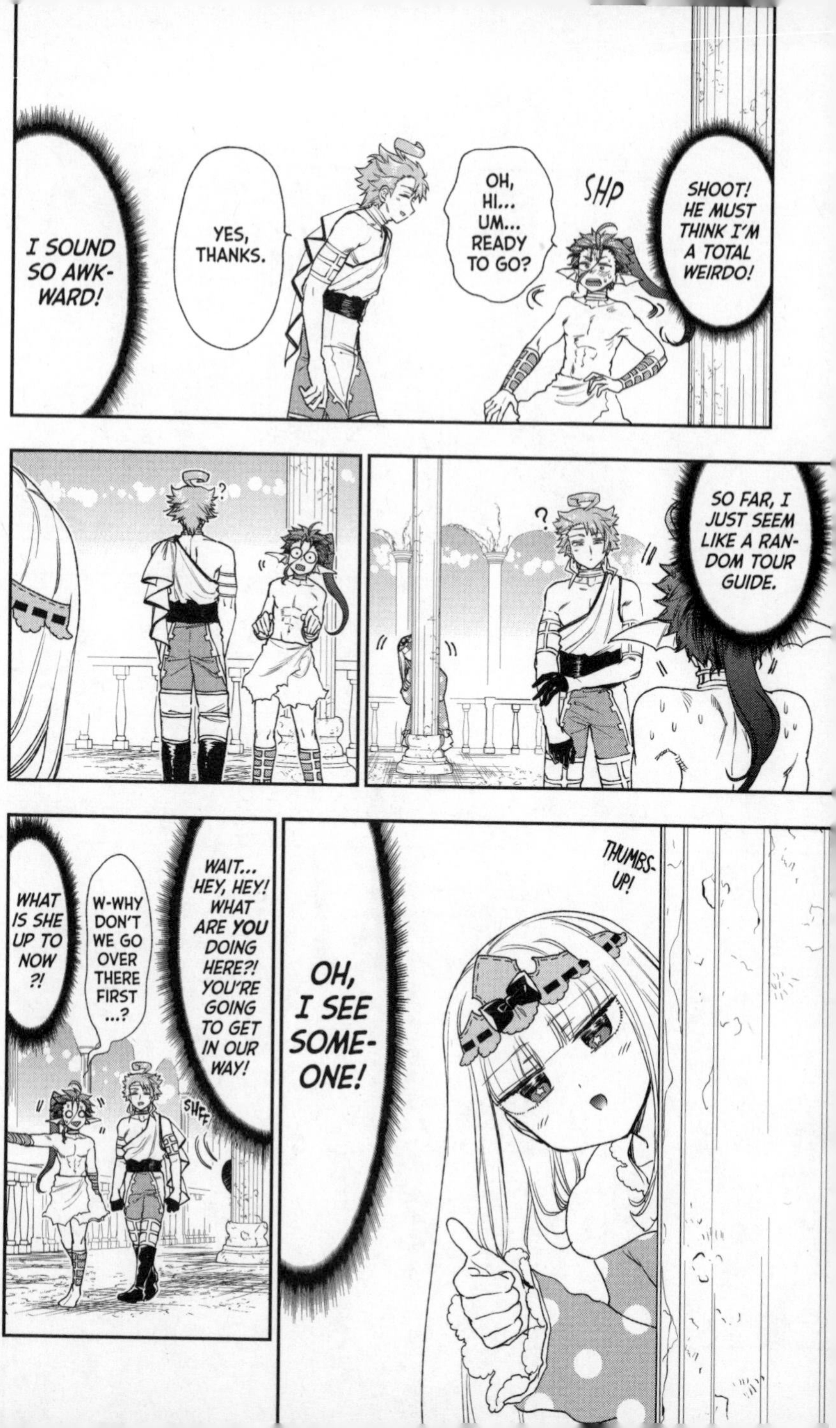
SHOOT! HE MUST THINK I'M A TOTAL WEIRDO!
SHP
OH, HI... UM... READY TO GO?
YES, THANKS.
I SOUND SO AWK-WARD!
SO FAR, I JUST SEEM LIKE A RAN-DOM TOUR GUIDE.
THUMBS-UP!
OH, I SEE SOME-ONE!
WAIT... HEY, HEY! WHAT ARE YOU DOING HERE?! YOU'RE GOING TO GET IN OUR WAY!
W-WHY DON'T WE GO OVER THERE FIRST ...?
SHFF
WHAT IS SHE UP TO NOW ?!

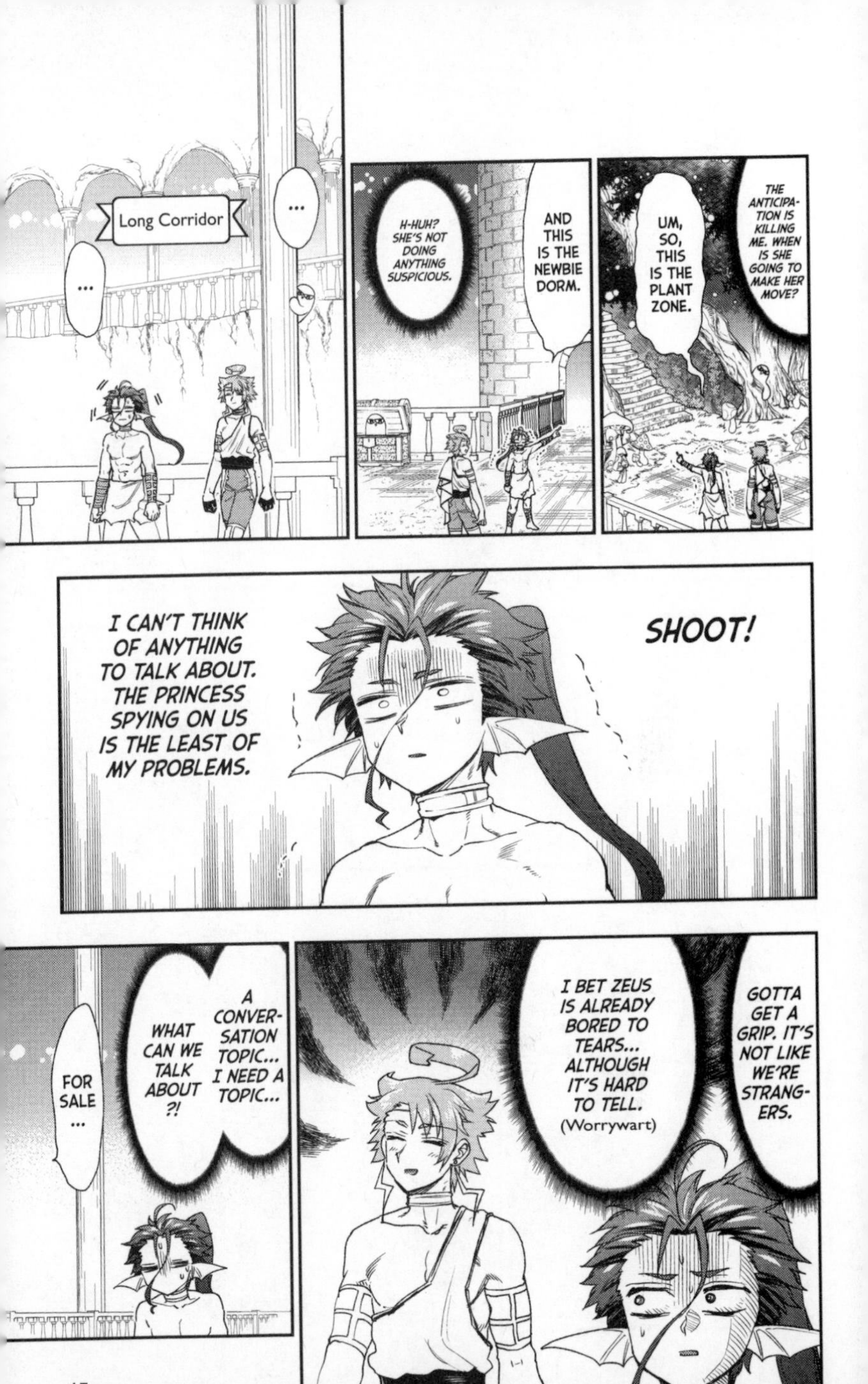
THE ANTICIPATION IS KILLING ME. WHEN IS SHE GOING TO MAKE HER MOVE?
UM, SO, THIS IS THE PLANT ZONE.
AND THIS IS THE NEWBIE DORM.
H-HUH? SHE'S NOT DOING ANYTHING SUSPICIOUS.
...
Long Corridor
...
SHOOT!
I CAN'T THINK OF ANYTHING TO TALK ABOUT. THE PRINCESS SPYING ON US IS THE LEAST OF MY PROBLEMS.
GOTTA GET A GRIP. IT'S NOT LIKE WE'RE STRANGERS.
I BET ZEUS IS ALREADY BORED TO TEARS... ALTHOUGH IT'S HARD TO TELL.
(Worrywart)
A CONVERSATION TOPIC... I NEED A TOPIC...
WHAT CAN WE TALK ABOUT?!
FOR SALE ...

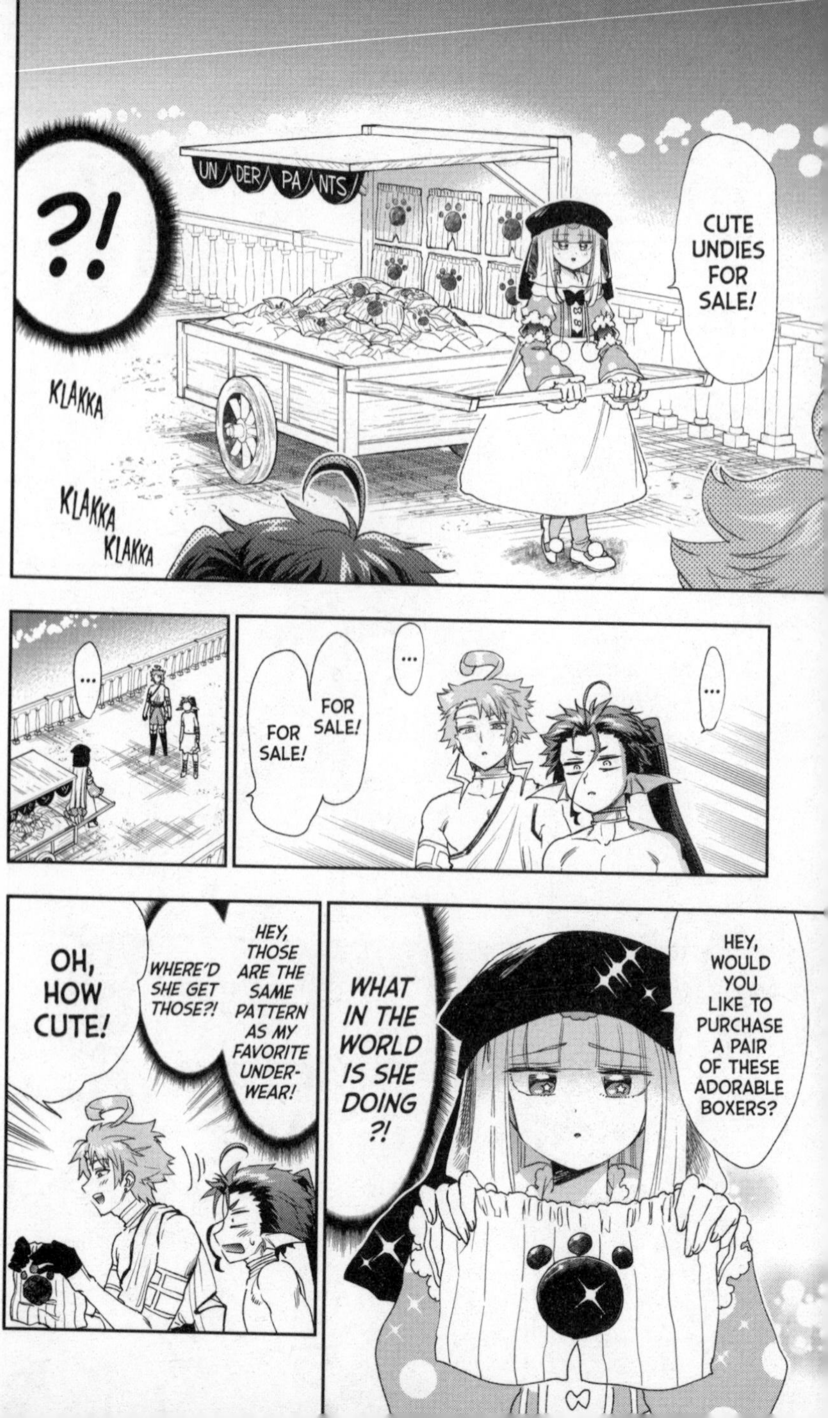
CUTE UNDIES FOR SALE!
UN DER PA NTS
?!
KLAKKA
KLAKKA KLAKKA
...
...
FOR SALE!
FOR SALE!
...
HEY, WOULD YOU LIKE TO PURCHASE A PAIR OF THESE ADORABLE BOXERS?
WHAT IN THE WORLD IS SHE DOING?!
HEY, THOSE ARE THE SAME PATTERN AS MY FAVORITE UNDER-WEAR!
WHERE'D SHE GET THOSE?!
OH, HOW CUTE!

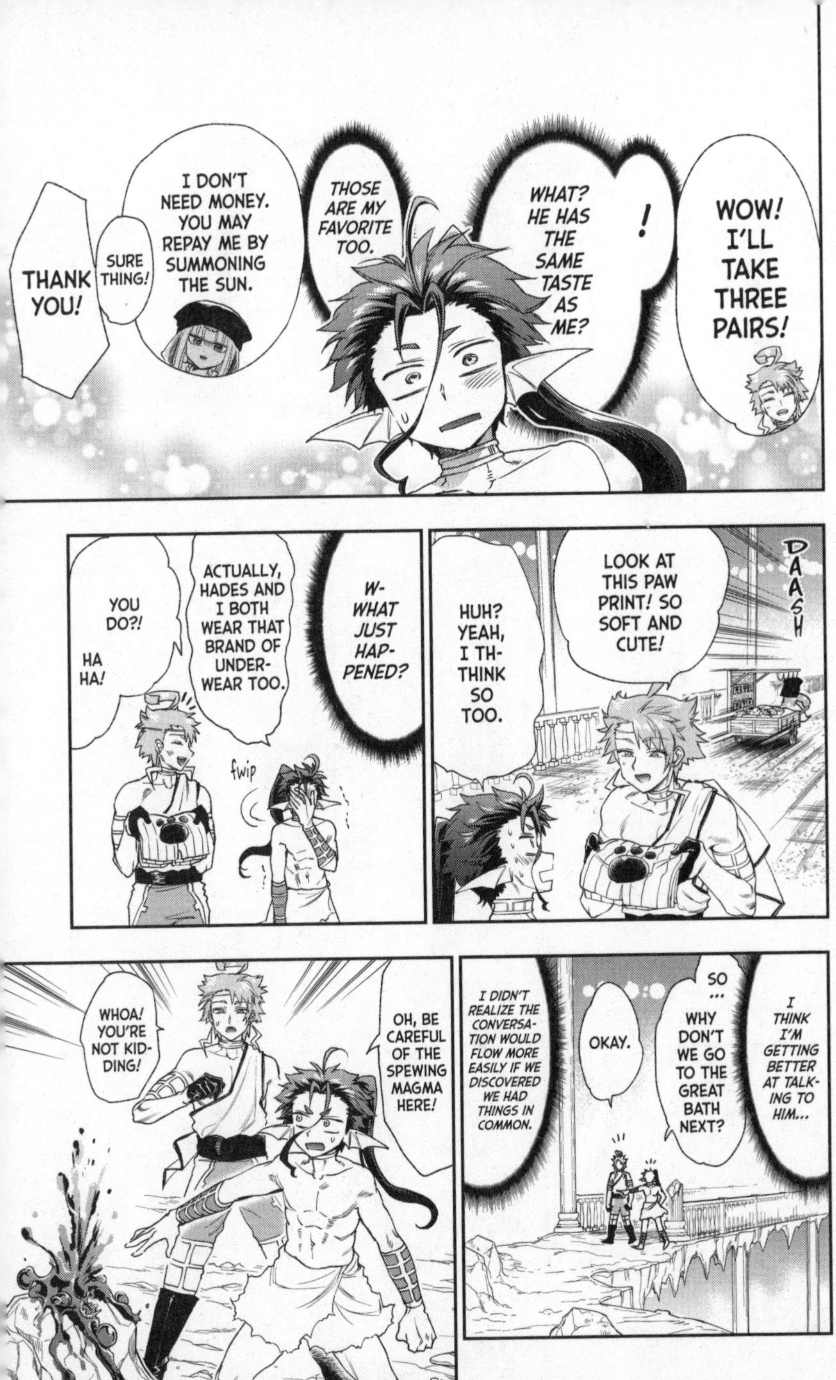
WOW! I'LL TAKE THREE PAIRS!
!
WHAT? HE HAS THE SAME TASTE AS ME?
THOSE ARE MY FAVORITE TOO.
I DON'T NEED MONEY. YOU MAY REPAY ME BY SUMMONING THE SUN.
SURE THING!
THANK YOU!
DAASH
LOOK AT THIS PAW PRINT! SO SOFT AND CUTE!
HUH? YEAH, I TH-THINK SO TOO.
W-WHAT JUST HAPPENED?
ACTUALLY, HADES AND I BOTH WEAR THAT BRAND OF UNDERWEAR TOO.
YOU DO?!
HA HA!
fwip
I THINK I'M GETTING BETTER AT TALKING TO HIM...
SO... WHY DON'T WE GO TO THE GREAT BATH NEXT?
OKAY.
I DIDN'T REALIZE THE CONVERSATION WOULD FLOW MORE EASILY IF WE DISCOVERED WE HAD THINGS IN COMMON.
OH, BE CAREFUL OF THE SPEWING MAGMA HERE!
WHOA! YOU'RE NOT KIDDING!

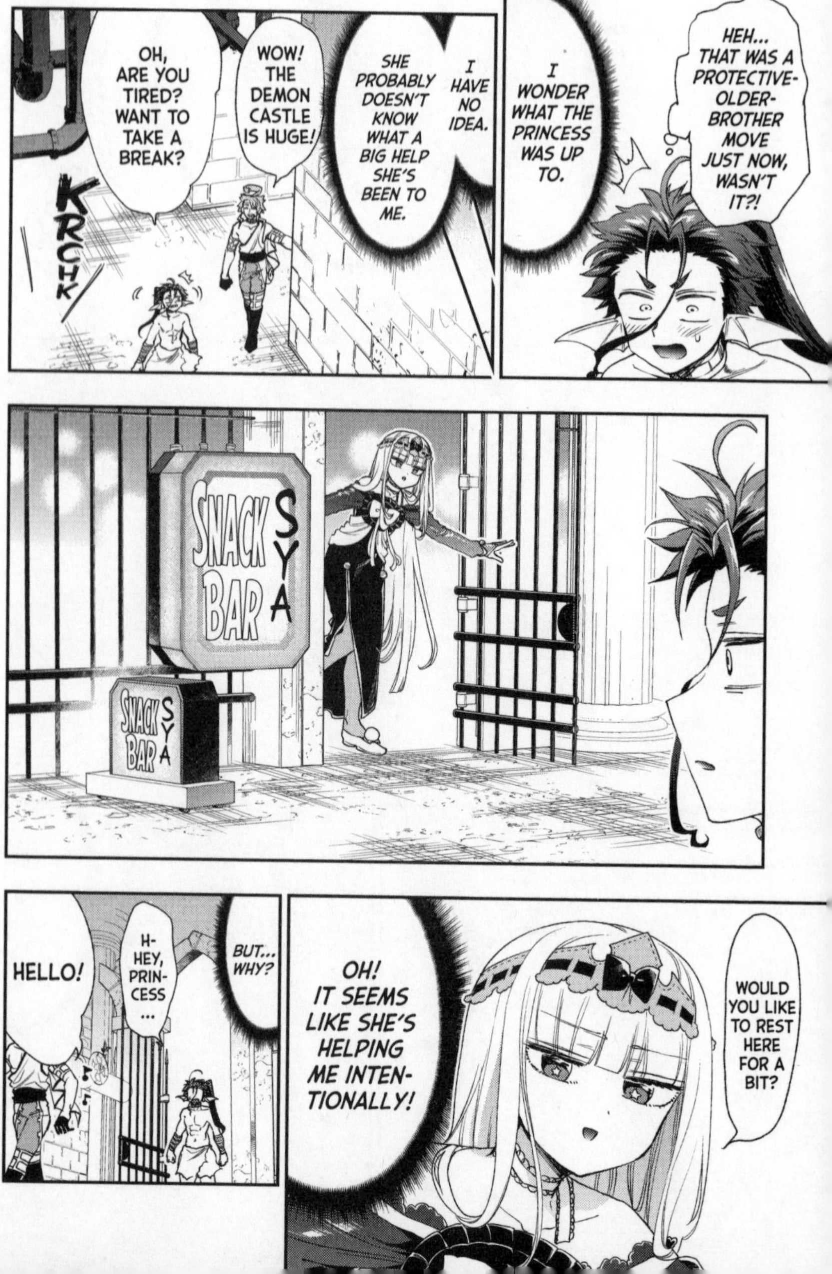
HEH... THAT WAS A PROTECTIVE-OLDER-BROTHER MOVE JUST NOW, WASN'T IT?!
I WONDER WHAT THE PRINCESS WAS UP TO.
I HAVE NO IDEA.
SHE PROBABLY DOESN'T KNOW WHAT A BIG HELP SHE'S BEEN TO ME.
WOW! THE DEMON CASTLE IS HUGE!
OH, ARE YOU TIRED? WANT TO TAKE A BREAK?
KRCHK
SNACK BAR SYA
SNACK BAR SYA
WOULD YOU LIKE TO REST HERE FOR A BIT?
OH! IT SEEMS LIKE SHE'S HELPING ME INTENTIONALLY!
BUT... WHY?
H-HEY, PRINCESS...
HELLO!

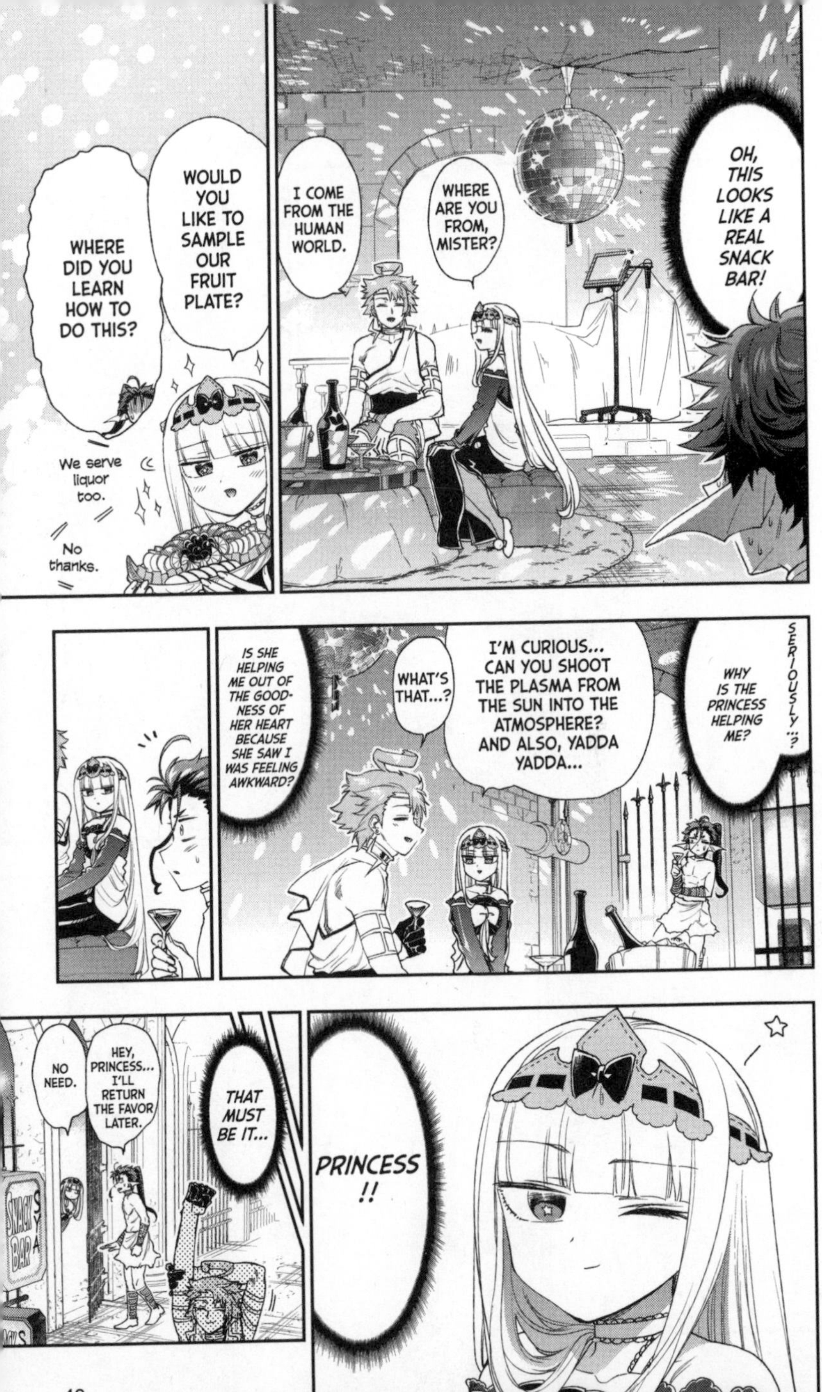
OH, THIS LOOKS LIKE A REAL SNACK BAR!
WHERE ARE YOU FROM, MISTER?
I COME FROM THE HUMAN WORLD.
WOULD YOU LIKE TO SAMPLE OUR FRUIT PLATE?
WHERE DID YOU LEARN HOW TO DO THIS?
We serve liquor too.
No thanks.
SERIOUSLY...?
WHY IS THE PRINCESS HELPING ME?
I'M CURIOUS... CAN YOU SHOOT THE PLASMA FROM THE SUN INTO THE ATMOSPHERE? AND ALSO, YADDA YADDA...
WHAT'S THAT...?
IS SHE HELPING ME OUT OF THE GOOD-NESS OF HER HEART BECAUSE SHE SAW I WAS FEELING AWKWARD?
PRINCESS !!
THAT MUST BE IT...
HEY, PRINCESS... I'LL RETURN THE FAVOR LATER.
NO NEED.
SNACK BAR

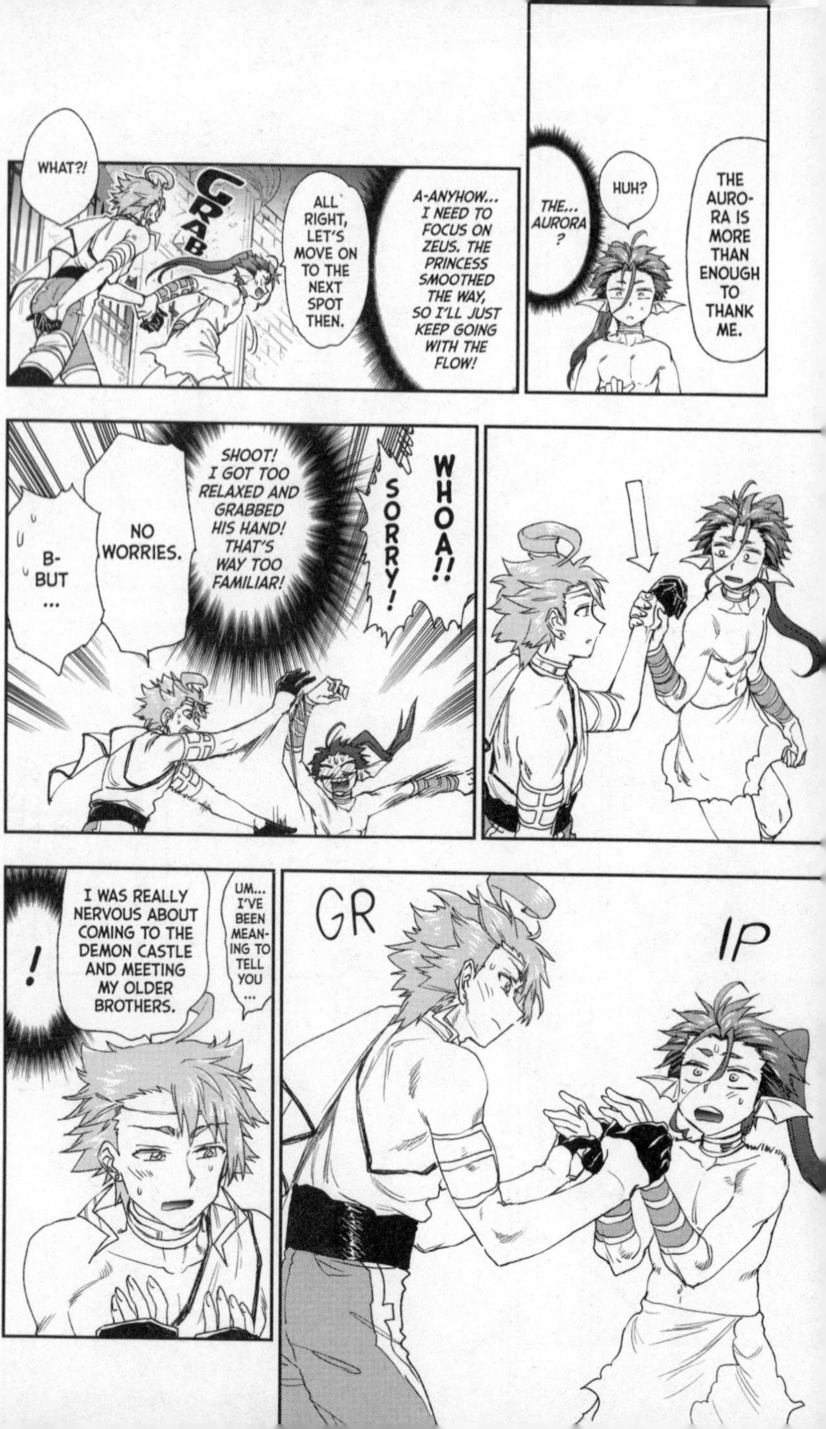
THE AURORA IS MORE THAN ENOUGH TO THANK ME.
HUH?
THE... AURORA?
A-ANYHOW... I NEED TO FOCUS ON ZEUS. THE PRINCESS SMOOTHED THE WAY, SO I'LL JUST KEEP GOING WITH THE FLOW!
ALL RIGHT, LET'S MOVE ON TO THE NEXT SPOT THEN.
GRAB
WHAT?!
WHOA!!
SORRY!
SHOOT! I GOT TOO RELAXED AND GRABBED HIS HAND! THAT'S WAY TOO FAMILIAR!
NO WORRIES.
B-BUT...
GR
IP
UM... I'VE BEEN MEANING TO TELL YOU...
I WAS REALLY NERVOUS ABOUT COMING TO THE DEMON CASTLE AND MEETING MY OLDER BROTHERS.
!

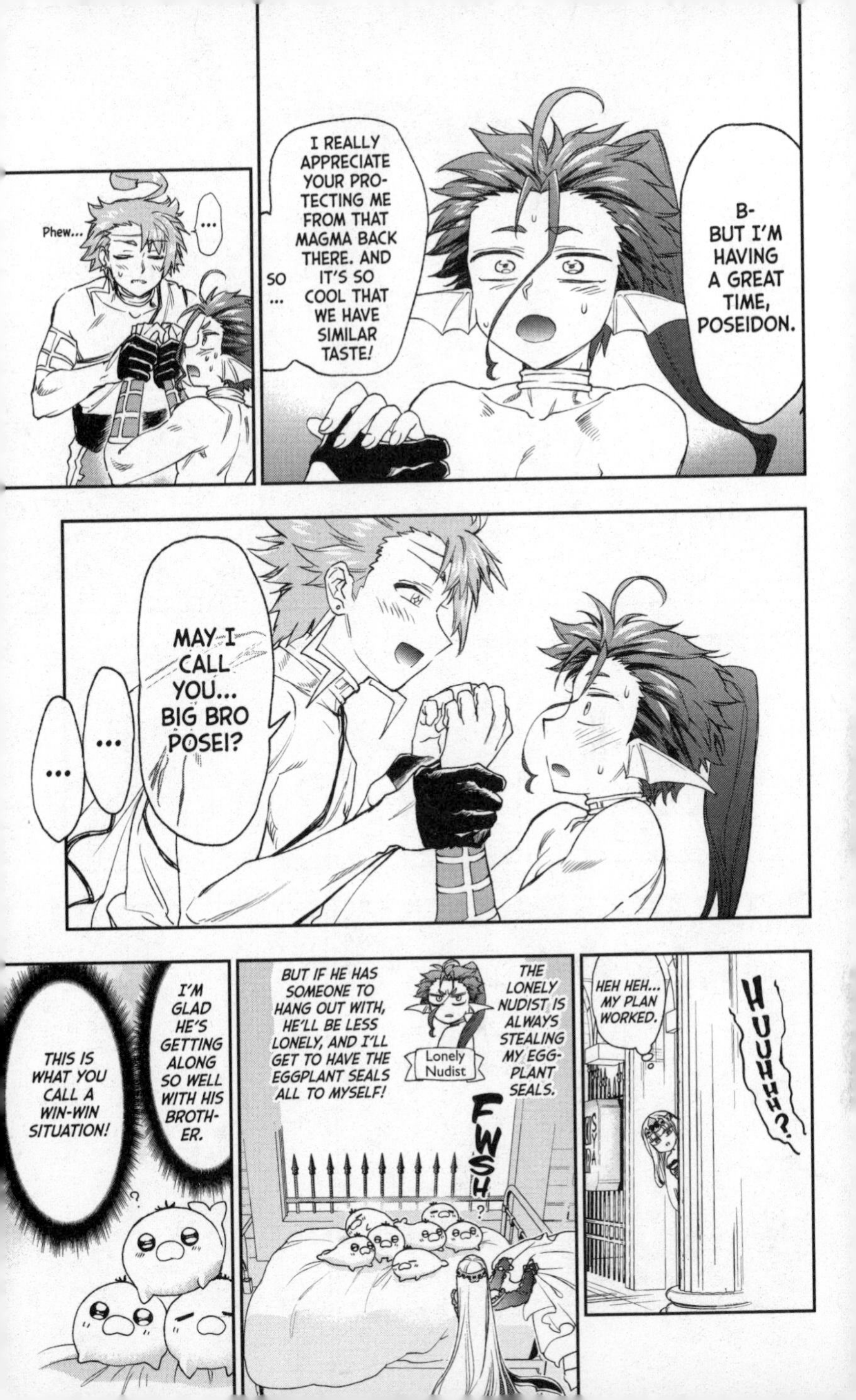
B- BUT I'M HAVING A GREAT TIME, POSEIDON.
I REALLY APPRECIATE YOUR PRO-TECTING ME FROM THAT MAGMA BACK THERE. AND IT'S SO COOL THAT WE HAVE SIMILAR TASTE!
SO ...
...
Phew...
MAY I CALL YOU... BIG BRO POSEI?
...
...
HUUUHH?
HEH HEH... MY PLAN WORKED.
THE LONELY NUDIST IS ALWAYS STEALING MY EGG-PLANT SEALS.
Lonely Nudist
BUT IF HE HAS SOMEONE TO HANG OUT WITH, HE'LL BE LESS LONELY, AND I'LL GET TO HAVE THE EGGPLANT SEALS ALL TO MYSELF!
FWSH
I'M GLAD HE'S GETTING ALONG SO WELL WITH HIS BROTH-ER.
THIS IS WHAT YOU CALL A WIN-WIN SITUATION!

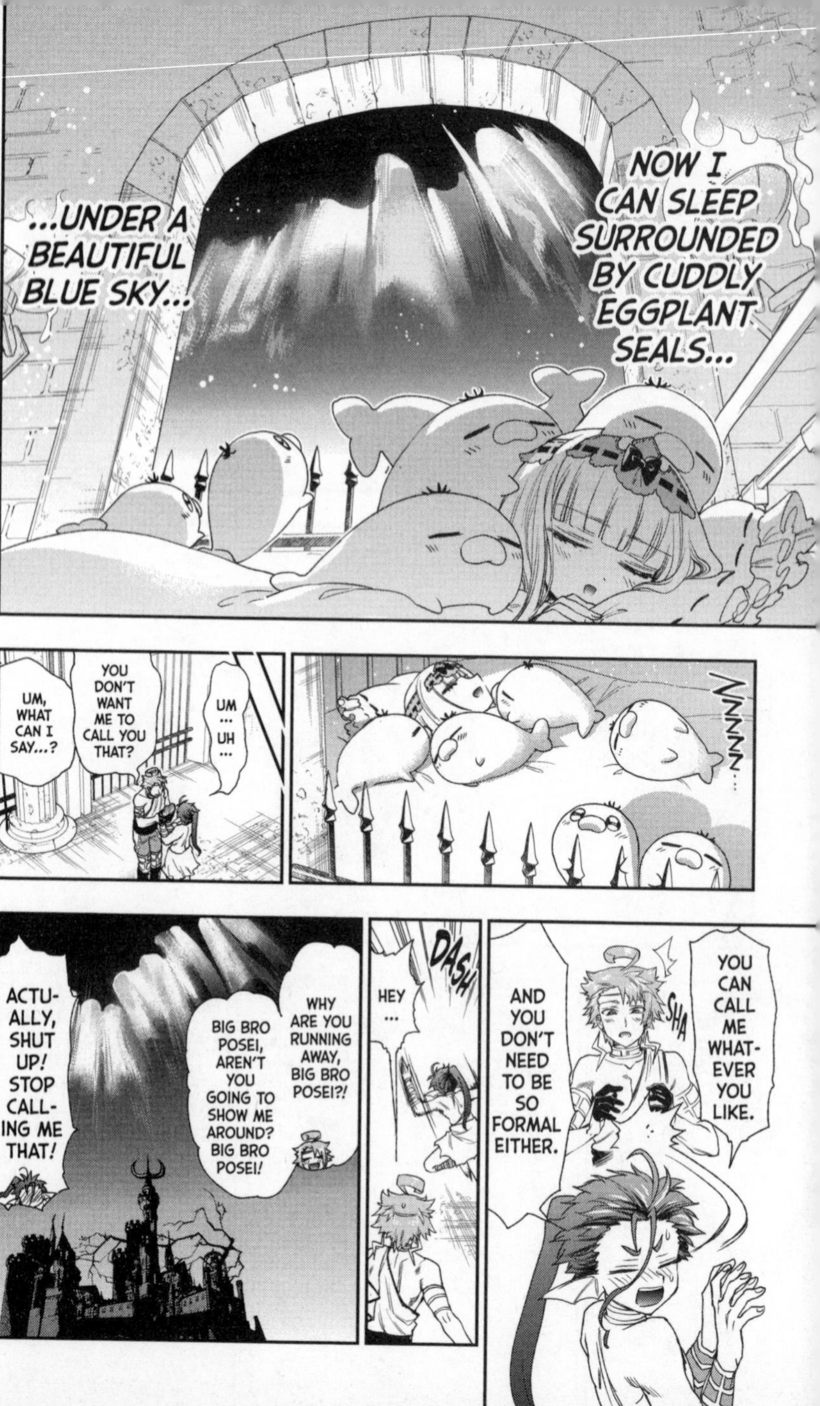
NOW I CAN SLEEP SURROUNDED BY CUDDLY EGGPLANT SEALS...
...UNDER A BEAUTIFUL BLUE SKY...
ZZZZ...
UM... UH...
YOU DON'T WANT ME TO CALL YOU THAT?
UM, WHAT CAN I SAY...?
YOU CAN CALL ME WHATEVER YOU LIKE.
SHA
AND YOU DON'T NEED TO BE SO FORMAL EITHER.
DASH
HEY...
WHY ARE YOU RUNNING AWAY, BIG BRO POSEI?!
BIG BRO POSEI, AREN'T YOU GOING TO SHOW ME AROUND? BIG BRO POSEI!
ACTUALLY, SHUT UP! STOP CALLING ME THAT!

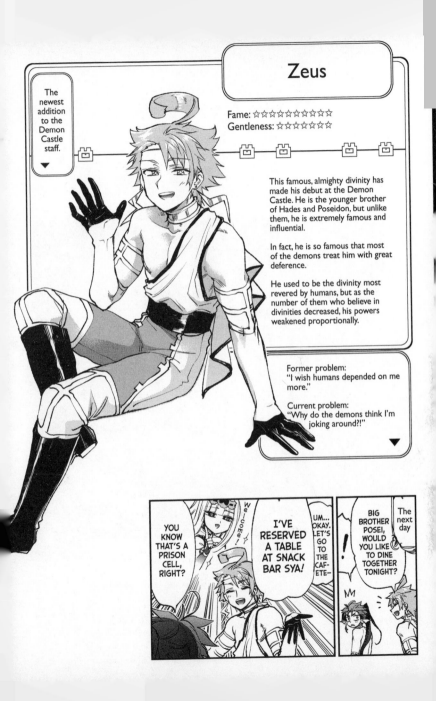

Zeus

The newest addition to the Demon Castle staff.

Fame: ☆☆☆☆☆☆☆☆☆☆☆
Gentleness: ☆☆☆☆☆☆☆

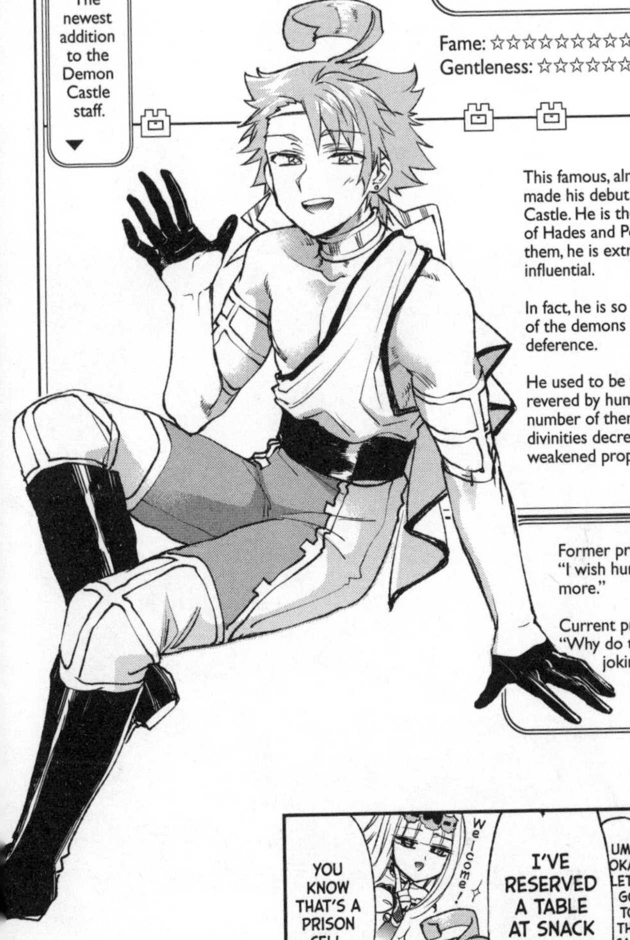

This famous, almighty divinity has made his debut at the Demon Castle. He is the younger brother of Hades and Poseidon, but unlike them, he is extremely famous and influential.

In fact, he is so famous that most of the demons treat him with great deference.

He used to be the divinity most revered by humans, but as the number of them who believe in divinities decreased, his powers weakened proportionally.

Former problem:
"I wish humans depended on me more."

Current problem:
"Why do the demons think I'm joking around?!"

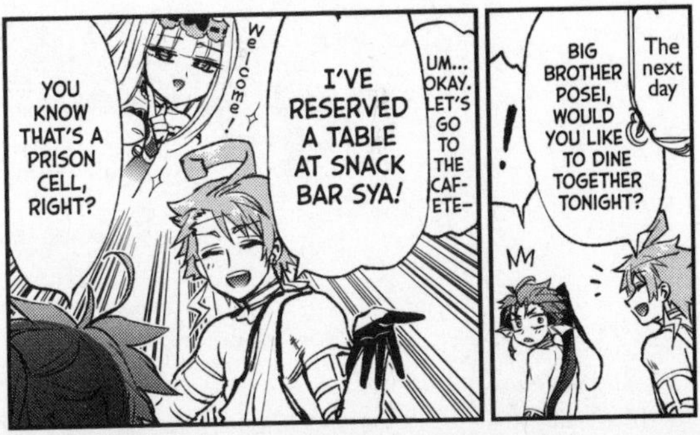
The next day
BIG BROTHER POSEI, WOULD YOU LIKE TO DINE TOGETHER TONIGHT?
!
UM... OKAY. LET'S GO TO THE CAFETE-
I'VE RESERVED A TABLE AT SNACK BAR SYA!
Welcome!
YOU KNOW THAT'S A PRISON CELL, RIGHT?

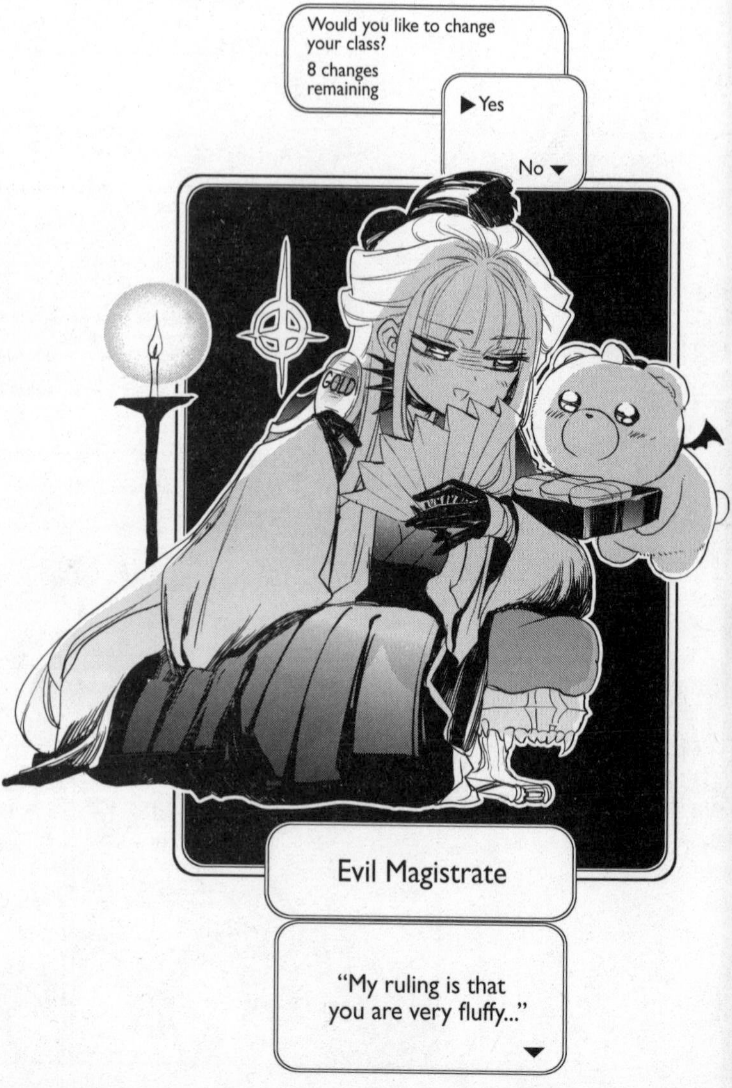
Would you like to change your class?
8 changes remaining
▶Yes
No
GOLD
Evil Magistrate
"My ruling is that you are very fluffy..."

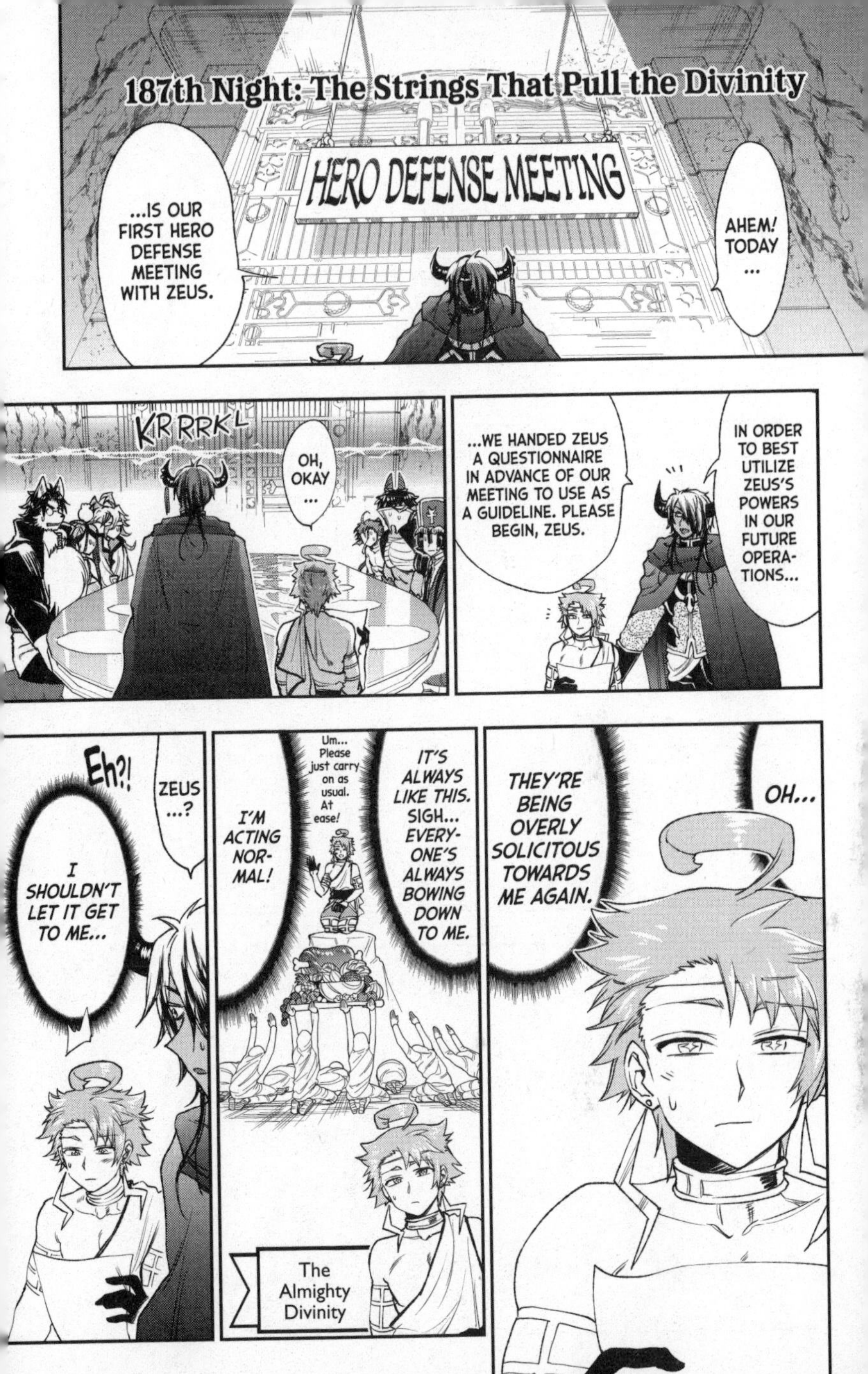
187th Night: The Strings That Pull the Divinity
HERO DEFENSE MEETING
AHEM! TODAY...
...IS OUR FIRST HERO DEFENSE MEETING WITH ZEUS.
IN ORDER TO BEST UTILIZE ZEUS'S POWERS IN OUR FUTURE OPERATIONS...
...WE HANDED ZEUS A QUESTIONNAIRE IN ADVANCE OF OUR MEETING TO USE AS A GUIDELINE. PLEASE BEGIN, ZEUS.
KRRRKL
OH, OKAY...
OH...
THEY'RE BEING OVERLY SOLICITOUS TOWARDS ME AGAIN.
IT'S ALWAYS LIKE THIS. SIGH... EVERYONE'S ALWAYS BOWING DOWN TO ME.
Um... Please just carry on as usual. At ease!
I'M ACTING NORMAL!
The Almighty Divinity
ZEUS...?
Eh?!
I SHOULDN'T LET IT GET TO ME...

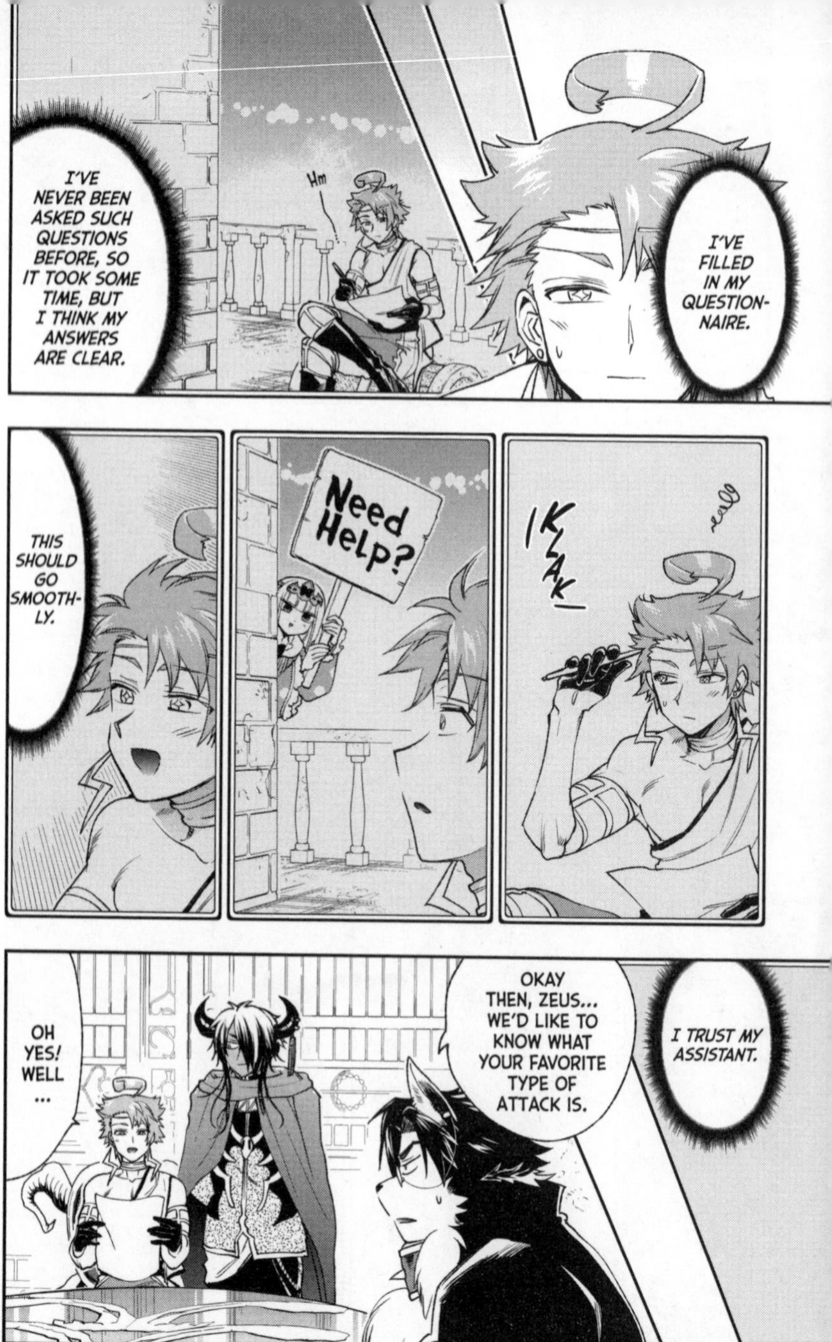
I'VE FILLED IN MY QUESTIONNAIRE.
Hm
I'VE NEVER BEEN ASKED SUCH QUESTIONS BEFORE, SO IT TOOK SOME TIME, BUT I THINK MY ANSWERS ARE CLEAR.
KLAK
Need Help?
THIS SHOULD GO SMOOTHLY.
I TRUST MY ASSISTANT.
OKAY THEN, ZEUS... WE'D LIKE TO KNOW WHAT YOUR FAVORITE TYPE OF ATTACK IS.
OH YES! WELL ...

187th Night: The Strings That Pull the Divinity

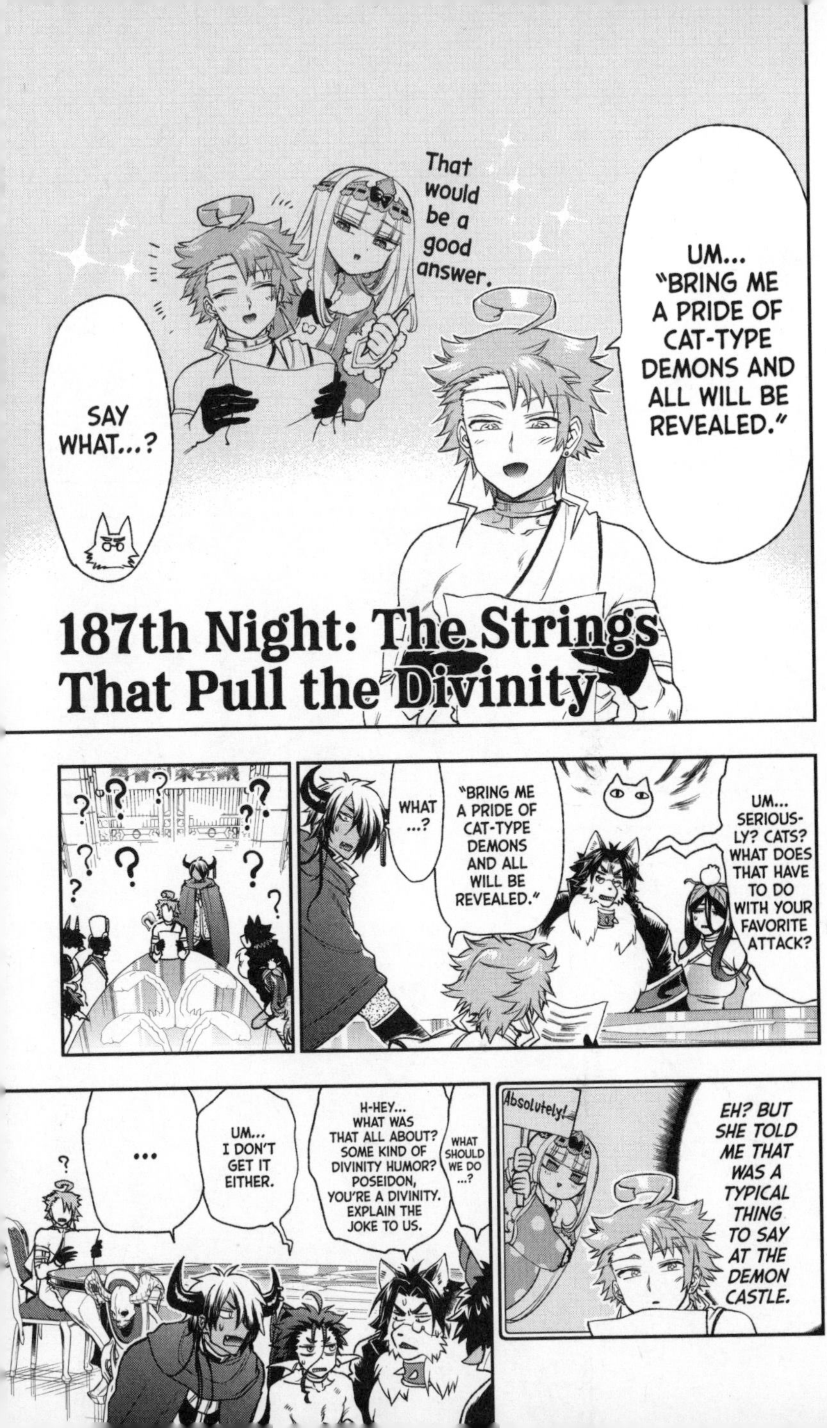
UM... "BRING ME A PRIDE OF CAT-TYPE DEMONS AND ALL WILL BE REVEALED."
That would be a good answer.
SAY WHAT...?
UM... SERIOUS-LY? CATS? WHAT DOES THAT HAVE TO DO WITH YOUR FAVORITE ATTACK?
"BRING ME A PRIDE OF CAT-TYPE DEMONS AND ALL WILL BE REVEALED."
WHAT ...?
EH? BUT SHE TOLD ME THAT WAS A TYPICAL THING TO SAY AT THE DEMON CASTLE.
Absolutely!
WHAT SHOULD WE DO ...?
H-HEY... WHAT WAS THAT ALL ABOUT? SOME KIND OF DIVINITY HUMOR? POSEIDON, YOU'RE A DIVINITY. EXPLAIN THE JOKE TO US.
UM... I DON'T GET IT EITHER.
...
?

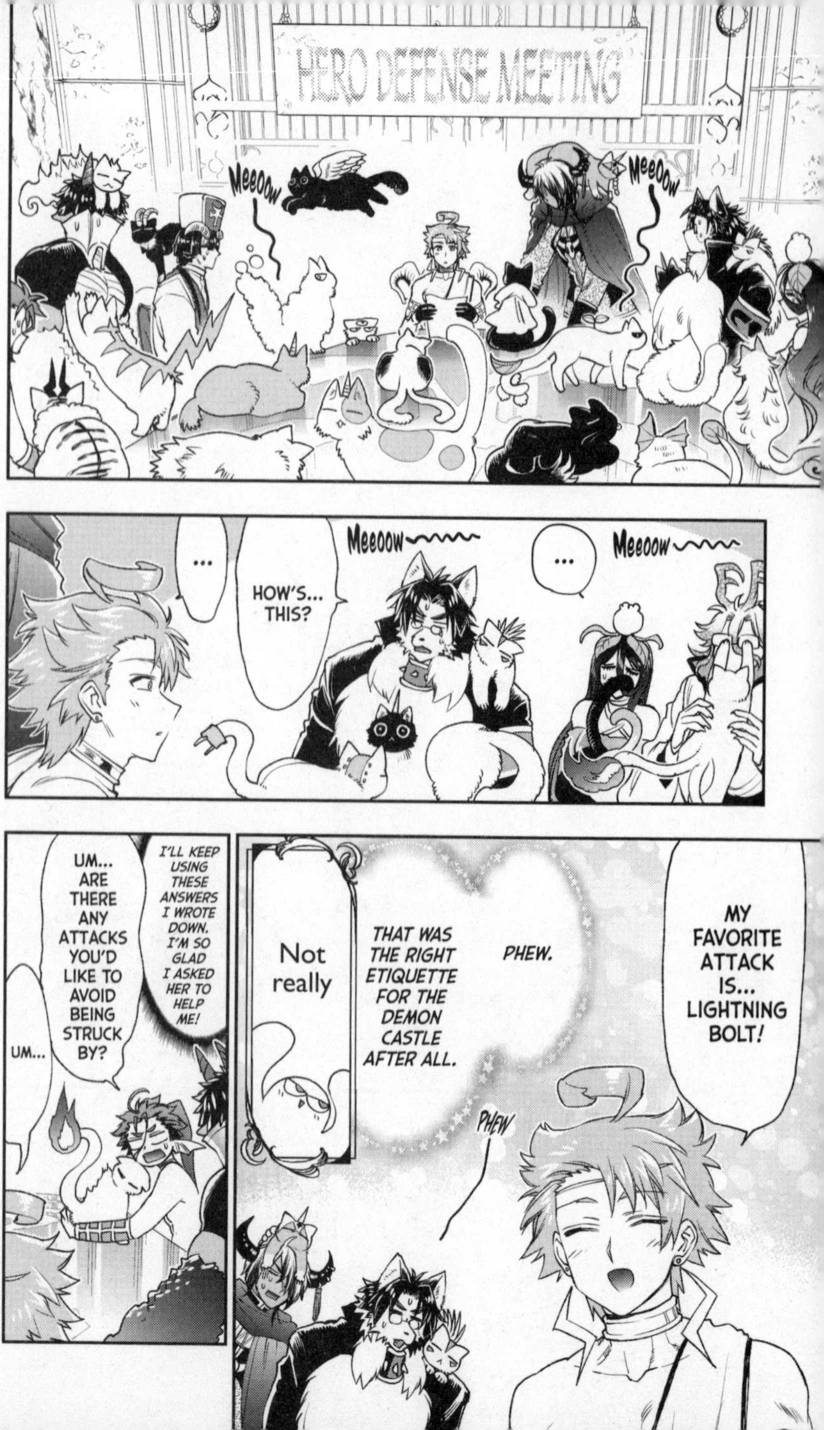
HERO DEFENSE MEETING
Meeoow
Meeoow
Meeoow
...
Meeoow
HOW'S... THIS?
...
MY FAVORITE ATTACK IS... LIGHTNING BOLT!
PHEW.
PHEW
THAT WAS THE RIGHT ETIQUETTE FOR THE DEMON CASTLE AFTER ALL.
Not really
I'LL KEEP USING THESE ANSWERS I WROTE DOWN. I'M SO GLAD I ASKED HER TO HELP ME!
UM... ARE THERE ANY ATTACKS YOU'D LIKE TO AVOID BEING STRUCK BY?
UM...

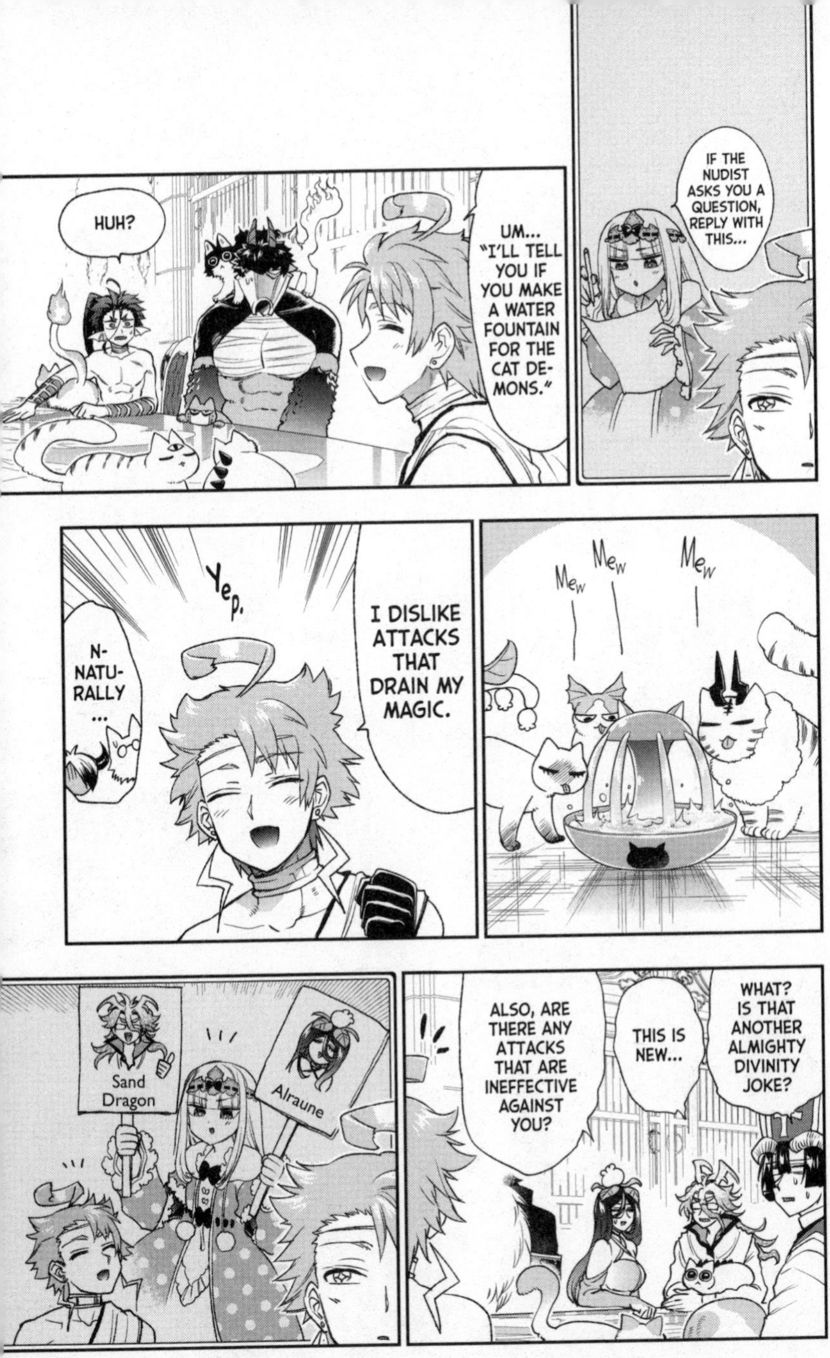
IF THE NUDIST ASKS YOU A QUESTION, REPLY WITH THIS...
UM... "I'LL TELL YOU IF YOU MAKE A WATER FOUNTAIN FOR THE CAT DE-MONS."
HUH?
Mew
Mew
Mew
I DISLIKE ATTACKS THAT DRAIN MY MAGIC.
Yep.
N-NATU-RALLY ...
WHAT? IS THAT ANOTHER ALMIGHTY DIVINITY JOKE?
THIS IS NEW...
ALSO, ARE THERE ANY ATTACKS THAT ARE INEFFECTIVE AGAINST YOU?
Alraune
Sand Dragon

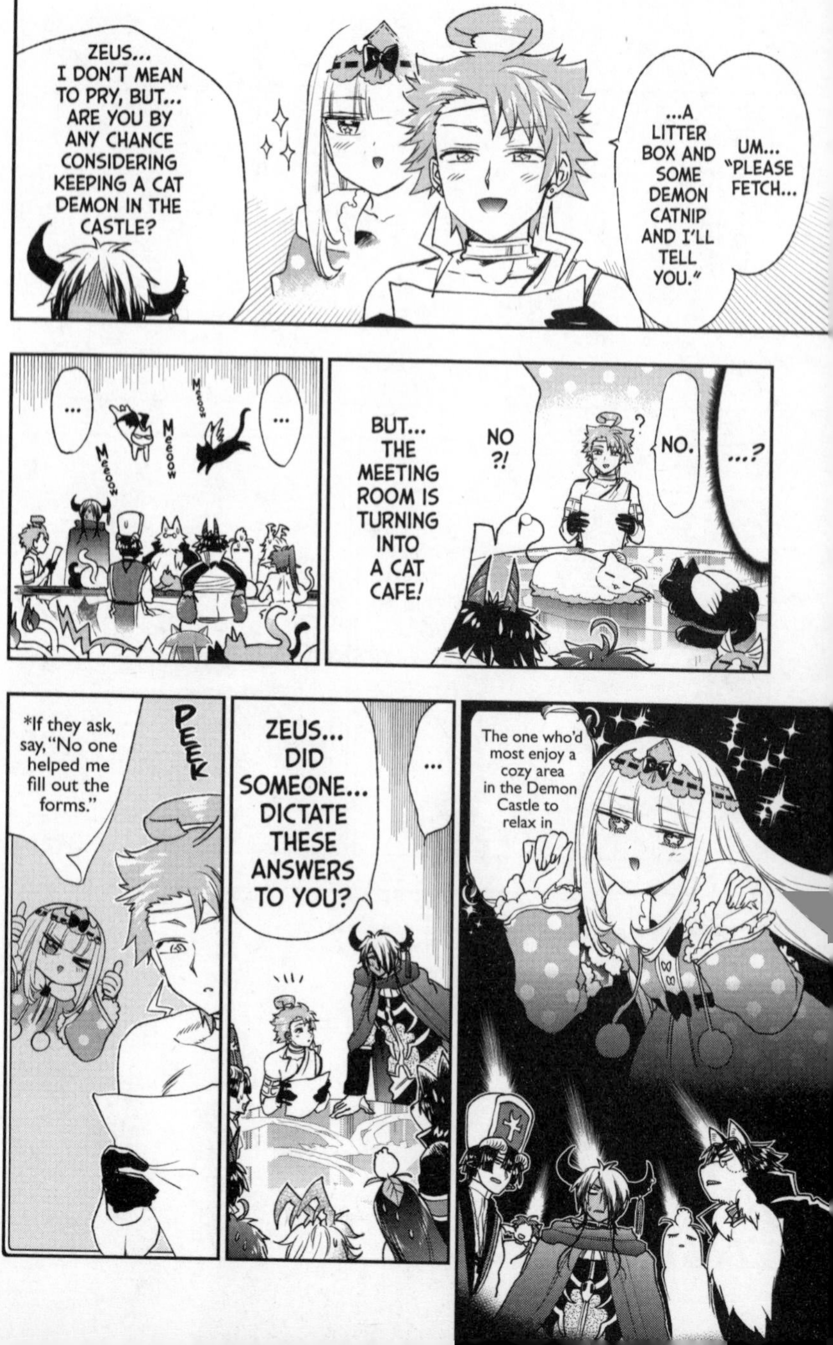
UM... "PLEASE FETCH...
...A LITTER BOX AND SOME DEMON CATNIP AND I'LL TELL YOU."
ZEUS... I DON'T MEAN TO PRY, BUT... ARE YOU BY ANY CHANCE CONSIDERING KEEPING A CAT DEMON IN THE CASTLE?
...?
NO.
NO ?!
BUT... THE MEETING ROOM IS TURNING INTO A CAT CAFE!
...
MEEOOW
Meeeow
Meeeow
...
The one who'd most enjoy a cozy area in the Demon Castle to relax in
...
ZEUS... DID SOMEONE... DICTATE THESE ANSWERS TO YOU?
PEEK
*If they ask, say, "No one helped me fill out the forms."

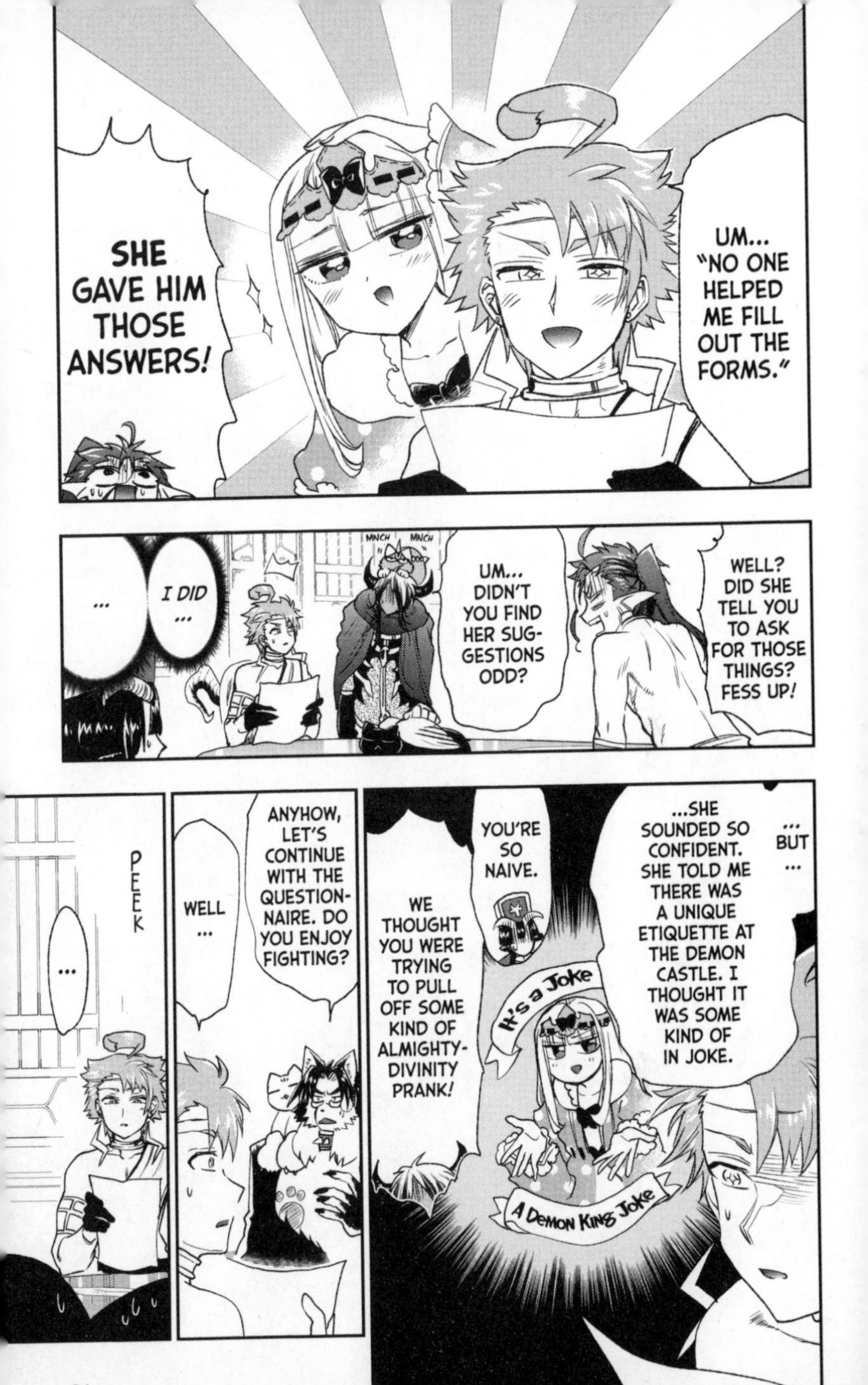
UM... "NO ONE HELPED ME FILL OUT THE FORMS."
SHE GAVE HIM THOSE ANSWERS!
WELL? DID SHE TELL YOU TO ASK FOR THOSE THINGS? FESS UP!
UM... DIDN'T YOU FIND HER SUG- GESTIONS ODD?
MNCH MNCH
I DID ...
...
... BUT ...
...SHE SOUNDED SO CONFIDENT. SHE TOLD ME THERE WAS A UNIQUE ETIQUETTE AT THE DEMON CASTLE. I THOUGHT IT WAS SOME KIND OF IN JOKE.
It's a Joke
A Demon King Joke
YOU'RE SO NAIVE.
WE THOUGHT YOU WERE TRYING TO PULL OFF SOME KIND OF ALMIGHTY- DIVINITY PRANK!
ANYHOW, LET'S CONTINUE WITH THE QUESTION- NAIRE. DO YOU ENJOY FIGHTING?
WELL ...
PEEK
...

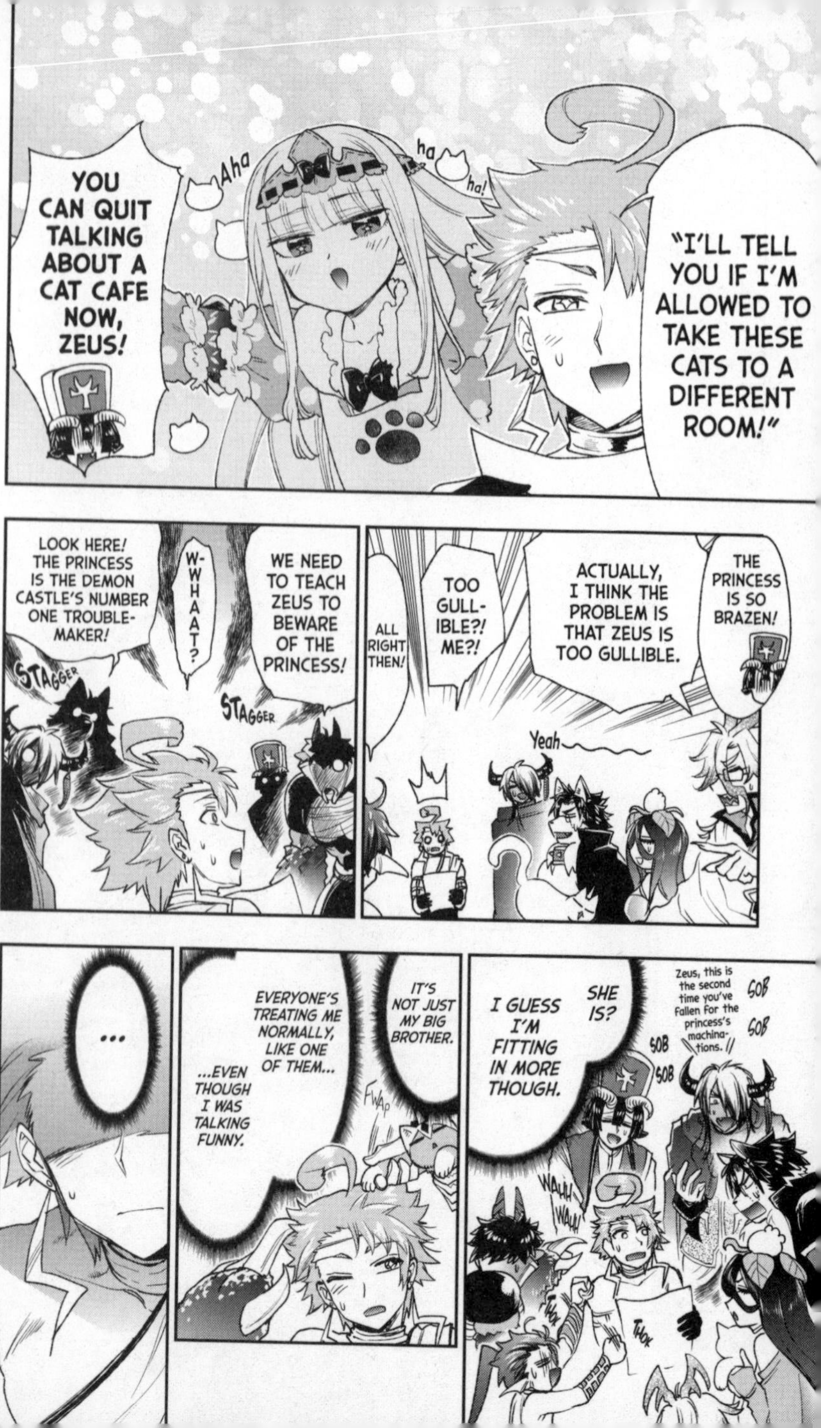
"I'LL TELL YOU IF I'M ALLOWED TO TAKE THESE CATS TO A DIFFERENT ROOM!"
ha
ha!
Aha
YOU CAN QUIT TALKING ABOUT A CAT CAFE NOW, ZEUS!
THE PRINCESS IS SO BRAZEN!
ACTUALLY, I THINK THE PROBLEM IS THAT ZEUS IS TOO GULLIBLE.
TOO GULL-IBLE?! ME?!
ALL RIGHT THEN!
Yeah
WE NEED TO TEACH ZEUS TO BEWARE OF THE PRINCESS!
W-WHAAT?
LOOK HERE! THE PRINCESS IS THE DEMON CASTLE'S NUMBER ONE TROUBLE-MAKER!
STAGGER
STAGGER
Zeus, this is the second time you've fallen for the princess's machinations.
SOB
SOB
SOB
SOB
SHE IS?
I GUESS I'M FITTING IN MORE THOUGH.
WAAH
WAAH
THOK
THOK
IT'S NOT JUST MY BIG BROTHER.
EVERYONE'S TREATING ME NORMALLY, LIKE ONE OF THEM...
...EVEN THOUGH I WAS TALKING FUNNY.
FWAP
...

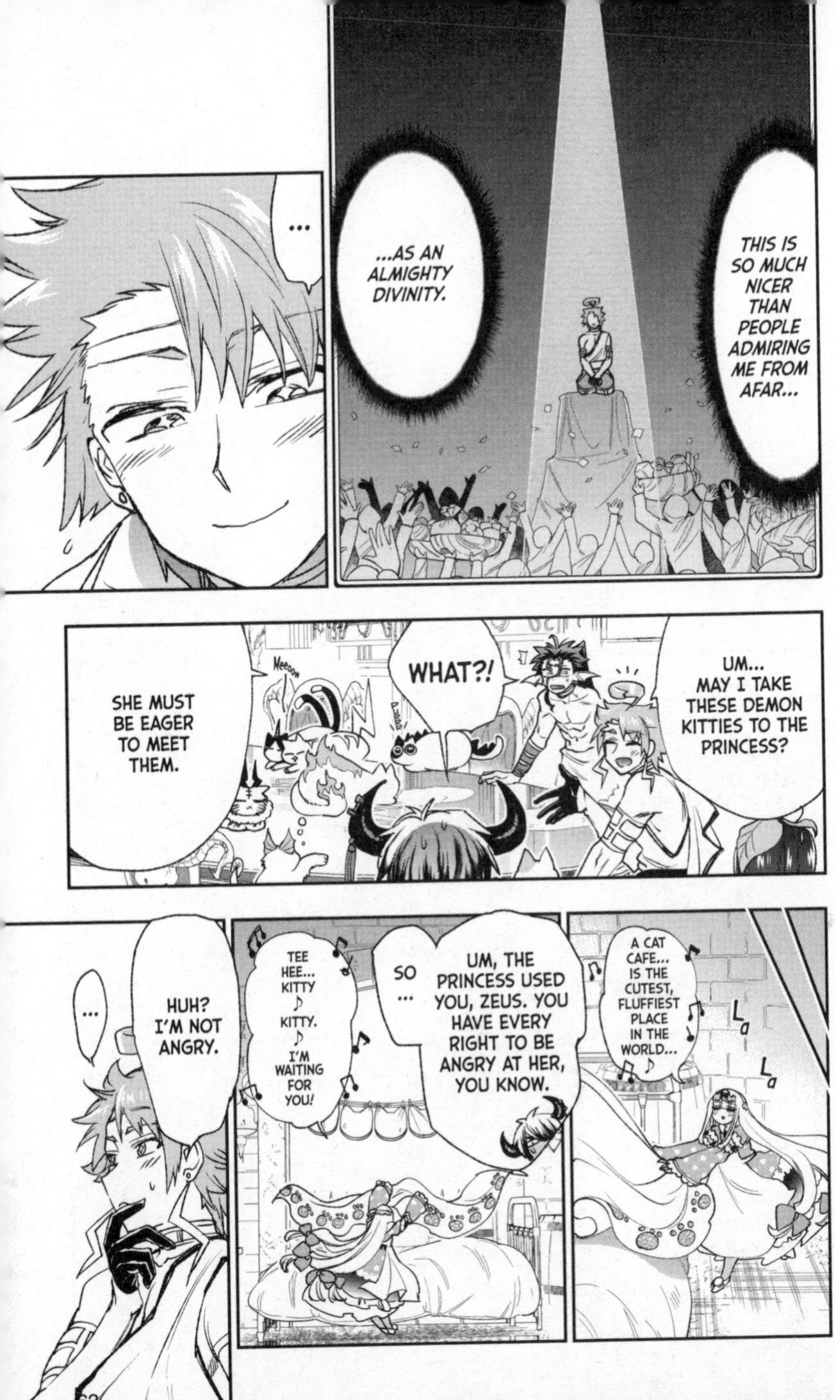
THIS IS SO MUCH NICER THAN PEOPLE ADMIRING ME FROM AFAR...
...AS AN ALMIGHTY DIVINITY.
...
UM... MAY I TAKE THESE DEMON KITTIES TO THE PRINCESS?
WHAT?!
Meeoow
SHE MUST BE EAGER TO MEET THEM.
A CAT CAFE... IS THE CUTEST, FLUFFIEST PLACE IN THE WORLD... ♪
La La
SO ... UM, THE PRINCESS USED YOU, ZEUS. YOU HAVE EVERY RIGHT TO BE ANGRY AT HER, YOU KNOW.
TEE HEE... KITTY ♪ KITTY. ♪ I'M WAITING FOR YOU!
HUH? I'M NOT ANGRY.
...

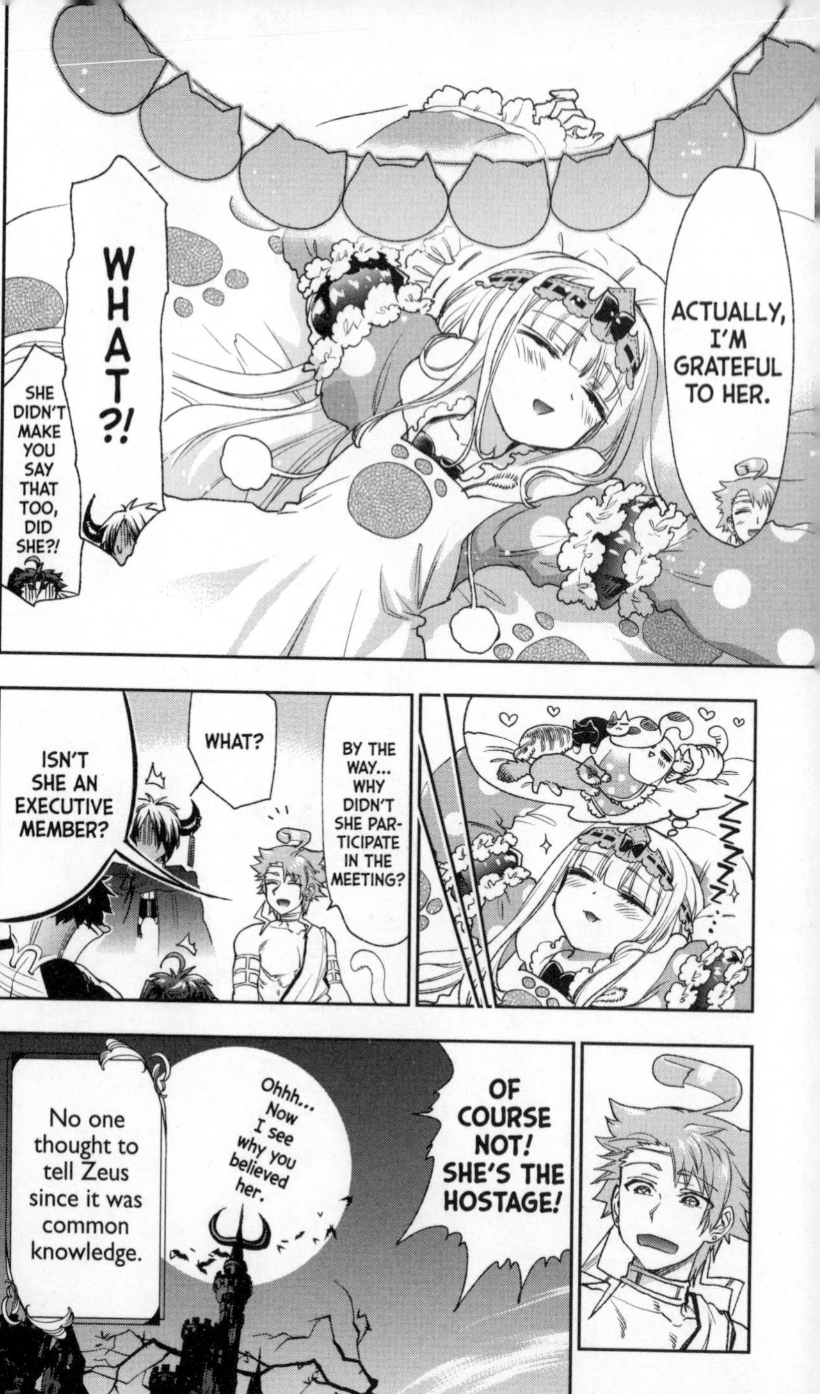
ACTUALLY, I'M GRATEFUL TO HER.
WHAT?!
SHE DIDN'T MAKE YOU SAY THAT TOO, DID SHE?!
BY THE WAY... WHY DIDN'T SHE PARTICIPATE IN THE MEETING?
WHAT?
ISN'T SHE AN EXECUTIVE MEMBER?
OF COURSE NOT! SHE'S THE HOSTAGE!
Ohhh... Now I see why you believed her.
No one thought to tell Zeus since it was common knowledge.

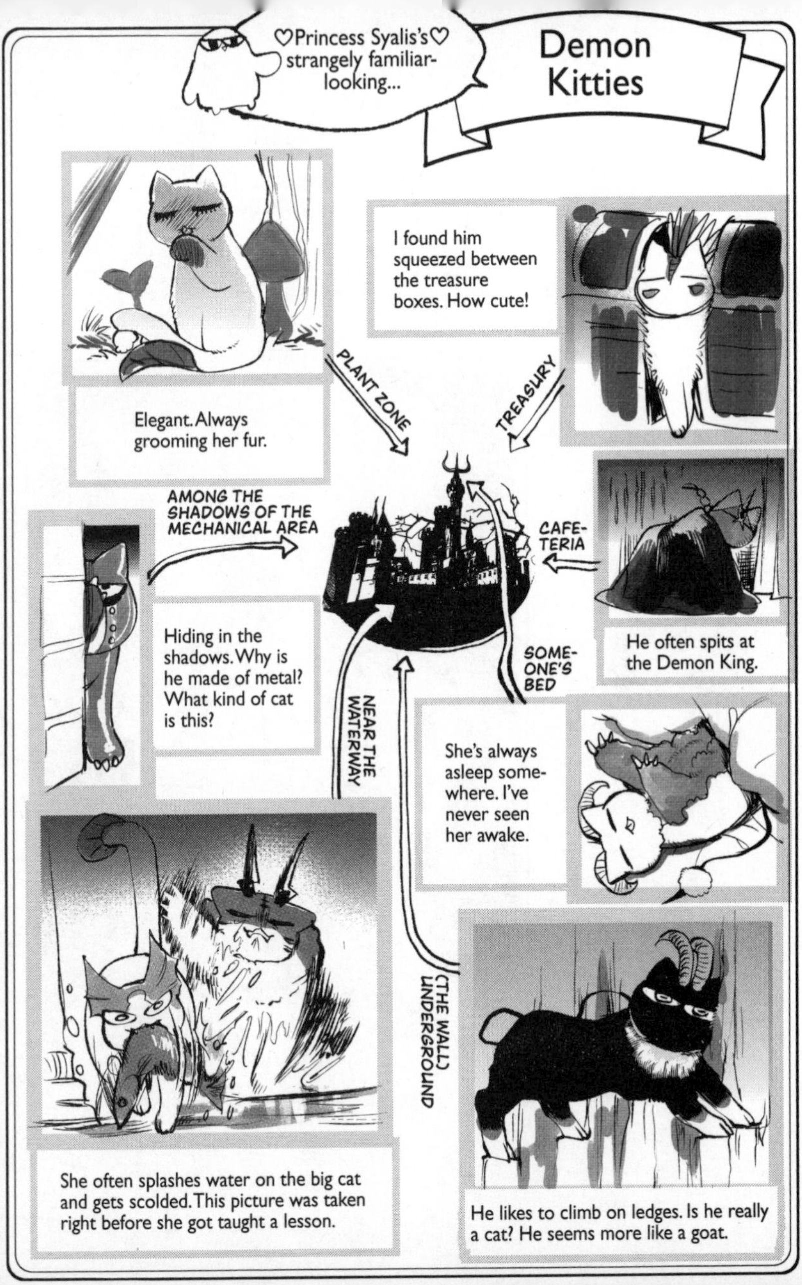
♡Princess Syalis's♡ strangely familiar-looking...
Demon Kitties
I found him squeezed between the treasure boxes. How cute!
TREASURY
Elegant. Always grooming her fur.
PLANT ZONE
CAFE-TERIA
He often spits at the Demon King.
AMONG THE SHADOWS OF THE MECHANICAL AREA
Hiding in the shadows. Why is he made of metal? What kind of cat is this?
SOME-ONE'S BED
She's always asleep some-where. I've never seen her awake.
NEAR THE WATERWAY
She often splashes water on the big cat and gets scolded. This picture was taken right before she got taught a lesson.
(THE WALL) UNDERGROUND
He likes to climb on ledges. Is he really a cat? He seems more like a goat.

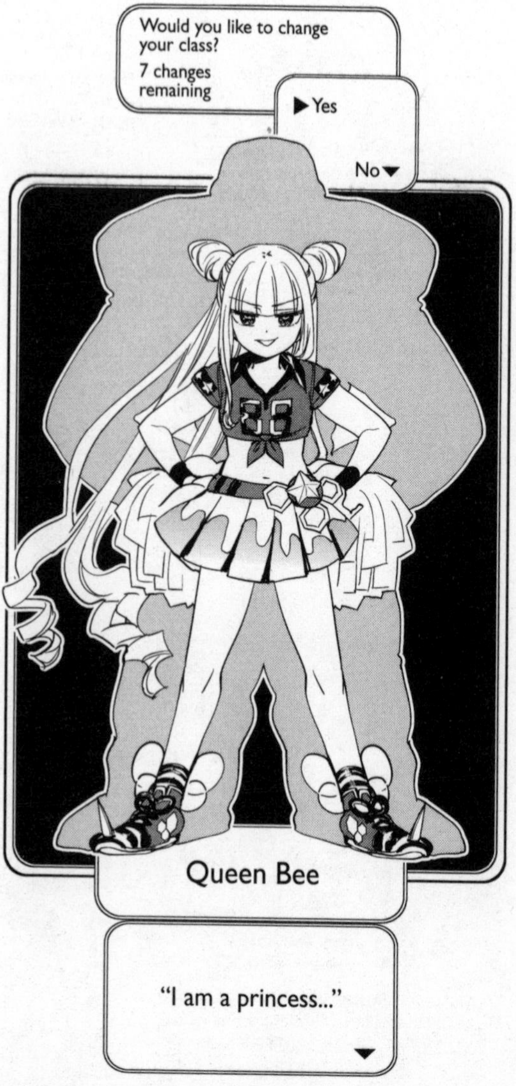
Would you like to change your class?
7 changes remaining
▶Yes
No▼
Queen Bee
“I am a princess...”

188th Night: Happy 50th Anniversary

☆Can you find Doraemon hidden in this chapter?

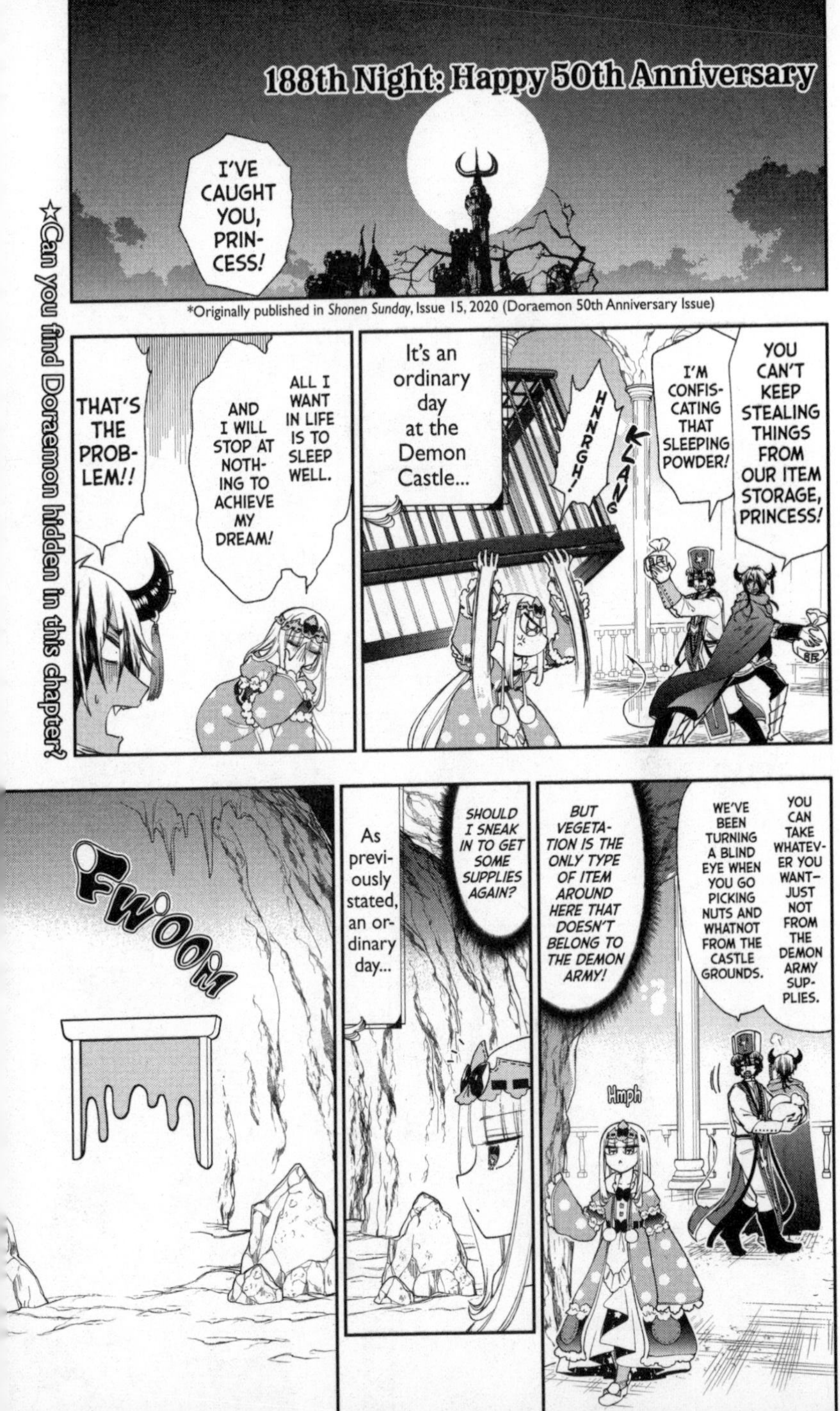
I'VE CAUGHT YOU, PRIN-CESS!
*Originally published in *Shonen Sunday*, Issue 15, 2020 (Doraemon 50th Anniversary Issue)
YOU CAN'T KEEP STEALING THINGS FROM OUR ITEM STORAGE, PRINCESS!
I'M CONFIS-CATING THAT SLEEPING POWDER!
KLANG
HNNRGH!
It's an ordinary day at the Demon Castle...
ALL I WANT IN LIFE IS TO SLEEP WELL.
AND I WILL STOP AT NOTH-ING TO ACHIEVE MY DREAM!
THAT'S THE PROB-LEM!!
YOU CAN TAKE WHATEV-ER YOU WANT—JUST NOT FROM THE DEMON ARMY SUP-PLIES.
WE'VE BEEN TURNING A BLIND EYE WHEN YOU GO PICKING NUTS AND WHATNOT FROM THE CASTLE GROUNDS.
BUT VEGETA-TION IS THE ONLY TYPE OF ITEM AROUND HERE THAT DOESN'T BELONG TO THE DEMON ARMY!
Hmph
SHOULD I SNEAK IN TO GET SOME SUPPLIES AGAIN?
As previ-ously stated, an or-dinary day...
FWOOM

188th Night: Happy 50th Anniversary

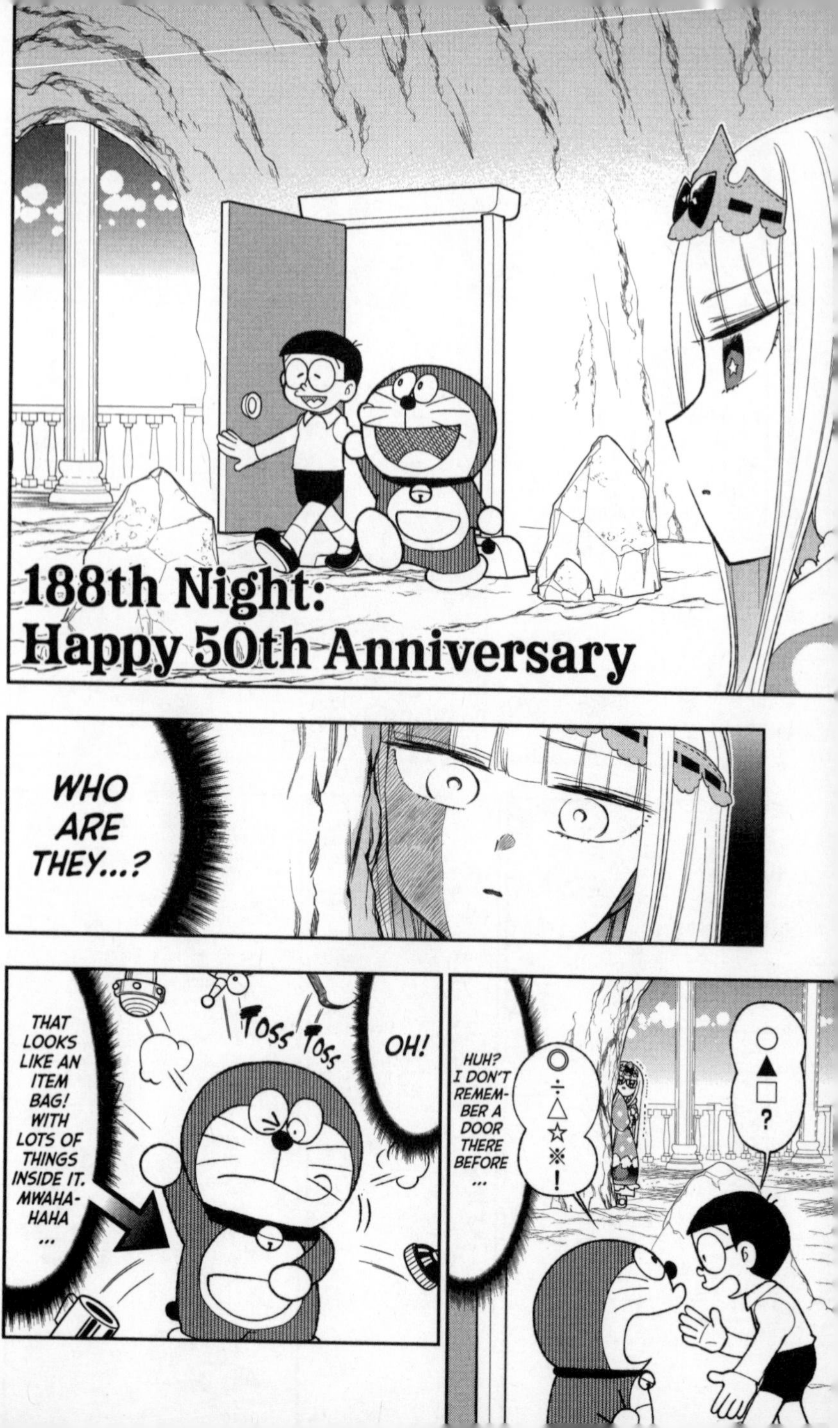
WHO ARE THEY...?
○▲□?
◎÷△☆※!
HUH? I DON'T REMEMBER A DOOR THERE BEFORE ...
OH!
TOSS TOSS
THAT LOOKS LIKE AN ITEM BAG! WITH LOTS OF THINGS INSIDE IT. MWAHAHAHA ...

AND LUCKILY, THAT CUTE BLUE RACCOON-DOG DOESN'T SEEM TO BE A DEMON ARMY SOLDIER. SO IT'S NOT EVEN OFF-LIMITS.

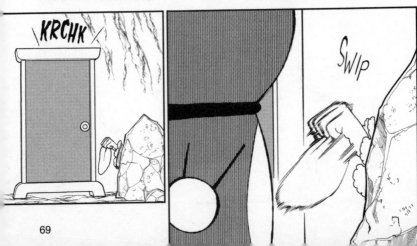

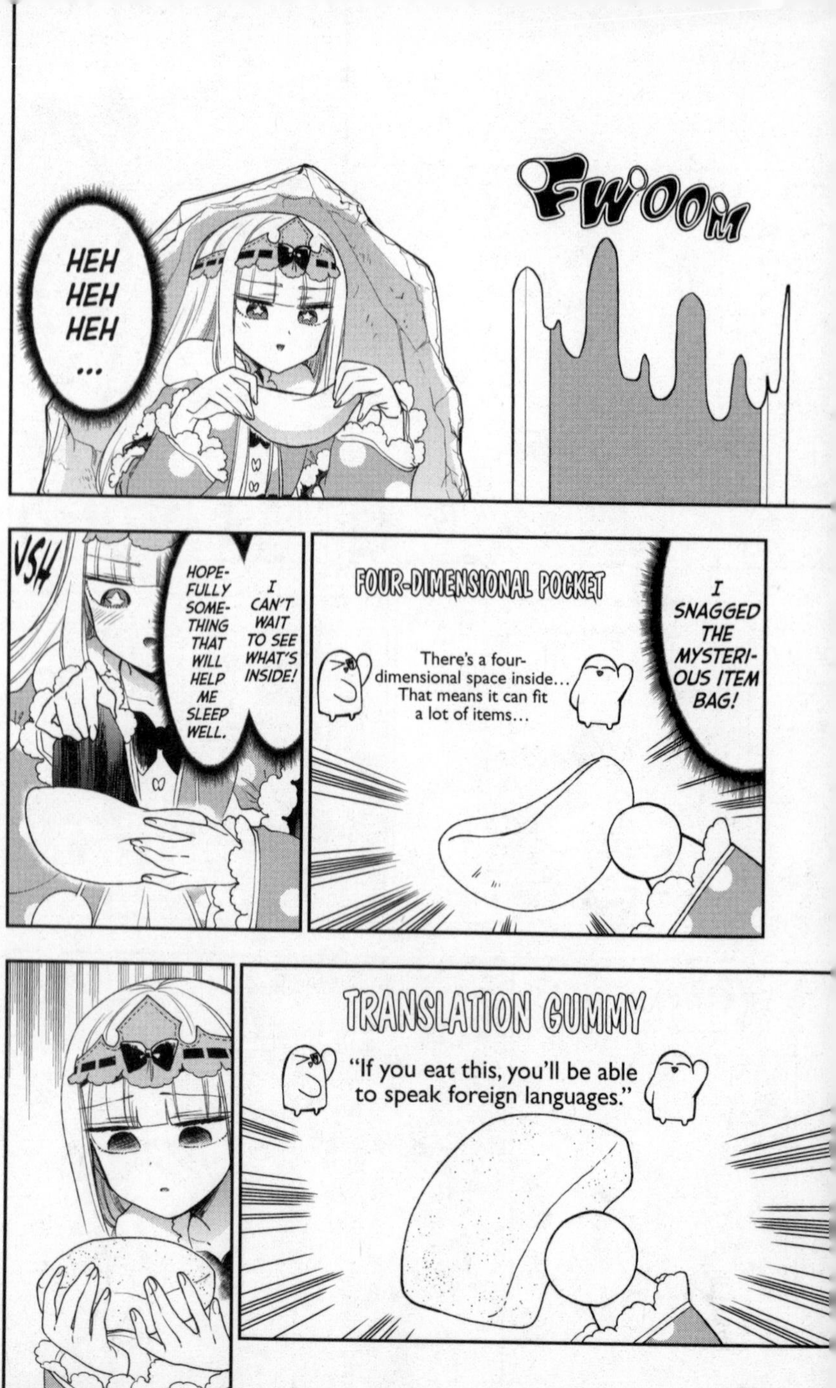
FWOOM
HEH HEH HEH...
I SNAGGED THE MYSTERIOUS ITEM BAG!
FOUR-DIMENSIONAL POCKET
There's a four-dimensional space inside... That means it can fit a lot of items...
I CAN'T WAIT TO SEE WHAT'S INSIDE!
HOPEFULLY SOMETHING THAT WILL HELP ME SLEEP WELL.
VSH
TRANSLATION GUMMY
"If you eat this, you'll be able to speak foreign languages."

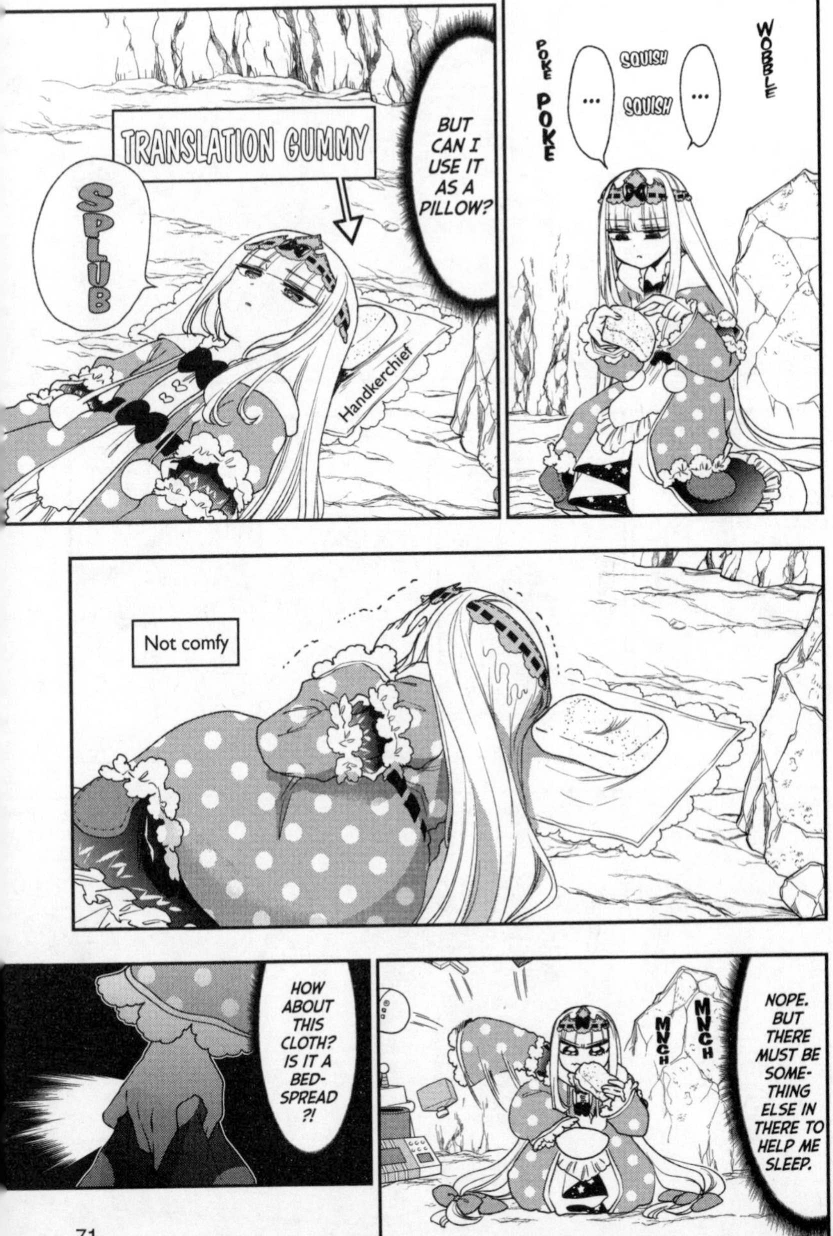
WOBBLE
...
SQUISH
SQUISH
...
POKE POKE
BUT CAN I USE IT AS A PILLOW?
TRANSLATION GUMMY
SPLUB
Handkerchief
Not comfy
NOPE. BUT THERE MUST BE SOME-THING ELSE IN THERE TO HELP ME SLEEP.
MNCH
MNCH
HOW ABOUT THIS CLOTH? IS IT A BED-SPREAD?!

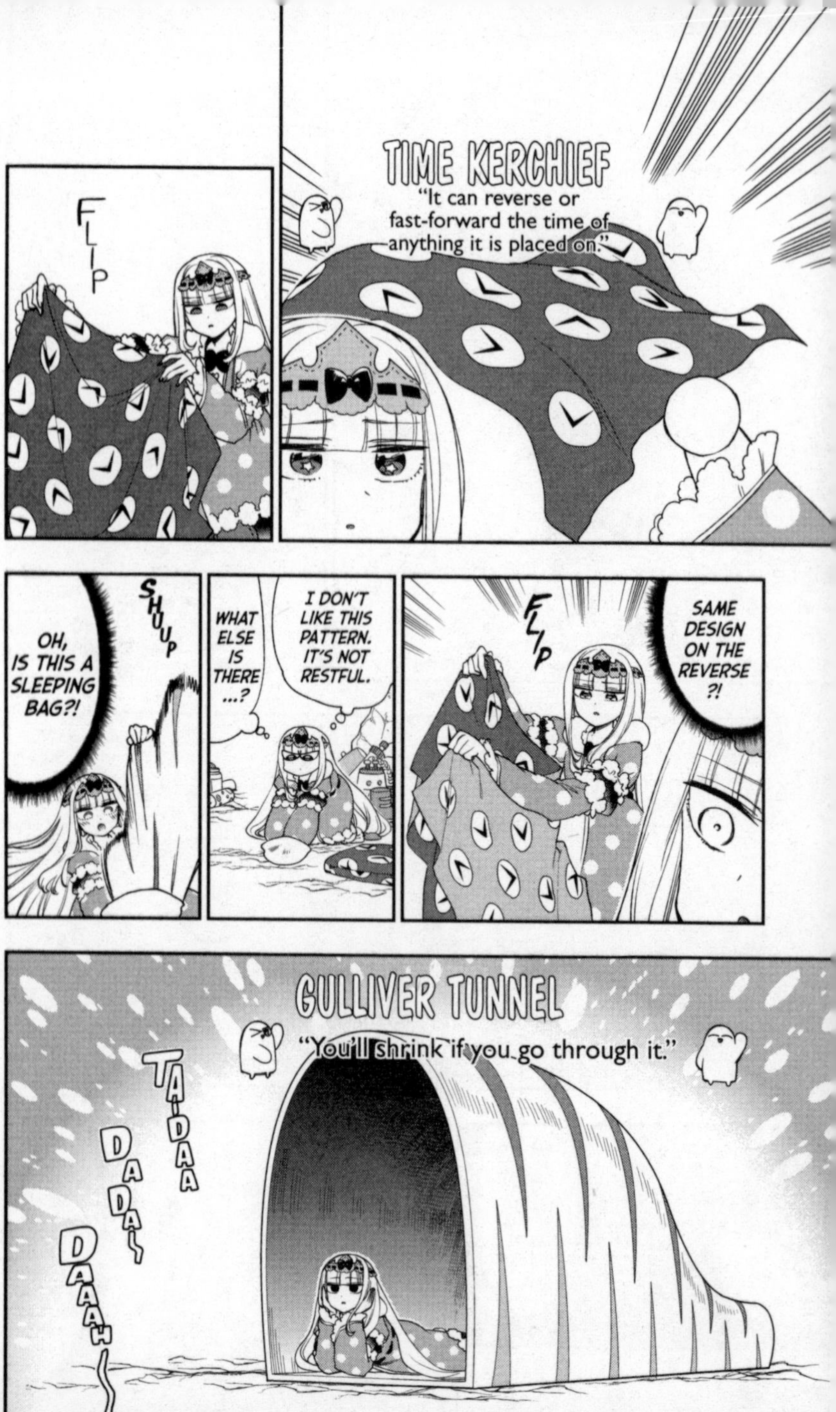
TIME KERCHIEF
"It can reverse or fast-forward the time of anything it is placed on."
FLIP
SAME DESIGN ON THE REVERSE?!
FLIP
I DON'T LIKE THIS PATTERN. IT'S NOT RESTFUL.
WHAT ELSE IS THERE...?
SHUUP
OH, IS THIS A SLEEPING BAG?!
GULLIVER TUNNEL
"You'll shrink if you go through it."
TADAA
DADA~
DAAAH~

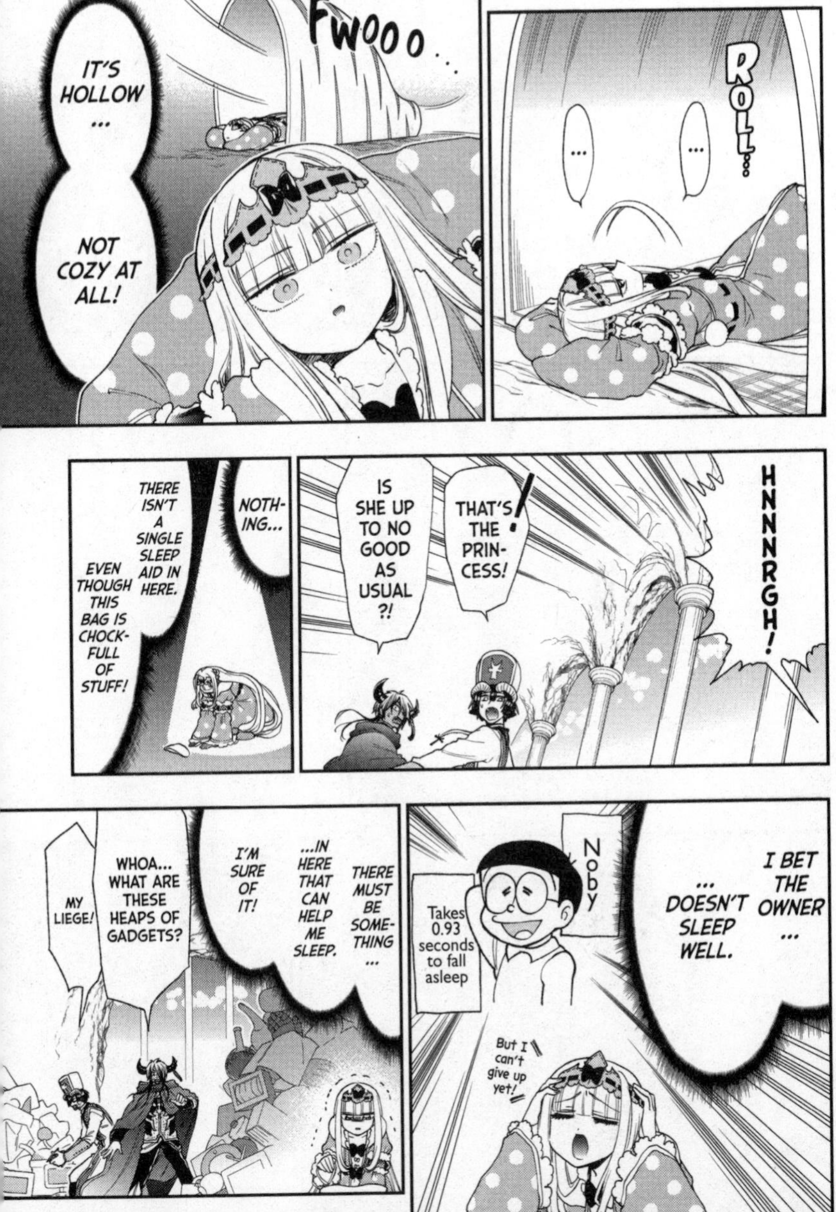
ROLL...
...
...
FWOOO...
IT'S HOLLOW...
NOT COZY AT ALL!
HNNNRGH!
THAT'S THE PRIN-CESS!
IS SHE UP TO NO GOOD AS USUAL?!
NOTH-ING...
THERE ISN'T A SINGLE SLEEP AID IN HERE.
EVEN THOUGH THIS BAG IS CHOCK-FULL OF STUFF!
I BET THE OWNER...
...DOESN'T SLEEP WELL.
Noby
Takes 0.93 seconds to fall asleep
But I can't give up yet!
THERE MUST BE SOME-THING...
...IN HERE THAT CAN HELP ME SLEEP.
I'M SURE OF IT!
WHOA... WHAT ARE THESE HEAPS OF GADGETS?
MY LIEGE!

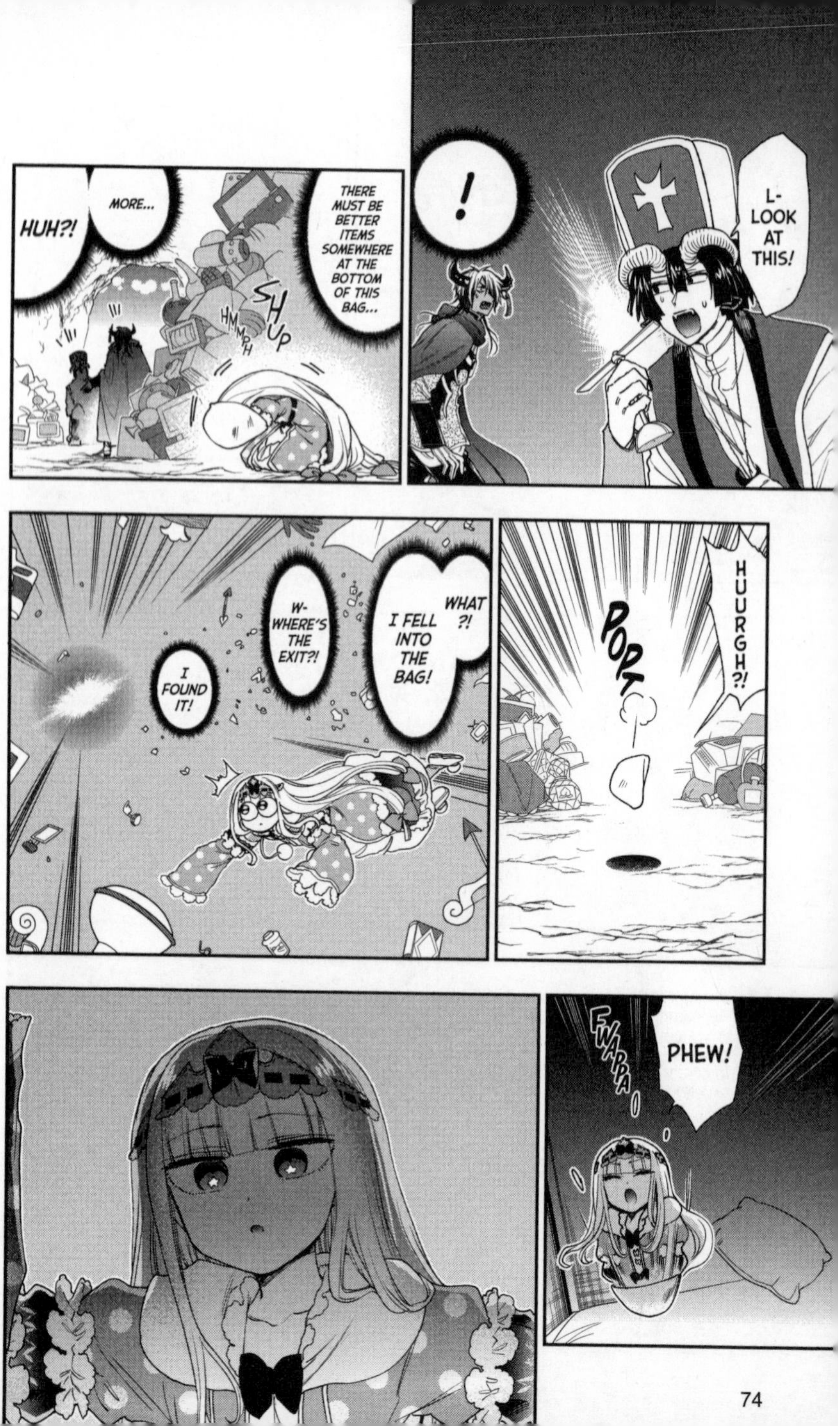
L-LOOK AT THIS!
!
THERE MUST BE BETTER ITEMS SOMEWHERE AT THE BOTTOM OF THIS BAG...
SHUP
HMMPH
MORE...
HUH?!
HUURGH?!
POP
WHAT?!
I FELL INTO THE BAG!
W-WHERE'S THE EXIT?!
I FOUND IT!
FWAPPA
PHEW!

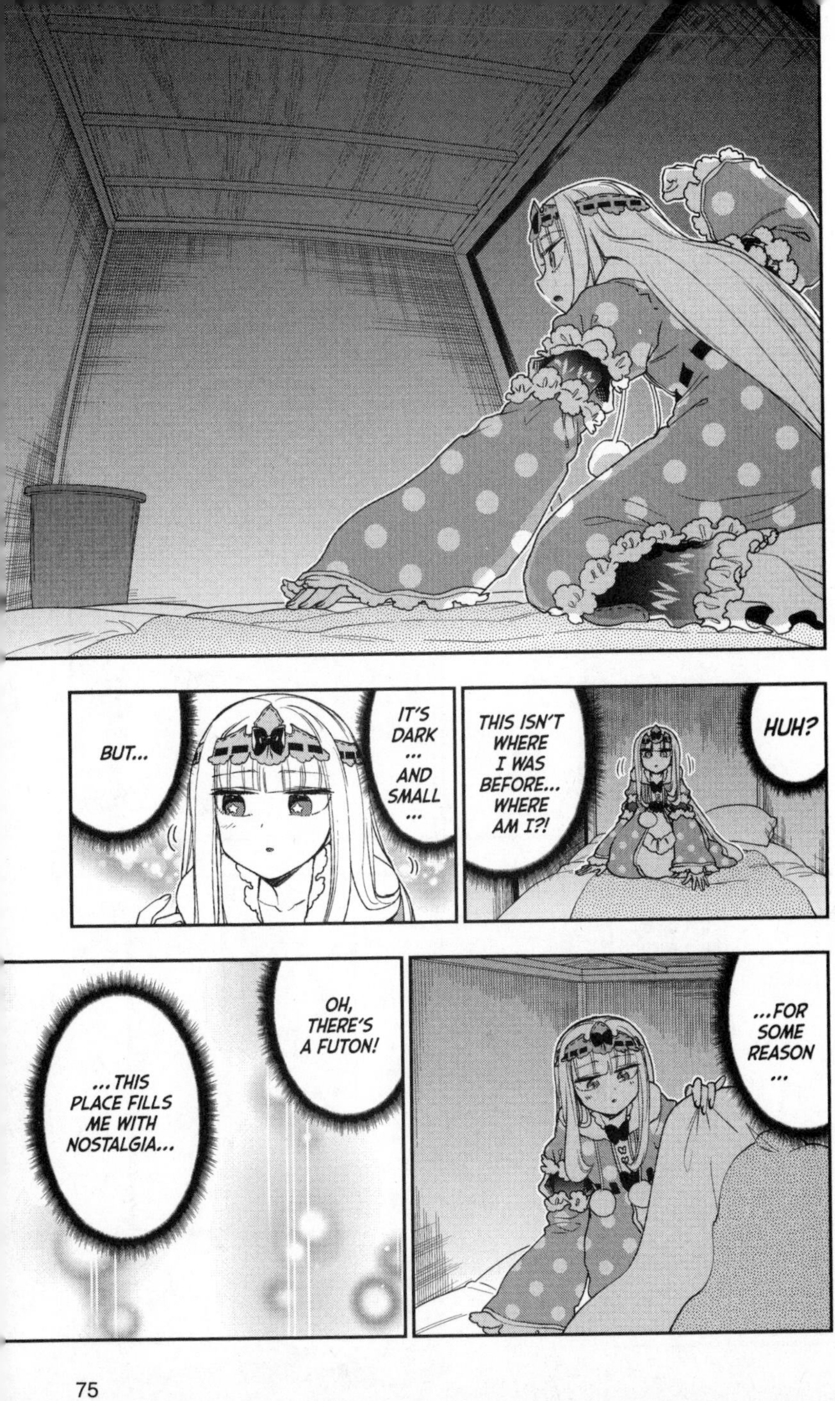
HUH?
THIS ISN'T WHERE I WAS BEFORE... WHERE AM I?!
IT'S DARK ... AND SMALL ...
BUT...
...FOR SOME REASON ...
OH, THERE'S A FUTON!
...THIS PLACE FILLS ME WITH NOSTALGIA...

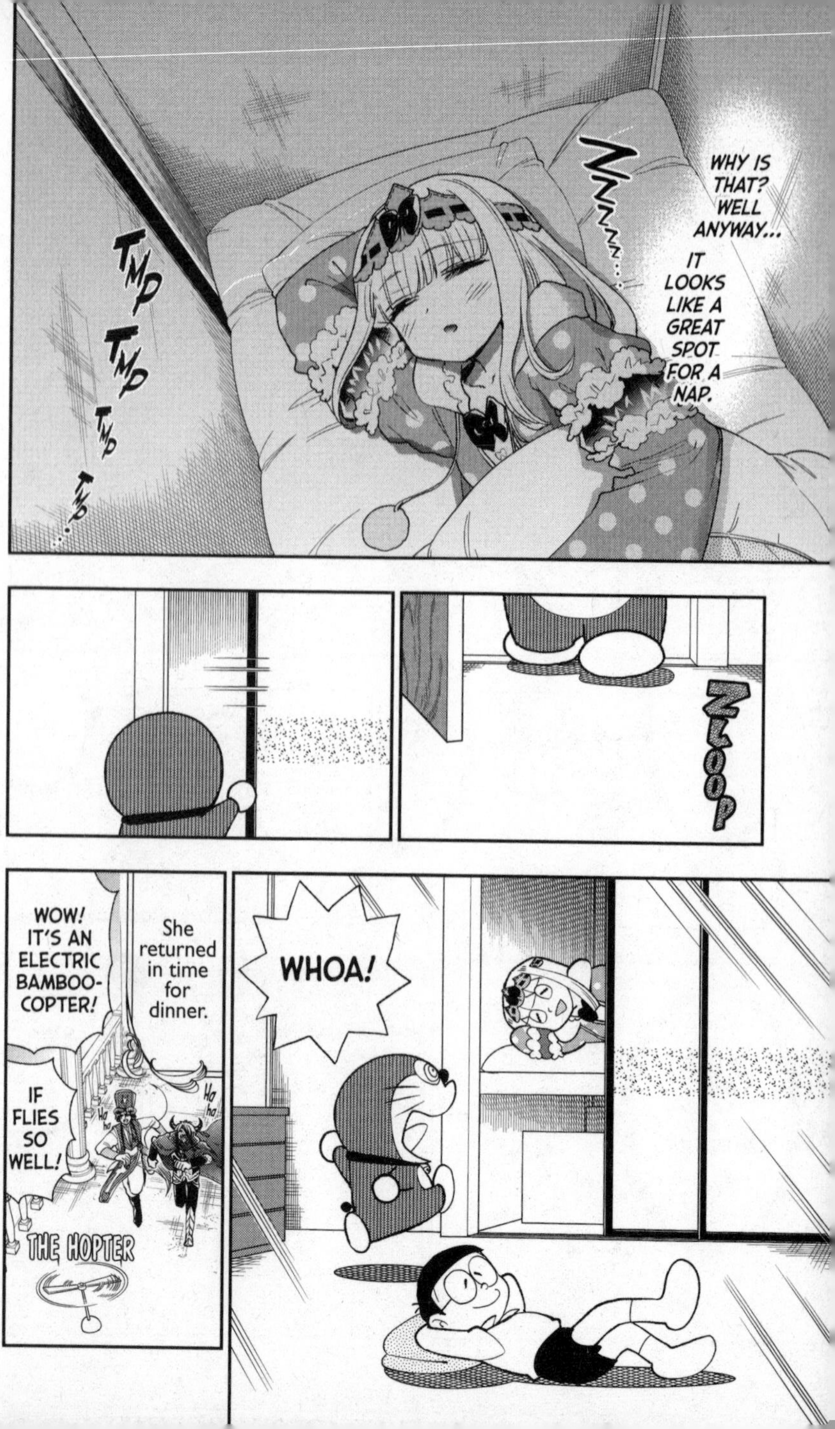
ZZZZZ...
WHY IS THAT? WELL ANYWAY...
IT LOOKS LIKE A GREAT SPOT FOR A NAP.
TMP TMP TMP TMP...
ZLOOP
WHOA!
She returned in time for dinner.
WOW! IT'S AN ELECTRIC BAMBOO-COPTER!
IF FLIES SO WELL!
THE HOPTER

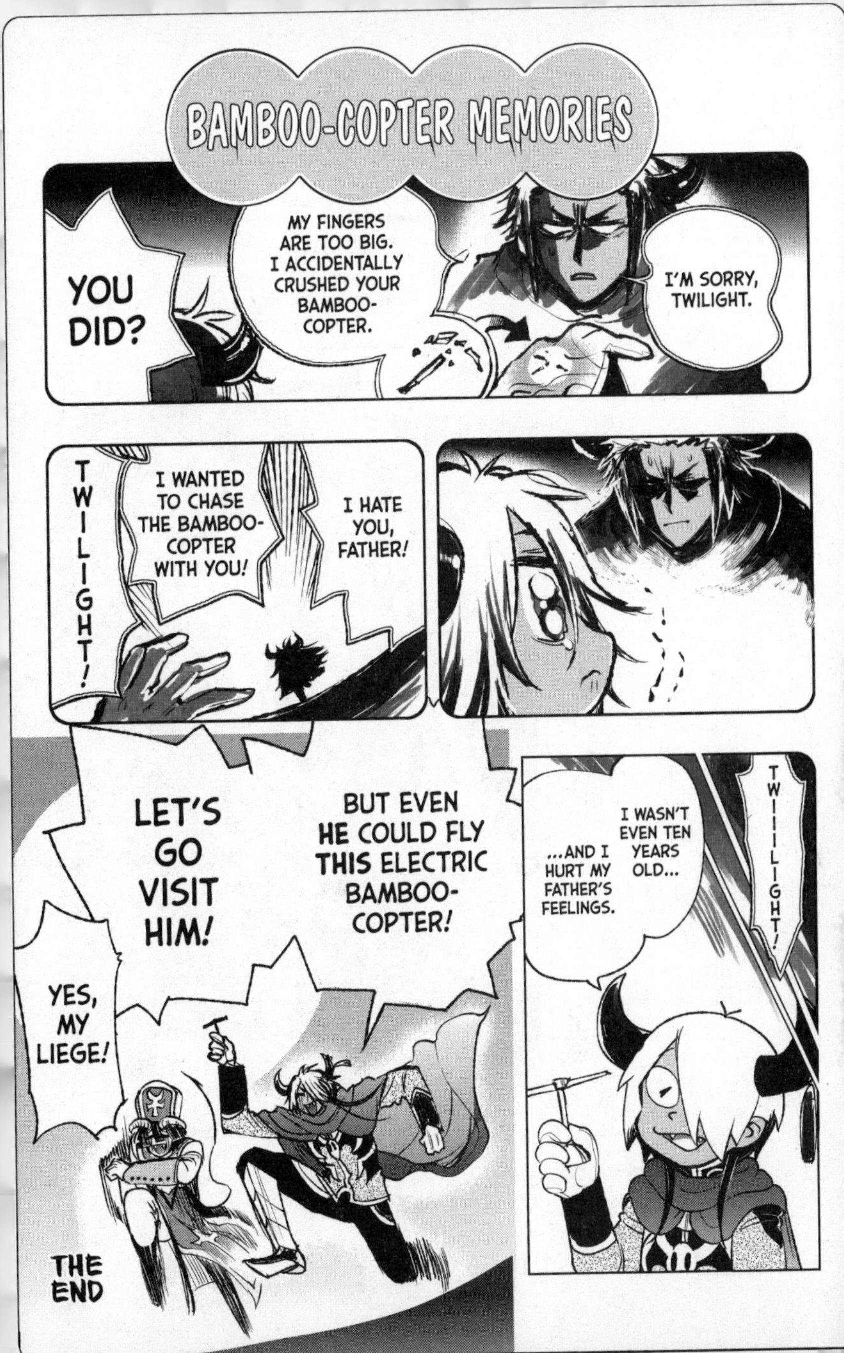
BAMBOO-COPTER MEMORIES
I'M SORRY, TWILIGHT.
MY FINGERS ARE TOO BIG. I ACCIDENTALLY CRUSHED YOUR BAMBOO-COPTER.
YOU DID?
I HATE YOU, FATHER!
I WANTED TO CHASE THE BAMBOO-COPTER WITH YOU!
TWILIGHT!
TWIIIILIGHT!
I WASN'T EVEN TEN YEARS OLD...
...AND I HURT MY FATHER'S FEELINGS.
BUT EVEN HE COULD FLY THIS ELECTRIC BAMBOO-COPTER!
LET'S GO VISIT HIM!
YES, MY LIEGE!
THE END

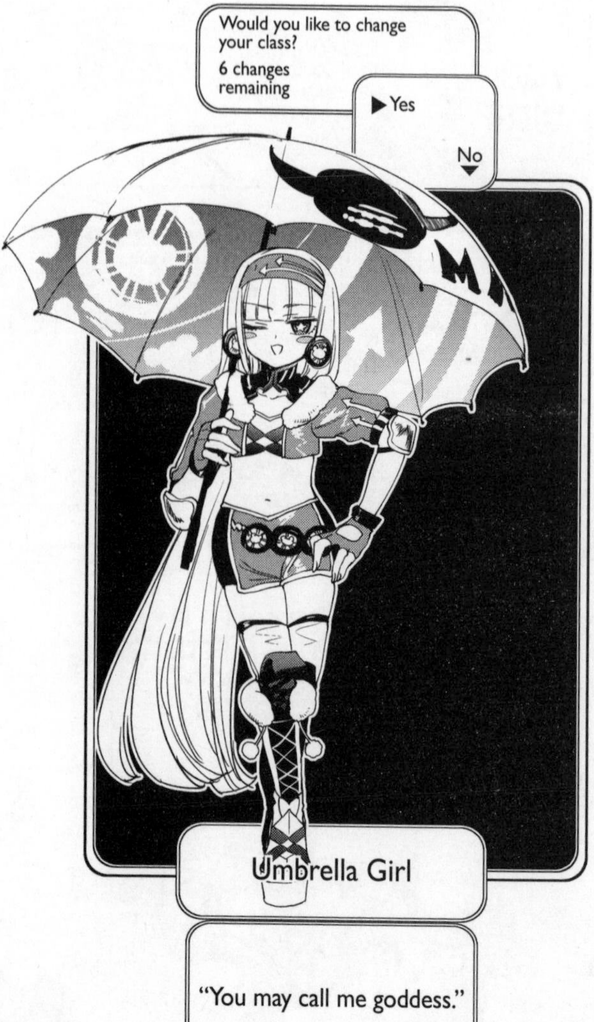
Would you like to change your class?
6 changes remaining
▶Yes
No
Umbrella Girl
“You may call me goddess.”

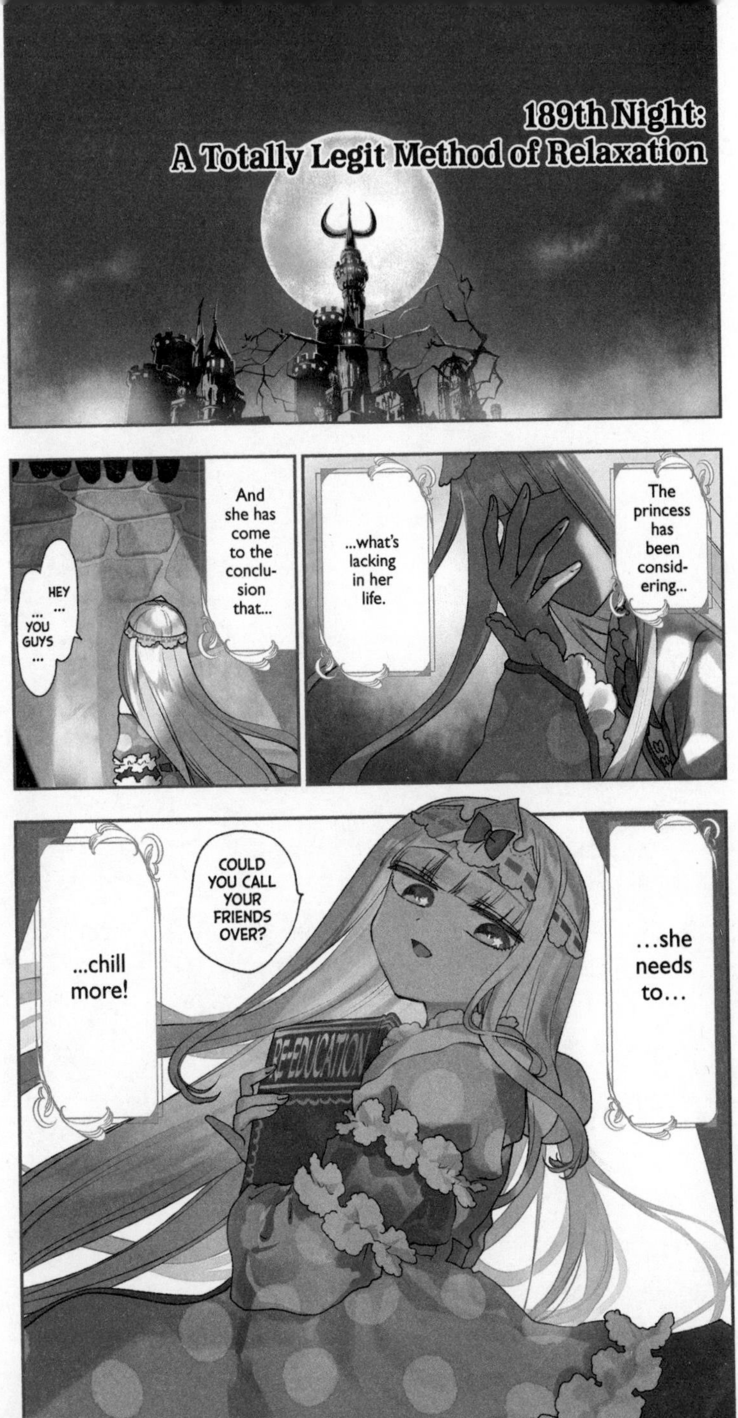
189th Night:
A Totally Legit Method of Relaxation
The princess has been consid-ering...
...what's lacking in her life.
And she has come to the conclu-sion that...
HEY... ...YOU GUYS...
...she needs to...
COULD YOU CALL YOUR FRIENDS OVER?
...chill more!
RE-EDUCATION

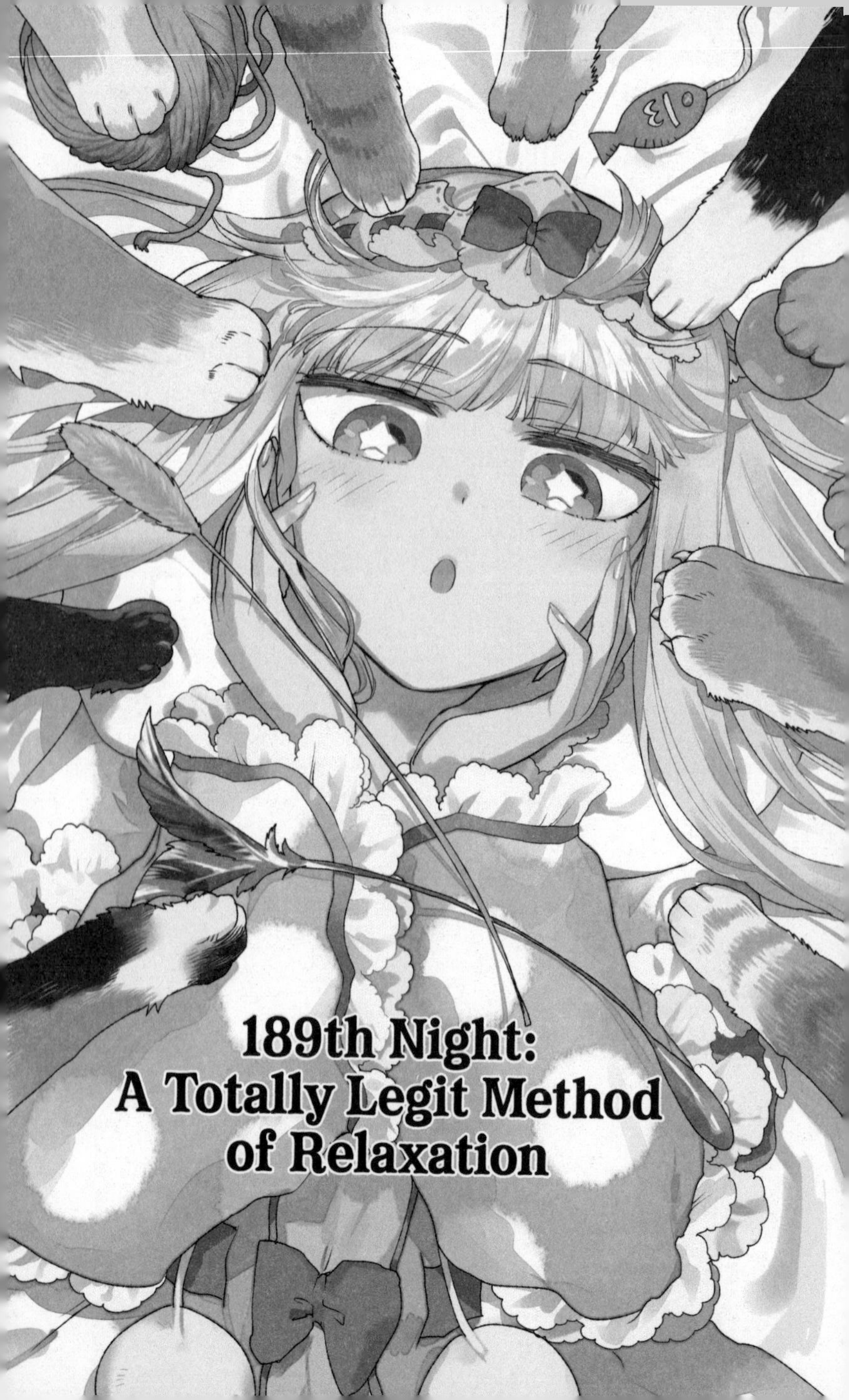
189th Night:
A Totally Legit Method
of Relaxation

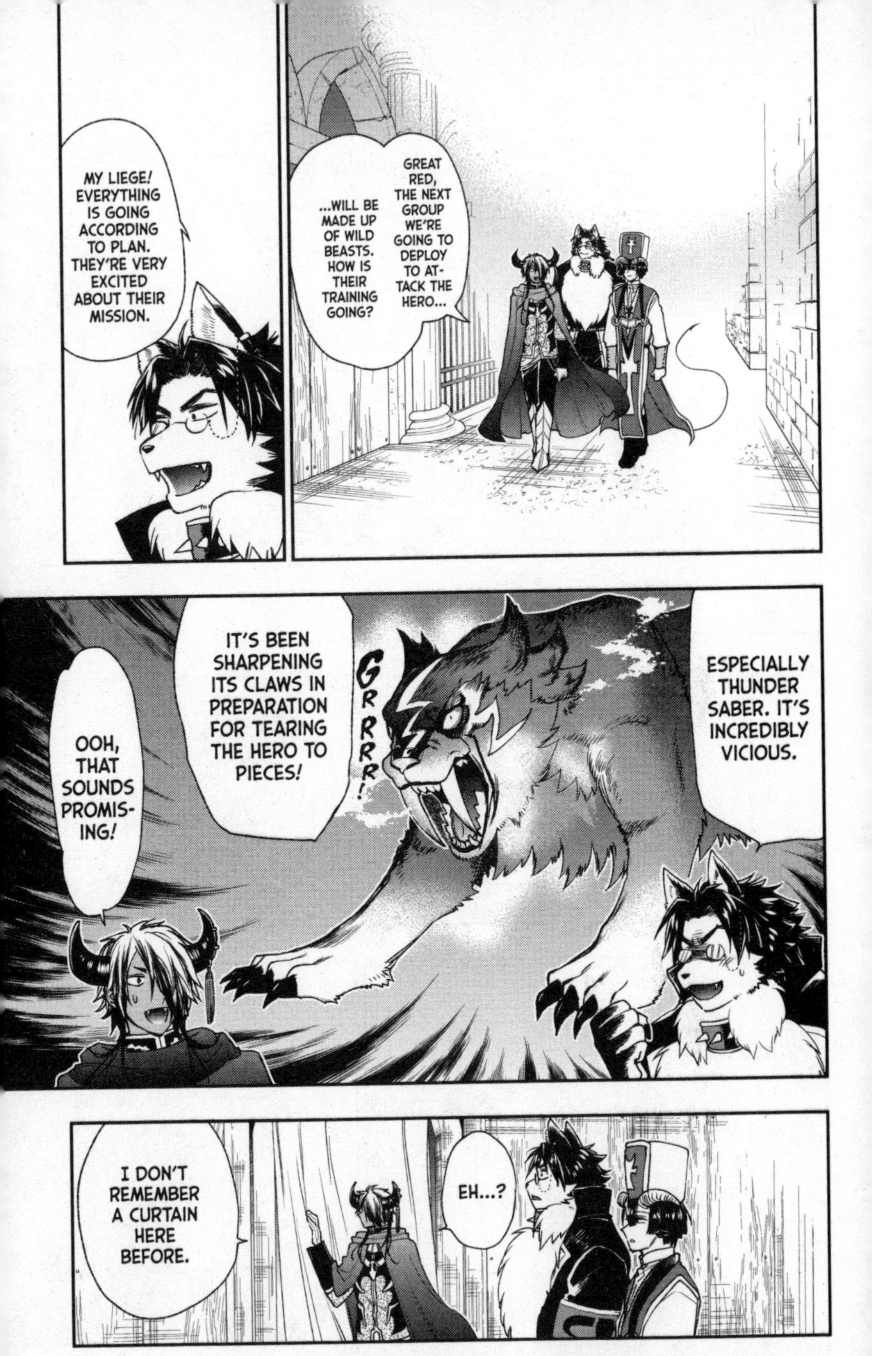
GREAT RED, THE NEXT GROUP WE'RE GOING TO DEPLOY TO ATTACK THE HERO...
...WILL BE MADE UP OF WILD BEASTS. HOW IS THEIR TRAINING GOING?
MY LIEGE! EVERYTHING IS GOING ACCORDING TO PLAN. THEY'RE VERY EXCITED ABOUT THEIR MISSION.
ESPECIALLY THUNDER SABER. IT'S INCREDIBLY VICIOUS.
IT'S BEEN SHARPENING ITS CLAWS IN PREPARATION FOR TEARING THE HERO TO PIECES!
GRRRR!
OOH, THAT SOUNDS PROMISING!
EH...?
I DON'T REMEMBER A CURTAIN HERE BEFORE.

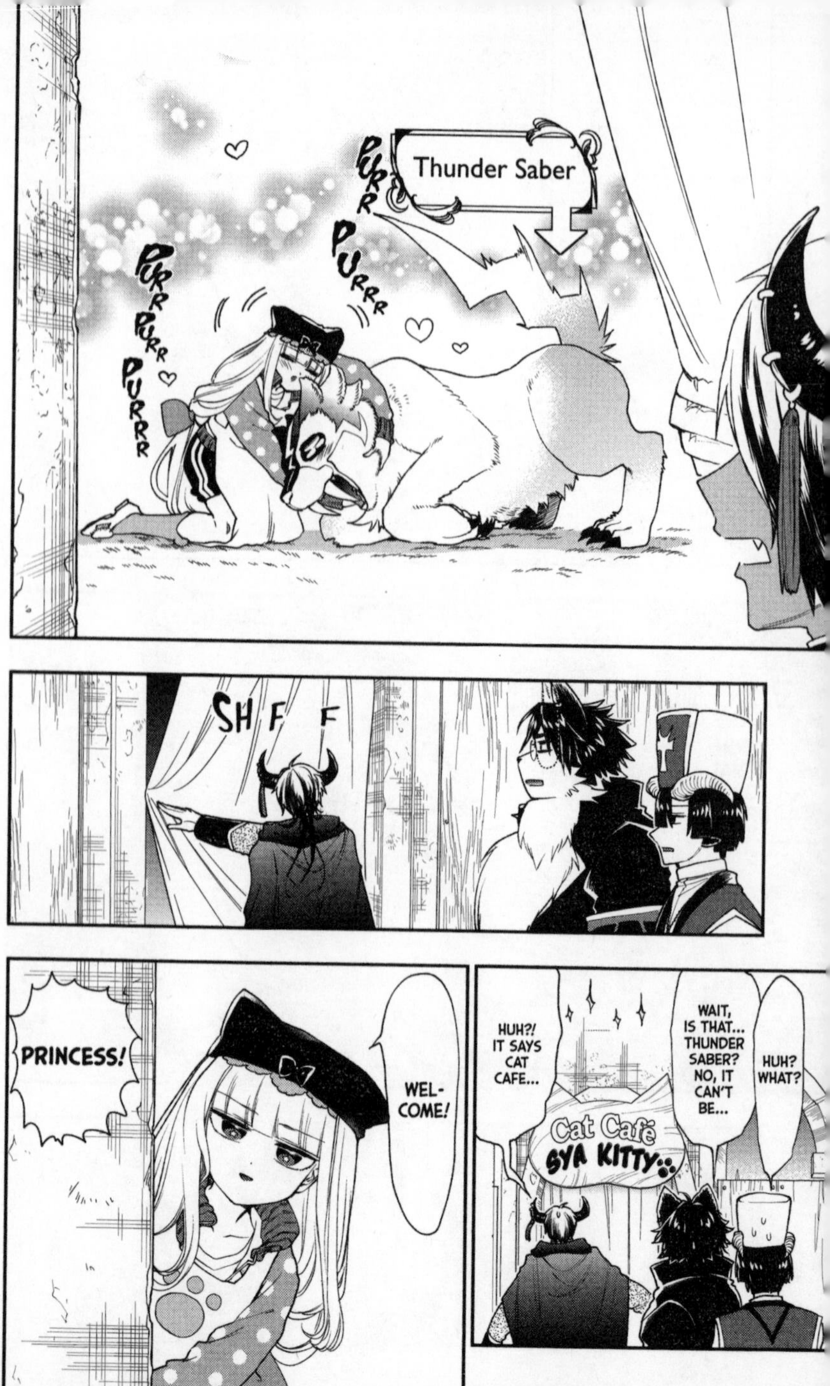
Thunder Saber
PURR PURRRR
PURR PURR PURRR
SHFF
HUH? WHAT?
WAIT, IS THAT... THUNDER SABER? NO, IT CAN'T BE...
HUH?! IT SAYS CAT CAFE...
Cat Café SYA KITTY
WEL-COME!
PRINCESS!

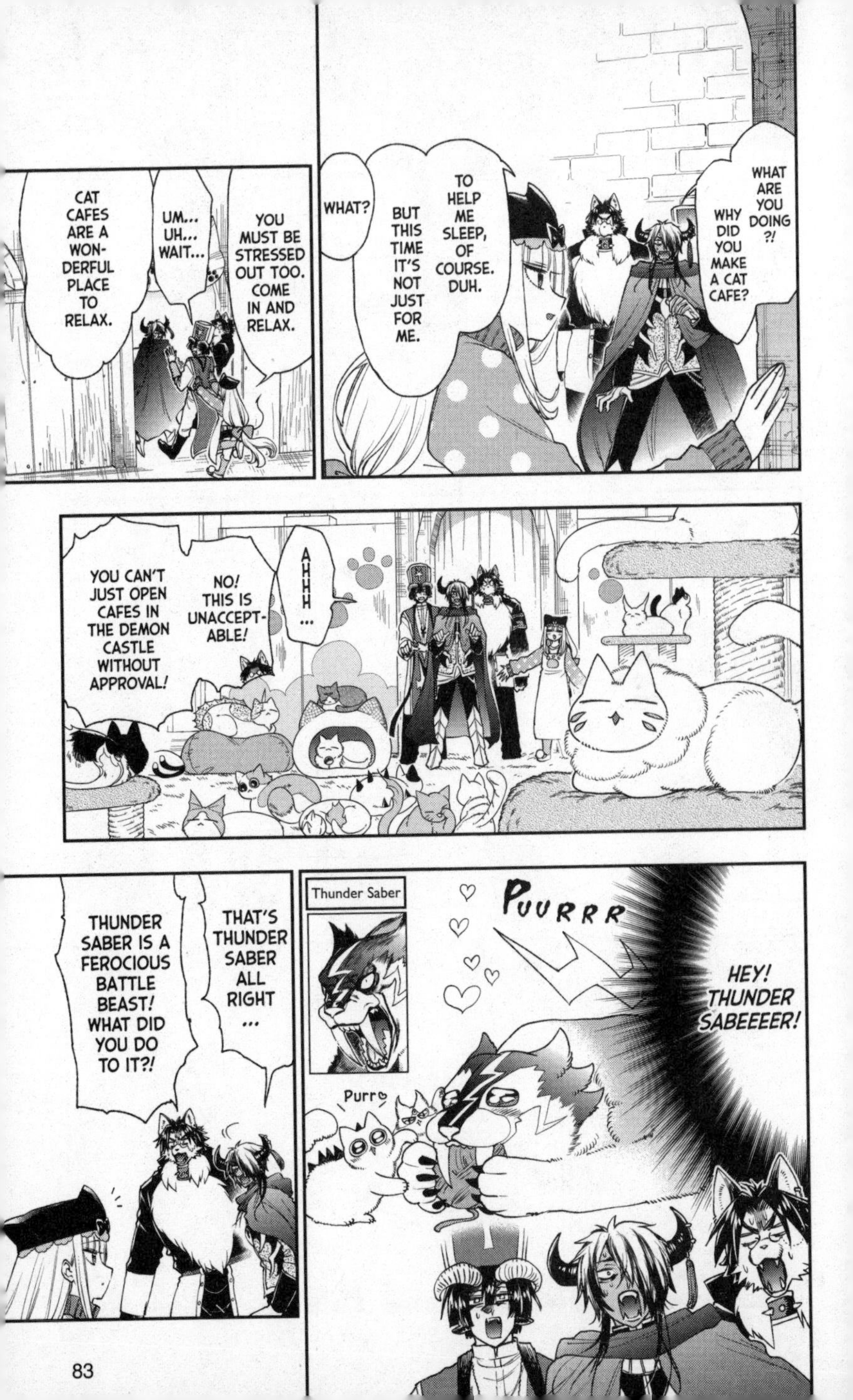
WHAT ARE YOU DOING?!
WHY DID YOU MAKE A CAT CAFE?
TO HELP ME SLEEP, OF COURSE. DUH.
WHAT?
BUT THIS TIME IT'S NOT JUST FOR ME.
YOU MUST BE STRESSED OUT TOO. COME IN AND RELAX.
UM... UH... WAIT...
CAT CAFES ARE A WONDERFUL PLACE TO RELAX.
AHHH...
NO! THIS IS UNACCEPTABLE!
YOU CAN'T JUST OPEN CAFES IN THE DEMON CASTLE WITHOUT APPROVAL!
HEY! THUNDER SABEEEER!
PUURRR
Thunder Saber
Purr♡
THAT'S THUNDER SABER ALL RIGHT...
THUNDER SABER IS A FEROCIOUS BATTLE BEAST! WHAT DID YOU DO TO IT?!

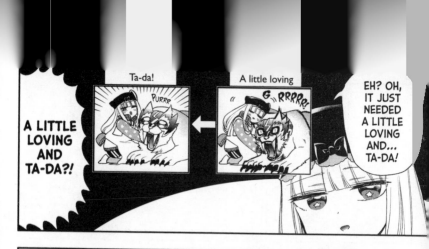

Ta-da!

PURRR

A little loving

G... RRRRR!

A LITTLE LOVING AND TA-DA?!

EH? OH, IT JUST NEEDED A LITTLE LOVING AND... TA-DA!

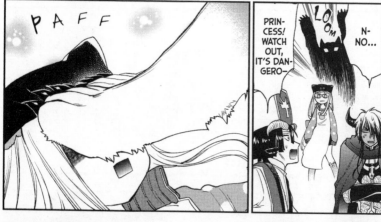

P A F F

PRINCESS! WATCH OUT, IT'S DANGERO~

LOOM

N-NO...

...

FLUFF

HEY...

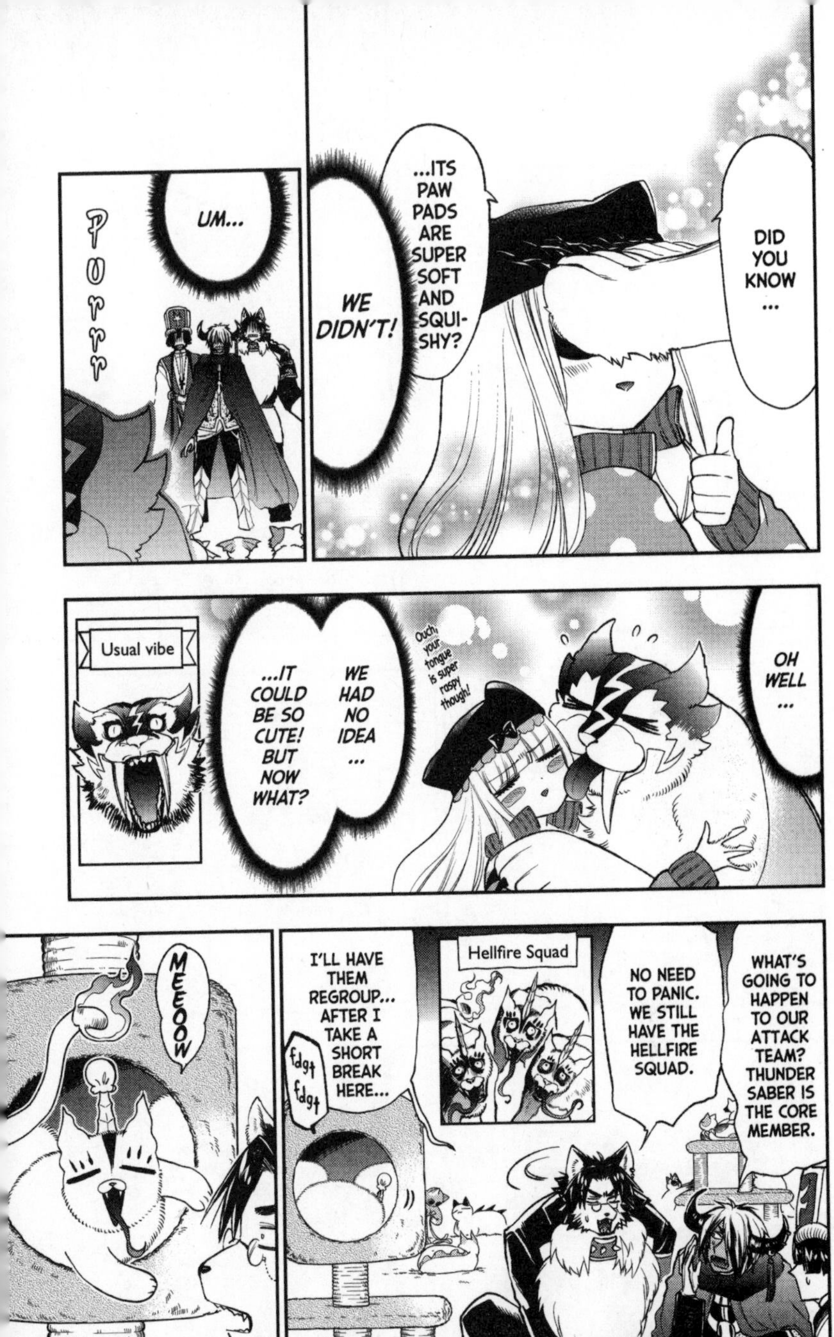
DID YOU KNOW ...
...ITS PAW PADS ARE SUPER SOFT AND SQUISHY?
WE DIDN'T!
UM...
Purrr
OH WELL ...
Ouch, your tongue is super raspy though!
WE HAD NO IDEA ...
...IT COULD BE SO CUTE! BUT NOW WHAT?
Usual vibe
WHAT'S GOING TO HAPPEN TO OUR ATTACK TEAM? THUNDER SABER IS THE CORE MEMBER.
NO NEED TO PANIC. WE STILL HAVE THE HELLFIRE SQUAD.
Hellfire Squad
I'LL HAVE THEM REGROUP... AFTER I TAKE A SHORT BREAK HERE...
fdgt fdgt
MEEOOOW

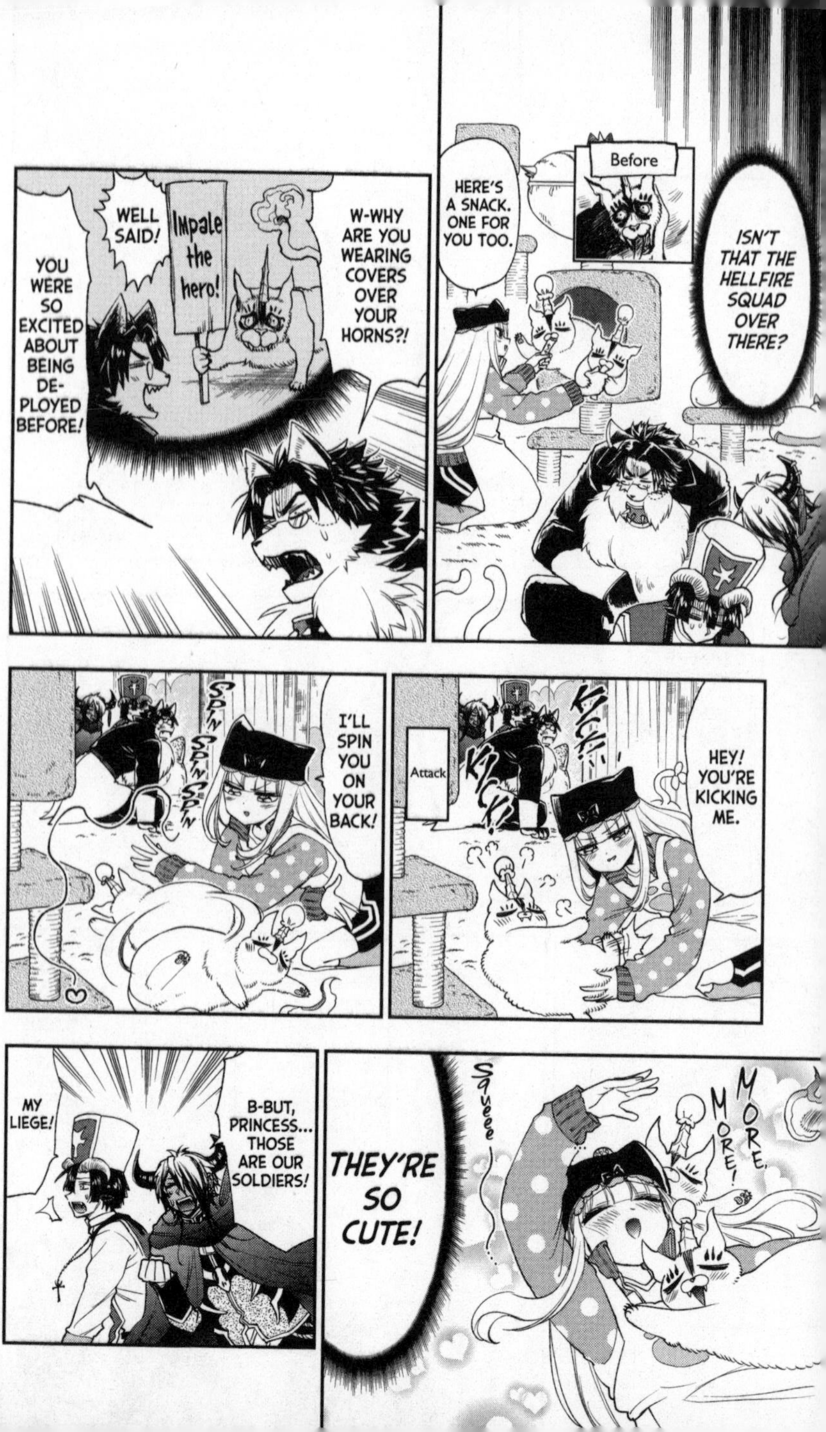
ISN'T THAT THE HELLFIRE SQUAD OVER THERE?
Before
HERE'S A SNACK. ONE FOR YOU TOO.
W-WHY ARE YOU WEARING COVERS OVER YOUR HORNS?!
WELL SAID!
Impale the hero!
YOU WERE SO EXCITED ABOUT BEING DE-PLOYED BEFORE!
HEY! YOU'RE KICKING ME.
KICK
KICK
Attack
I'LL SPIN YOU ON YOUR BACK!
SPIN SPIN SPIN
MORE, MORE!
Squeee
THEY'RE SO CUTE!
B-BUT, PRINCESS... THOSE ARE OUR SOLDIERS!
MY LIEGE!

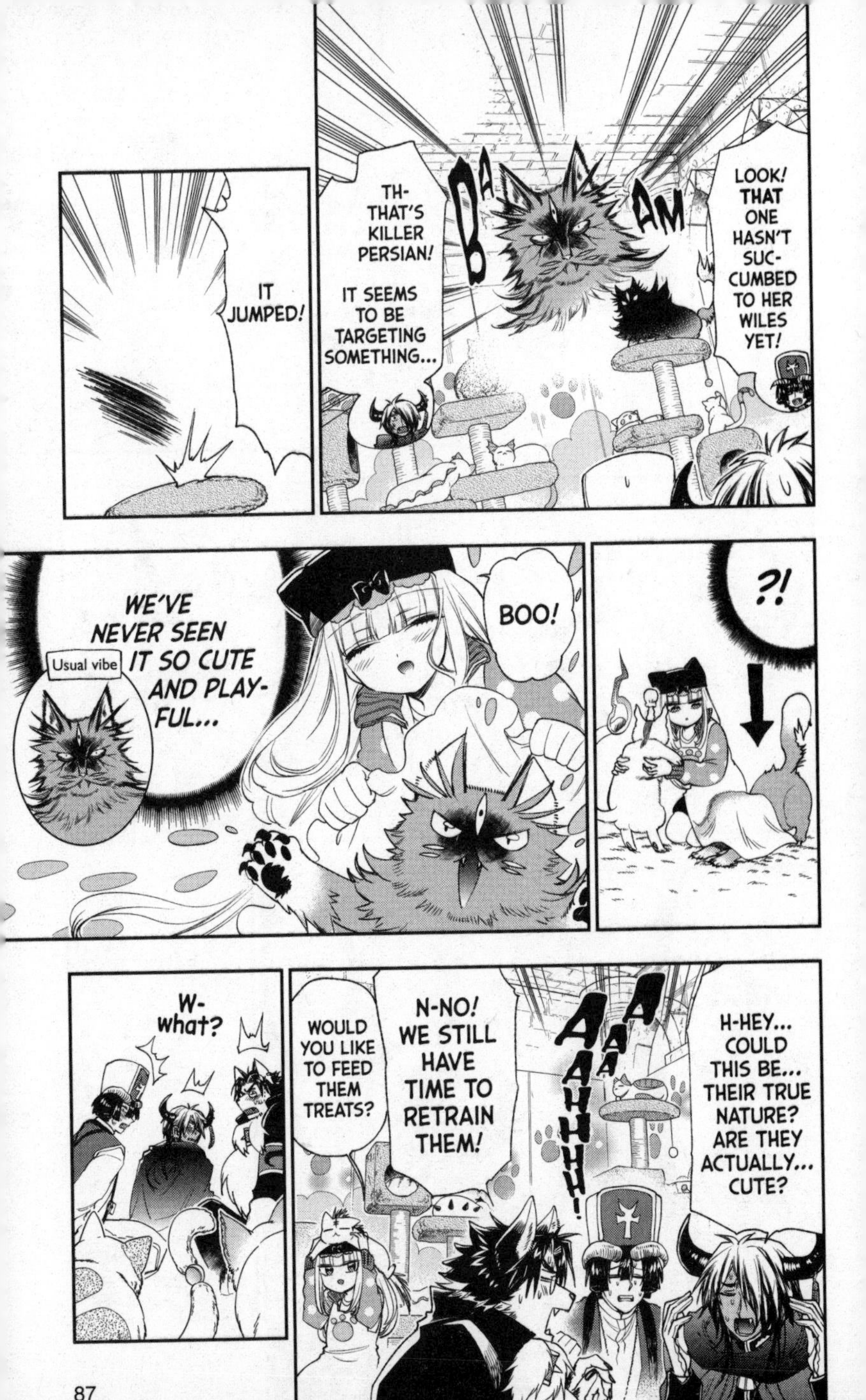

LOOK! THAT ONE HASN'T SUC-CUMBED TO HER WILES YET!
BAM
TH- THAT'S KILLER PERSIAN!
IT SEEMS TO BE TARGETING SOMETHING...
IT JUMPED!
?!
BOO!
WE'VE NEVER SEEN IT SO CUTE AND PLAY-FUL...
Usual vibe
H-HEY... COULD THIS BE... THEIR TRUE NATURE? ARE THEY ACTUALLY... CUTE?
AAAAAHHHH!
N-NO! WE STILL HAVE TIME TO RETRAIN THEM!
WOULD YOU LIKE TO FEED THEM TREATS?
W- what?

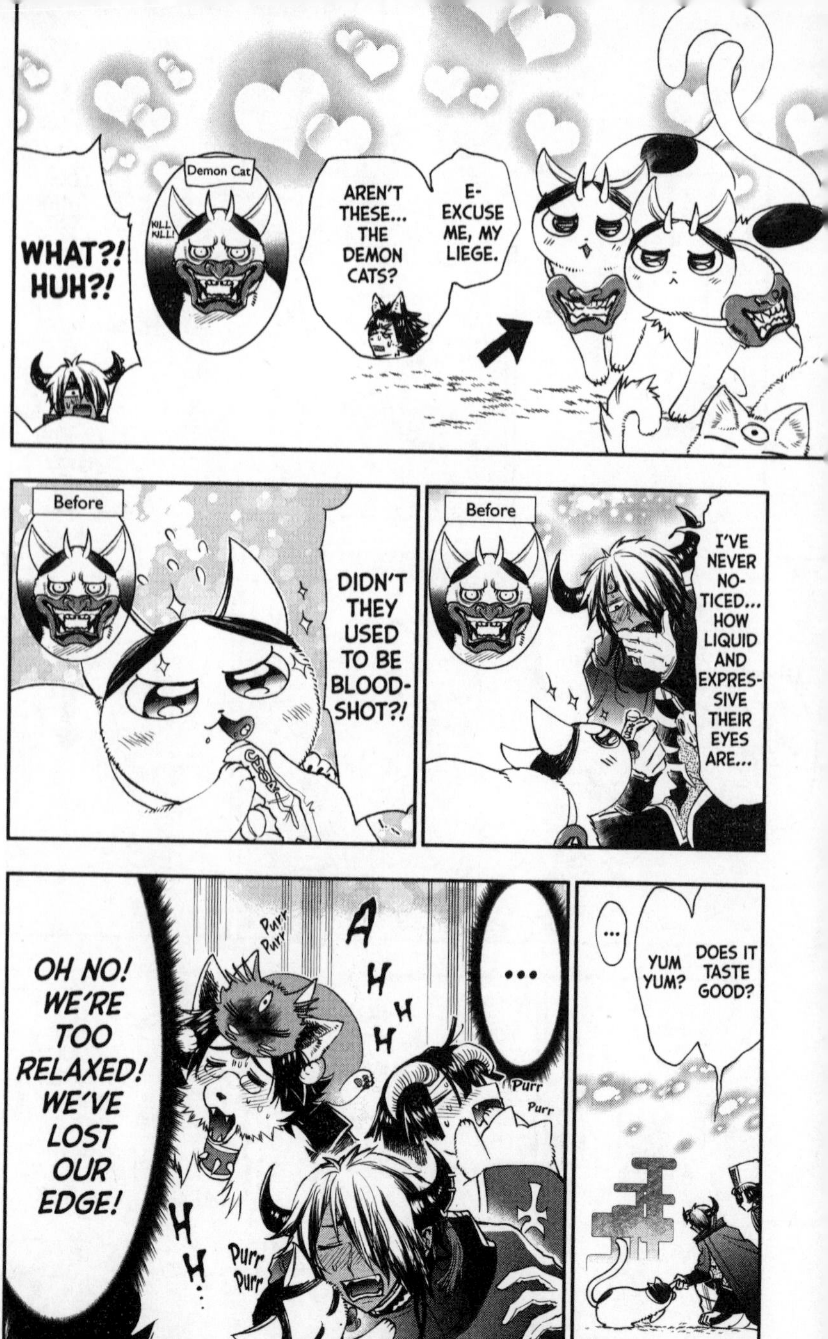
E-EXCUSE ME, MY LIEGE.
AREN'T THESE... THE DEMON CATS?
Demon Cat
KILL KILL!
WHAT?! HUH?!
Before
I'VE NEVER NOTICED... HOW LIQUID AND EXPRESSIVE THEIR EYES ARE...
Before
DIDN'T THEY USED TO BE BLOODSHOT?!
DOES IT TASTE GOOD?
YUM YUM?
...
...
AHHHH
Purr Purr
Purr Purr
OH NO! WE'RE TOO RELAXED! WE'VE LOST OUR EDGE!
HH...
Purr Purr

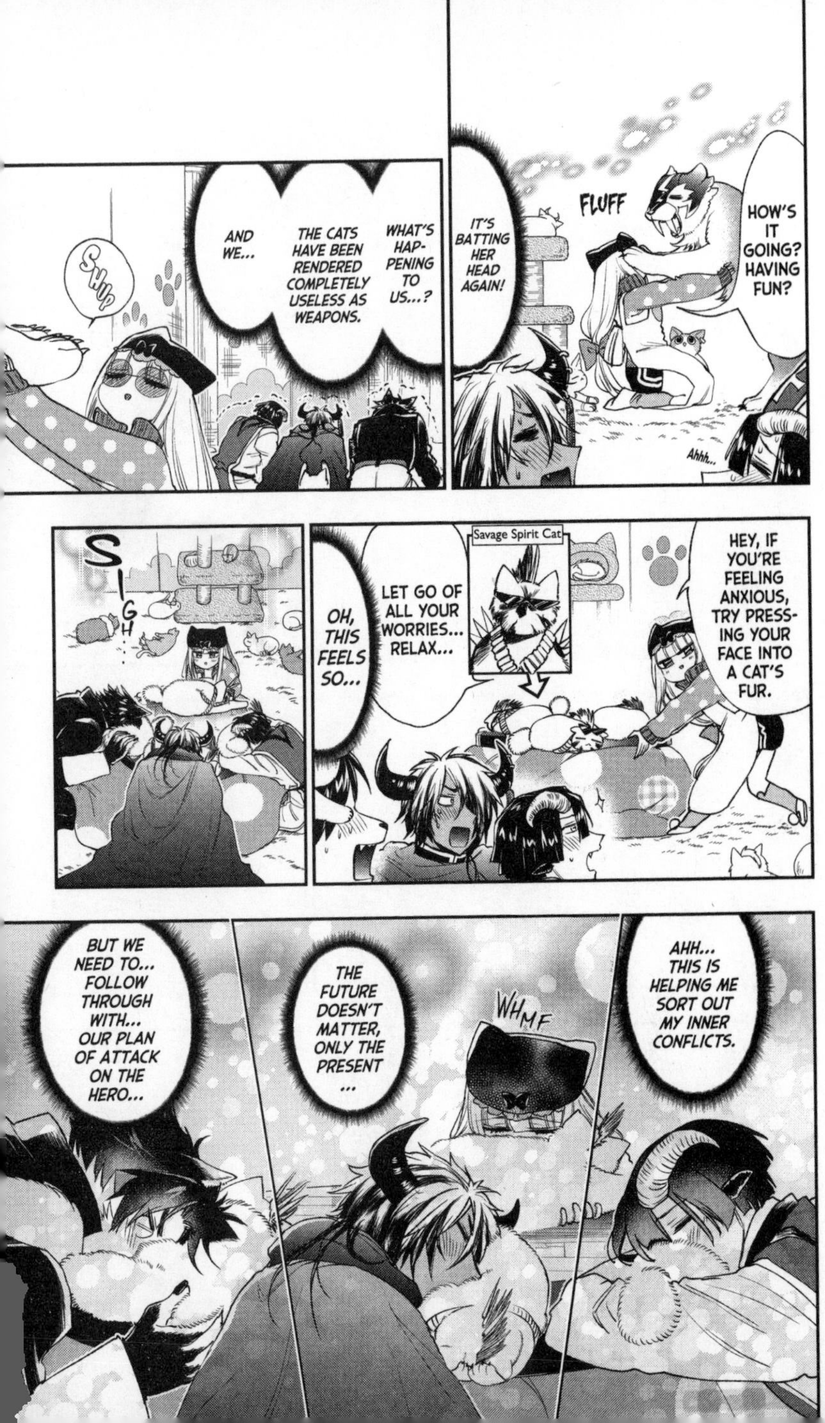
HOW'S IT GOING? HAVING FUN?
FLUFF
IT'S BATTING HER HEAD AGAIN!
Ahhh...
WHAT'S HAPPENING TO US...?
THE CATS HAVE BEEN RENDERED COMPLETELY USELESS AS WEAPONS.
AND WE...
SHUP
HEY, IF YOU'RE FEELING ANXIOUS, TRY PRESSING YOUR FACE INTO A CAT'S FUR.
Savage Spirit Cat
LET GO OF ALL YOUR WORRIES... RELAX...
OH, THIS FEELS SO...
SIGH...
AHH... THIS IS HELPING ME SORT OUT MY INNER CONFLICTS.
WHMF
THE FUTURE DOESN'T MATTER, ONLY THE PRESENT ...
BUT WE NEED TO... FOLLOW THROUGH WITH... OUR PLAN OF ATTACK ON THE HERO...

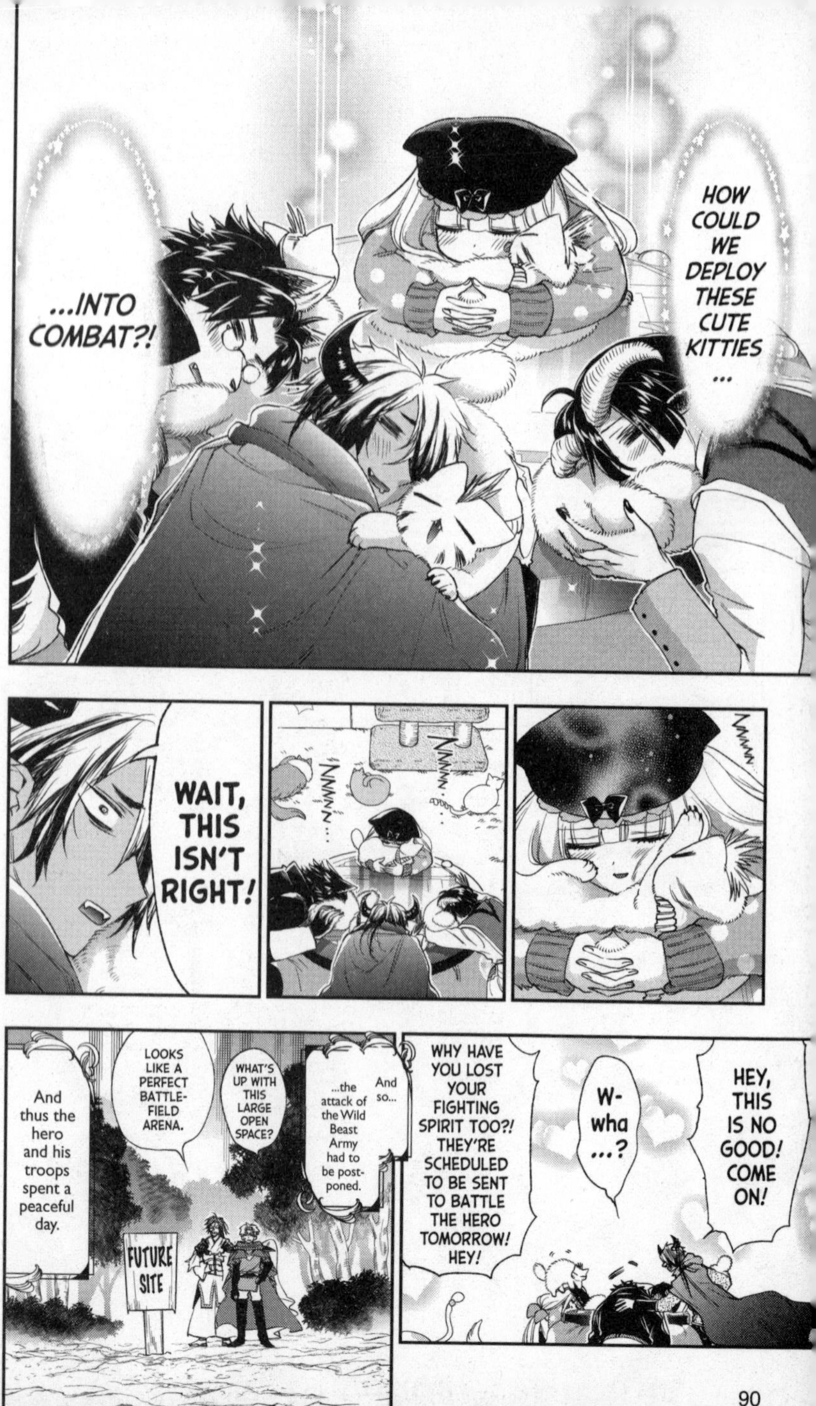
HOW COULD WE DEPLOY THESE CUTE KITTIES ...
...INTO COMBAT?!
WAIT, THIS ISN'T RIGHT!
HEY, THIS IS NO GOOD! COME ON!
W- wha ...?
WHY HAVE YOU LOST YOUR FIGHTING SPIRIT TOO?! THEY'RE SCHEDULED TO BE SENT TO BATTLE THE HERO TOMORROW! HEY!
And so...
...the attack of the Wild Beast Army had to be postponed.
WHAT'S UP WITH THIS LARGE OPEN SPACE?
LOOKS LIKE A PERFECT BATTLEFIELD ARENA.
FUTURE SITE
And thus the hero and his troops spent a peaceful day.

③

Demon Castle Question Corner

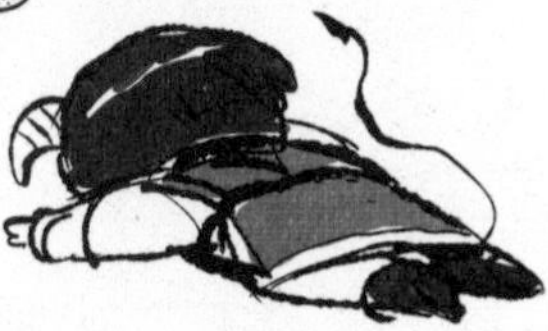

Q Are Teddy Demons and Fallen Panda Angels related?

A If they were dogs, they'd be different breeds.

Q Poseidon's battle against the hero ended in a draw. Will there be a rematch?

A He seems to want a rematch.

Q Are there any zones that haven't appeared in the manga yet?

A The Desert Zone and Underworld Zone might make an appearance.

Q Does the Demon Castle cafeteria serve sushi? If not, where do they get it?

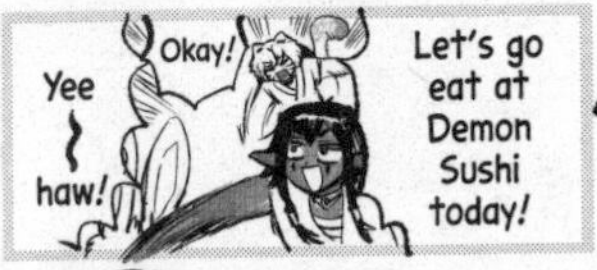

Let's go eat at Demon Sushi today!
Okay!
Yee ~ haw!

A In addition to the cafeteria, there are small bars and specialty restaurants throughout the Demon Castle.

Q Do Harpy and the Cursed Musician get along?

A They're not super close or anything, but they have a typical sibling relationship.

Q Are Master Hypnos and Demon Cleric related in some way? Also, Master Hypnos doesn't seem to do any work, so what is his role at the Old Demon Castle, and how does he get paid? Does he battle...?

A No relation whatsoever. Hypnos sleeps 20 hours a day, but he is capable of accessing the dream world while he's asleep, so he does work that can only be accomplished there (like creating and infiltrating others' dreams, etc...). But most of the time he just sleeps.

Q What's an ordinary day's schedule for Teddy Demon?

A

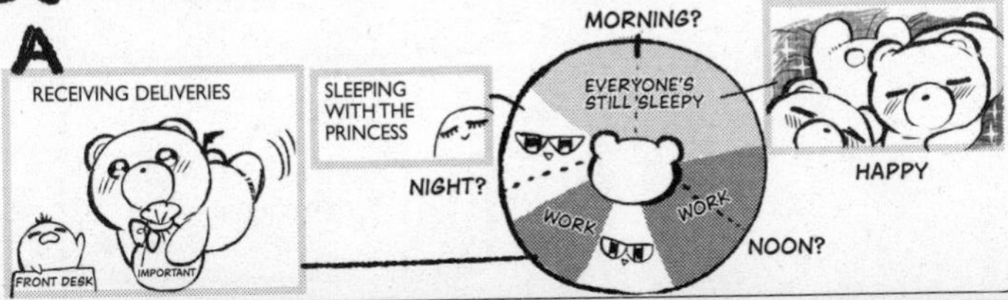

MORNING?
EVERYONE'S STILL SLEEPY
HAPPY
WORK
WORK
NOON?
NIGHT?
SLEEPING WITH THE PRINCESS
RECEIVING DELIVERIES
FRONT DESK
IMPORTANT

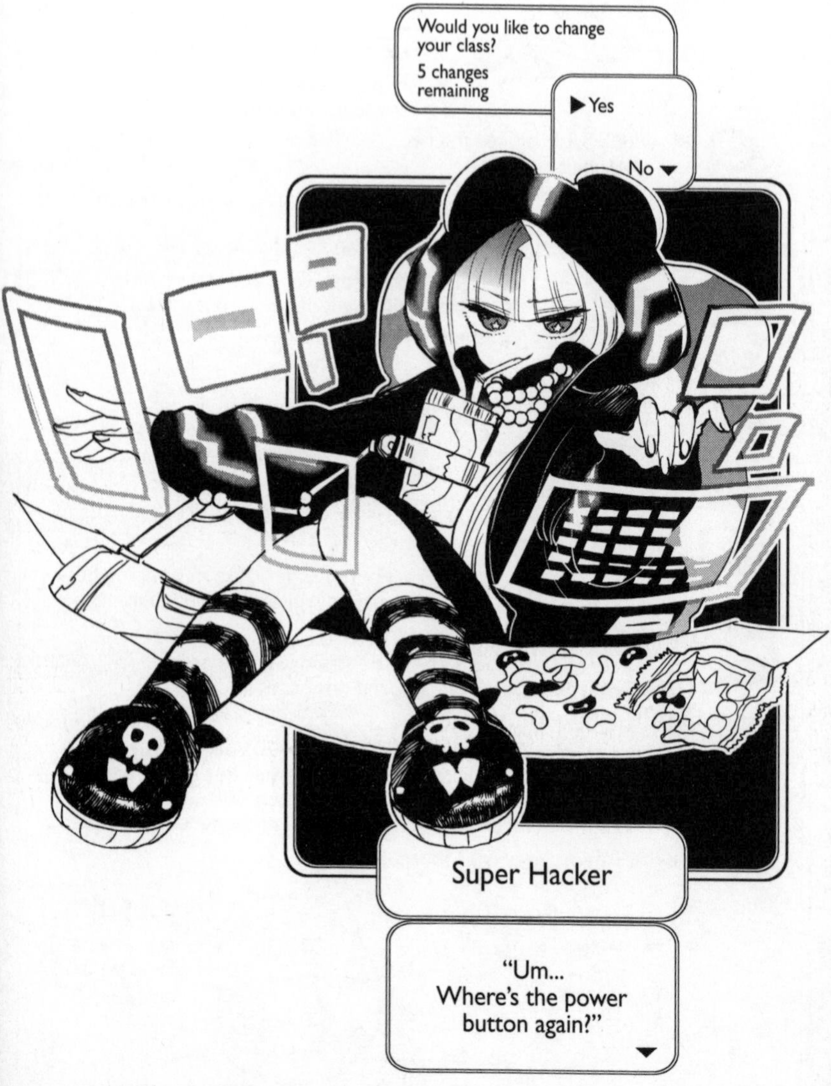

Would you like to change your class?
5 changes remaining
▶Yes
No
Super Hacker
"Um...
Where's the power button again?"

190th Night: *Sleepy Princess in the Demon Castle* Prologue

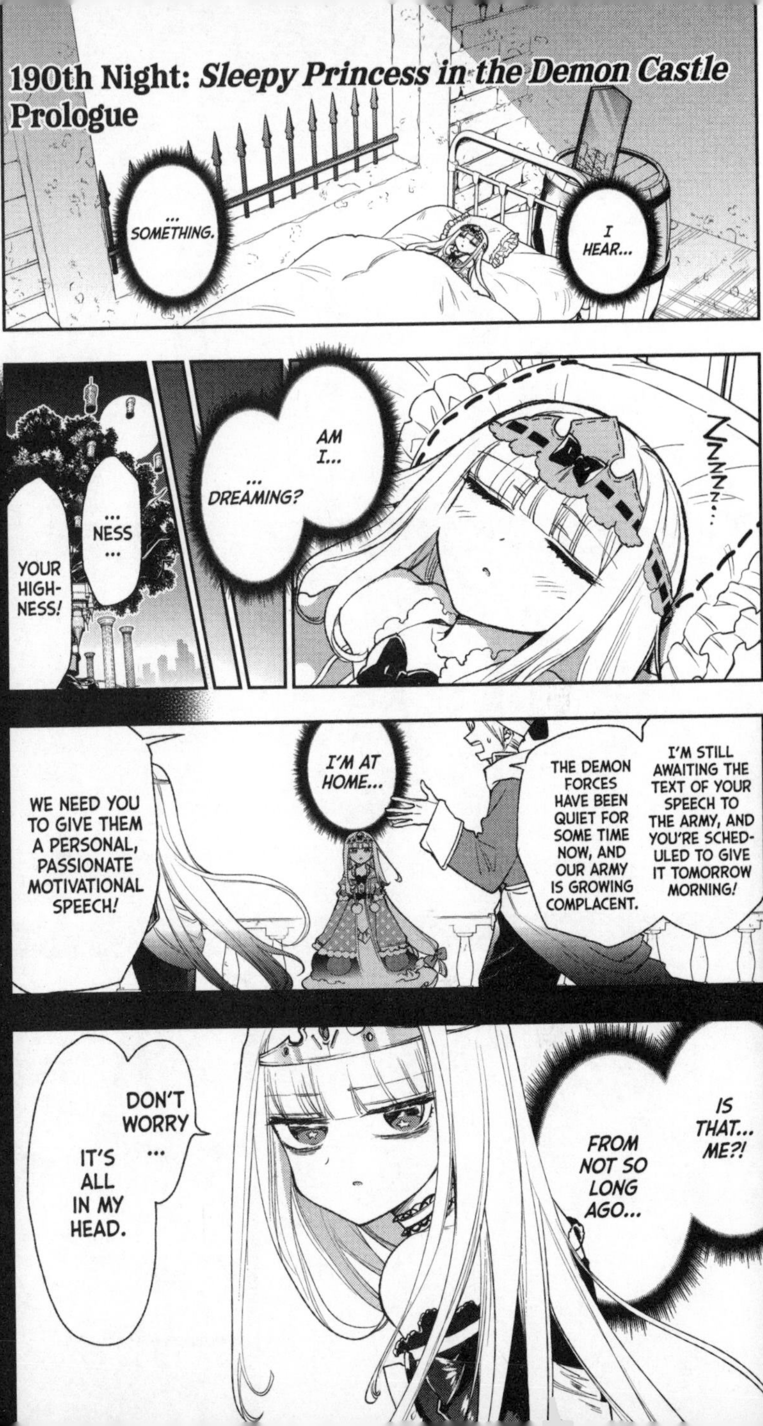
I HEAR...
... SOMETHING.
ZZZZZ...
AM I... ... DREAMING?
... NESS ...
YOUR HIGHNESS!
I'M STILL AWAITING THE TEXT OF YOUR SPEECH TO THE ARMY, AND YOU'RE SCHEDULED TO GIVE IT TOMORROW MORNING!
THE DEMON FORCES HAVE BEEN QUIET FOR SOME TIME NOW, AND OUR ARMY IS GROWING COMPLACENT.
I'M AT HOME...
WE NEED YOU TO GIVE THEM A PERSONAL, PASSIONATE MOTIVATIONAL SPEECH!
IS THAT... ME?!
FROM NOT SO LONG AGO...
DON'T WORRY ...
IT'S ALL IN MY HEAD.

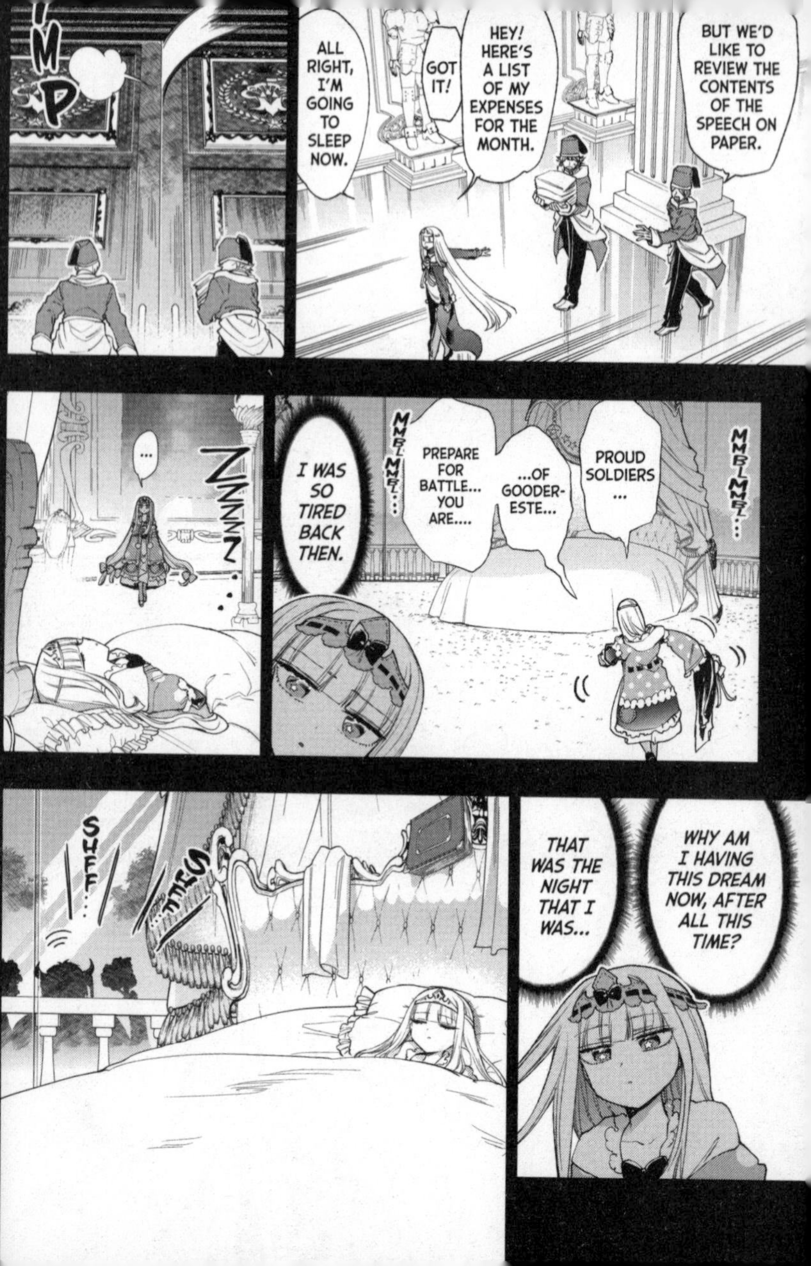
BUT WE'D LIKE TO REVIEW THE CONTENTS OF THE SPEECH ON PAPER.
HEY! HERE'S A LIST OF MY EXPENSES FOR THE MONTH.
GOT IT!
ALL RIGHT, I'M GOING TO SLEEP NOW.
MP
MMBL MMBL...
PROUD SOLDIERS...
...OF GOODER-ESTE...
PREPARE FOR BATTLE... YOU ARE....
MMBL MMBL...
I WAS SO TIRED BACK THEN.
...
ZZZZZ
WHY AM I HAVING THIS DREAM NOW, AFTER ALL THIS TIME?
THAT WAS THE NIGHT THAT I WAS...
SHFF...
SHFF...

190th Night: *Sleepy Princess in the Demon Castle* Prologue

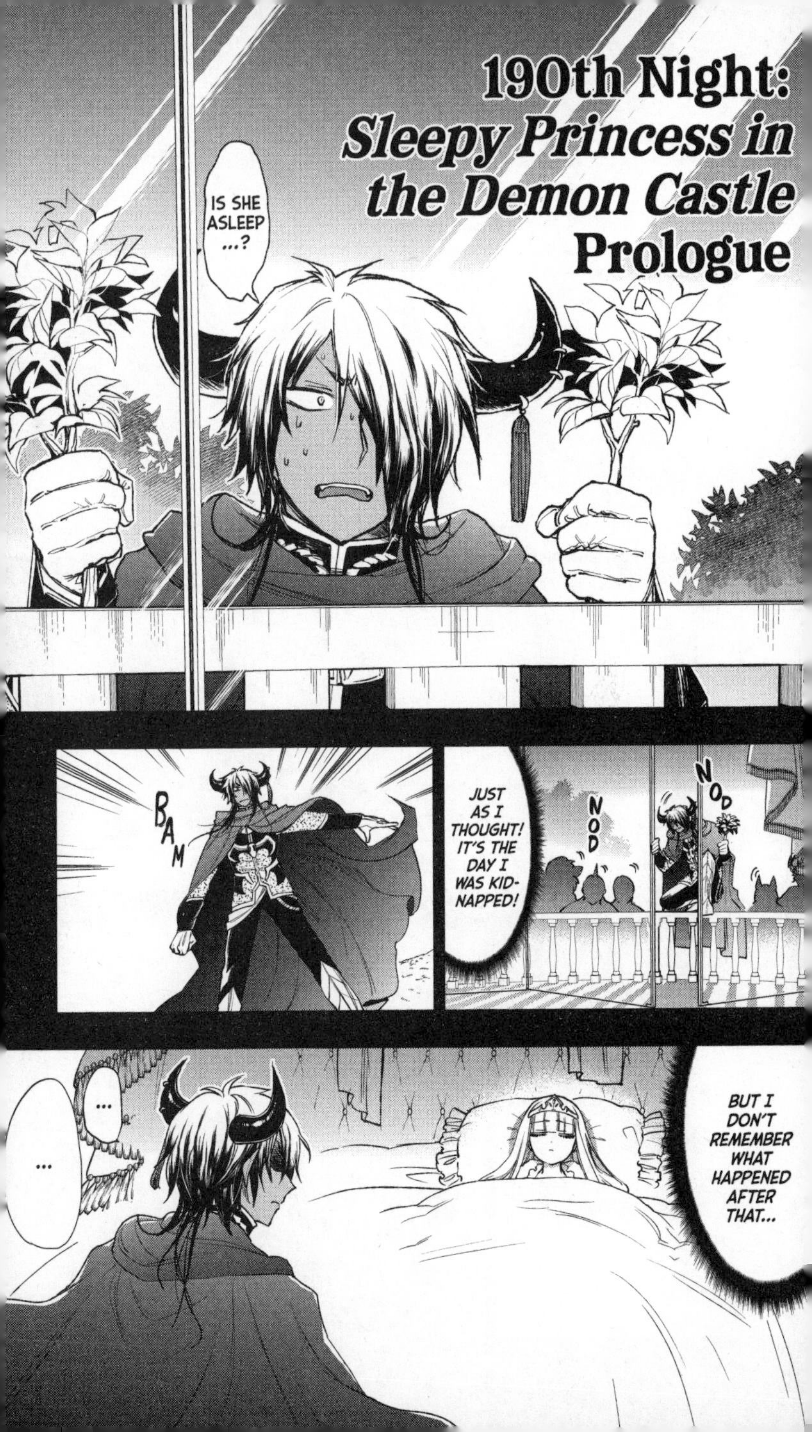
IS SHE ASLEEP ...?
JUST AS I THOUGHT! IT'S THE DAY I WAS KID-NAPPED!
NOD
NOD
BAM
BUT I DON'T REMEMBER WHAT HAPPENED AFTER THAT...
...
...

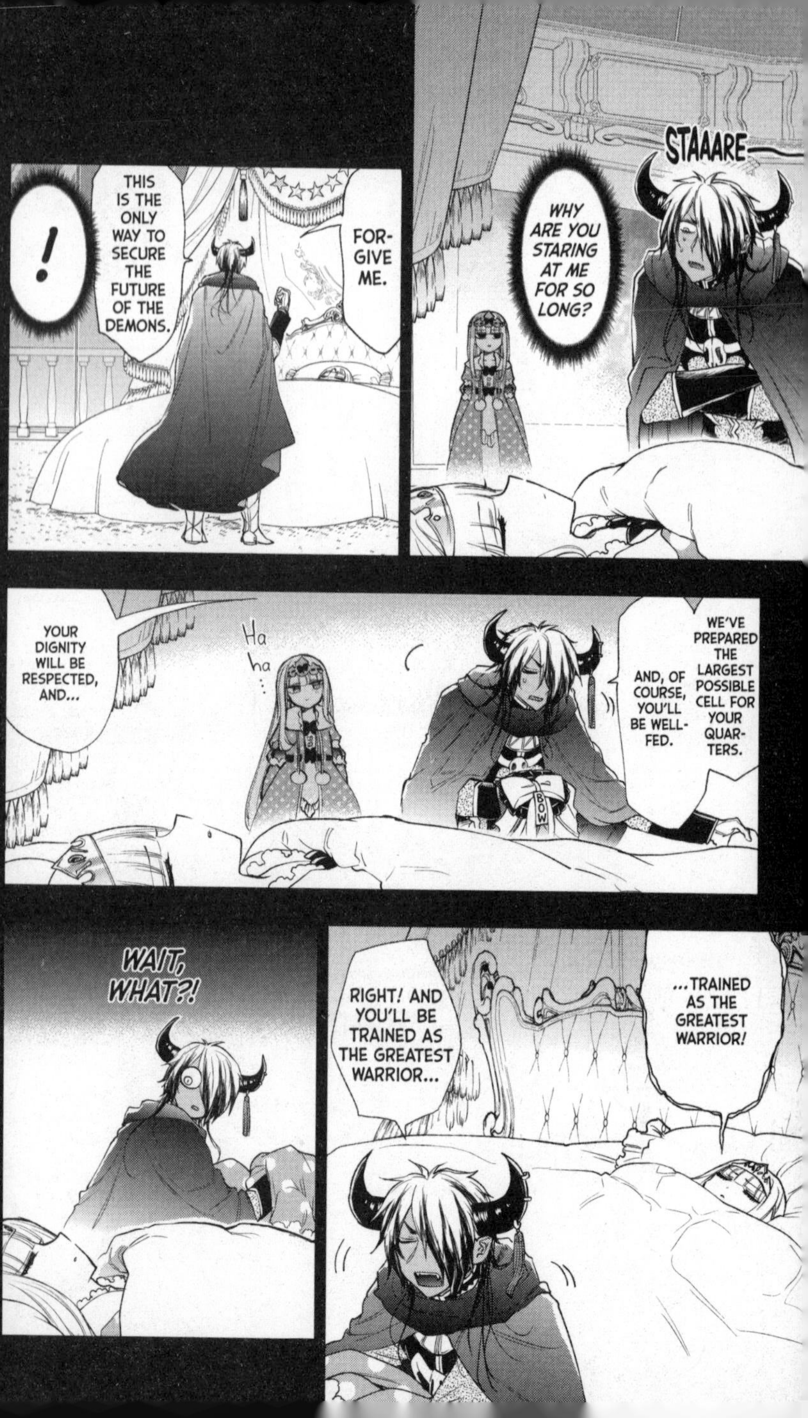
STAAARE
WHY ARE YOU STARING AT ME FOR SO LONG?
FOR-GIVE ME.
THIS IS THE ONLY WAY TO SECURE THE FUTURE OF THE DEMONS.
!
WE'VE PREPARED THE LARGEST POSSIBLE CELL FOR YOUR QUARTERS.
AND, OF COURSE, YOU'LL BE WELL-FED.
Ha ha...
YOUR DIGNITY WILL BE RESPECTED, AND...
BOW
...TRAINED AS THE GREATEST WARRIOR!
RIGHT! AND YOU'LL BE TRAINED AS THE GREATEST WARRIOR...
WAIT, WHAT?!

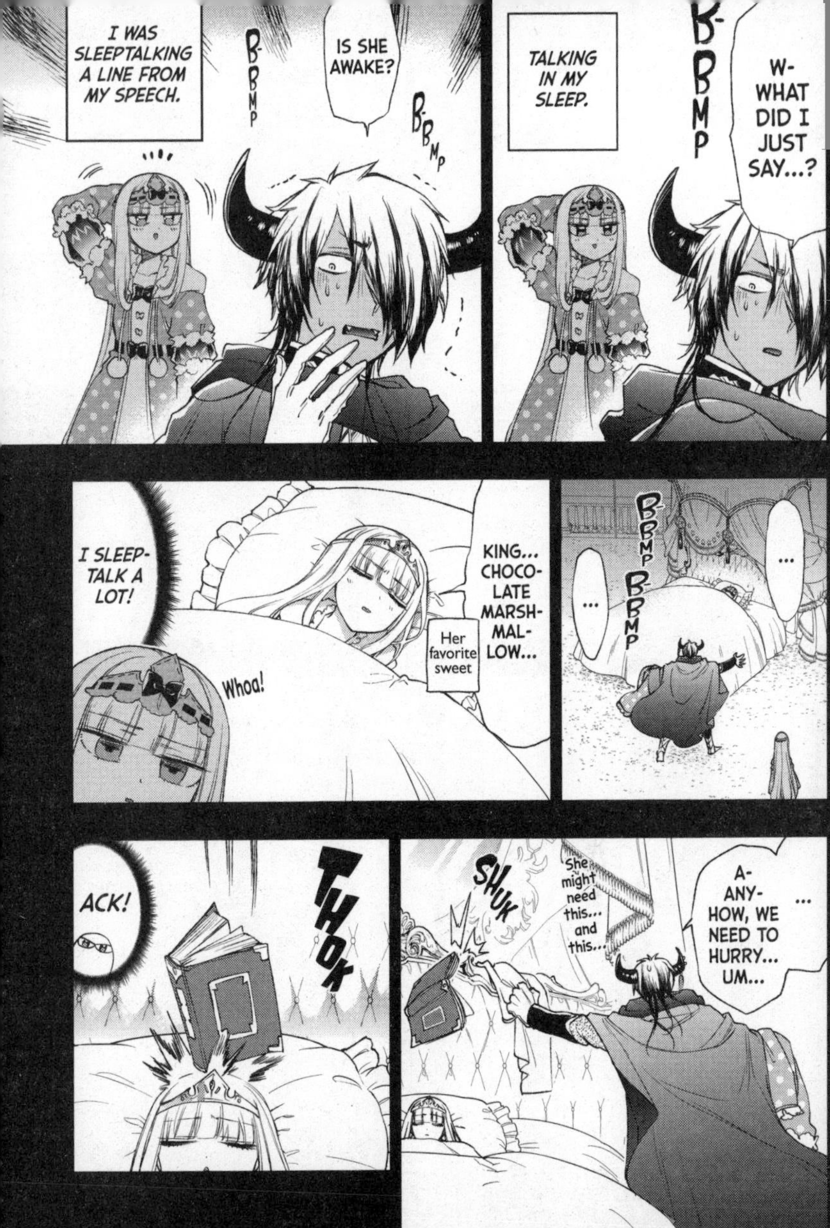
TALKING IN MY SLEEP.
B-BMP
W-WHAT DID I JUST SAY...?
I WAS SLEEPTALKING A LINE FROM MY SPEECH.
B-BMP
IS SHE AWAKE?
B-BMP
...
B-BMP B-BMP
...
KING... CHOCOLATE MARSHMALLOW...
Her favorite sweet
I SLEEP-TALK A LOT!
Whoa!
A-ANYHOW, WE NEED TO HURRY... UM...
...
SHUK
She might need this... and this...
THOK
ACK!

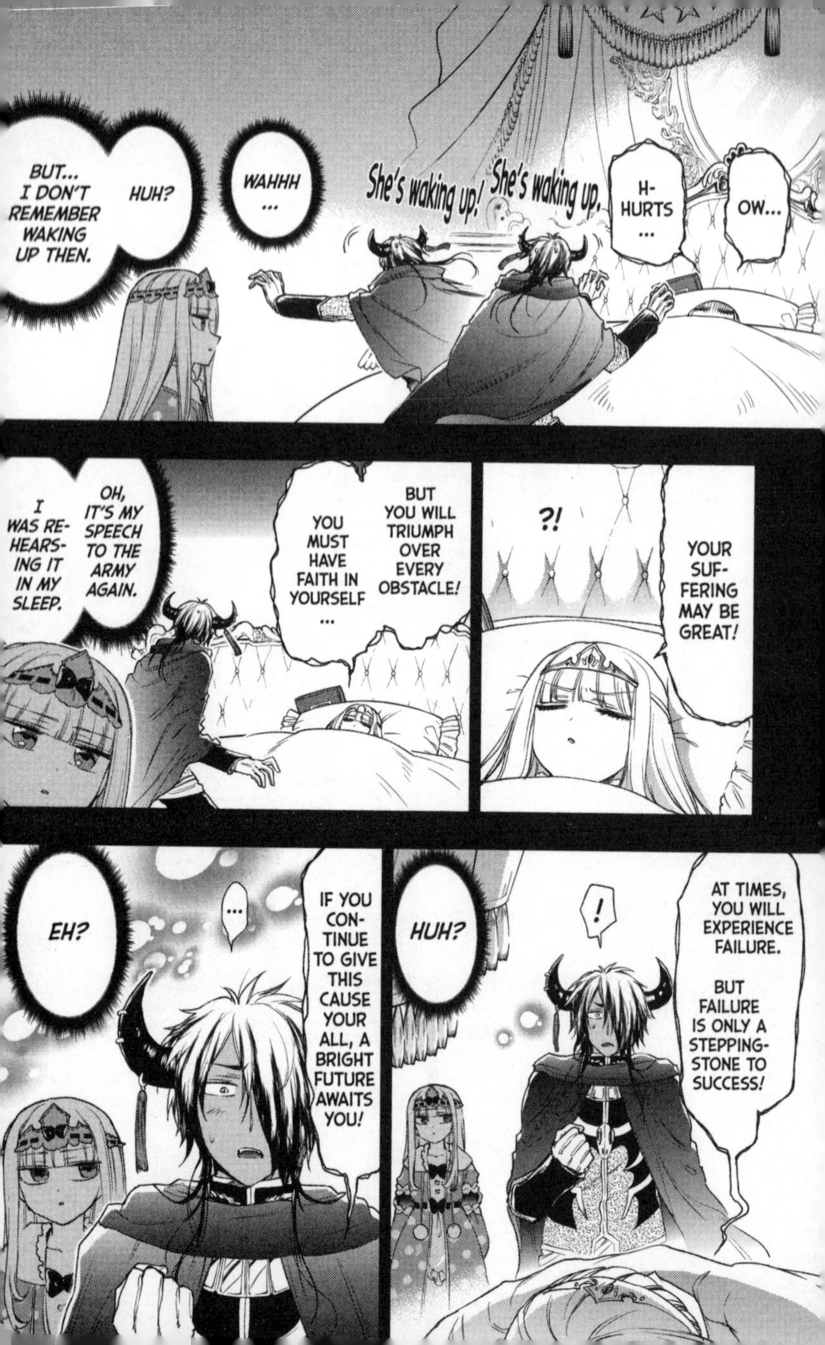
OW...
H-HURTS...
She's waking up.
She's waking up!
WAHHH...
HUH?
BUT... I DON'T REMEMBER WAKING UP THEN.
YOUR SUFFERING MAY BE GREAT!
?!
BUT YOU WILL TRIUMPH OVER EVERY OBSTACLE!
YOU MUST HAVE FAITH IN YOURSELF...
OH, IT'S MY SPEECH TO THE ARMY AGAIN.
I WAS REHEARSING IT IN MY SLEEP.
AT TIMES, YOU WILL EXPERIENCE FAILURE.
BUT FAILURE IS ONLY A STEPPING-STONE TO SUCCESS!
!
HUH?
IF YOU CONTINUE TO GIVE THIS CAUSE YOUR ALL, A BRIGHT FUTURE AWAITS YOU!
...
EH?

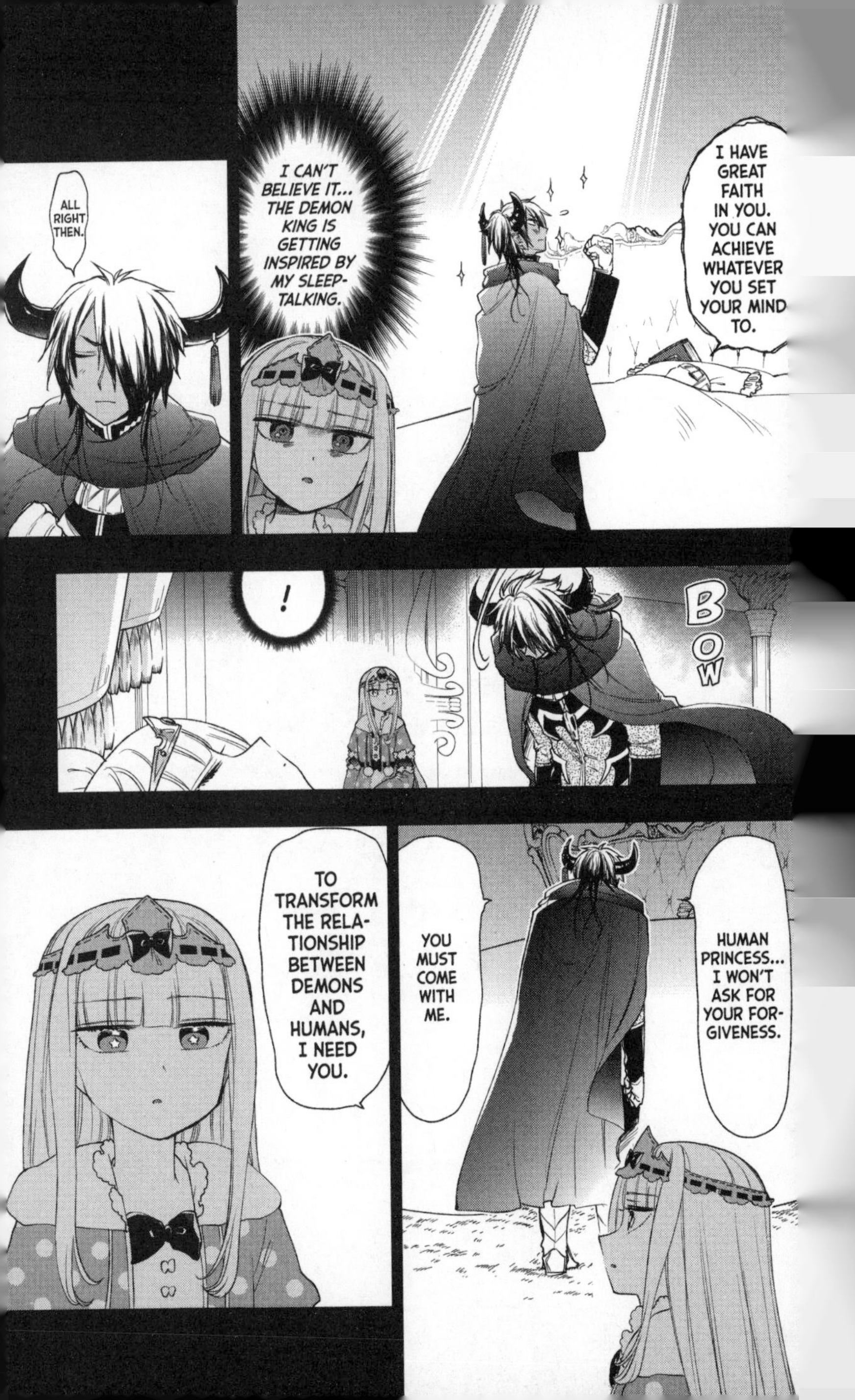
I HAVE GREAT FAITH IN YOU. YOU CAN ACHIEVE WHATEVER YOU SET YOUR MIND TO.
I CAN'T BELIEVE IT... THE DEMON KING IS GETTING INSPIRED BY MY SLEEP-TALKING.
ALL RIGHT THEN.
BOW
!
HUMAN PRINCESS... I WON'T ASK FOR YOUR FOR-GIVENESS.
YOU MUST COME WITH ME.
TO TRANSFORM THE RELA-TIONSHIP BETWEEN DEMONS AND HUMANS, I NEED YOU.

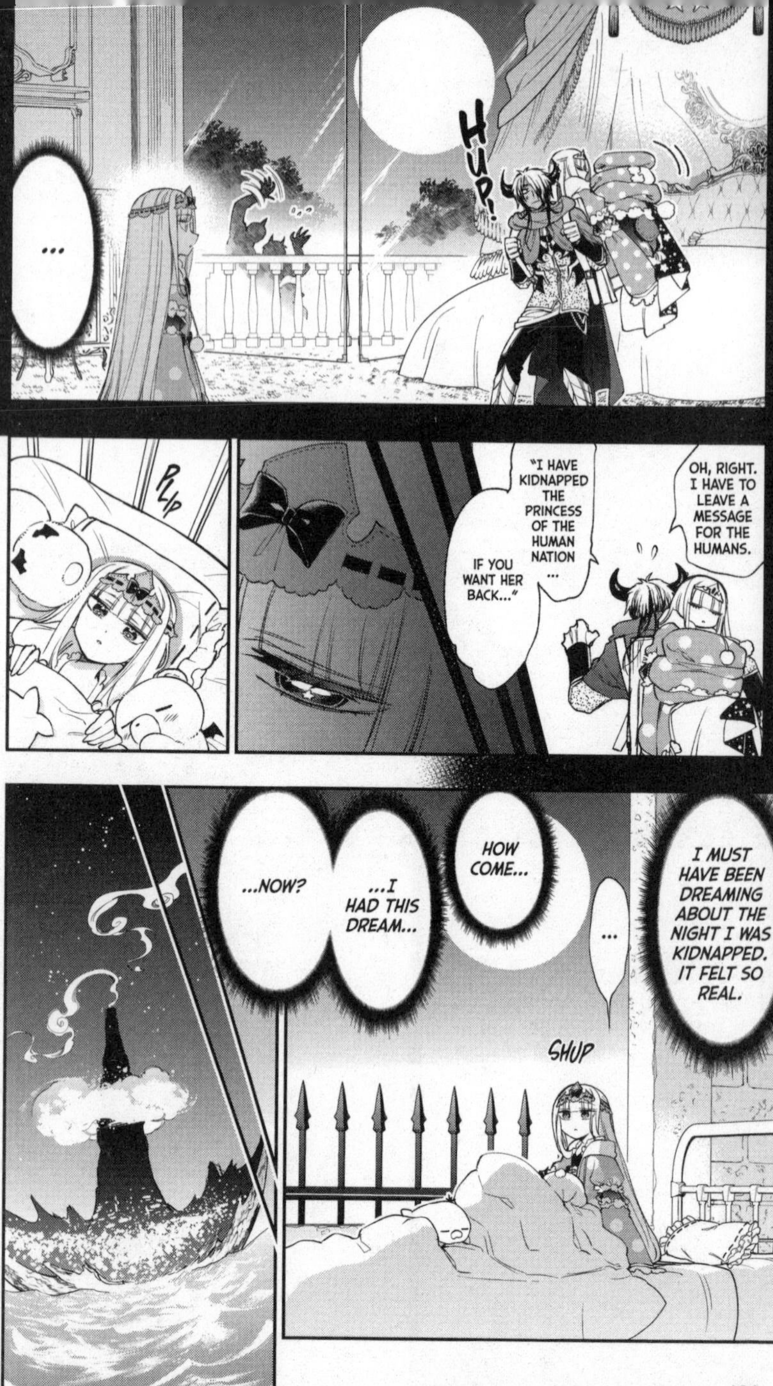
HUP!
...
OH, RIGHT. I HAVE TO LEAVE A MESSAGE FOR THE HUMANS.
"I HAVE KIDNAPPED THE PRINCESS OF THE HUMAN NATION ...
IF YOU WANT HER BACK..."
PLIP
I MUST HAVE BEEN DREAMING ABOUT THE NIGHT I WAS KIDNAPPED. IT FELT SO REAL.
...
SHUP
HOW COME...
...I HAD THIS DREAM...
...NOW?

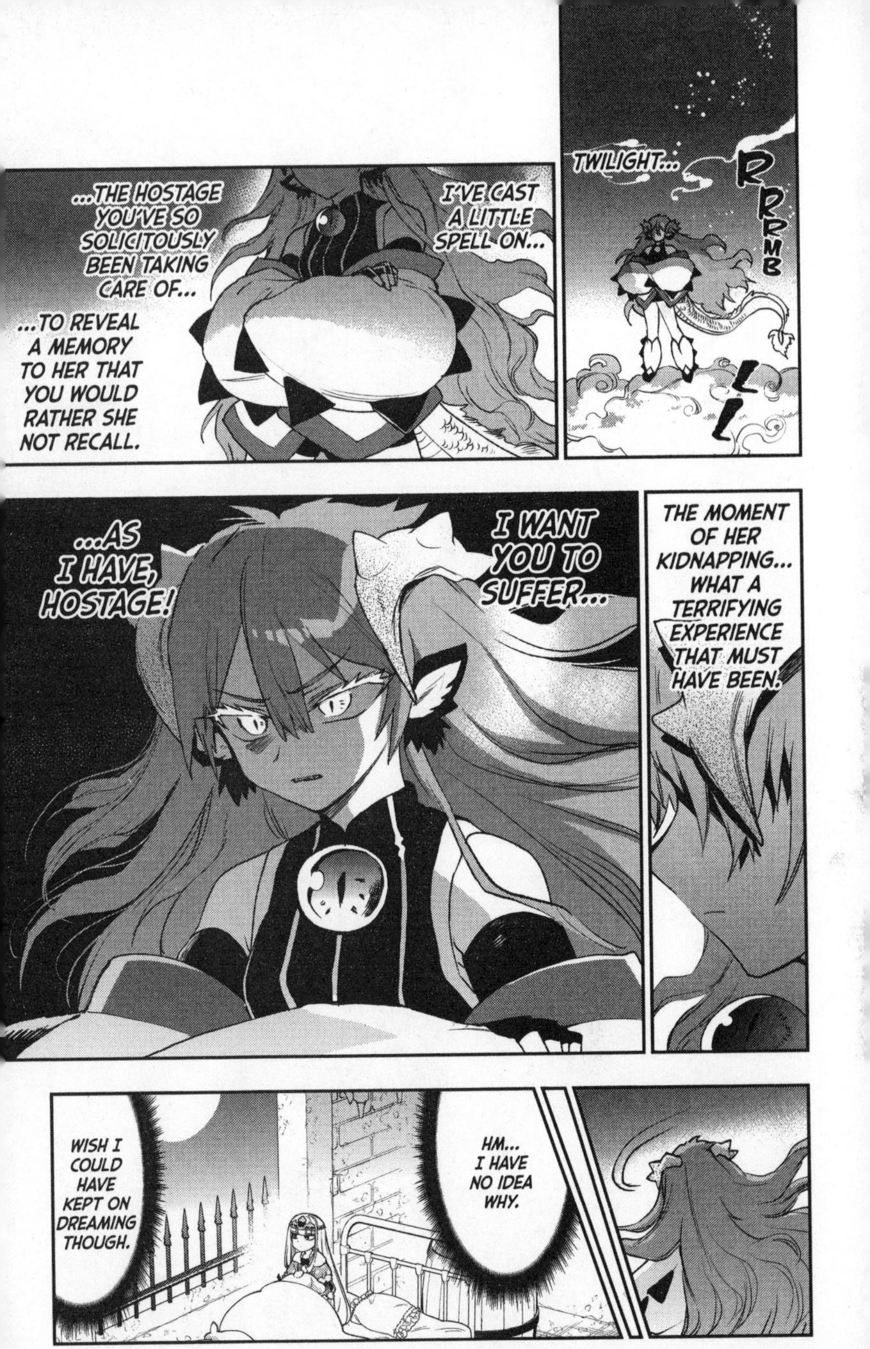
TWILIGHT...
RRRMB
I'VE CAST A LITTLE SPELL ON...
...THE HOSTAGE YOU'VE SO SOLICITOUSLY BEEN TAKING CARE OF...
...TO REVEAL A MEMORY TO HER THAT YOU WOULD RATHER SHE NOT RECALL.
THE MOMENT OF HER KIDNAPPING... WHAT A TERRIFYING EXPERIENCE THAT MUST HAVE BEEN.
I WANT YOU TO SUFFER...
...AS I HAVE, HOSTAGE!
HM... I HAVE NO IDEA WHY.
WISH I COULD HAVE KEPT ON DREAMING THOUGH.

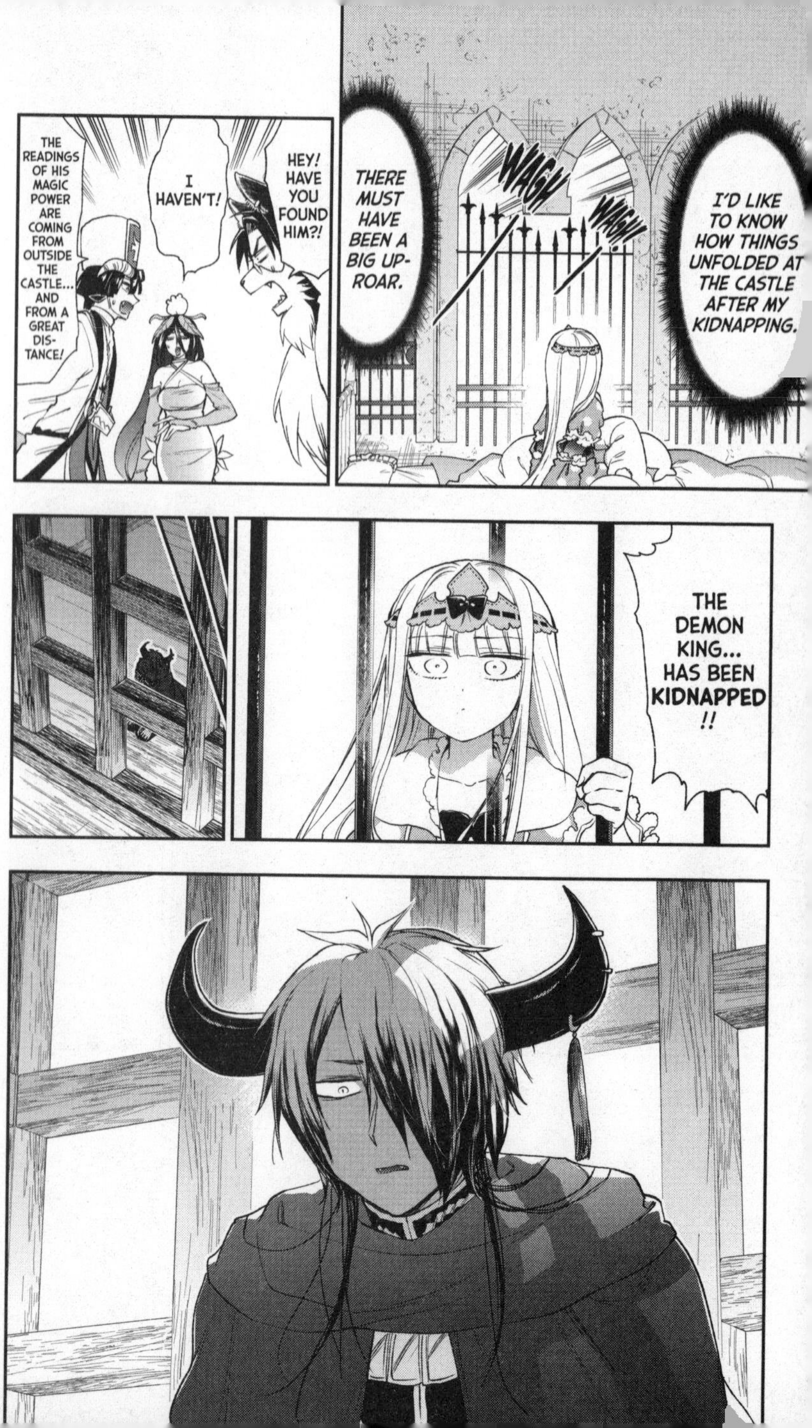
I'D LIKE TO KNOW HOW THINGS UNFOLDED AT THE CASTLE AFTER MY KIDNAPPING.
WAGH
WAGH!
THERE MUST HAVE BEEN A BIG UP-ROAR.
HEY! HAVE YOU FOUND HIM?!
I HAVEN'T!
THE READINGS OF HIS MAGIC POWER ARE COMING FROM OUTSIDE THE CASTLE... AND FROM A GREAT DIS-TANCE!
THE DEMON KING... HAS BEEN KIDNAPPED !!

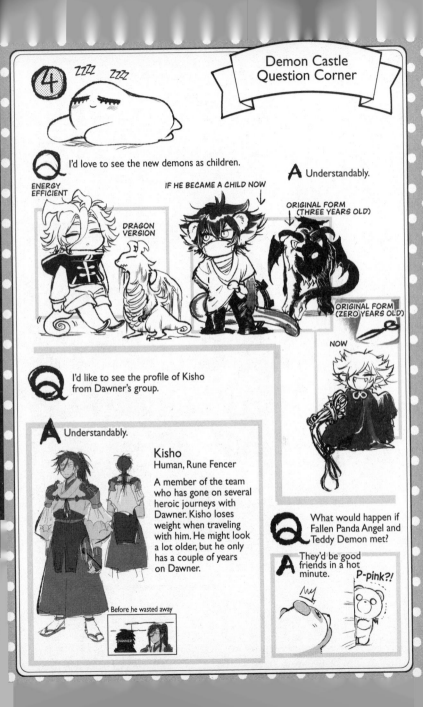

Demon Castle Question Corner

4

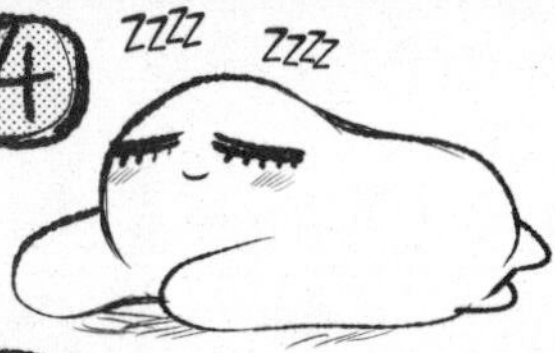
ZZZZ
ZZZZ

Q I'd love to see the new demons as children.

A Understandably.

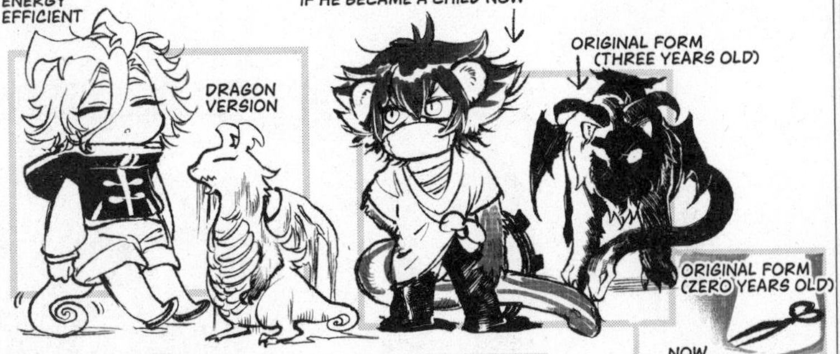
ENERGY EFFICIENT
DRAGON VERSION
IF HE BECAME A CHILD NOW
ORIGINAL FORM (THREE YEARS OLD)
ORIGINAL FORM (ZERO YEARS OLD)

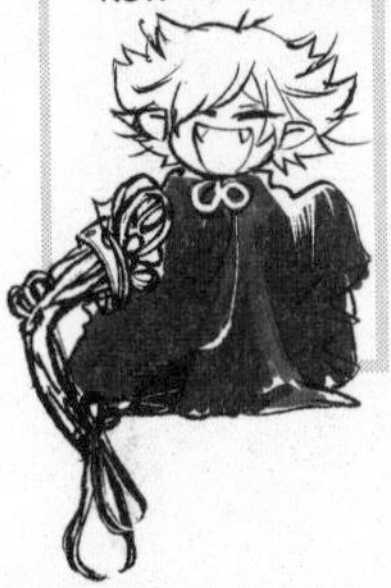
NOW

Q I'd like to see the profile of Kisho from Dawner's group.

A Understandably.

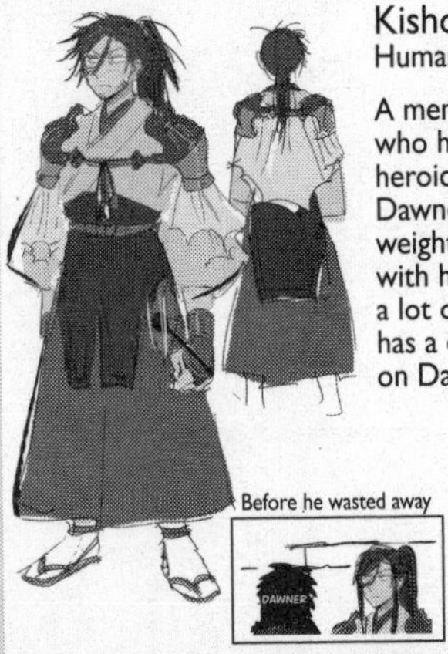
Before he wasted away
DAWNER

Kisho
Human, Rune Fencer

A member of the team who has gone on several heroic journeys with Dawner. Kisho loses weight when traveling with him. He might look a lot older, but he only has a couple of years on Dawner.

Q What would happen if Fallen Panda Angel and Teddy Demon met?

A They'd be good friends in a hot minute.

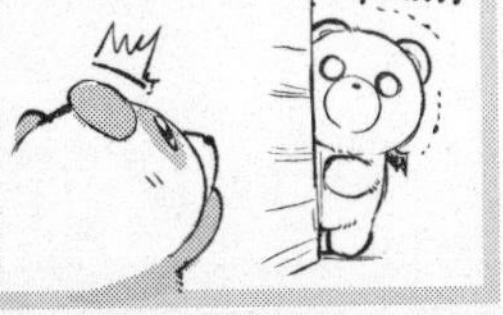
P-pink?!

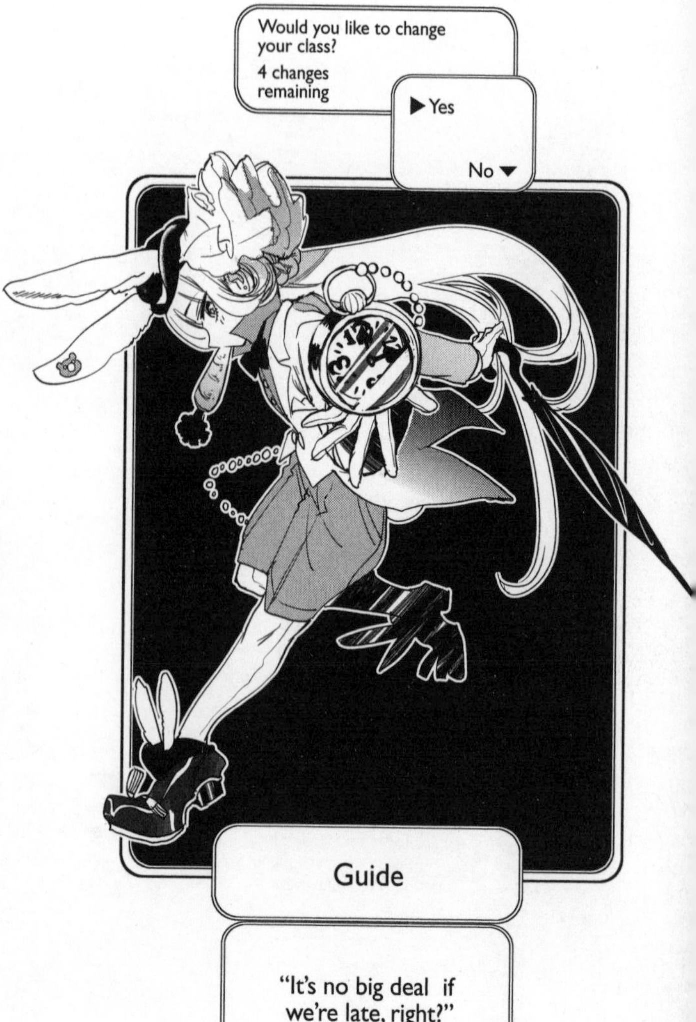
Would you like to change your class?
4 changes remaining
▶Yes
No ▼
Guide
"It's no big deal if we're late, right?"

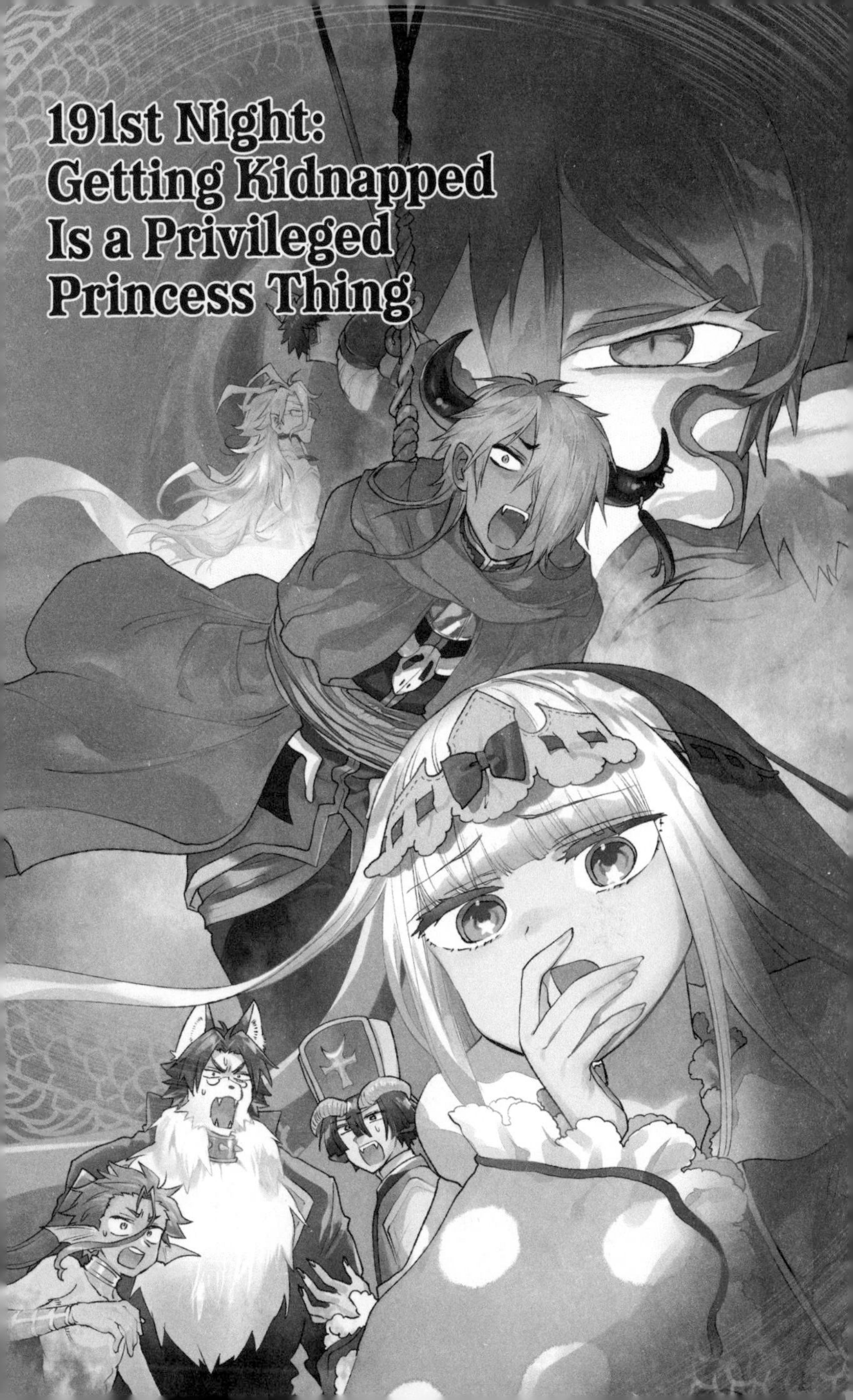
191st Night:
Getting Kidnapped
Is a Privileged
Princess Thing

SLEEPY PRINCESS
IN THE DEMON CASTLE

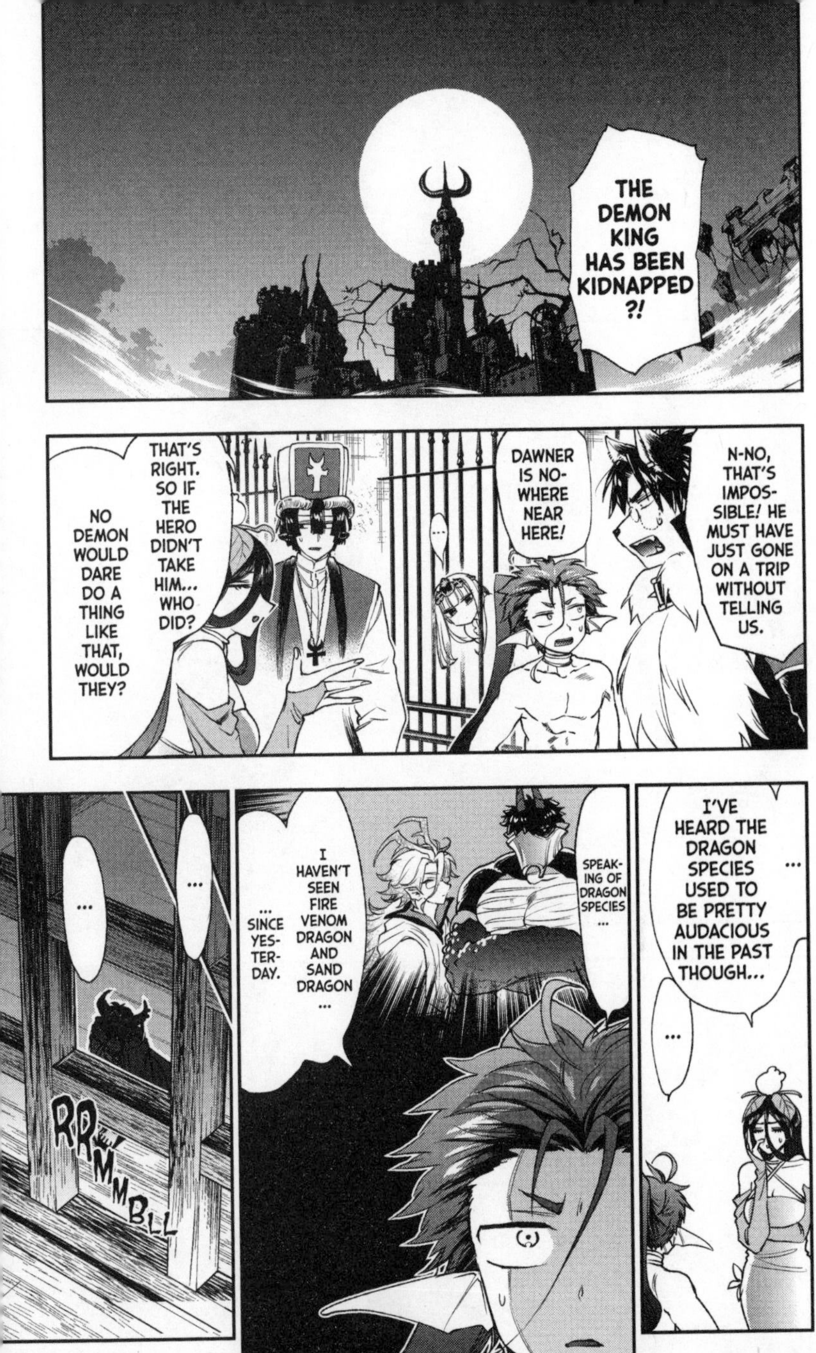
THE DEMON KING HAS BEEN KIDNAPPED?!
N-NO, THAT'S IMPOSSIBLE! HE MUST HAVE JUST GONE ON A TRIP WITHOUT TELLING US.
DAWNER IS NO-WHERE NEAR HERE!
...
THAT'S RIGHT. SO IF THE HERO DIDN'T TAKE HIM... WHO DID?
NO DEMON WOULD DARE DO A THING LIKE THAT, WOULD THEY?
I'VE HEARD THE DRAGON SPECIES USED TO BE PRETTY AUDACIOUS IN THE PAST THOUGH...
...
...
SPEAK-ING OF DRAGON SPECIES ...
I HAVEN'T SEEN FIRE VENOM DRAGON AND SAND DRAGON ...
... SINCE YES-TER-DAY.
...
...
RRMMBLL

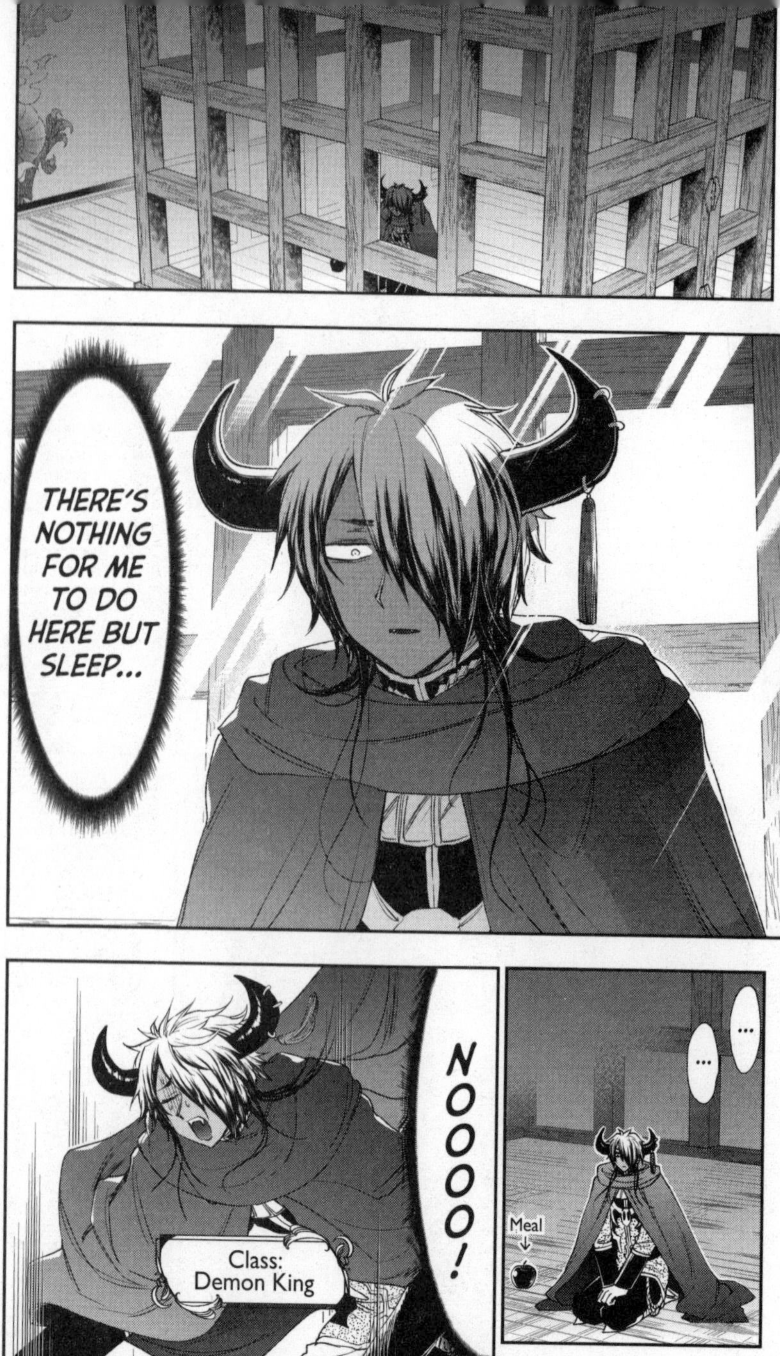
THERE'S NOTHING FOR ME TO DO HERE BUT SLEEP...
...
...
Meal
NOOOOO!
Class: Demon King

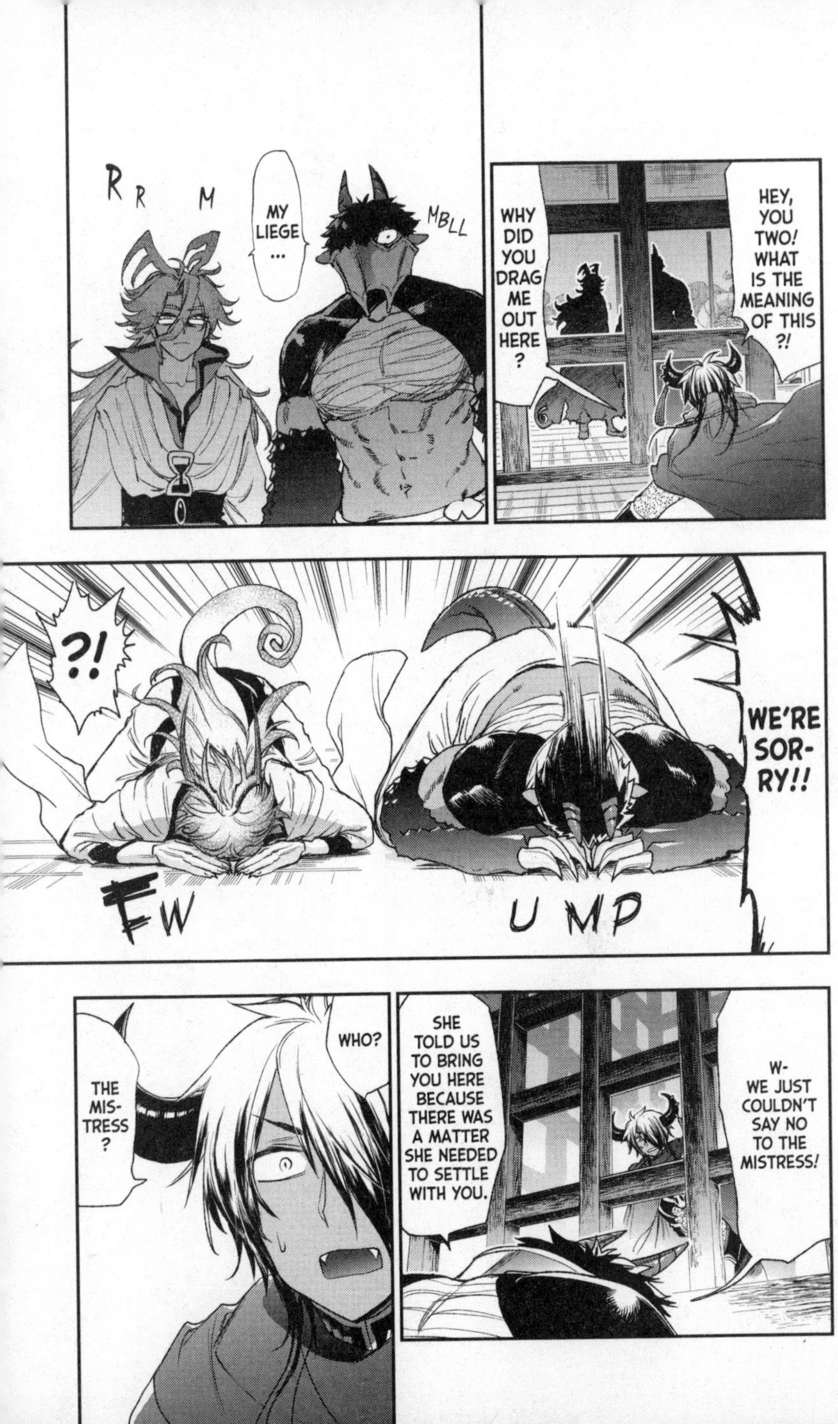
HEY, YOU TWO! WHAT IS THE MEANING OF THIS?!
WHY DID YOU DRAG ME OUT HERE?
MBLL
MY LIEGE...
RRM
WE'RE SORRY!!
?!
FW UMP
W- WE JUST COULDN'T SAY NO TO THE MISTRESS!
SHE TOLD US TO BRING YOU HERE BECAUSE THERE WAS A MATTER SHE NEEDED TO SETTLE WITH YOU.
WHO?
THE MISTRESS?

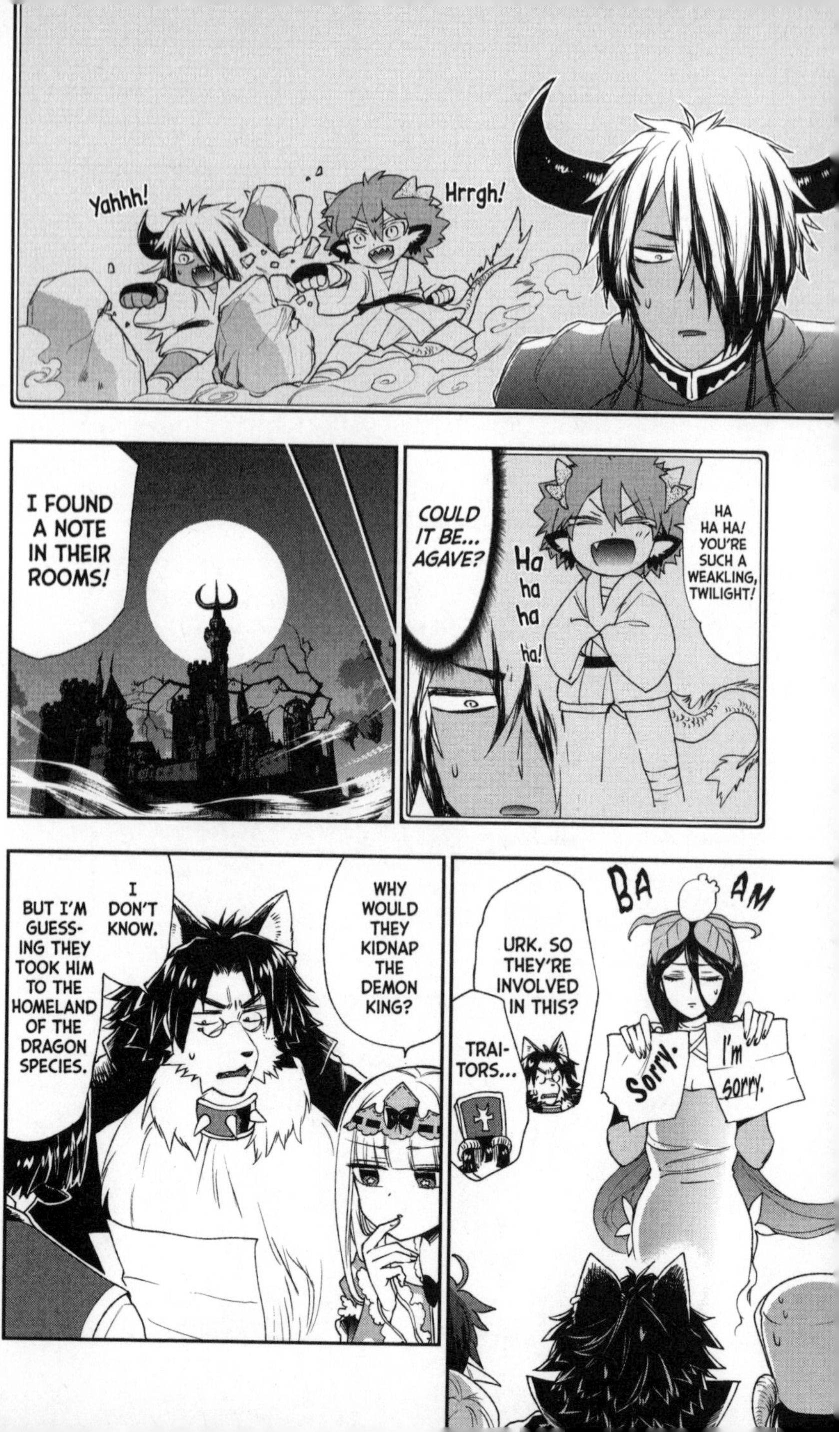
Hrrgh!
Yahhh!
HA HA HA! YOU'RE SUCH A WEAKLING, TWILIGHT!
Ha ha ha ha!
COULD IT BE... AGAVE?
I FOUND A NOTE IN THEIR ROOMS!
BAAM
URK. SO THEY'RE INVOLVED IN THIS?
TRAITORS...
Sorry.
I'm sorry.
WHY WOULD THEY KIDNAP THE DEMON KING?
I DON'T KNOW.
BUT I'M GUESSING THEY TOOK HIM TO THE HOMELAND OF THE DRAGON SPECIES.

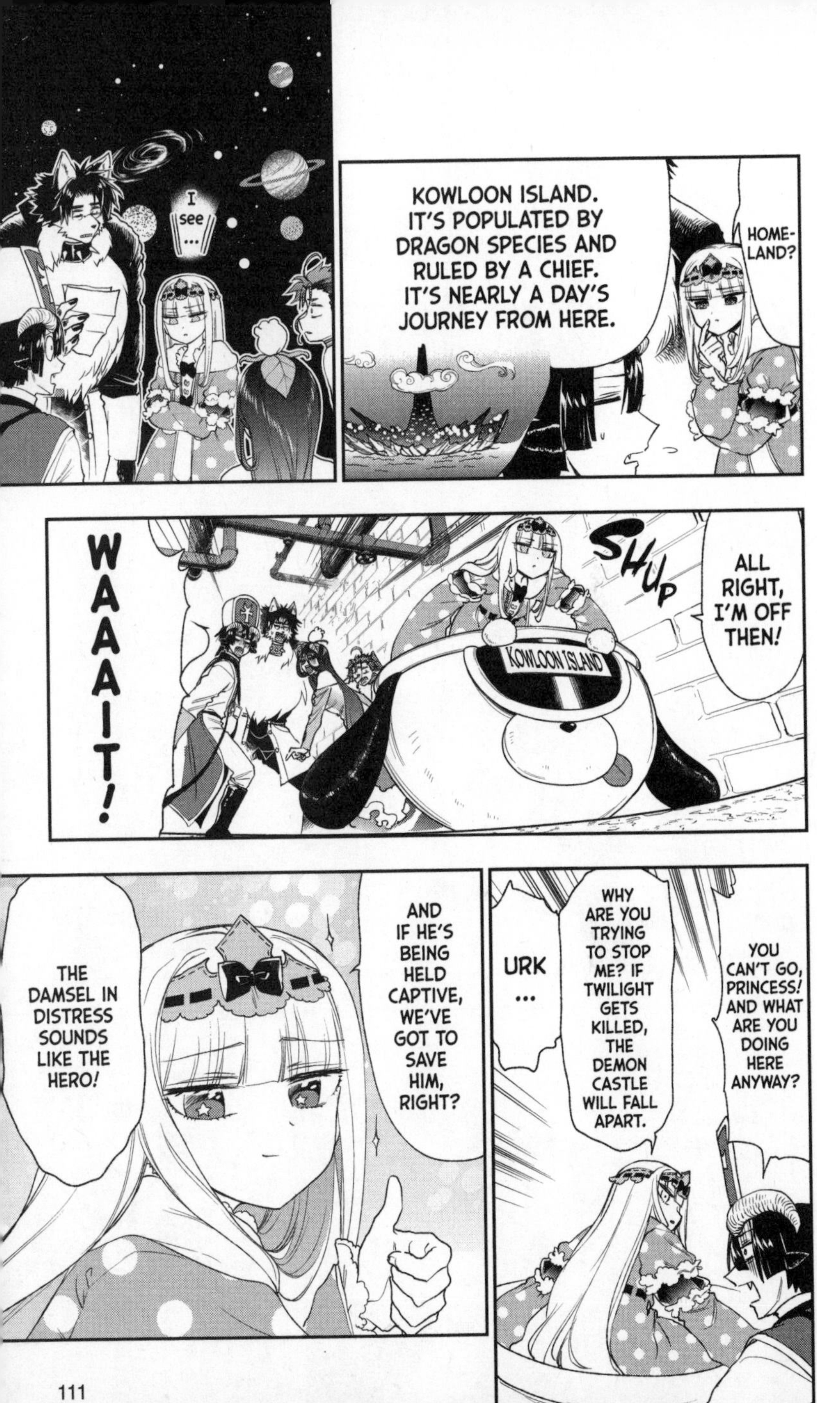
HOME-LAND?
KOWLOON ISLAND. IT'S POPULATED BY DRAGON SPECIES AND RULED BY A CHIEF. IT'S NEARLY A DAY'S JOURNEY FROM HERE.
I see ...
ALL RIGHT, I'M OFF THEN!
SHUP
KOWLOON ISLAND
WAAAAIT!
YOU CAN'T GO, PRINCESS! AND WHAT ARE YOU DOING HERE ANYWAY?
WHY ARE YOU TRYING TO STOP ME? IF TWILIGHT GETS KILLED, THE DEMON CASTLE WILL FALL APART.
URK ...
AND IF HE'S BEING HELD CAPTIVE, WE'VE GOT TO SAVE HIM, RIGHT?
THE DAMSEL IN DISTRESS SOUNDS LIKE THE HERO!

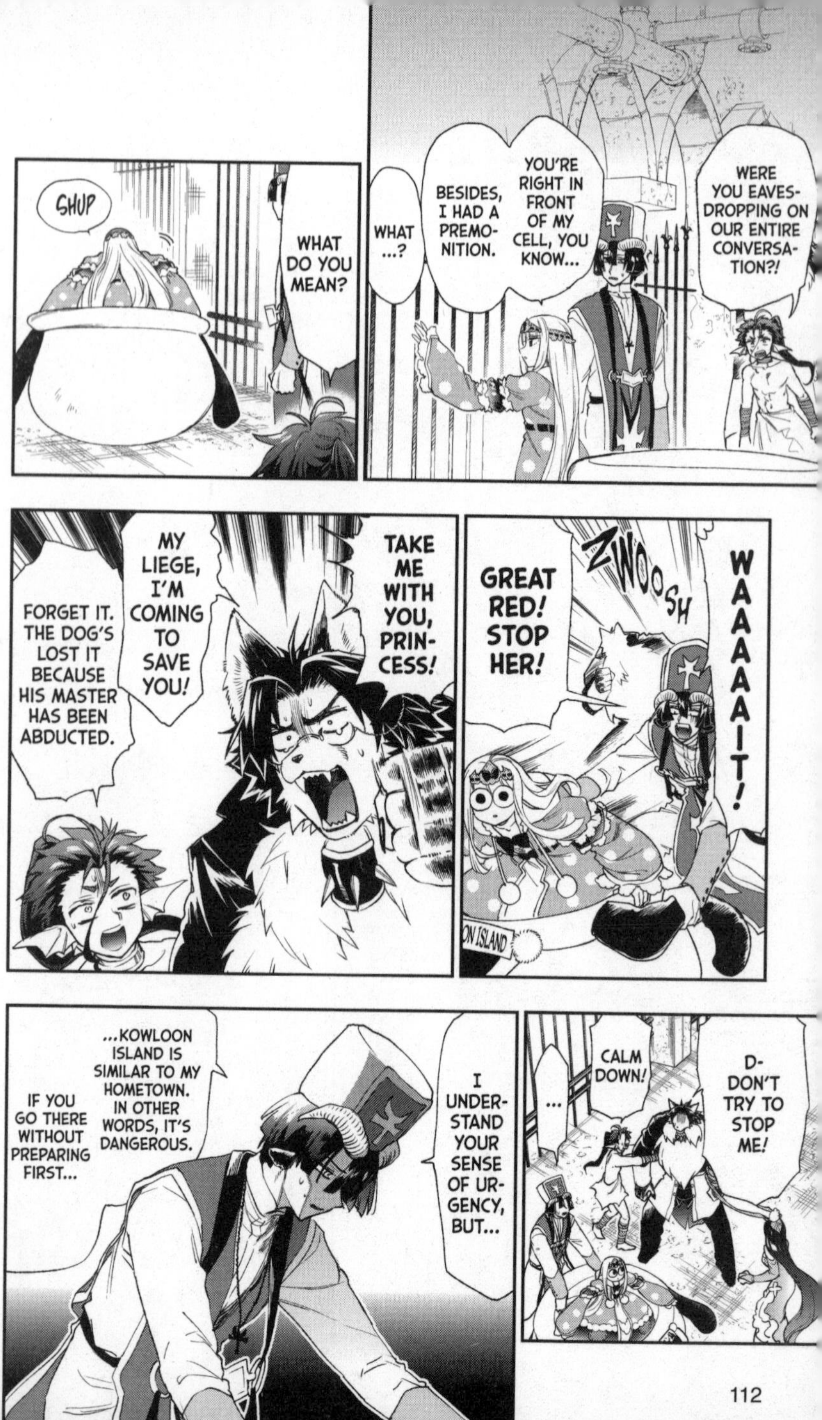
WERE YOU EAVES-DROPPING ON OUR ENTIRE CONVERSA-TION?!
YOU'RE RIGHT IN FRONT OF MY CELL, YOU KNOW...
BESIDES, I HAD A PREMO-NITION.
WHAT ...?
WHAT DO YOU MEAN?
SHUP
WAAAAAAIT!
ZWOOSH
GREAT RED! STOP HER!
ON ISLAND
TAKE ME WITH YOU, PRIN-CESS!
MY LIEGE, I'M COMING TO SAVE YOU!
FORGET IT. THE DOG'S LOST IT BECAUSE HIS MASTER HAS BEEN ABDUCTED.
D-DON'T TRY TO STOP ME!
CALM DOWN!
...
I UNDER-STAND YOUR SENSE OF UR-GENCY, BUT...
...KOWLOON ISLAND IS SIMILAR TO MY HOMETOWN. IN OTHER WORDS, IT'S DANGEROUS.
IF YOU GO THERE WITHOUT PREPARING FIRST...

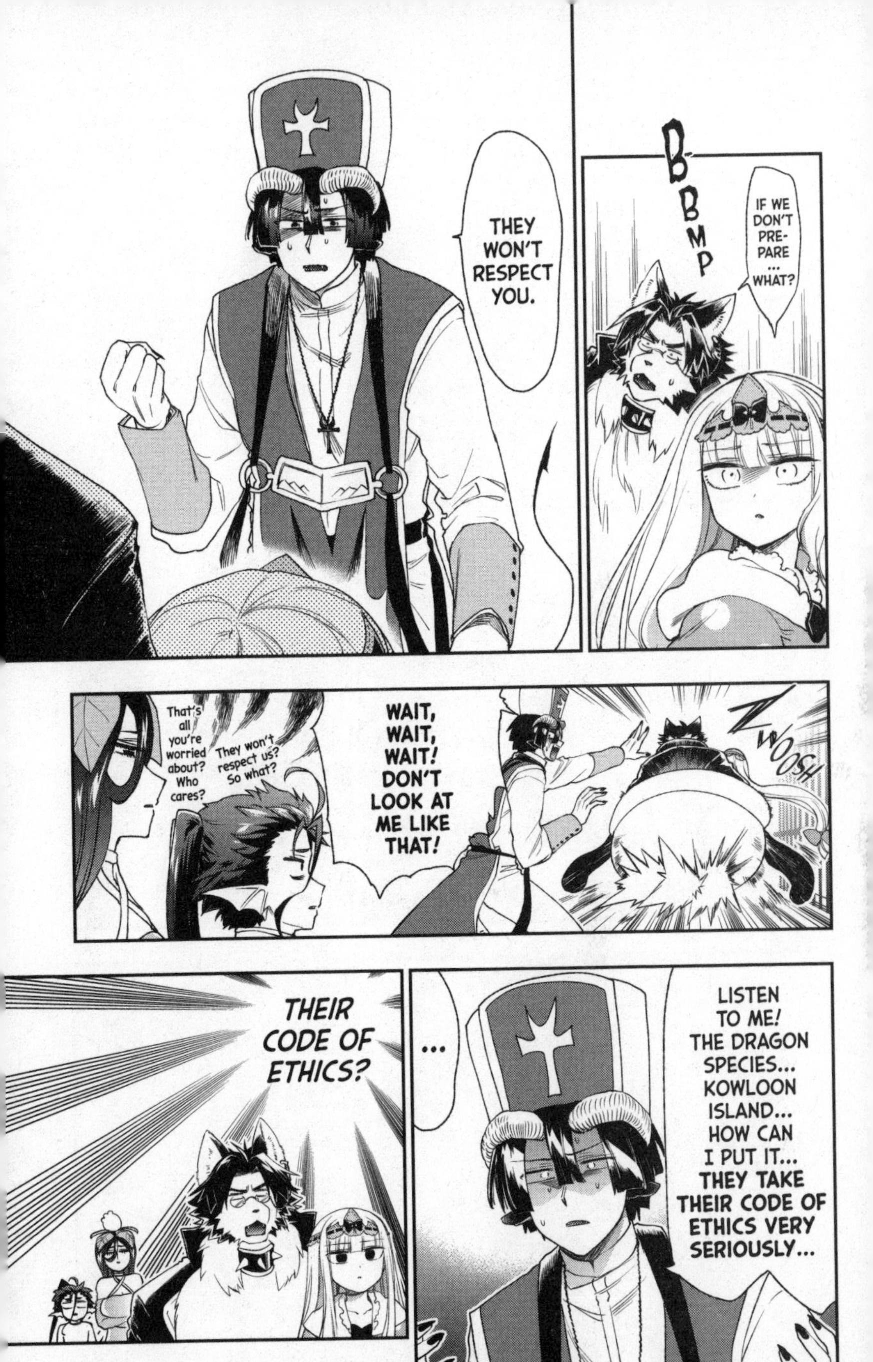
BBMP
IF WE DON'T PRE-PARE ... WHAT?
THEY WON'T RESPECT YOU.
WHOOSH
WAIT, WAIT, WAIT! DON'T LOOK AT ME LIKE THAT!
They won't respect us? So what?
That's all you're worried about? Who cares?
LISTEN TO ME! THE DRAGON SPECIES... KOWLOON ISLAND... HOW CAN I PUT IT... THEY TAKE THEIR CODE OF ETHICS VERY SERIOUSLY...
...
THEIR CODE OF ETHICS?

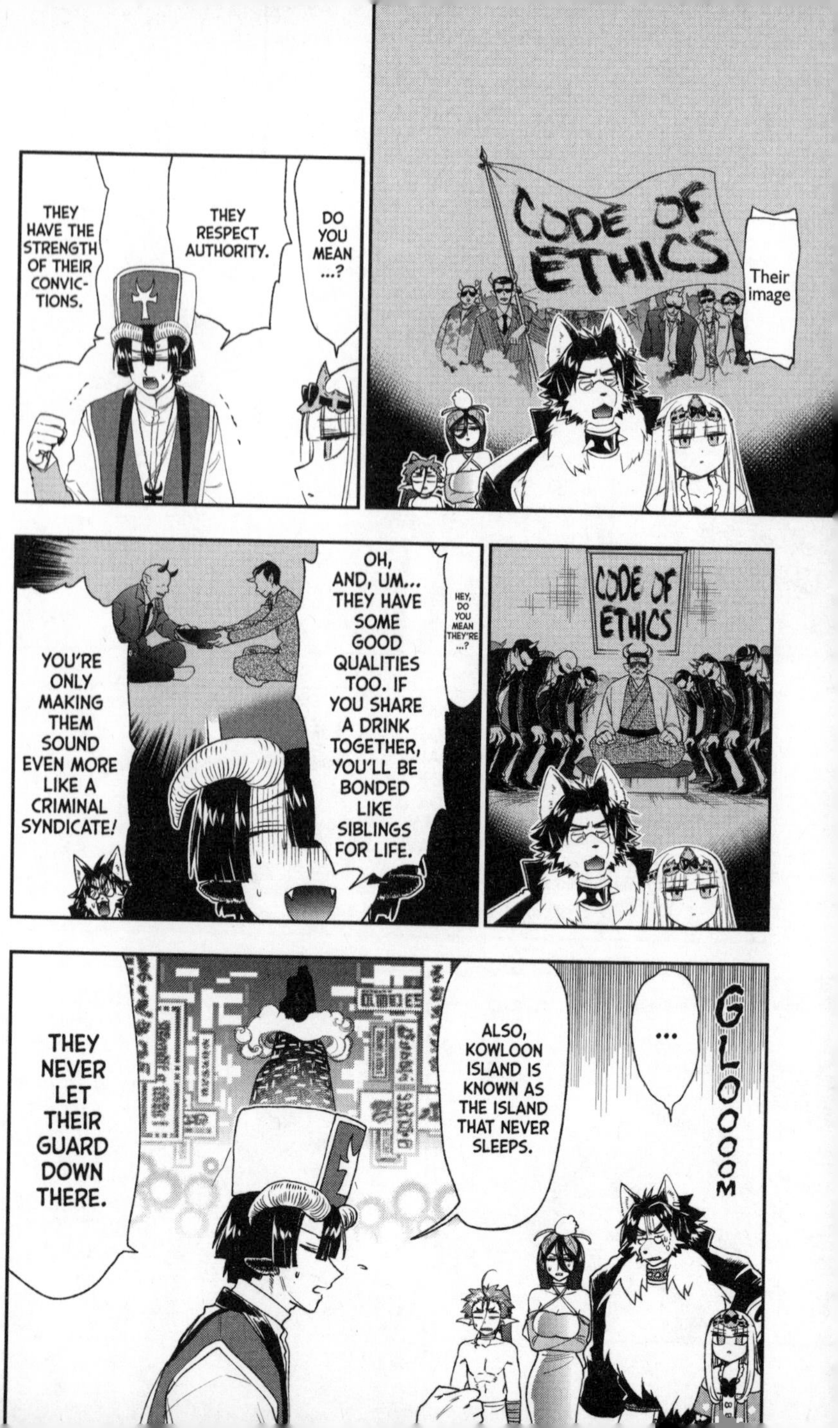
CODE OF ETHICS
Their image
DO YOU MEAN ...?
THEY RESPECT AUTHORITY.
THEY HAVE THE STRENGTH OF THEIR CONVIC- TIONS.
CODE OF ETHICS
HEY, DO YOU MEAN THEY'RE ...?
OH, AND, UM... THEY HAVE SOME GOOD QUALITIES TOO. IF YOU SHARE A DRINK TOGETHER, YOU'LL BE BONDED LIKE SIBLINGS FOR LIFE.
YOU'RE ONLY MAKING THEM SOUND EVEN MORE LIKE A CRIMINAL SYNDICATE!
GLOOOOOM
...
ALSO, KOWLOON ISLAND IS KNOWN AS THE ISLAND THAT NEVER SLEEPS.
THEY NEVER LET THEIR GUARD DOWN THERE.

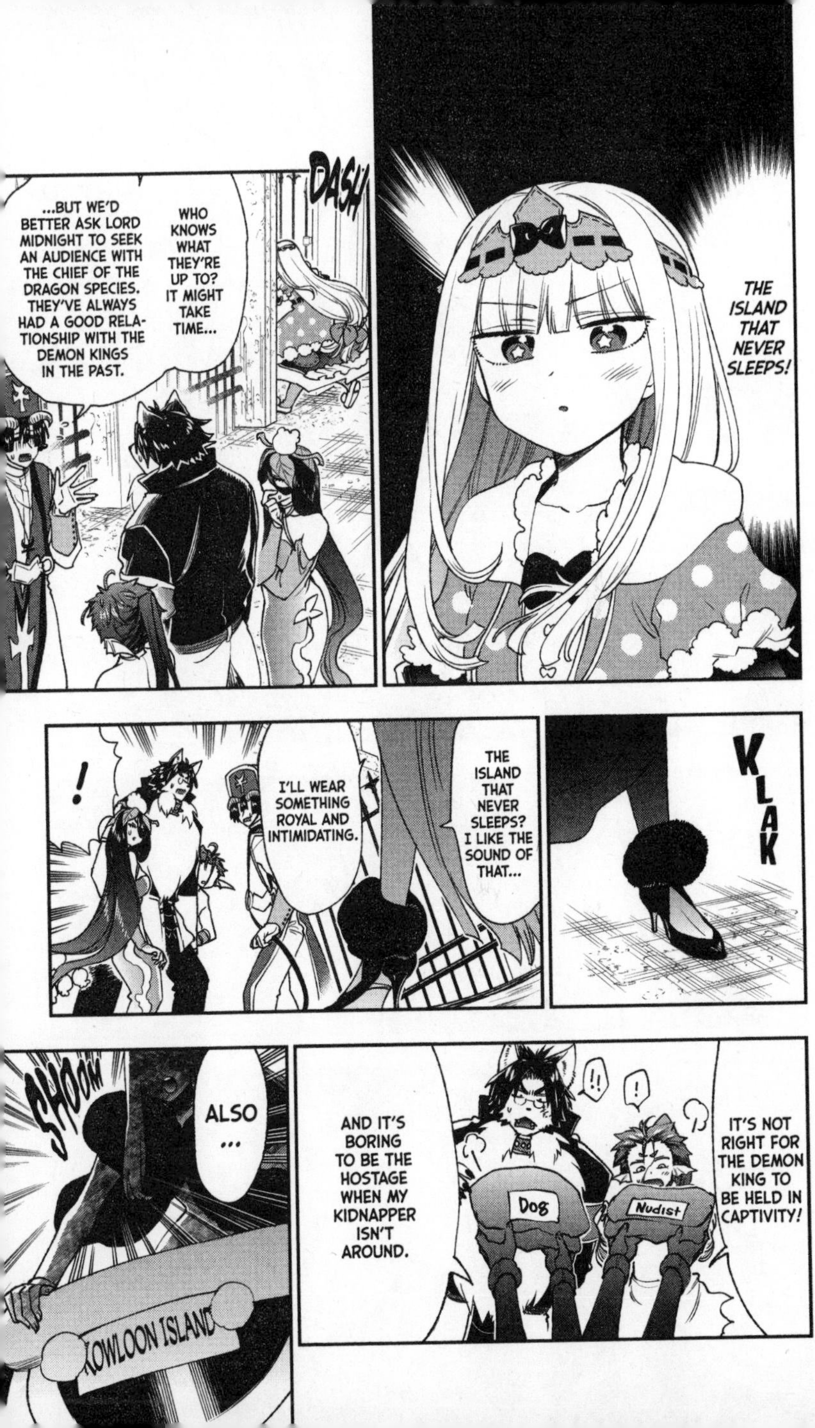
THE ISLAND THAT NEVER SLEEPS!
DASH
WHO KNOWS WHAT THEY'RE UP TO? IT MIGHT TAKE TIME...
...BUT WE'D BETTER ASK LORD MIDNIGHT TO SEEK AN AUDIENCE WITH THE CHIEF OF THE DRAGON SPECIES. THEY'VE ALWAYS HAD A GOOD RELA-TIONSHIP WITH THE DEMON KINGS IN THE PAST.
KLAK
THE ISLAND THAT NEVER SLEEPS? I LIKE THE SOUND OF THAT...
I'LL WEAR SOMETHING ROYAL AND INTIMIDATING.
!
IT'S NOT RIGHT FOR THE DEMON KING TO BE HELD IN CAPTIVITY!
!
!!
Nudist
Dog
AND IT'S BORING TO BE THE HOSTAGE WHEN MY KIDNAPPER ISN'T AROUND.
ALSO...
SHOOM
KOWLOON ISLAND

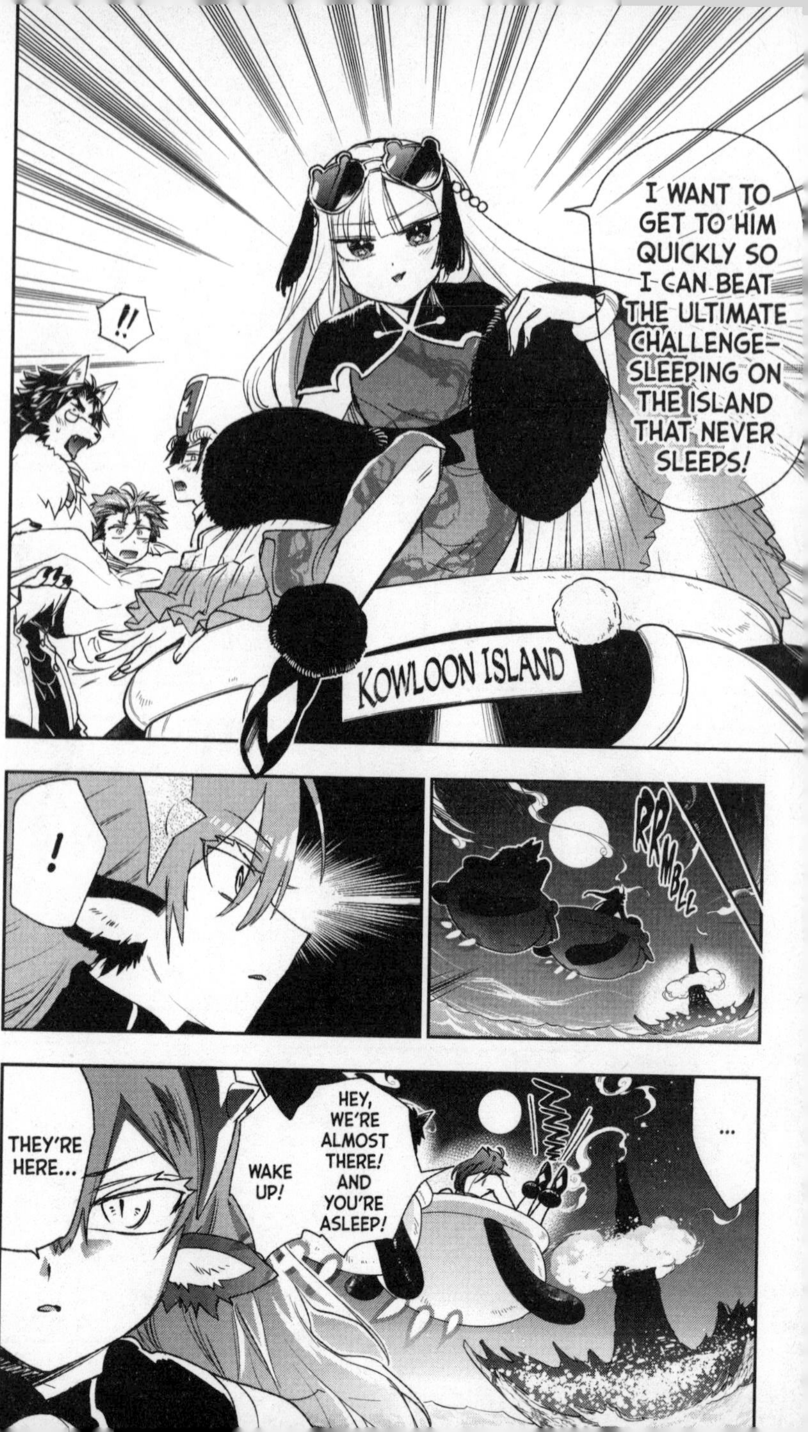
I WANT TO GET TO HIM QUICKLY SO I CAN BEAT THE ULTIMATE CHALLENGE—SLEEPING ON THE ISLAND THAT NEVER SLEEPS!
!!
KOWLOON ISLAND
RRMBLL
!
...
HEY, WE'RE ALMOST THERE! AND YOU'RE ASLEEP!
WAKE UP!
THEY'RE HERE...

5

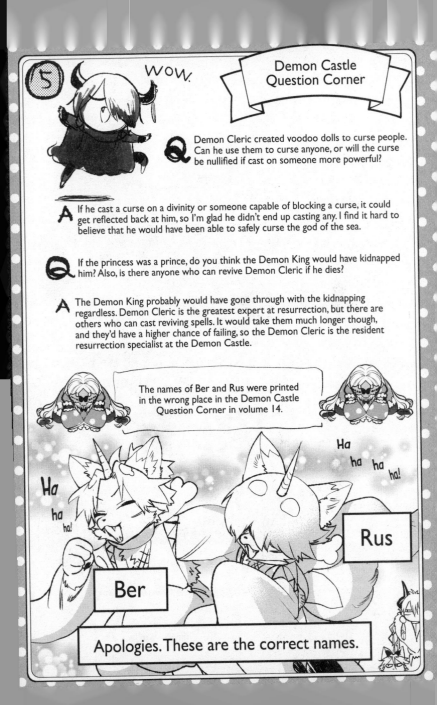

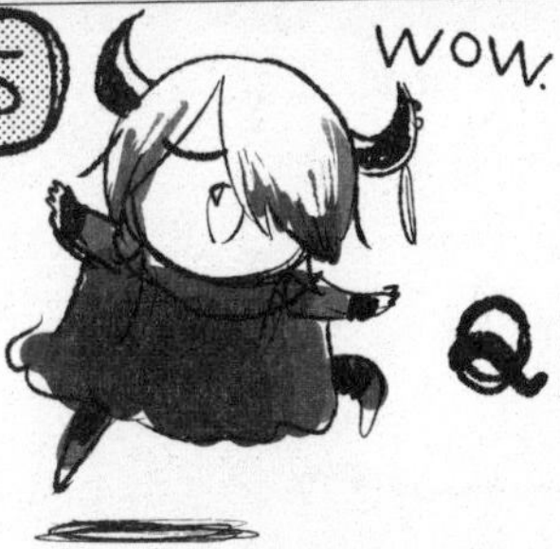
WOW.

Demon Castle Question Corner

Q Demon Cleric created voodoo dolls to curse people. Can he use them to curse anyone, or will the curse be nullified if cast on someone more powerful?

A If he cast a curse on a divinity or someone capable of blocking a curse, it could get reflected back at him, so I'm glad he didn't end up casting any. I find it hard to believe that he would have been able to safely curse the god of the sea.

Q If the princess was a prince, do you think the Demon King would have kidnapped him? Also, is there anyone who can revive Demon Cleric if he dies?

A The Demon King probably would have gone through with the kidnapping regardless. Demon Cleric is the greatest expert at resurrection, but there are others who can cast reviving spells. It would take them much longer though, and they'd have a higher chance of failing, so the Demon Cleric is the resident resurrection specialist at the Demon Castle.

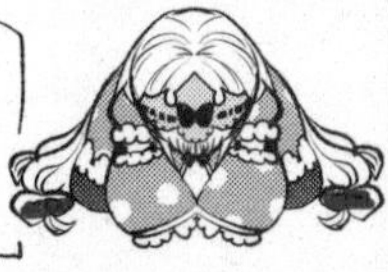

The names of Ber and Rus were printed in the wrong place in the Demon Castle Question Corner in volume 14.

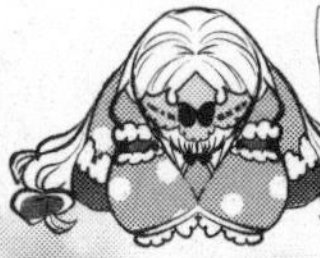

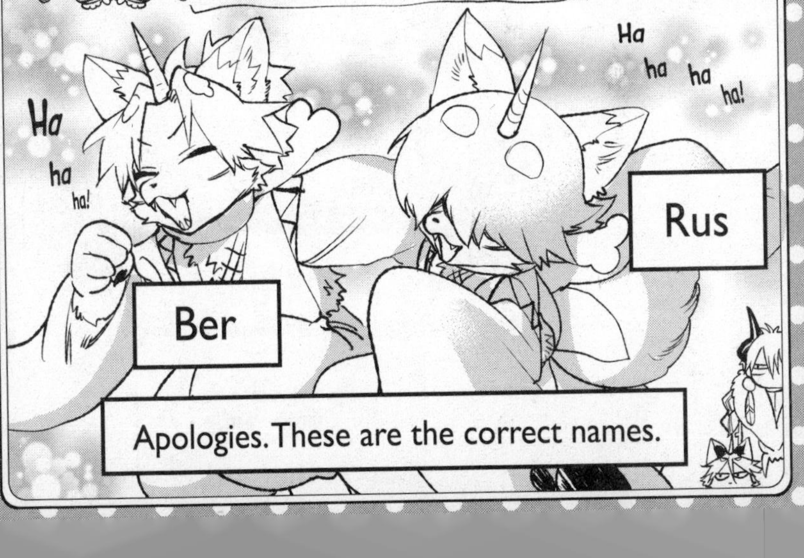
Ha ha ha ha!
Rus
Ha ha ha!
Ber
Apologies. These are the correct names.

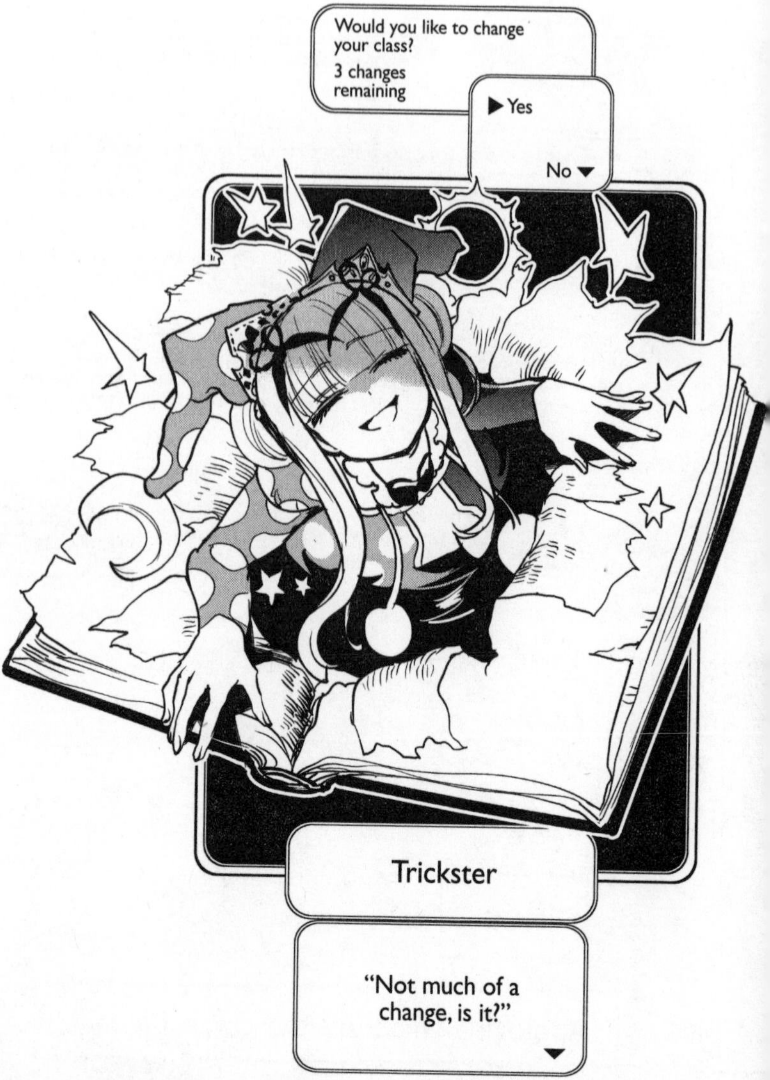
Would you like to change your class?
3 changes remaining
▶Yes
No
Trickster
"Not much of a change, is it?"

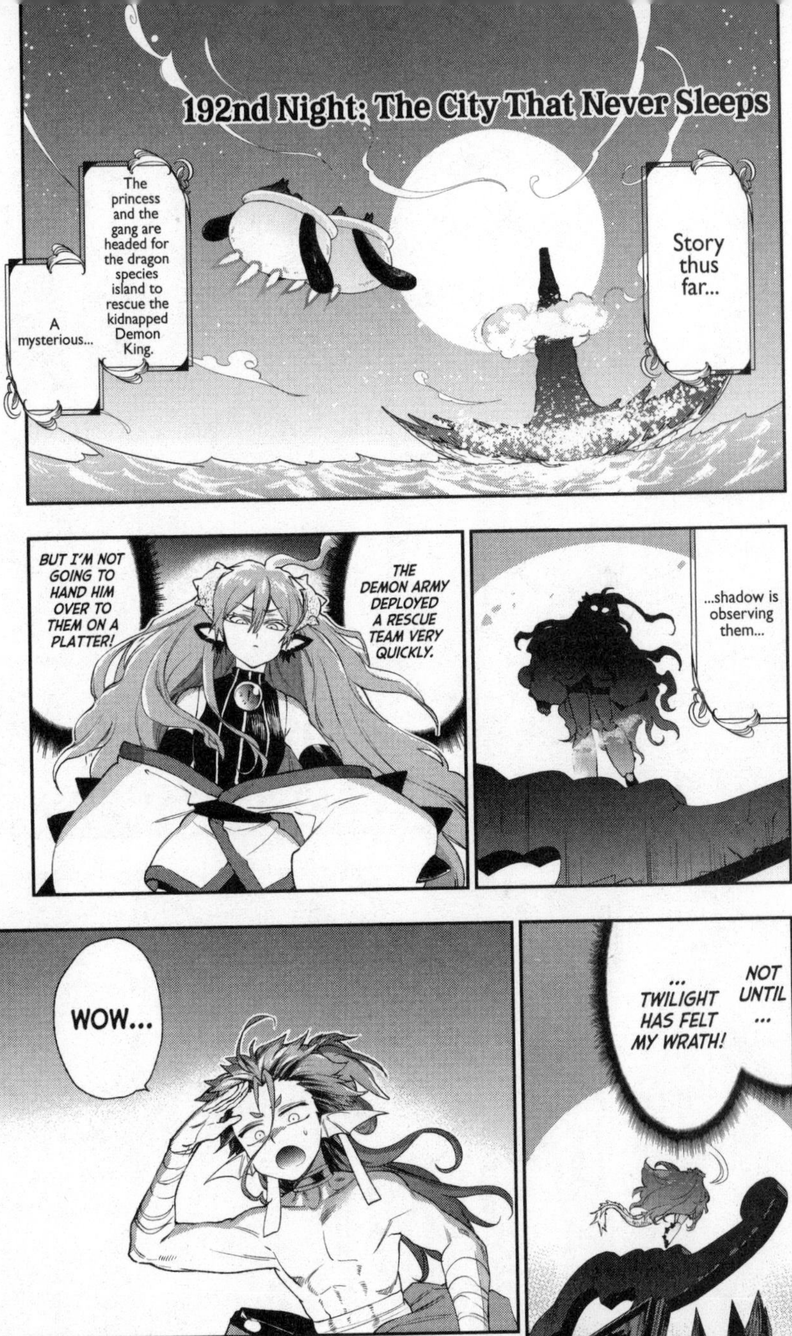
192nd Night: The City That Never Sleeps
Story thus far...
The princess and the gang are headed for the dragon species island to rescue the kidnapped Demon King.
A mysterious...
...shadow is observing them...
THE DEMON ARMY DEPLOYED A RESCUE TEAM VERY QUICKLY.
BUT I'M NOT GOING TO HAND HIM OVER TO THEM ON A PLATTER!
NOT UNTIL ...
... TWILIGHT HAS FELT MY WRATH!
WOW...

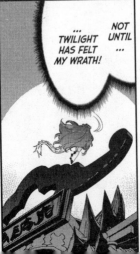

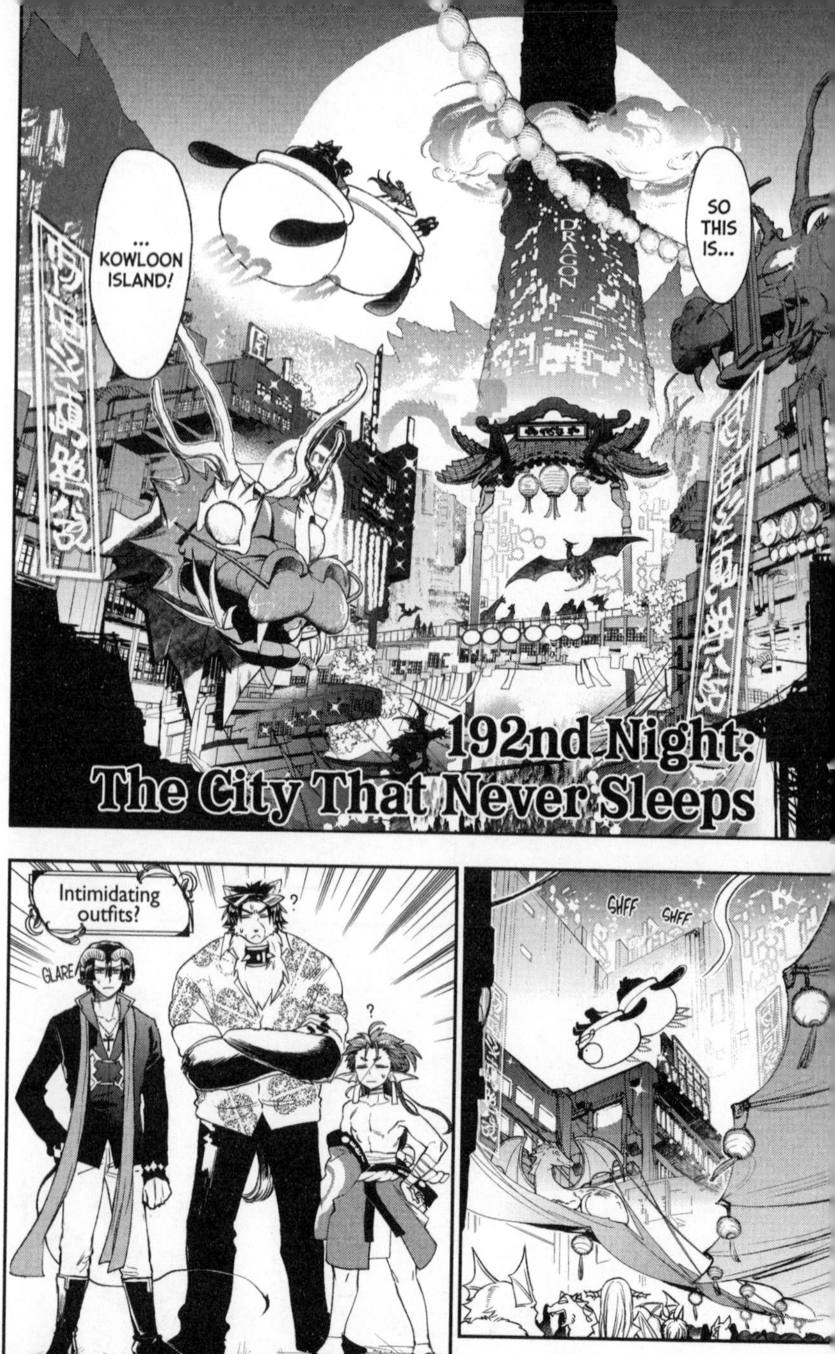
SO THIS IS...
... KOWLOON ISLAND!
DRAGON
192nd Night:
The City That Never Sleeps
SHFF
SHFF
Intimidating outfits?
GLARE
?
?

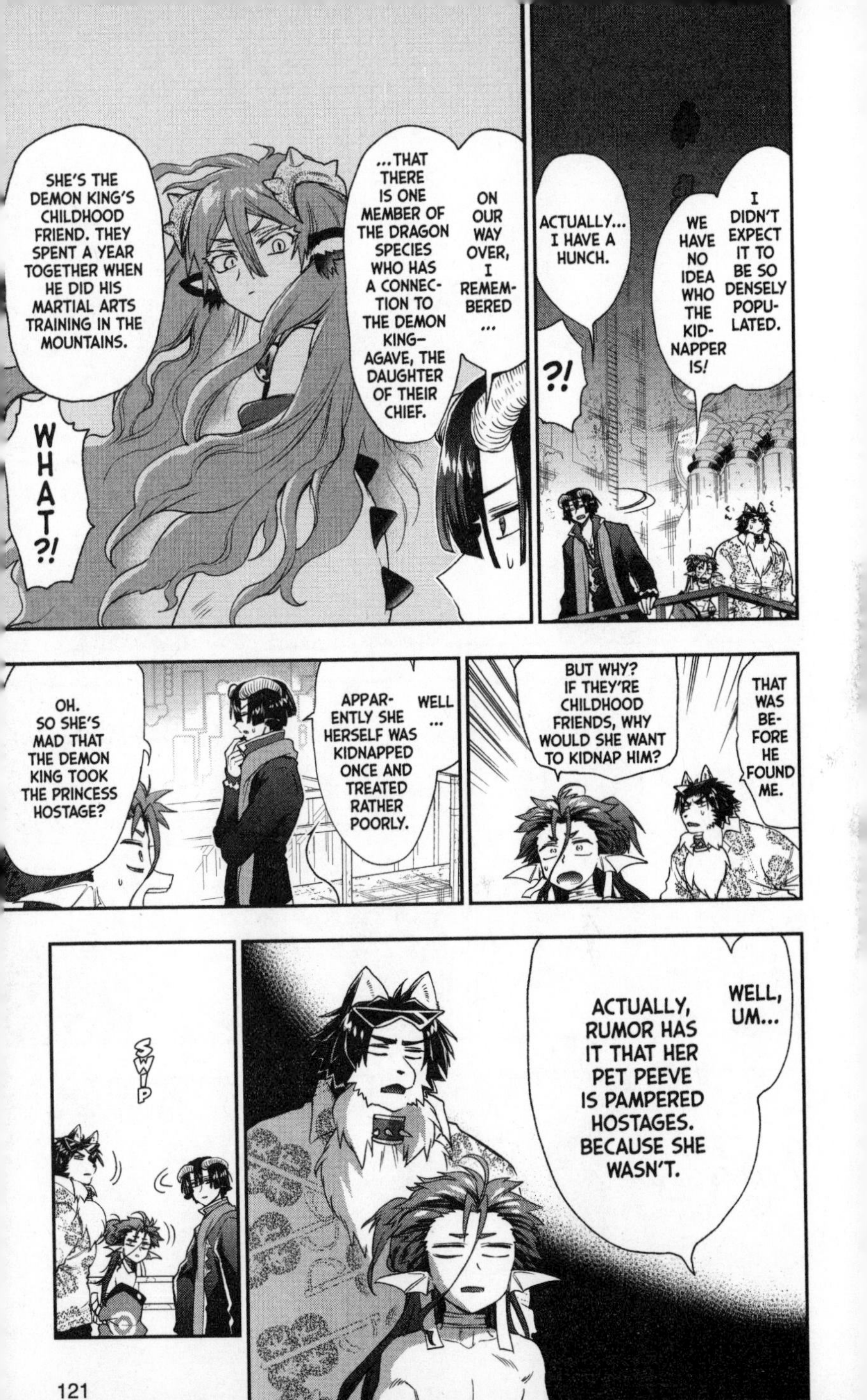
I DIDN'T EXPECT IT TO BE SO DENSELY POPULATED.
WE HAVE NO IDEA WHO THE KIDNAPPER IS!
ACTUALLY... I HAVE A HUNCH.
?!
ON OUR WAY OVER, I REMEMBERED...
...THAT THERE IS ONE MEMBER OF THE DRAGON SPECIES WHO HAS A CONNECTION TO THE DEMON KING—AGAVE, THE DAUGHTER OF THEIR CHIEF.
SHE'S THE DEMON KING'S CHILDHOOD FRIEND. THEY SPENT A YEAR TOGETHER WHEN HE DID HIS MARTIAL ARTS TRAINING IN THE MOUNTAINS.
WHAT?!
THAT WAS BEFORE HE FOUND ME.
BUT WHY? IF THEY'RE CHILDHOOD FRIENDS, WHY WOULD SHE WANT TO KIDNAP HIM?
WELL...
APPARENTLY SHE HERSELF WAS KIDNAPPED ONCE AND TREATED RATHER POORLY.
OH. SO SHE'S MAD THAT THE DEMON KING TOOK THE PRINCESS HOSTAGE?
WELL, UM...
ACTUALLY, RUMOR HAS IT THAT HER PET PEEVE IS PAMPERED HOSTAGES. BECAUSE SHE WASN'T.
SWIP

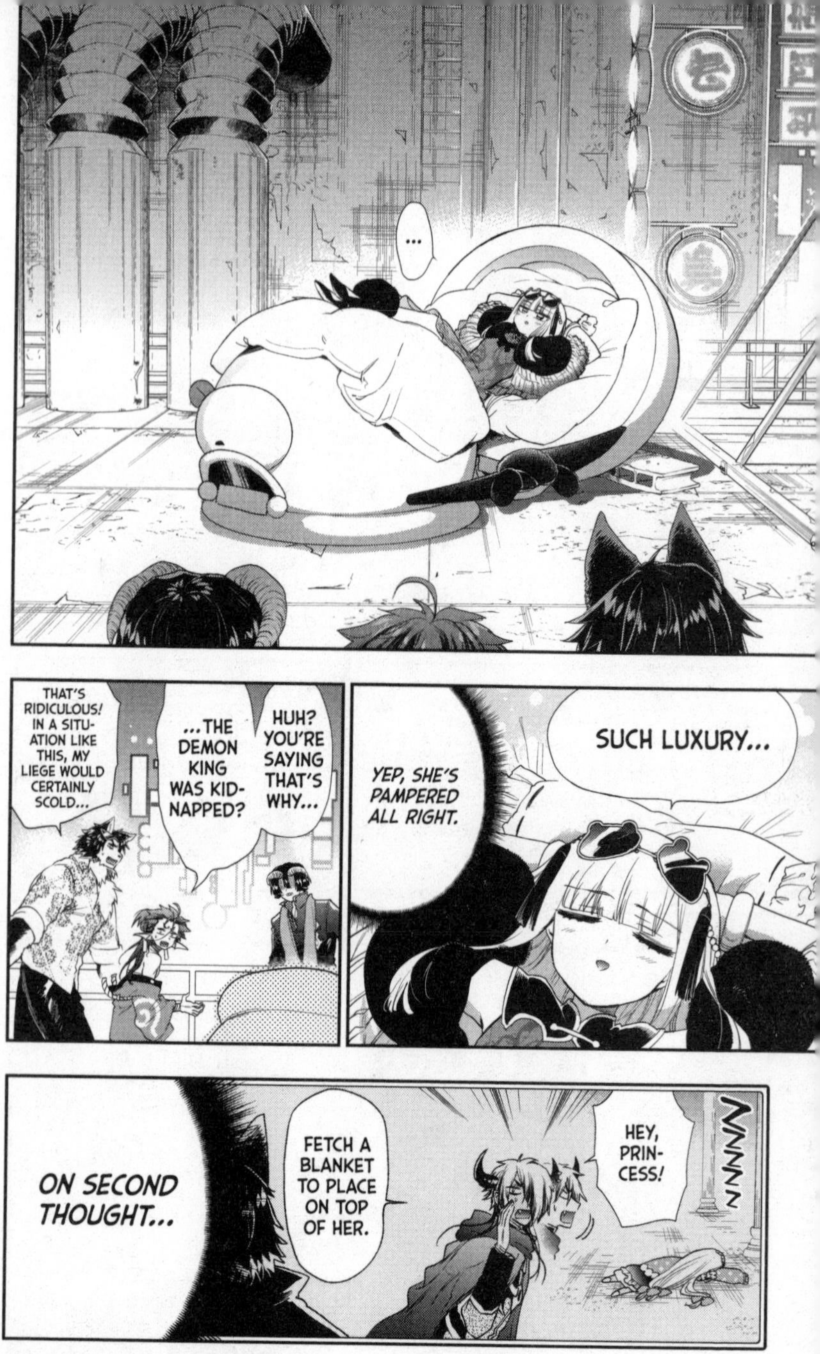
...
SUCH LUXURY...
YEP, SHE'S PAMPERED ALL RIGHT.
HUH? YOU'RE SAYING THAT'S WHY...
...THE DEMON KING WAS KID-NAPPED?
THAT'S RIDICULOUS! IN A SITU-ATION LIKE THIS, MY LIEGE WOULD CERTAINLY SCOLD...
HEY, PRIN-CESS!
FETCH A BLANKET TO PLACE ON TOP OF HER.
ON SECOND THOUGHT...

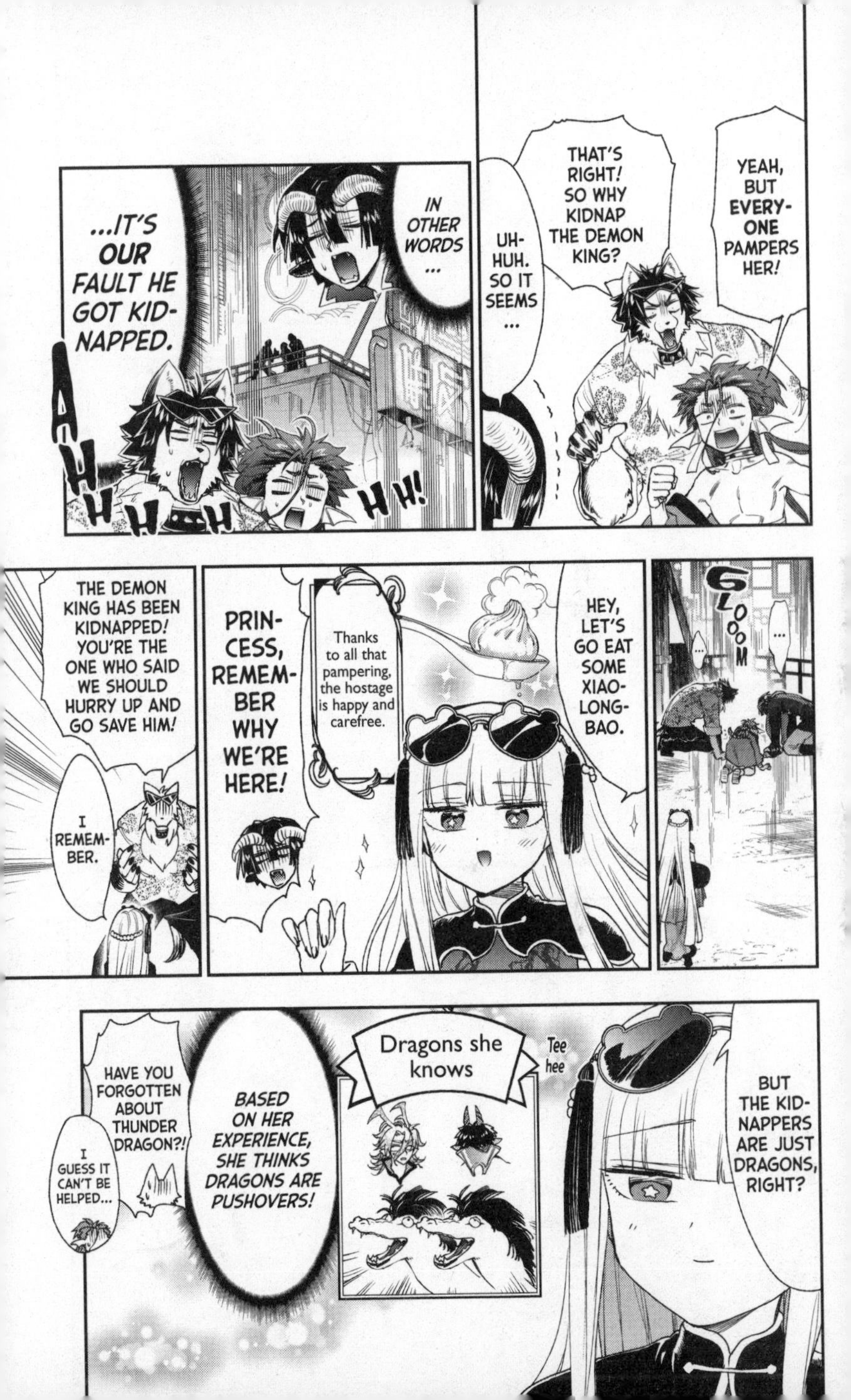
YEAH, BUT EVERYONE PAMPERS HER!
THAT'S RIGHT! SO WHY KIDNAP THE DEMON KING?
UH-HUH. SO IT SEEMS...
IN OTHER WORDS...
...IT'S OUR FAULT HE GOT KIDNAPPED.
AHHHHHHH!
...
...
GLOOOM
HEY, LET'S GO EAT SOME XIAOLONGBAO.
Thanks to all that pampering, the hostage is happy and carefree.
PRINCESS, REMEMBER WHY WE'RE HERE!
THE DEMON KING HAS BEEN KIDNAPPED! YOU'RE THE ONE WHO SAID WE SHOULD HURRY UP AND GO SAVE HIM!
I REMEMBER.
BUT THE KIDNAPPERS ARE JUST DRAGONS, RIGHT?
Tee hee
Dragons she knows
BASED ON HER EXPERIENCE, SHE THINKS DRAGONS ARE PUSHOVERS!
HAVE YOU FORGOTTEN ABOUT THUNDER DRAGON?!
I GUESS IT CAN'T BE HELPED...

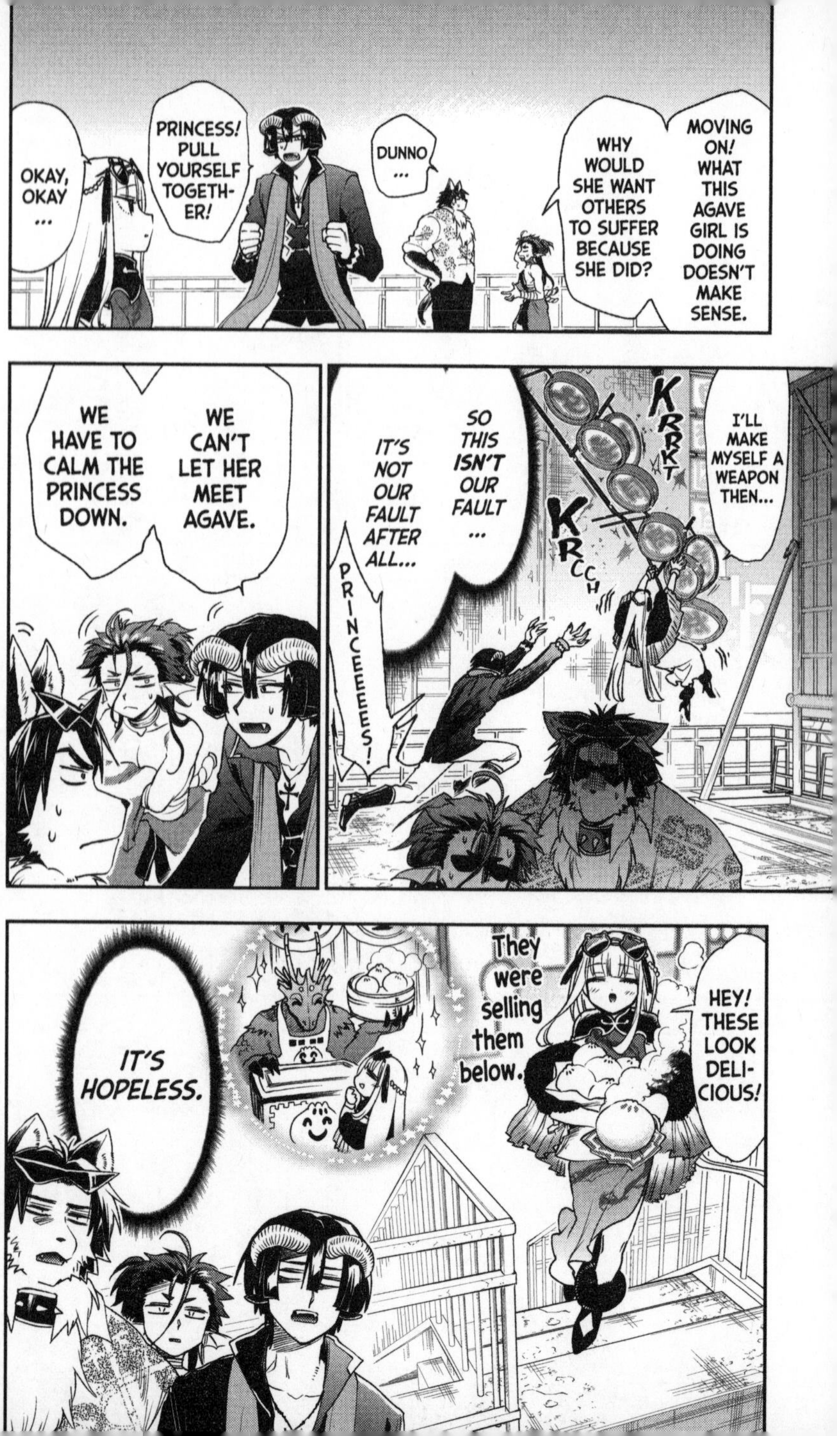
MOVING ON! WHAT THIS AGAVE GIRL IS DOING DOESN'T MAKE SENSE.
WHY WOULD SHE WANT OTHERS TO SUFFER BECAUSE SHE DID?
DUNNO...
PRINCESS! PULL YOURSELF TOGETH-ER!
OKAY, OKAY...
I'LL MAKE MYSELF A WEAPON THEN...
KRRKT
KRCCH
SO THIS ISN'T OUR FAULT...
IT'S NOT OUR FAULT AFTER ALL...
PRINCEEEEES!
WE CAN'T LET HER MEET AGAVE.
WE HAVE TO CALM THE PRINCESS DOWN.
HEY! THESE LOOK DELI-CIOUS!
They were selling them below.
IT'S HOPELESS.

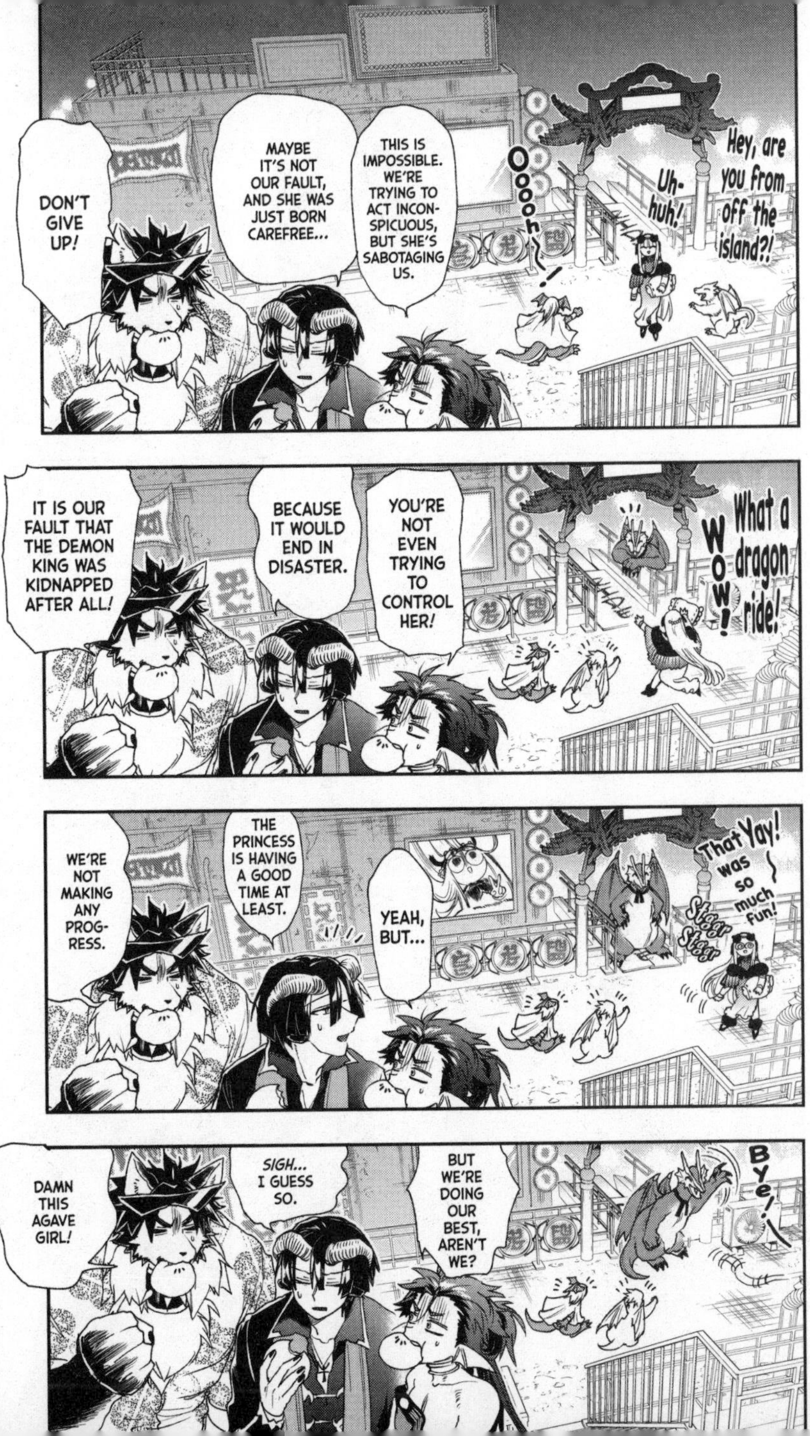
Hey, are you from off the island?!
Uh-huh!
Ooooh~!
THIS IS IMPOSSIBLE. WE'RE TRYING TO ACT INCON-SPICUOUS, BUT SHE'S SABOTAGING US.
MAYBE IT'S NOT OUR FAULT, AND SHE WAS JUST BORN CAREFREE...
DON'T GIVE UP!
What a dragon ride!
WOW!
YOU'RE NOT EVEN TRYING TO CONTROL HER!
BECAUSE IT WOULD END IN DISASTER.
IT IS OUR FAULT THAT THE DEMON KING WAS KIDNAPPED AFTER ALL!
Yay!
That was so much fun!
Stggr Stggr
YEAH, BUT...
THE PRINCESS IS HAVING A GOOD TIME AT LEAST.
WE'RE NOT MAKING ANY PROG-RESS.
Bye!
BUT WE'RE DOING OUR BEST, AREN'T WE?
SIGH... I GUESS SO.
DAMN THIS AGAVE GIRL!

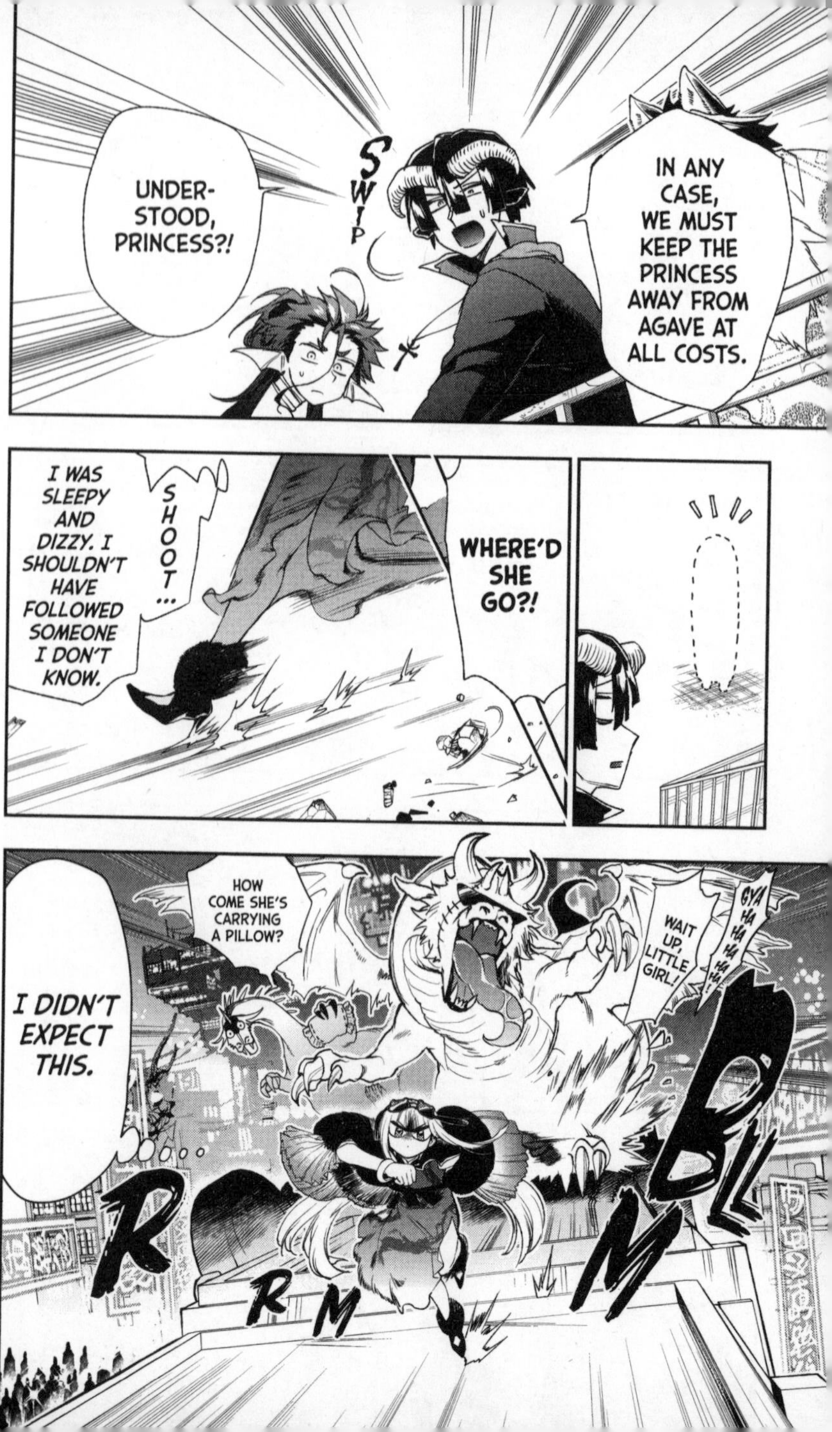
IN ANY CASE, WE MUST KEEP THE PRINCESS AWAY FROM AGAVE AT ALL COSTS.
SWIP
UNDER-STOOD, PRINCESS?!
WHERE'D SHE GO?!
SHOOT...
I WAS SLEEPY AND DIZZY. I SHOULDN'T HAVE FOLLOWED SOMEONE I DON'T KNOW.
GYAHAHAHAHAHA!
WAIT UP, LITTLE GIRL!
HOW COME SHE'S CARRYING A PILLOW?
I DIDN'T EXPECT THIS.
RRMMBL

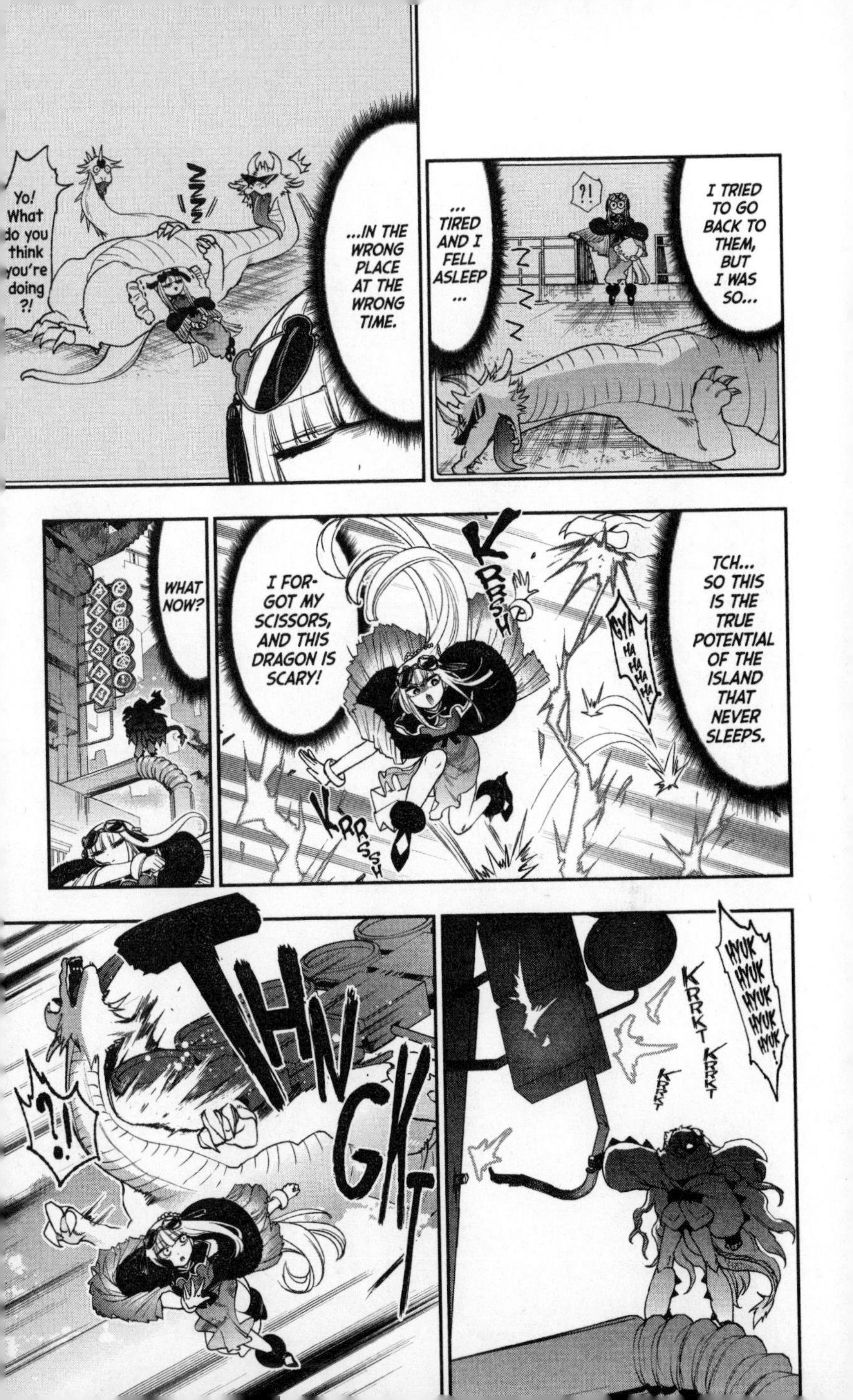
I TRIED TO GO BACK TO THEM, BUT I WAS SO...
... TIRED AND I FELL ASLEEP ...
?!
ZZZ
...IN THE WRONG PLACE AT THE WRONG TIME.
ZZZZ
Yo! What do you think you're doing ?!
TCH... SO THIS IS THE TRUE POTENTIAL OF THE ISLAND THAT NEVER SLEEPS.
GYA HA HA HA HA!
KRRSSH
I FOR- GOT MY SCISSORS, AND THIS DRAGON IS SCARY!
KRRSSH
WHAT NOW?
HYUK HYUK HYUK HYUK HYUK!
KRRKT KRRKT KRRKT
THNGKT
?!!

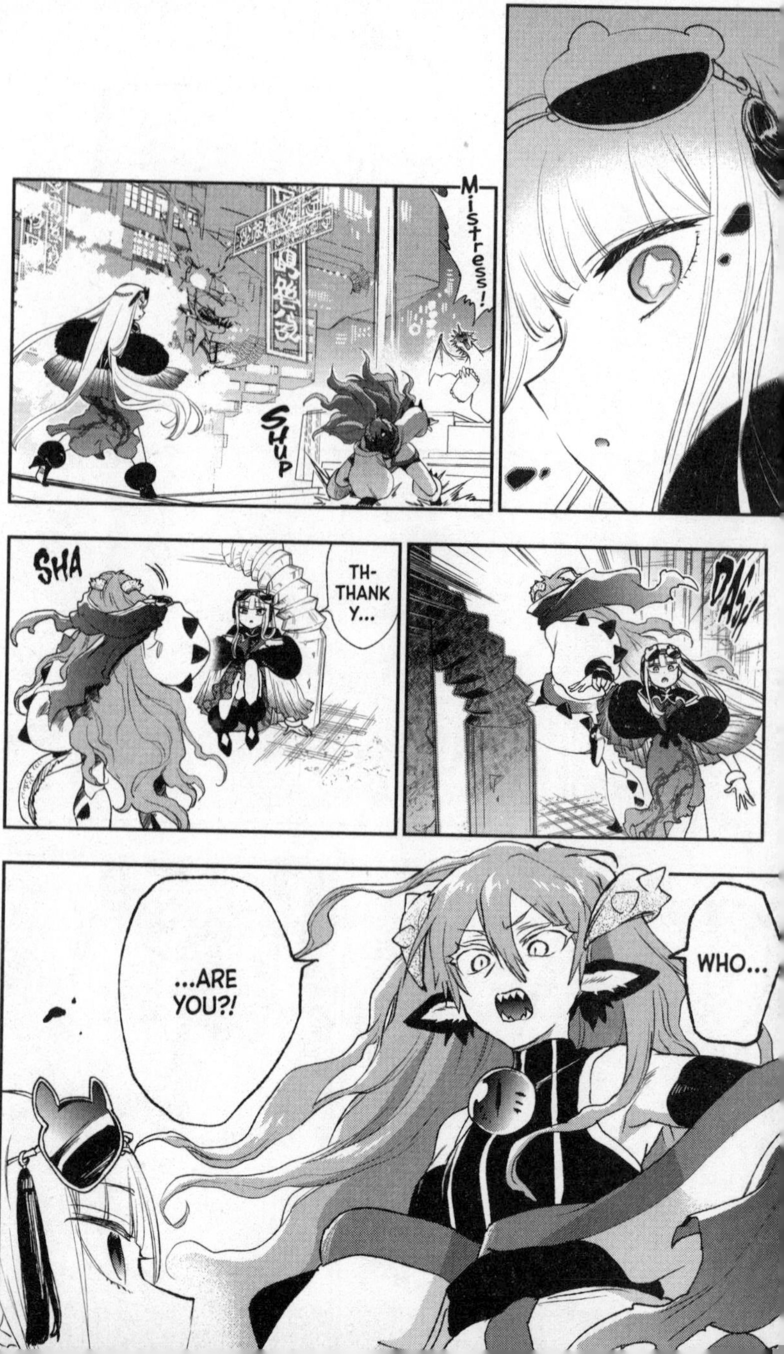
Mistress!
SHUP
TH-THANK Y...
DASH
SHA
WHO...
...ARE YOU?!

Kowloon Island

Density: ☆☆☆☆☆☆☆☆☆
Public Safety: ☆☆☆

The island of the dragons.

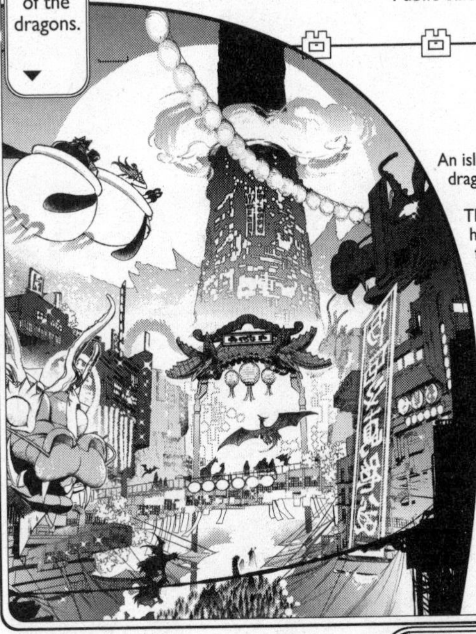

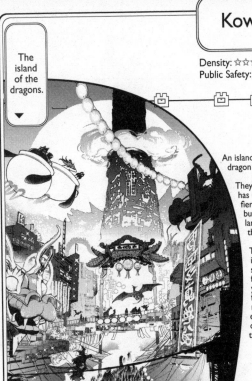

An island of the dragon species, by the dragon species, for the dragon species.

They have a unique culture. The island has numerous organizations engaged in fierce competition with one another, but they are all subsidiaries of one larger organization led by the chief of the dragon species.

The other characteristic of note is their foodie culture. If you enjoy stir-fried, deep-fried or steamed foods, this place will be paradise for you. The island is filled with food stalls that would be highly recommended for any gourmet—except that the island is too crime ridden for defenseless tourists to visit.

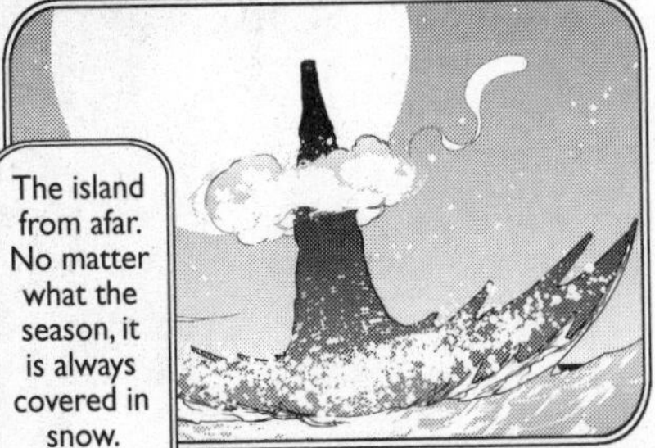

The island from afar. No matter what the season, it is always covered in snow.

Due to the island's odd shape, legend has it that an ancient chief of the dragon species threw a massive amount of magical power into the sea, and it solidified and formed an island.

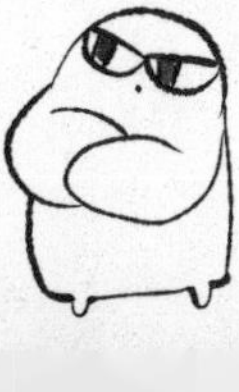
It has an urban vibe.
And it's densely populated.

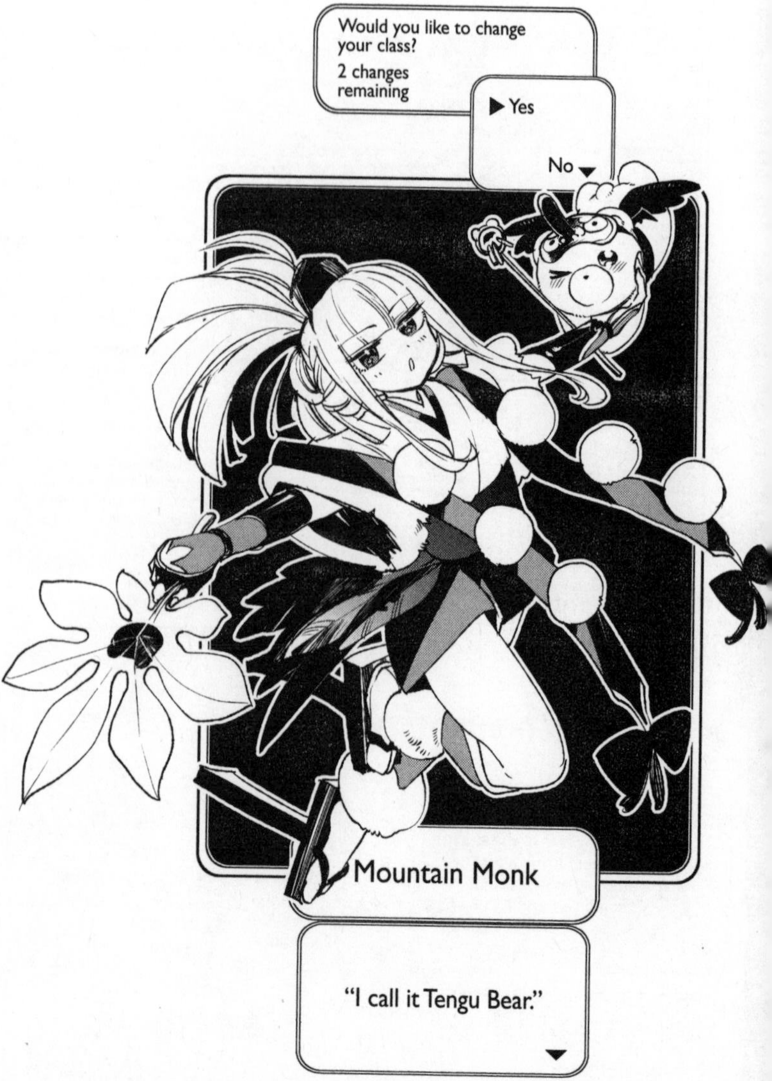
Would you like to change your class?
2 changes remaining
▶Yes
No
Mountain Monk
"I call it Tengu Bear."

193rd Night: Hostage Sympathy

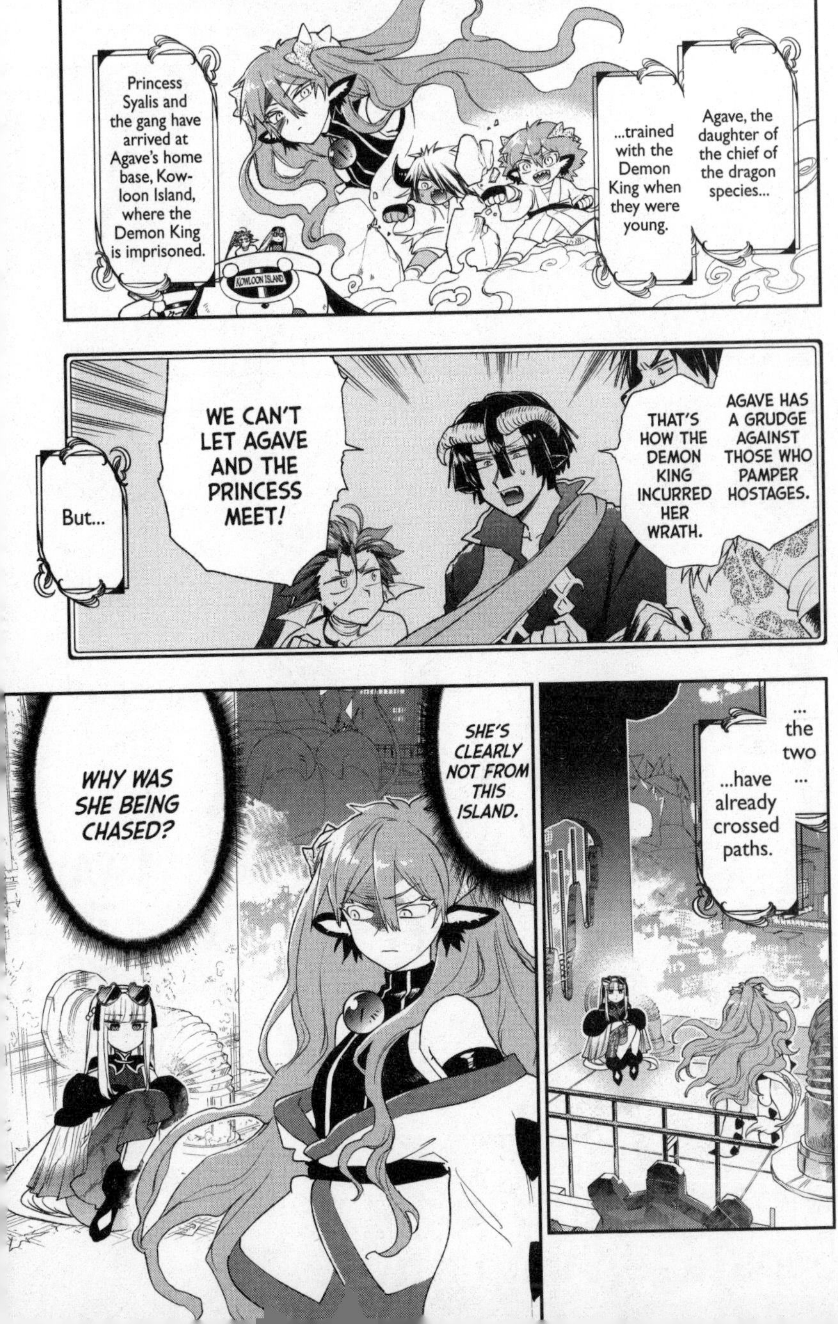
Agave, the daughter of the chief of the dragon species...
...trained with the Demon King when they were young.
Princess Syalis and the gang have arrived at Agave's home base, Kowloon Island, where the Demon King is imprisoned.
KOWLOON ISLAND
AGAVE HAS A GRUDGE AGAINST THOSE WHO PAMPER HOSTAGES.
THAT'S HOW THE DEMON KING INCURRED HER WRATH.
WE CAN'T LET AGAVE AND THE PRINCESS MEET!
But...
... the two ...
...have already crossed paths.
SHE'S CLEARLY NOT FROM THIS ISLAND.
WHY WAS SHE BEING CHASED?

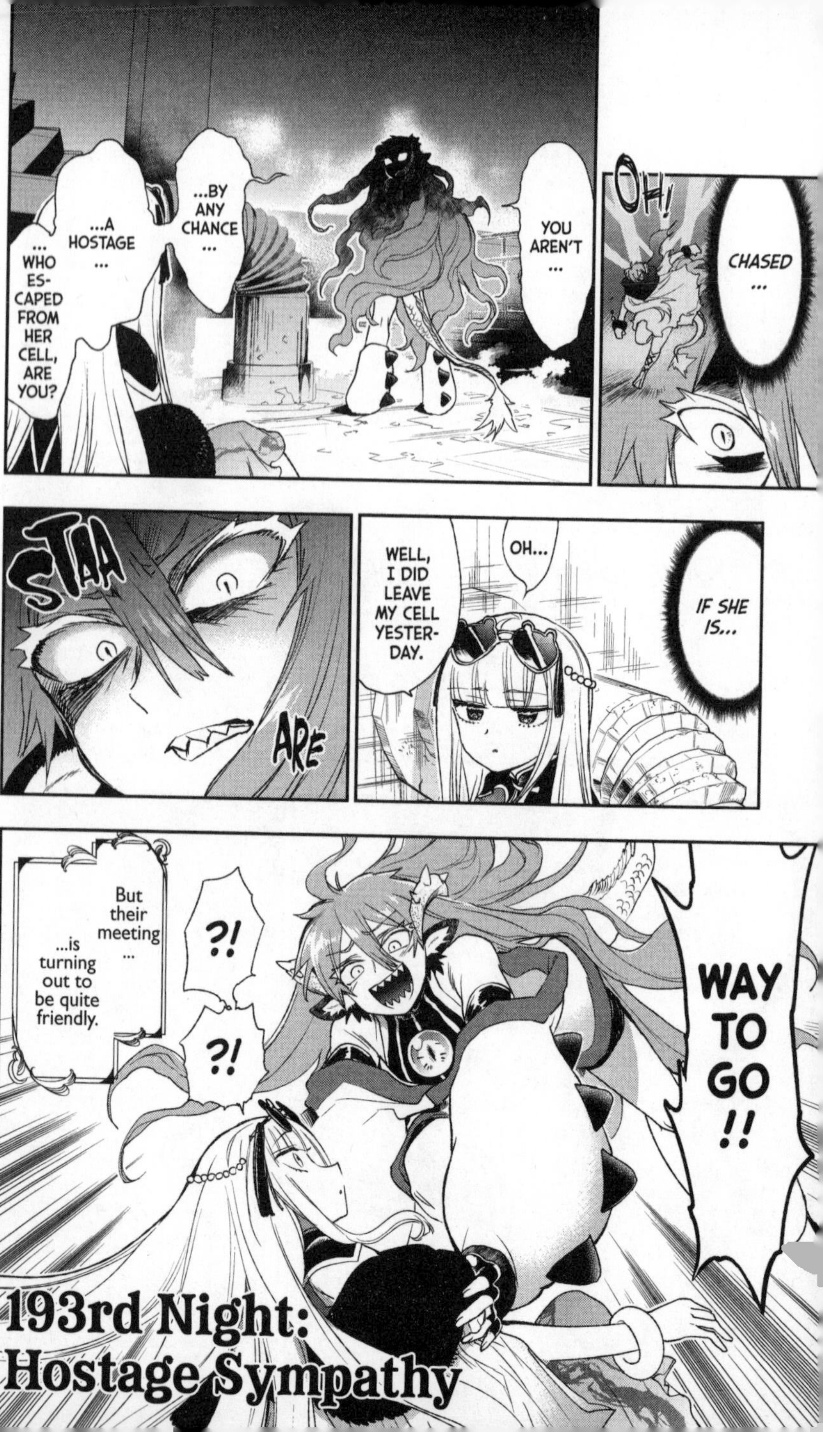
OH!
CHASED ...
YOU AREN'T ...
...BY ANY CHANCE ...
...A HOSTAGE ...
... WHO ES-CAPED FROM HER CELL, ARE YOU?
IF SHE IS...
OH...
WELL, I DID LEAVE MY CELL YESTER-DAY.
STAA
ARE
WAY TO GO !!
?!
?!
But their meeting ...
...is turning out to be quite friendly.

193rd Night: Hostage Sympathy

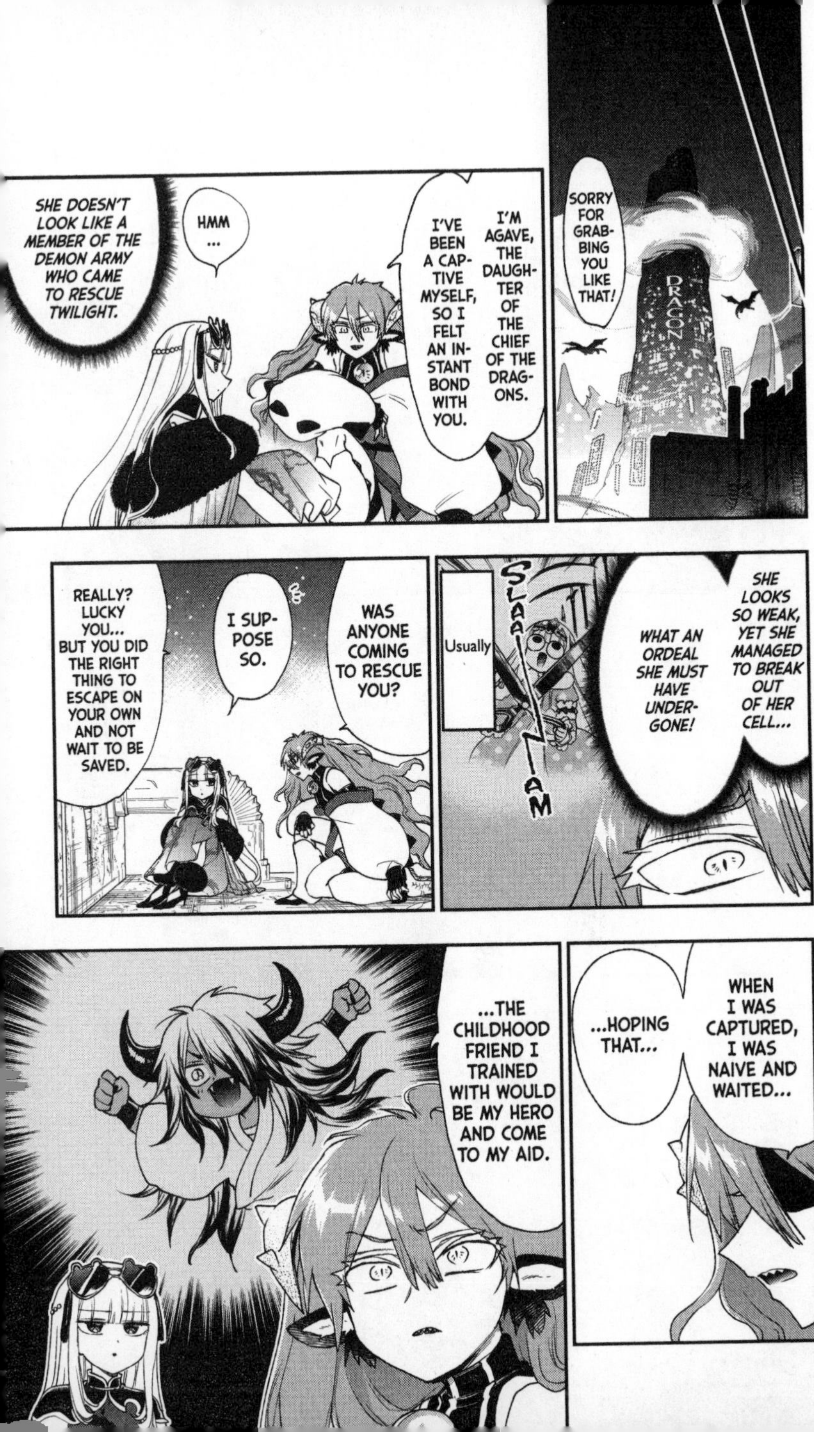
SORRY FOR GRABBING YOU LIKE THAT!
DRAGON
I'M AGAVE, THE DAUGHTER OF THE CHIEF OF THE DRAGONS.
I'VE BEEN A CAPTIVE MYSELF, SO I FELT AN INSTANT BOND WITH YOU.
HMM...
SHE DOESN'T LOOK LIKE A MEMBER OF THE DEMON ARMY WHO CAME TO RESCUE TWILIGHT.
SHE LOOKS SO WEAK, YET SHE MANAGED TO BREAK OUT OF HER CELL...
WHAT AN ORDEAL SHE MUST HAVE UNDERGONE!
SLAAAAM
Usually
WAS ANYONE COMING TO RESCUE YOU?
I SUPPOSE SO.
REALLY? LUCKY YOU... BUT YOU DID THE RIGHT THING TO ESCAPE ON YOUR OWN AND NOT WAIT TO BE SAVED.
WHEN I WAS CAPTURED, I WAS NAIVE AND WAITED...
...HOPING THAT...
...THE CHILDHOOD FRIEND I TRAINED WITH WOULD BE MY HERO AND COME TO MY AID.

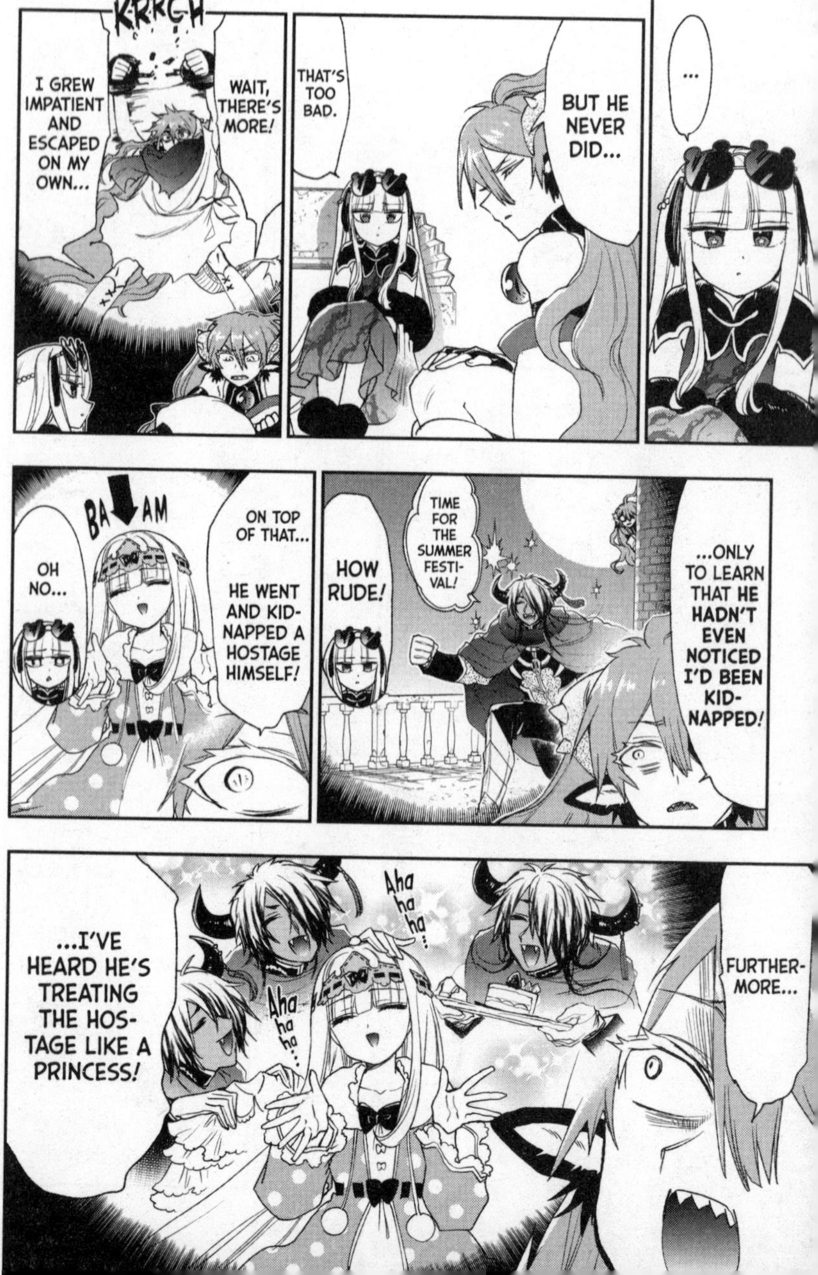
...
BUT HE NEVER DID...
THAT'S TOO BAD.
WAIT, THERE'S MORE!
KRRCH
I GREW IMPATIENT AND ESCAPED ON MY OWN...
...ONLY TO LEARN THAT HE HADN'T EVEN NOTICED I'D BEEN KID-NAPPED!
TIME FOR THE SUMMER FESTI-VAL!
HOW RUDE!
ON TOP OF THAT...
HE WENT AND KID-NAPPED A HOSTAGE HIMSELF!
BAAM
OH NO...
FURTHER-MORE...
Ahahaha...
Ahahaha...
...I'VE HEARD HE'S TREATING THE HOS-TAGE LIKE A PRINCESS!

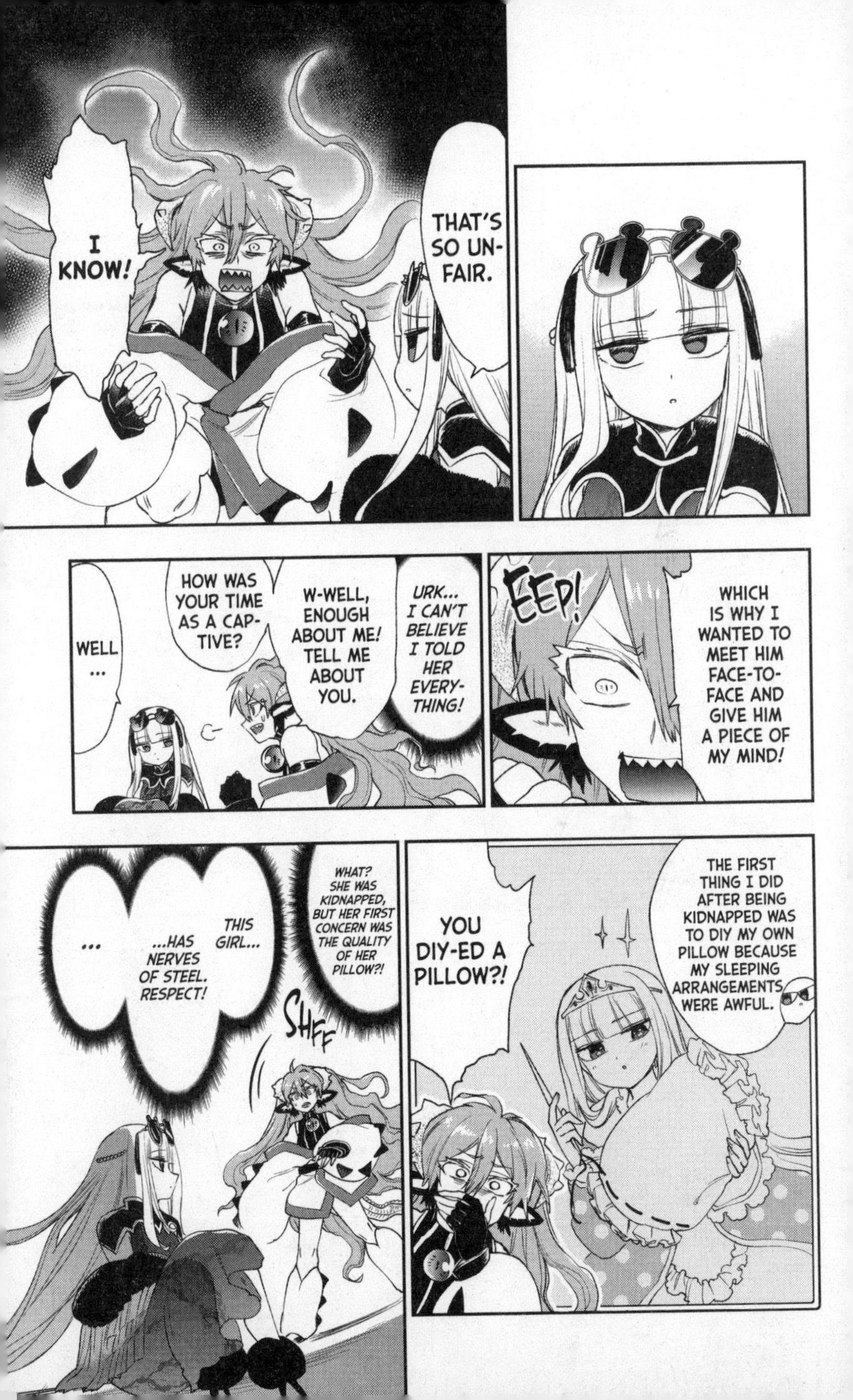

THAT'S SO UN-FAIR.
I KNOW!
EEP!
WHICH IS WHY I WANTED TO MEET HIM FACE-TO-FACE AND GIVE HIM A PIECE OF MY MIND!
URK... I CAN'T BELIEVE I TOLD HER EVERY-THING!
W-WELL, ENOUGH ABOUT ME! TELL ME ABOUT YOU.
HOW WAS YOUR TIME AS A CAP-TIVE?
WELL ...
THE FIRST THING I DID AFTER BEING KIDNAPPED WAS TO DIY MY OWN PILLOW BECAUSE MY SLEEPING ARRANGEMENTS WERE AWFUL.
YOU DIY-ED A PILLOW?!
WHAT? SHE WAS KIDNAPPED, BUT HER FIRST CONCERN WAS THE QUALITY OF HER PILLOW?!
THIS GIRL...
...HAS NERVES OF STEEL. RESPECT!
...
SHFF

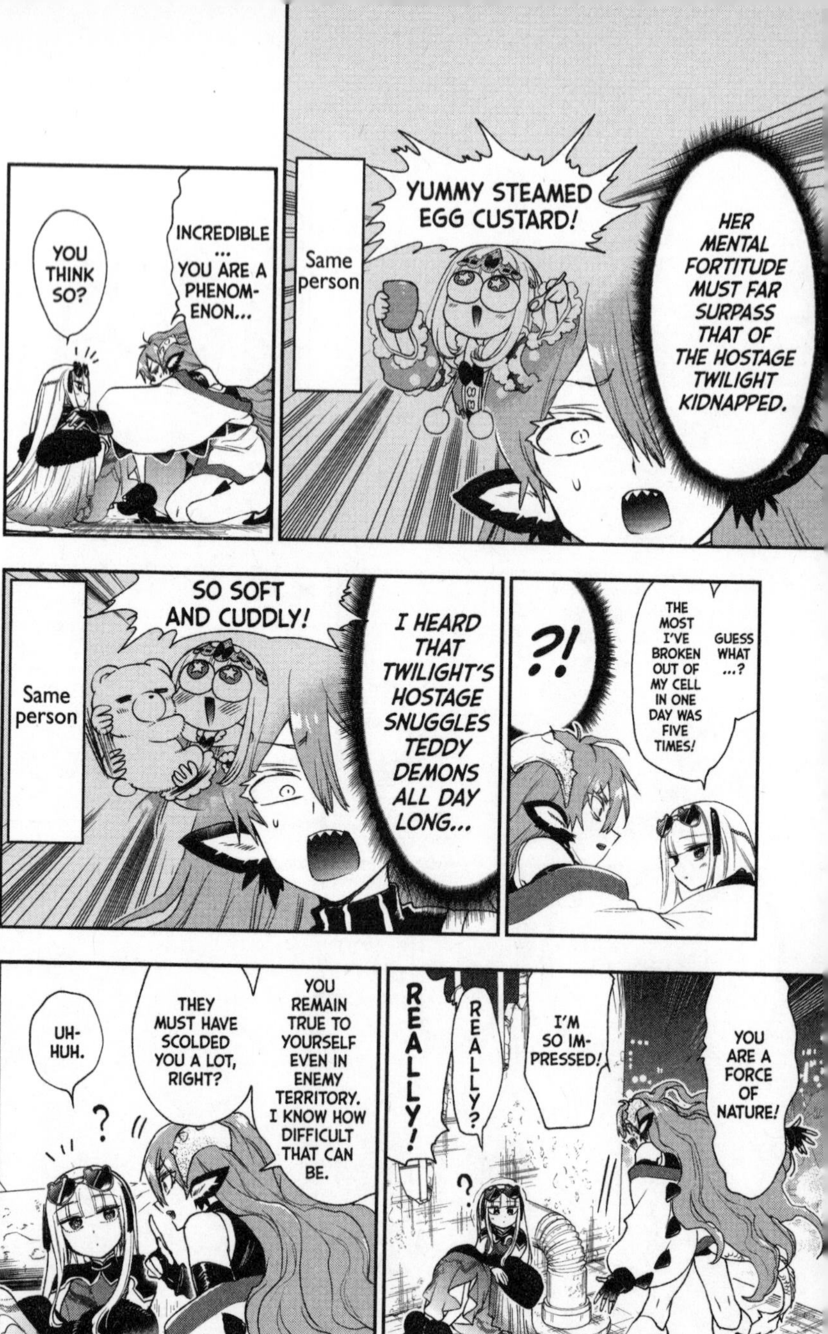
HER MENTAL FORTITUDE MUST FAR SURPASS THAT OF THE HOSTAGE TWILIGHT KIDNAPPED.
YUMMY STEAMED EGG CUSTARD!
Same person
INCREDIBLE ... YOU ARE A PHENOM-ENON...
YOU THINK SO?
GUESS WHAT ...?
THE MOST I'VE BROKEN OUT OF MY CELL IN ONE DAY WAS FIVE TIMES!
?!
I HEARD THAT TWILIGHT'S HOSTAGE SNUGGLES TEDDY DEMONS ALL DAY LONG...
SO SOFT AND CUDDLY!
Same person
YOU ARE A FORCE OF NATURE!
I'M SO IM-PRESSED!
REALLY?
REALLY!
?
YOU REMAIN TRUE TO YOURSELF EVEN IN ENEMY TERRITORY. I KNOW HOW DIFFICULT THAT CAN BE.
THEY MUST HAVE SCOLDED YOU A LOT, RIGHT?
UH-HUH.
?

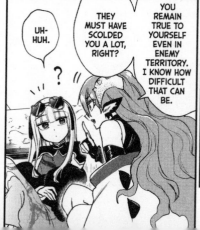

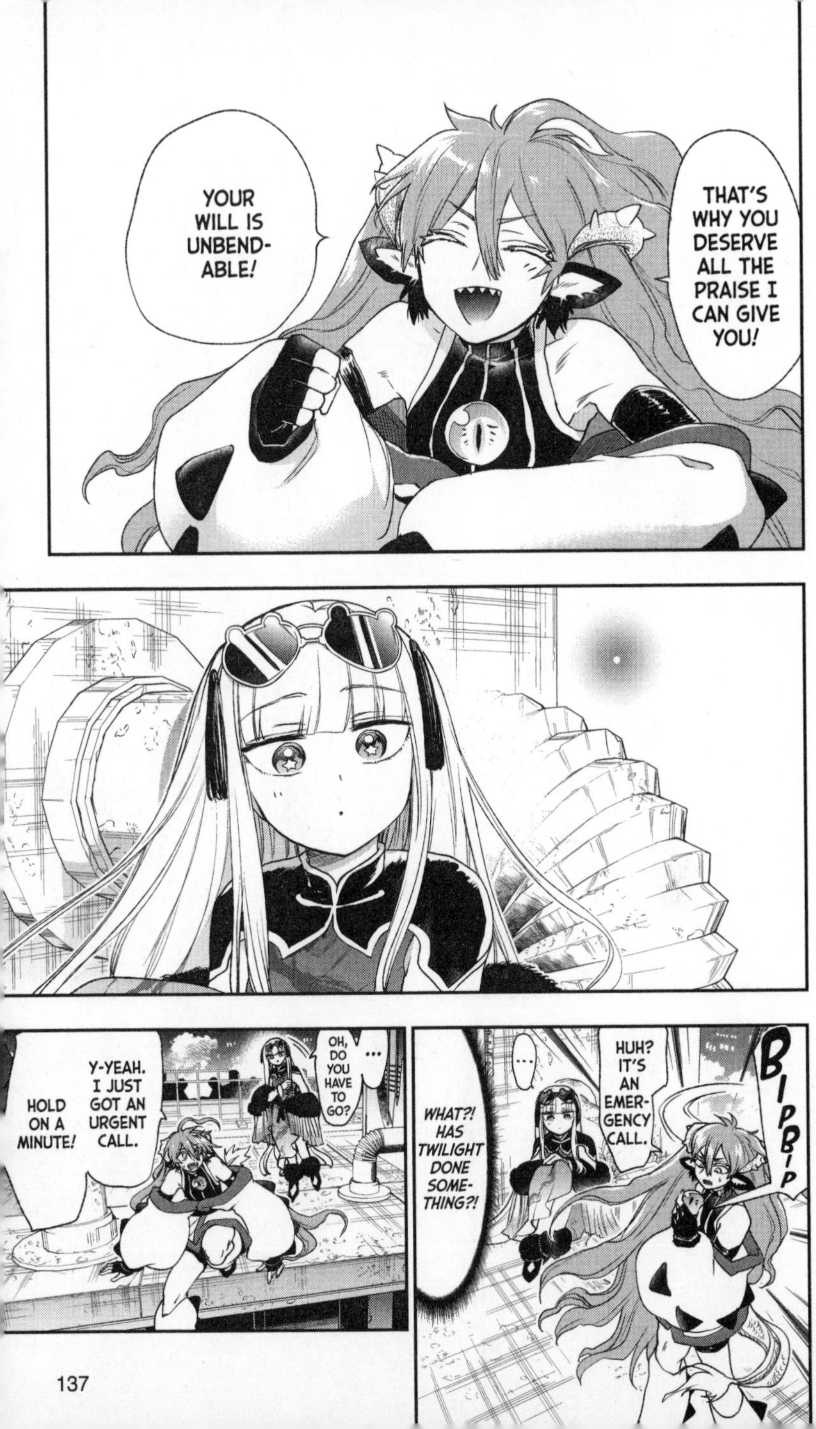
YOUR WILL IS UNBEND-ABLE!
THAT'S WHY YOU DESERVE ALL THE PRAISE I CAN GIVE YOU!
BIPBIP
HUH? IT'S AN EMER-GENCY CALL.
...
WHAT?! HAS TWILIGHT DONE SOME-THING?!
...
OH, DO YOU HAVE TO GO?
Y-YEAH. I JUST GOT AN URGENT CALL.
HOLD ON A MINUTE!

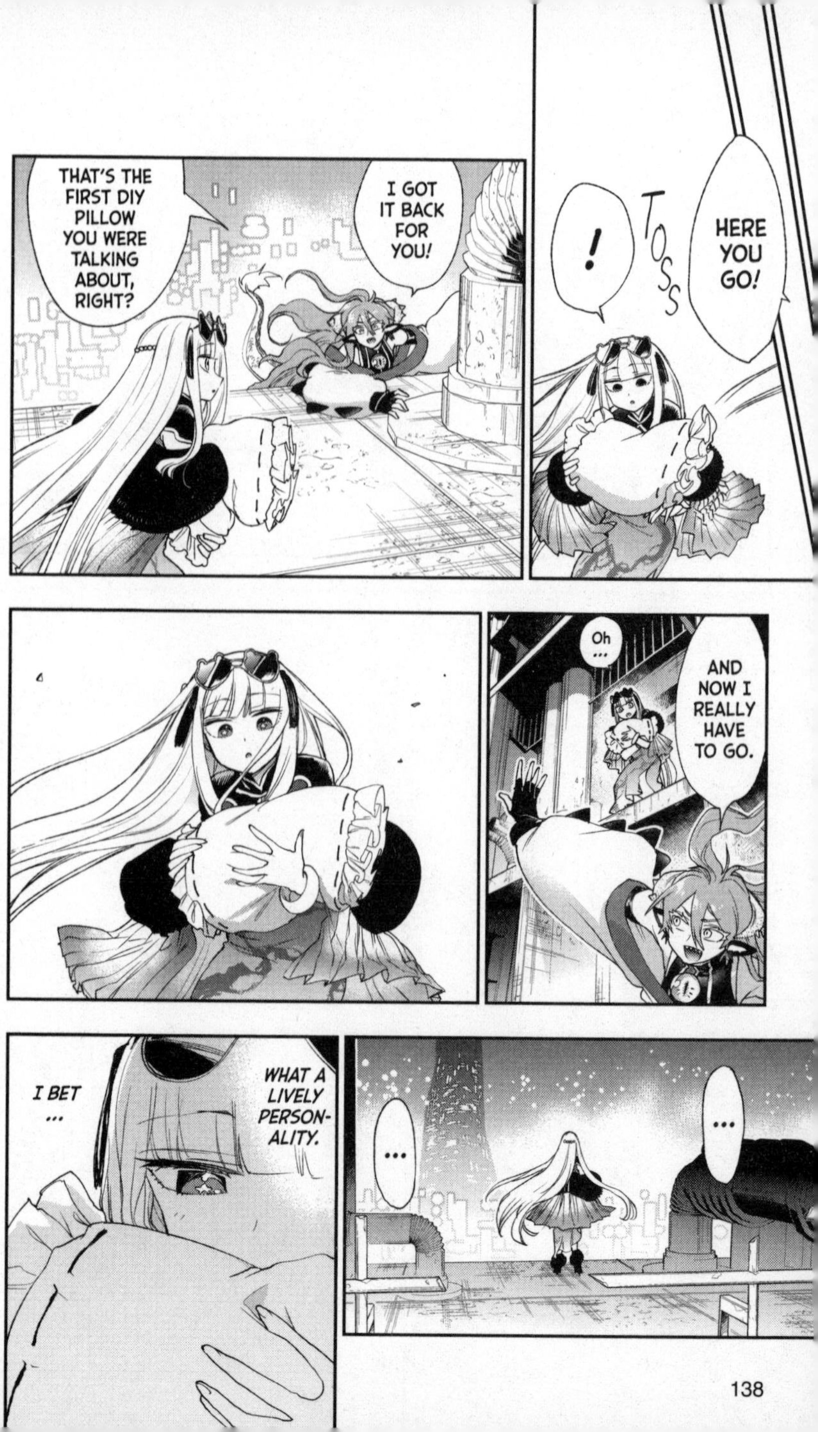
HERE YOU GO!
TOSS
!
I GOT IT BACK FOR YOU!
THAT'S THE FIRST DIY PILLOW YOU WERE TALKING ABOUT, RIGHT?
AND NOW I REALLY HAVE TO GO.
Oh ...
...
...
WHAT A LIVELY PERSONALITY.
I BET ...

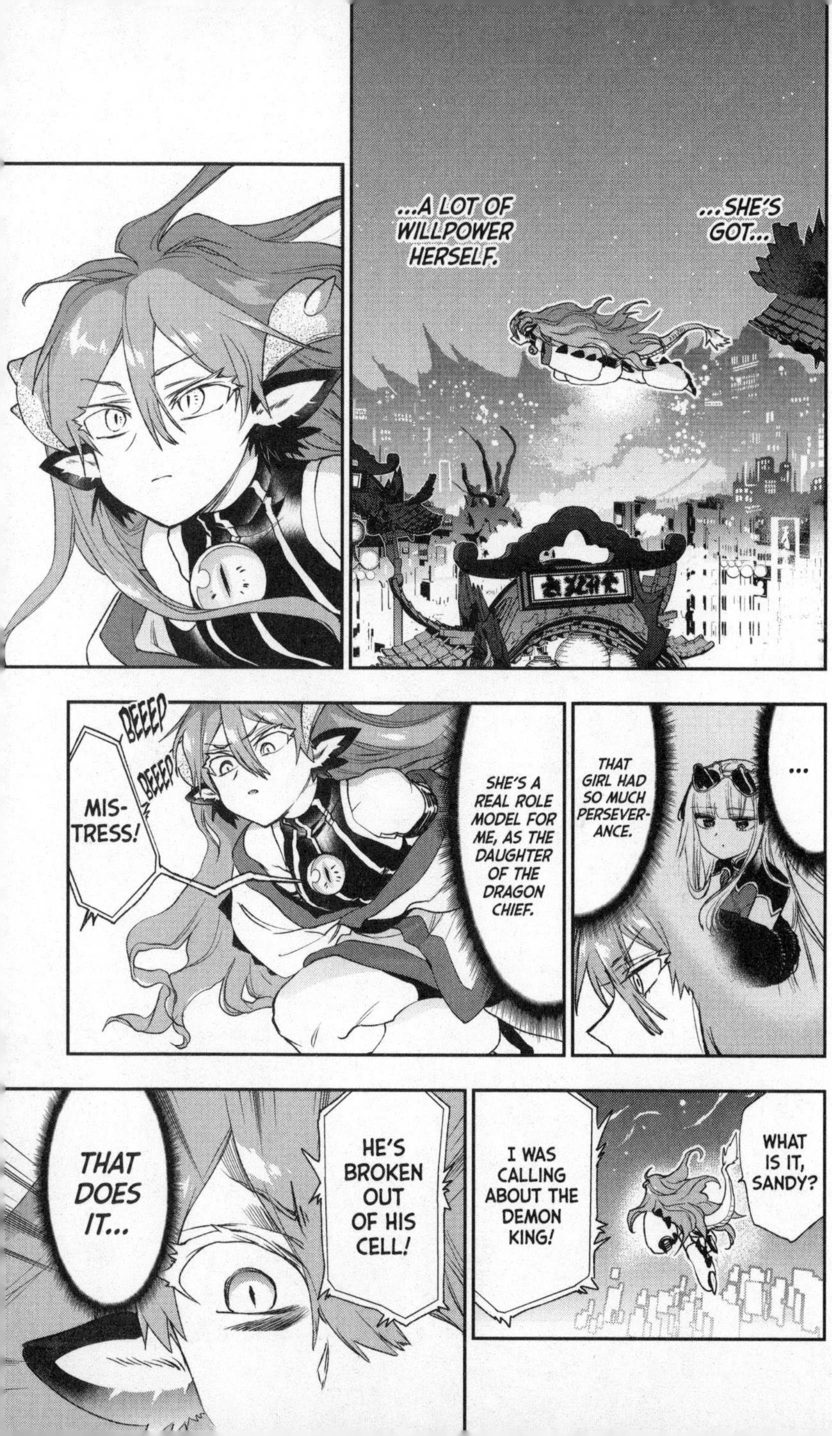
...SHE'S GOT...
...A LOT OF WILLPOWER HERSELF.
...
THAT GIRL HAD SO MUCH PERSEVERANCE.
SHE'S A REAL ROLE MODEL FOR ME, AS THE DAUGHTER OF THE DRAGON CHIEF.
BEEEP
BEEEP
MISTRESS!
WHAT IS IT, SANDY?
I WAS CALLING ABOUT THE DEMON KING!
HE'S BROKEN OUT OF HIS CELL!
THAT DOES IT...

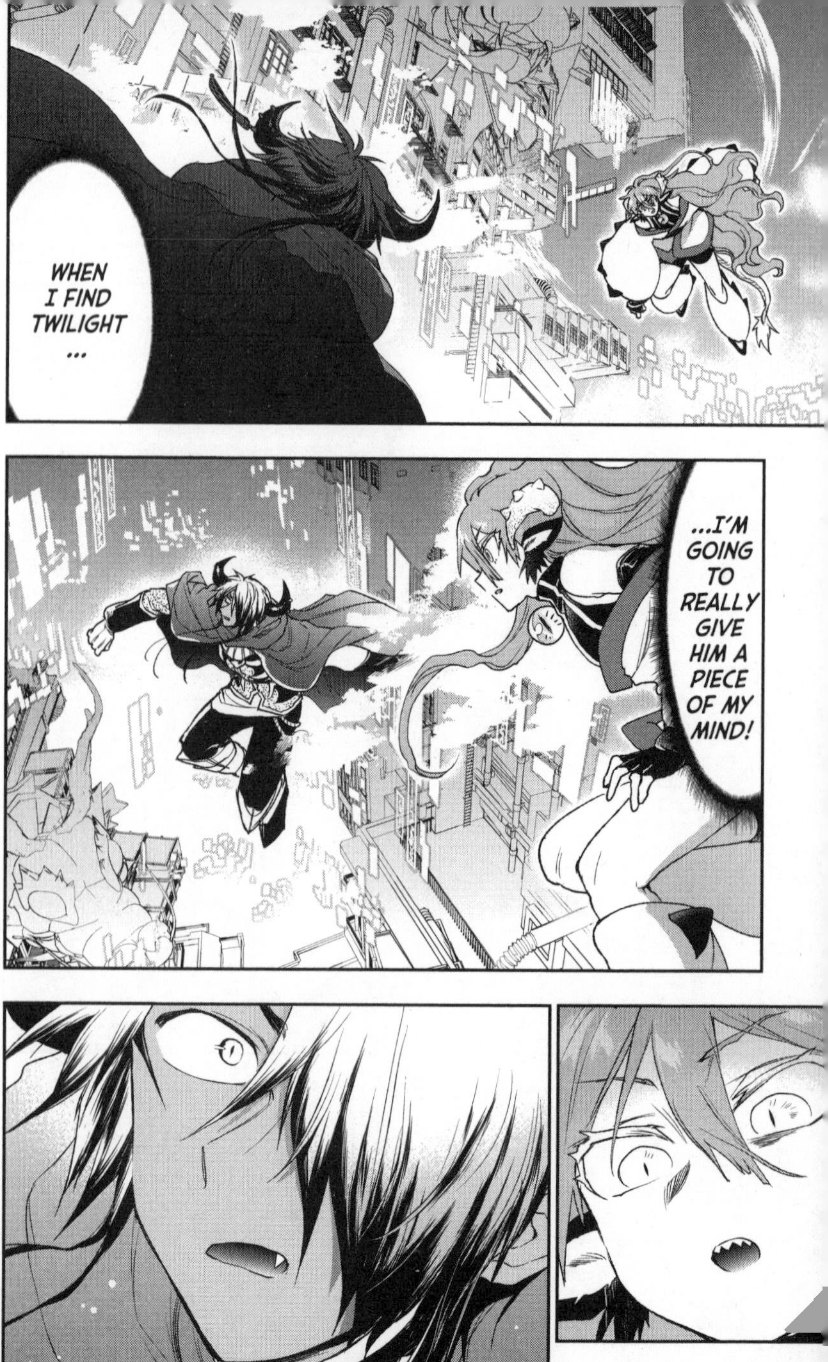
WHEN I FIND TWILIGHT ...
...I'M GOING TO REALLY GIVE HIM A PIECE OF MY MIND!

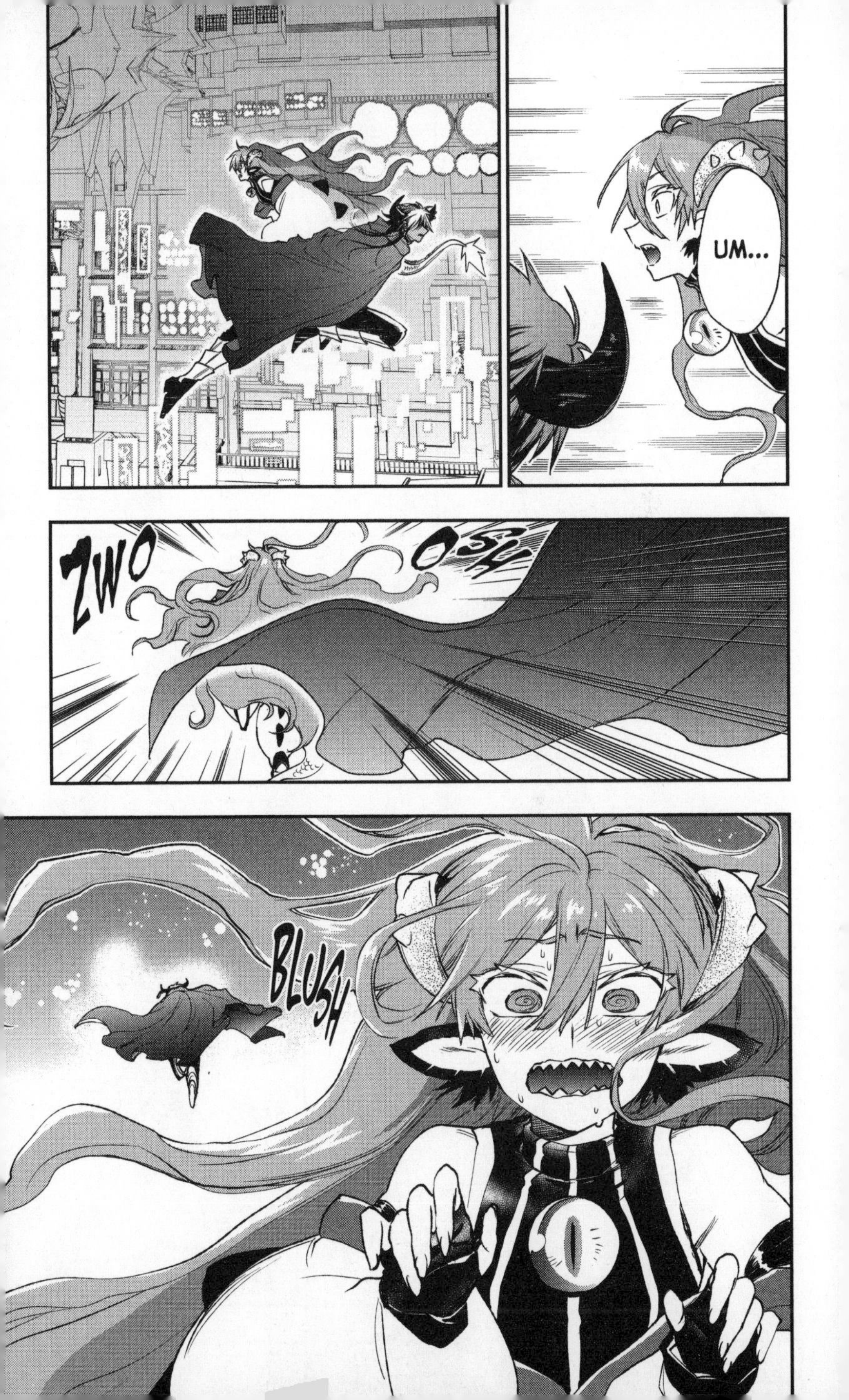
UM...
ZWOOSH
BLUSH

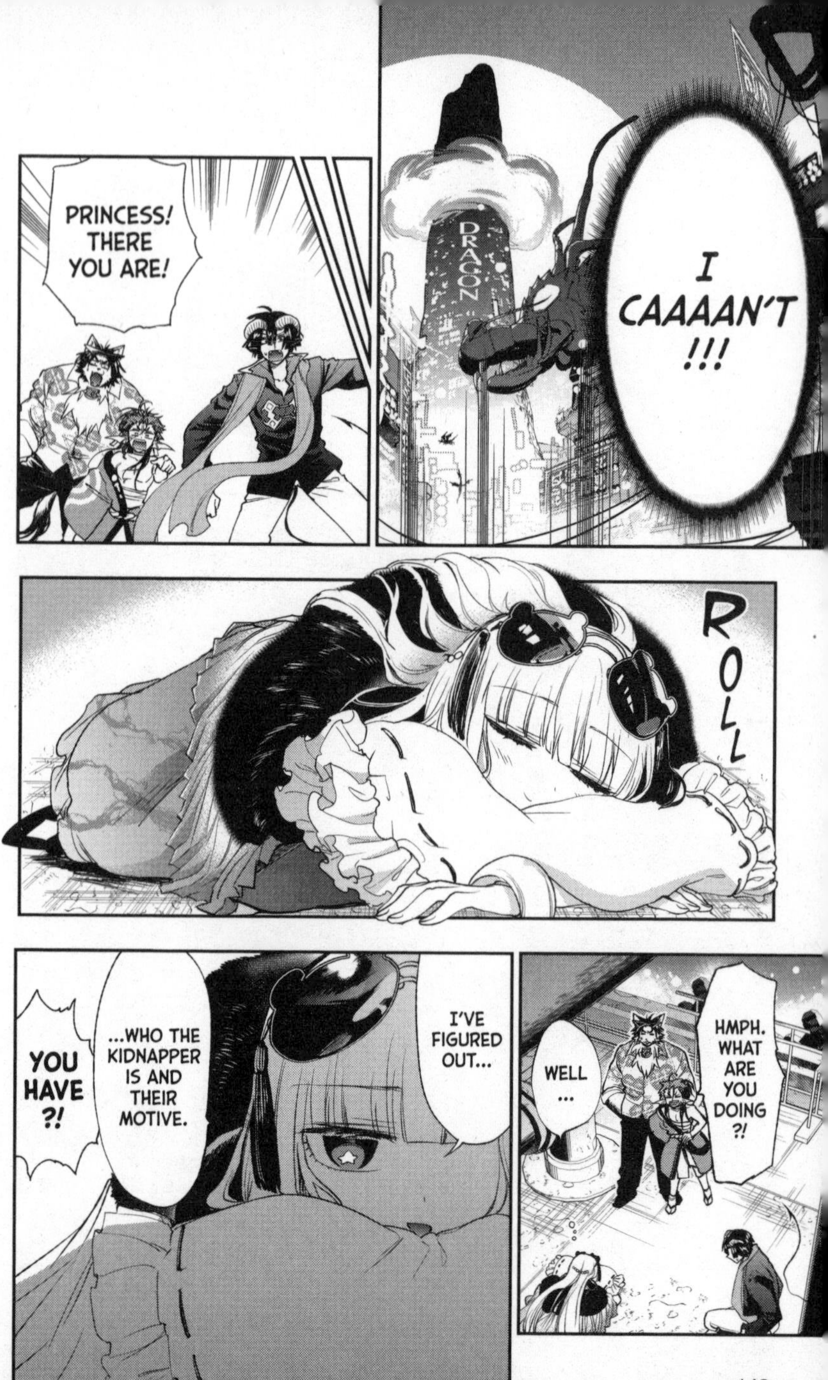
I CAAAAN'T !!!
PRINCESS! THERE YOU ARE!
ROLL
HMPH. WHAT ARE YOU DOING ?!
WELL ...
I'VE FIGURED OUT...
...WHO THE KIDNAPPER IS AND THEIR MOTIVE.
YOU HAVE ?!

Agave

Passionate dragon girl

Brute Strength: ☆☆☆☆☆☆☆☆☆☆
Naivety: ∞

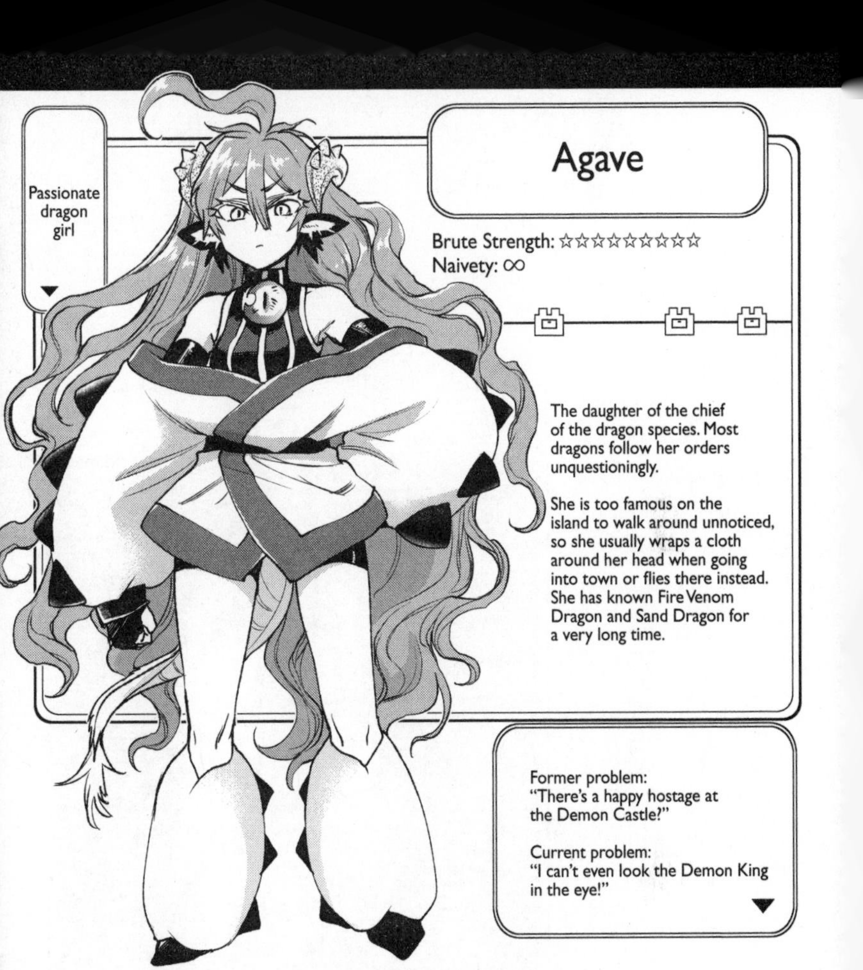

The daughter of the chief of the dragon species. Most dragons follow her orders unquestioningly.

She is too famous on the island to walk around unnoticed, so she usually wraps a cloth around her head when going into town or flies there instead. She has known Fire Venom Dragon and Sand Dragon for a very long time.

Former problem:
"There's a happy hostage at the Demon Castle?"

Current problem:
"I can't even look the Demon King in the eye!"

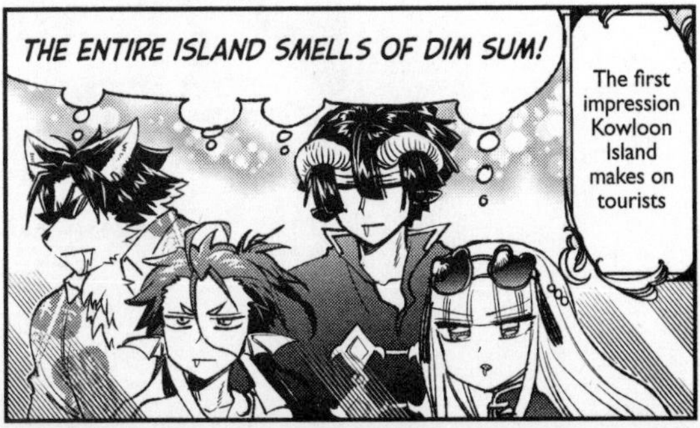
The first impression Kowloon Island makes on tourists
THE ENTIRE ISLAND SMELLS OF DIM SUM!

Would you like to change your class?
1 change remaining
▶Yes
No
Hanged Man
"You're cute even upside down..."

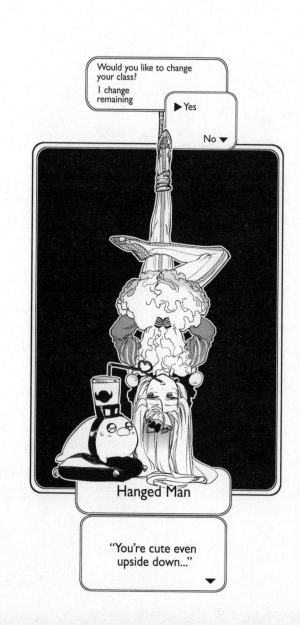

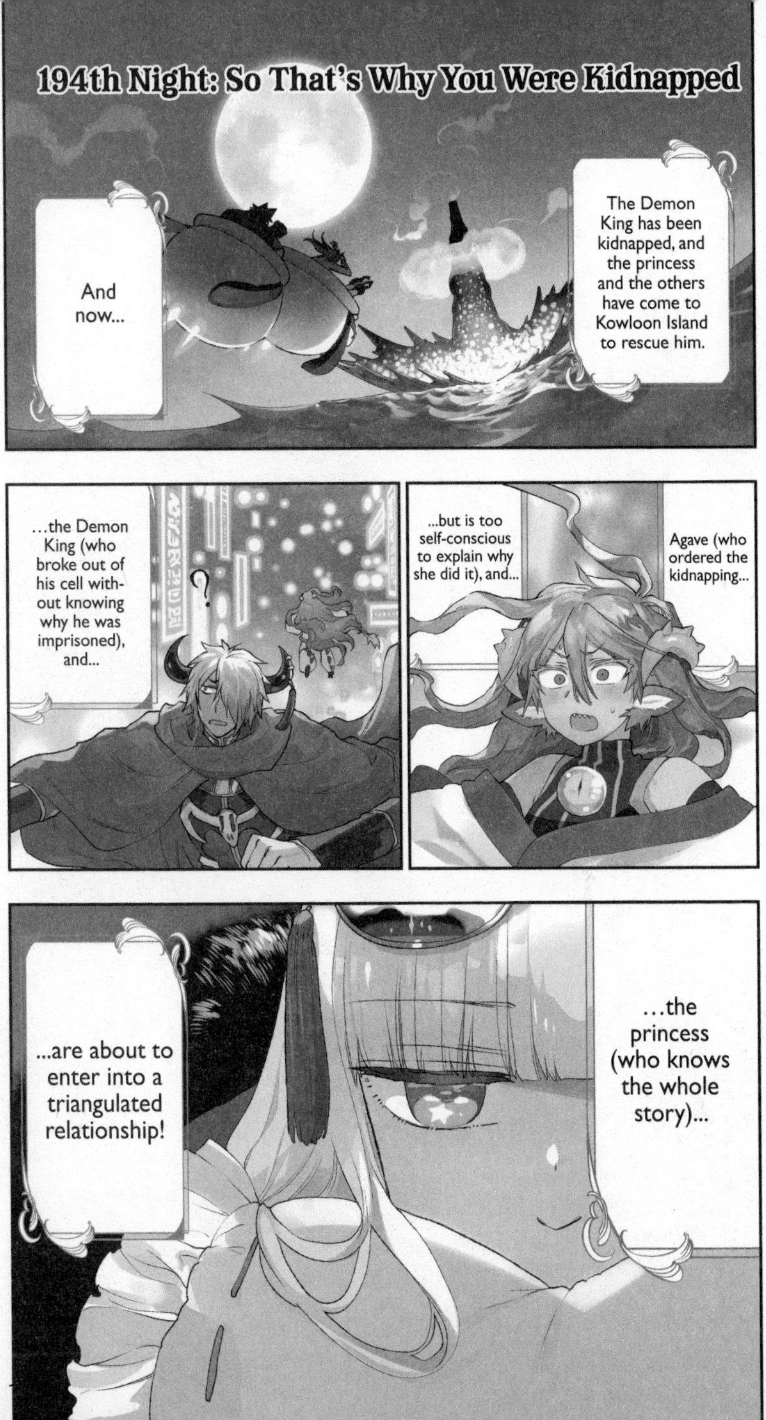
194th Night: So That's Why You Were Kidnapped
The Demon King has been kidnapped, and the princess and the others have come to Kowloon Island to rescue him.
And now...
Agave (who ordered the kidnapping...
...but is too self-conscious to explain why she did it), and...
...the Demon King (who broke out of his cell without knowing why he was imprisoned), and...
...the princess (who knows the whole story)...
...are about to enter into a triangulated relationship!

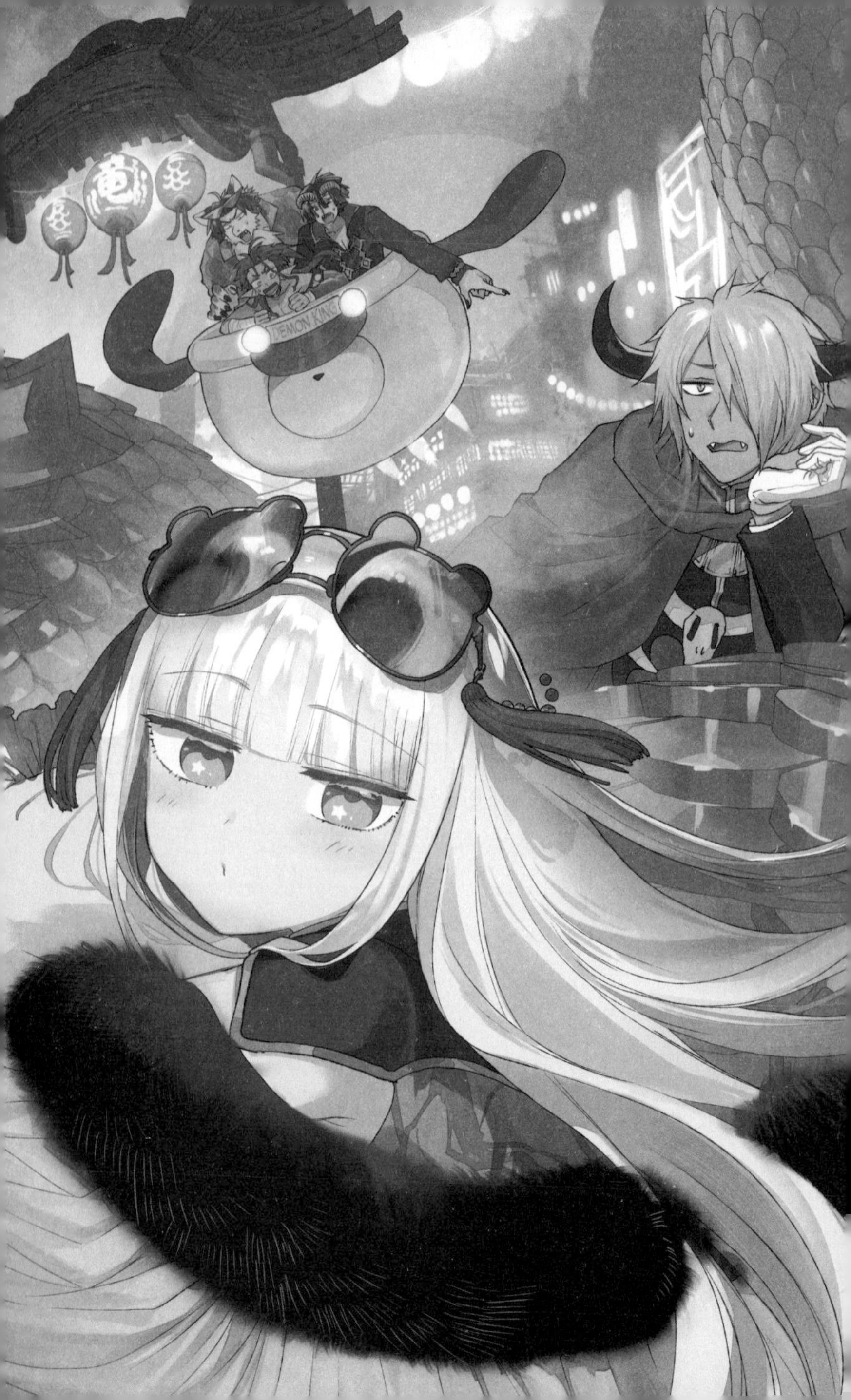
DEMON KING

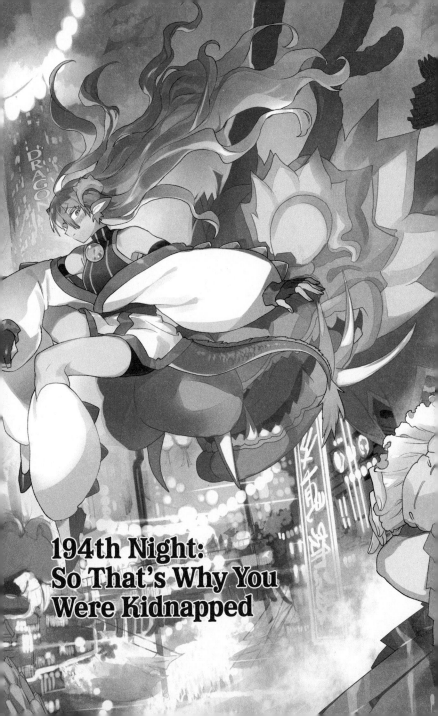

194th Night:
So That's Why You
Were Kidnapped

SLEEPY PRINCESS
IN THE DEMON CASTLE

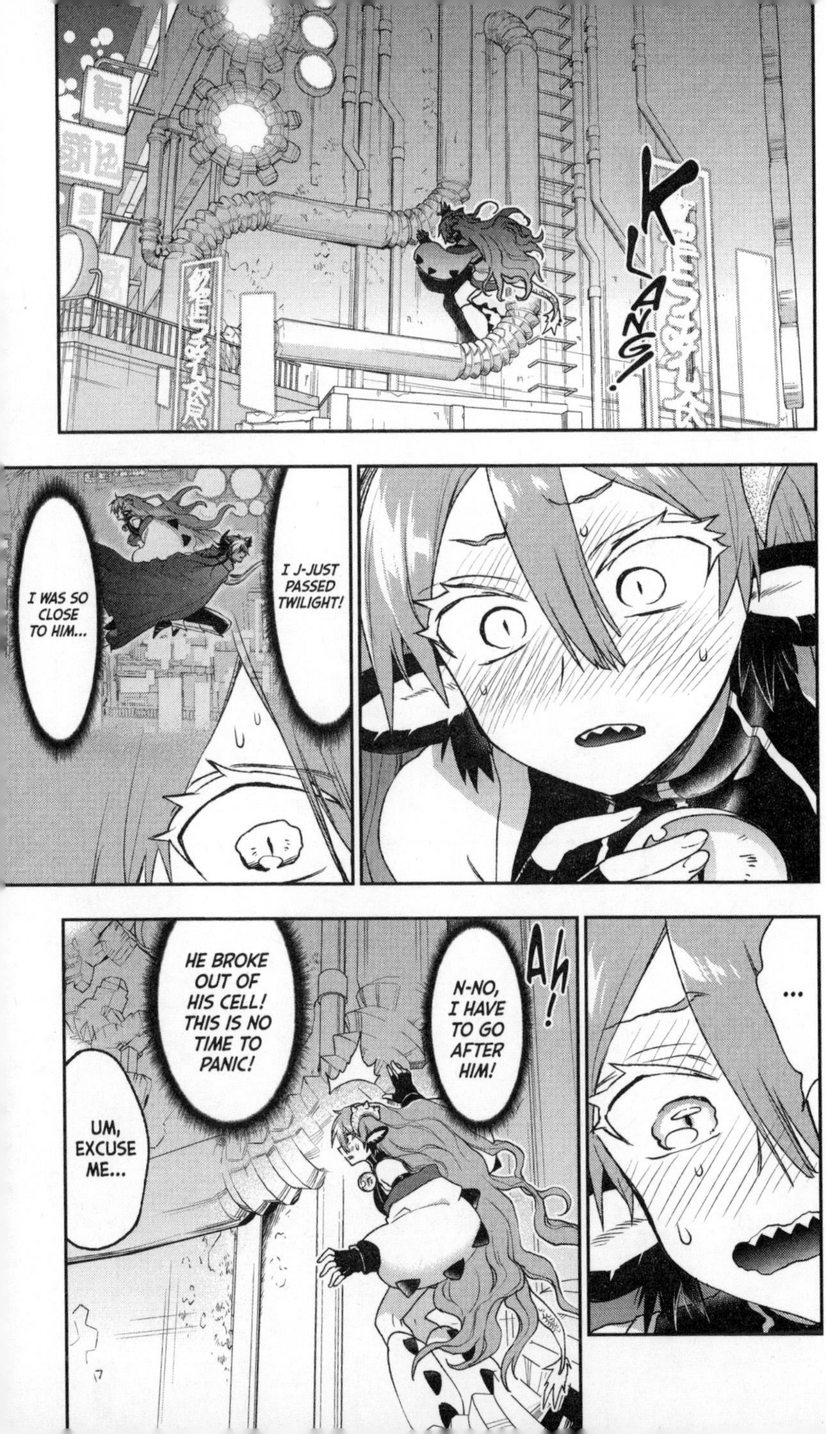
KLANG!
I J-JUST PASSED TWILIGHT!
I WAS SO CLOSE TO HIM...
...
AH!
N-NO, I HAVE TO GO AFTER HIM!
HE BROKE OUT OF HIS CELL! THIS IS NO TIME TO PANIC!
UM, EXCUSE ME...

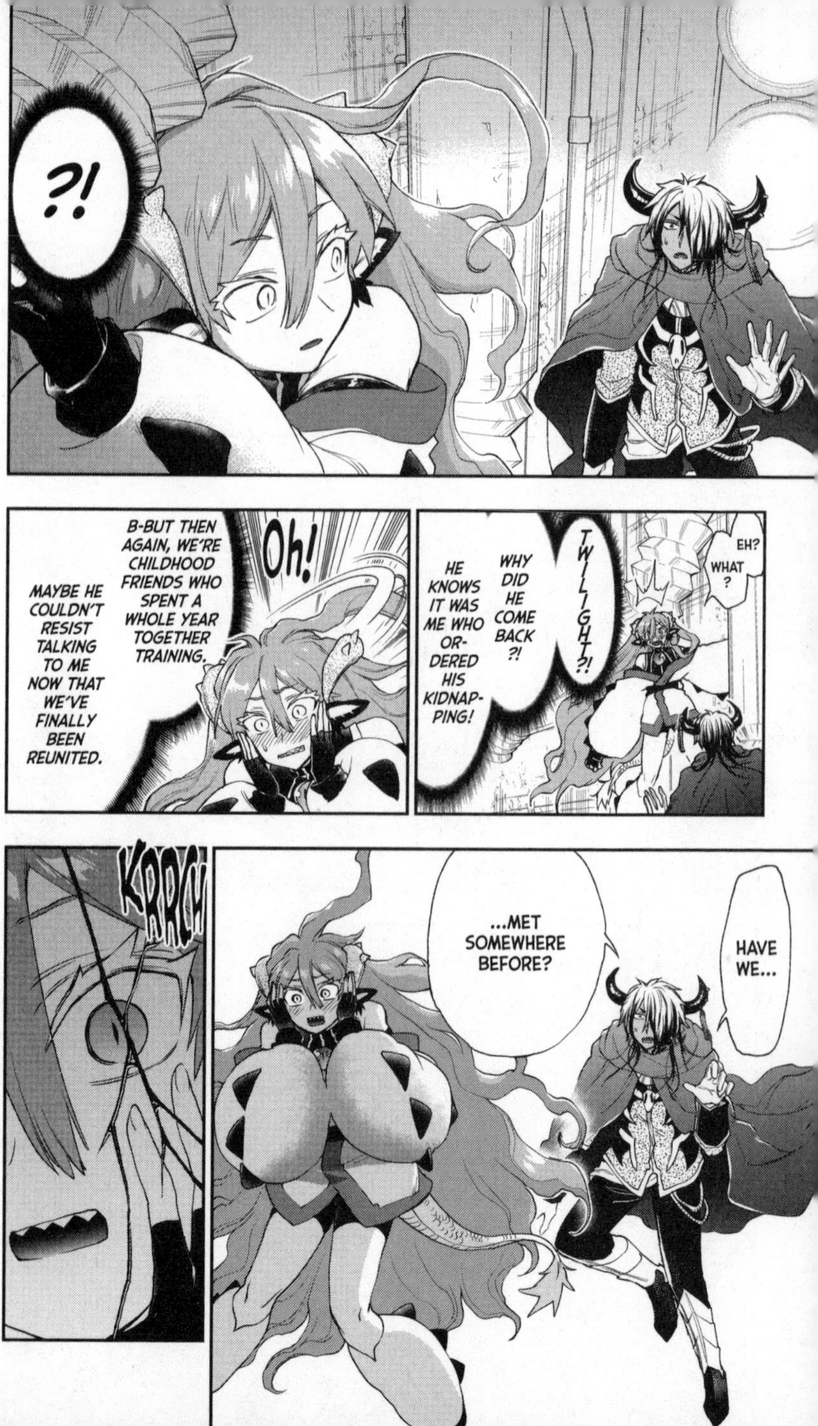
?!
EH? WHAT?
TWILIGHT?!
WHY DID HE COME BACK?!
HE KNOWS IT WAS ME WHO ORDERED HIS KIDNAPPING!
Oh!
B-BUT THEN AGAIN, WE'RE CHILDHOOD FRIENDS WHO SPENT A WHOLE YEAR TOGETHER TRAINING.
MAYBE HE COULDN'T RESIST TALKING TO ME NOW THAT WE'VE FINALLY BEEN REUNITED.
HAVE WE...
...MET SOMEWHERE BEFORE?
KRRCH

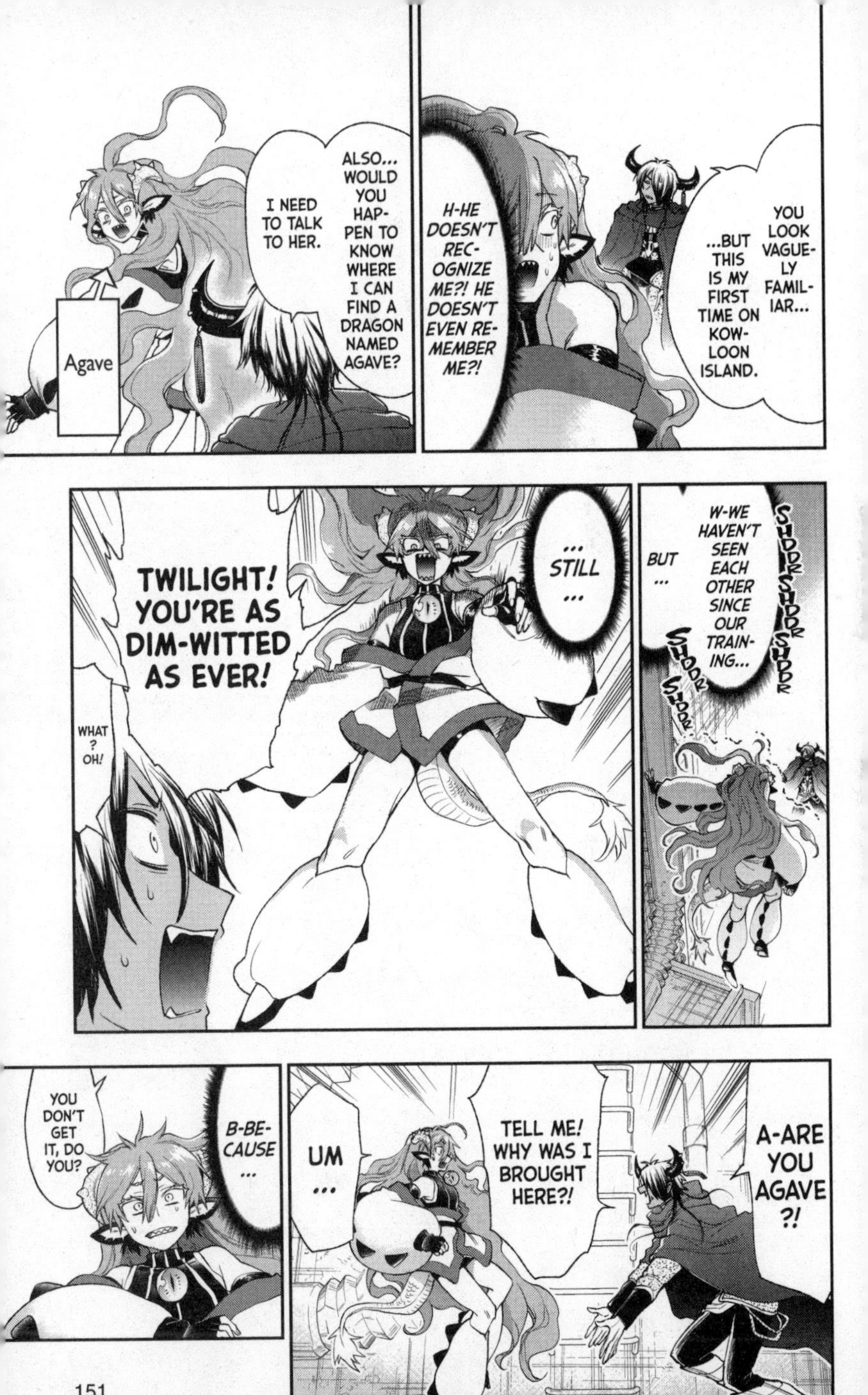
YOU LOOK VAGUELY FAMILIAR...
...BUT THIS IS MY FIRST TIME ON KOWLOON ISLAND.
H-HE DOESN'T RECOGNIZE ME?! HE DOESN'T EVEN REMEMBER ME?!
ALSO... WOULD YOU HAPPEN TO KNOW WHERE I CAN FIND A DRAGON NAMED AGAVE?
I NEED TO TALK TO HER.
Agave
SHDDR SHDDR SHDDR
W-WE HAVEN'T SEEN EACH OTHER SINCE OUR TRAINING...
BUT ...
SHDDR SHDDR
... STILL ...
TWILIGHT! YOU'RE AS DIM-WITTED AS EVER!
WHAT? OH!
A-ARE YOU AGAVE?!
TELL ME! WHY WAS I BROUGHT HERE?!
UM ...
B-BECAUSE ...
YOU DON'T GET IT, DO YOU?

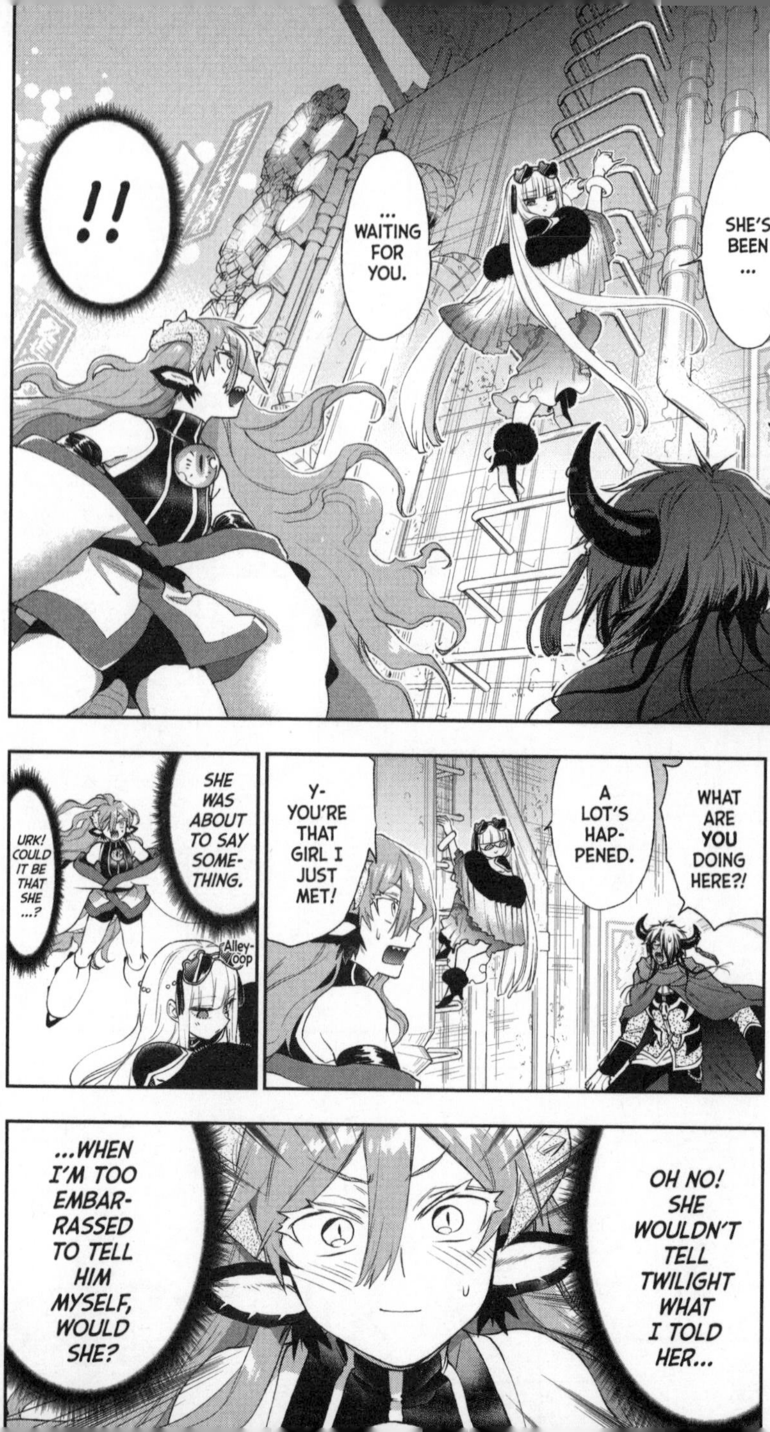
SHE'S BEEN ...
... WAITING FOR YOU.
!!
WHAT ARE YOU DOING HERE?!
A LOT'S HAPPENED.
Y-YOU'RE THAT GIRL I JUST MET!
SHE WAS ABOUT TO SAY SOMETHING.
URK! COULD IT BE THAT SHE ...?
Alley-Oop
OH NO! SHE WOULDN'T TELL TWILIGHT WHAT I TOLD HER...
...WHEN I'M TOO EMBARRASSED TO TELL HIM MYSELF, WOULD SHE?

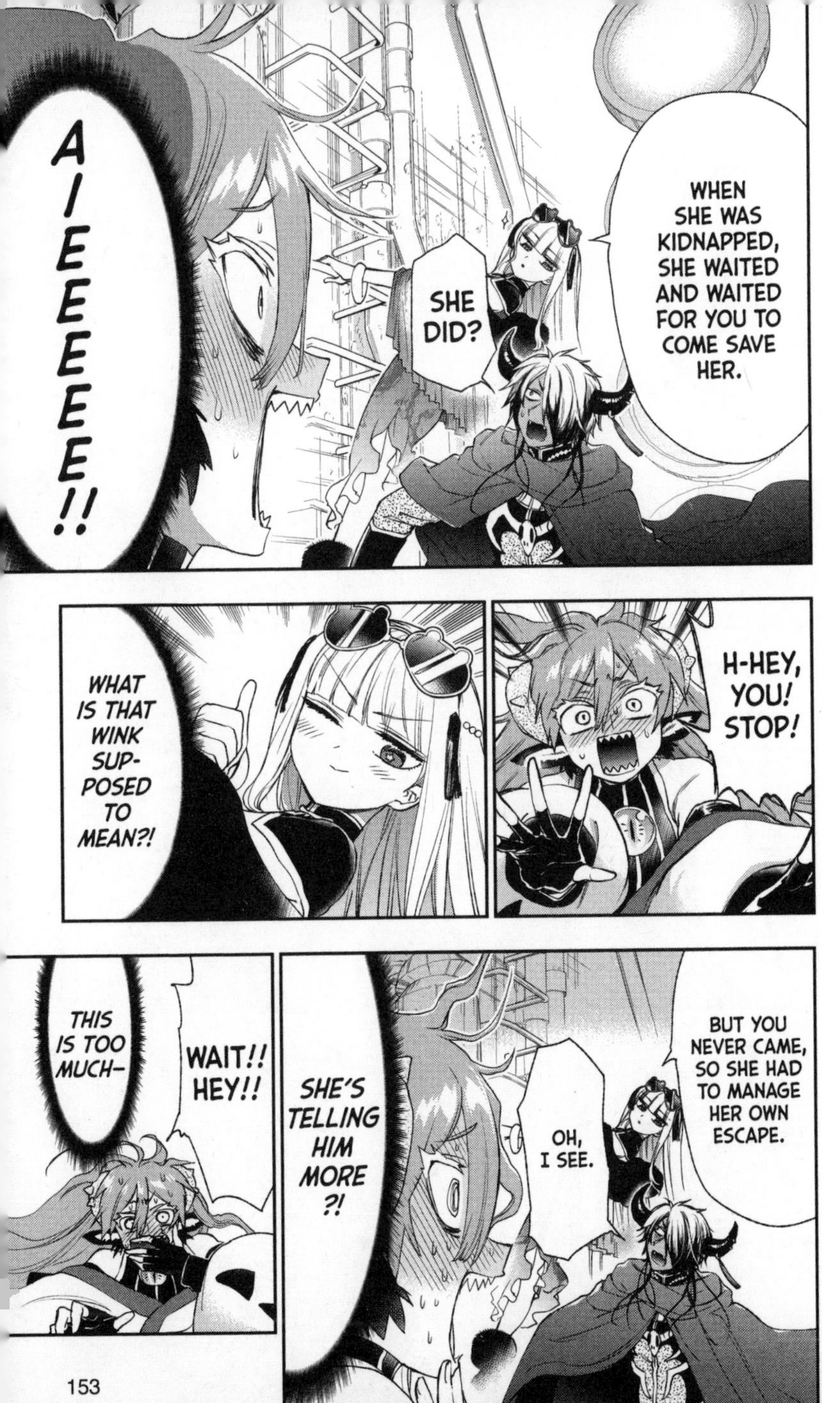
WHEN SHE WAS KIDNAPPED, SHE WAITED AND WAITED FOR YOU TO COME SAVE HER.
SHE DID?
AIEEEEEEE!!
H-HEY, YOU! STOP!
WHAT IS THAT WINK SUP-POSED TO MEAN?!
BUT YOU NEVER CAME, SO SHE HAD TO MANAGE HER OWN ESCAPE.
OH, I SEE.
SHE'S TELLING HIM MORE?!
WAIT!! HEY!!
THIS IS TOO MUCH–

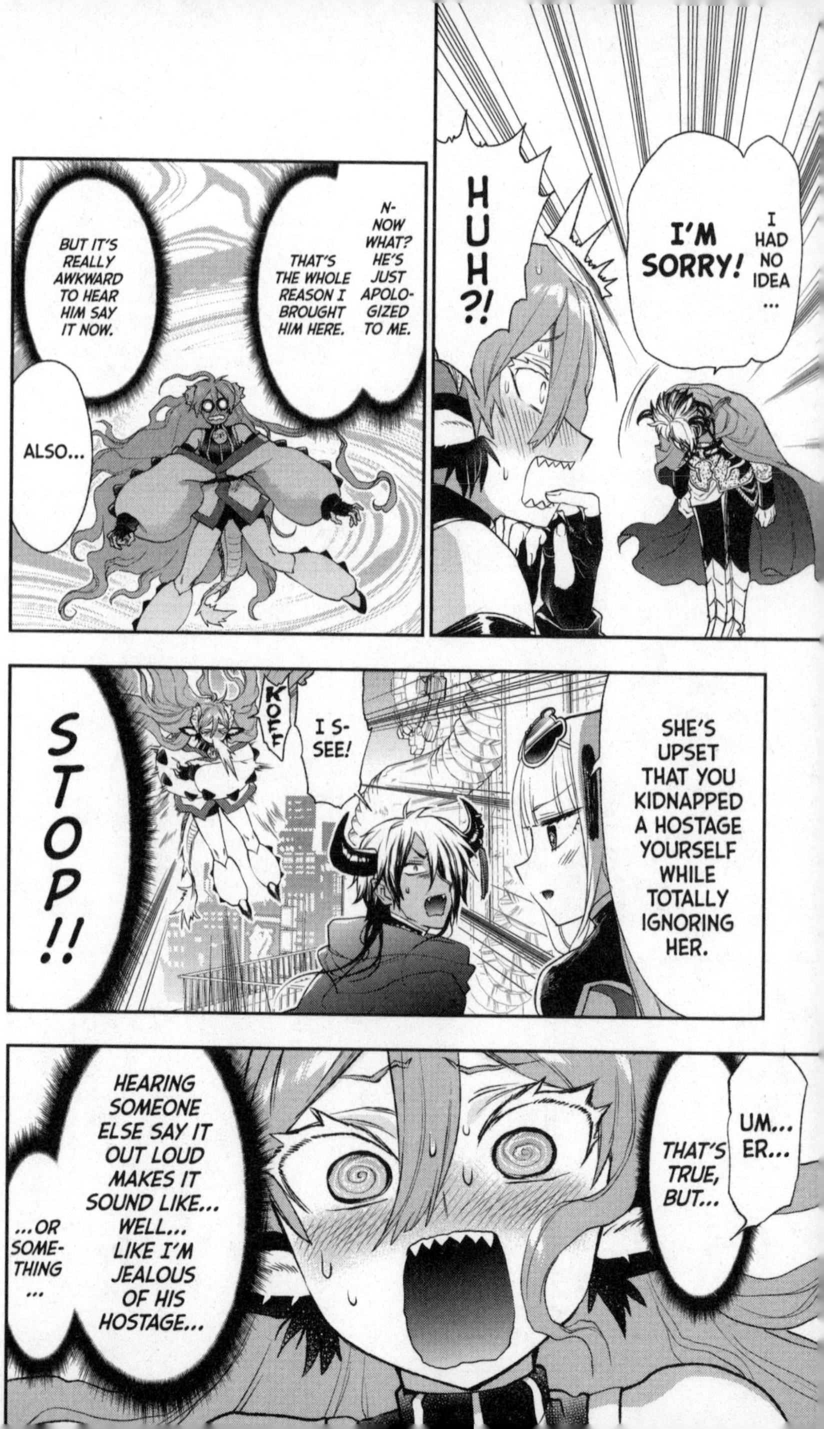
I'M SORRY! I HAD NO IDEA...
HUH?!
N-NOW WHAT? HE'S JUST APOLOGIZED TO ME.
THAT'S THE WHOLE REASON I BROUGHT HIM HERE.
BUT IT'S REALLY AWKWARD TO HEAR HIM SAY IT NOW.
ALSO...
SHE'S UPSET THAT YOU KIDNAPPED A HOSTAGE YOURSELF WHILE TOTALLY IGNORING HER.
I S-SEE!
KOFF
STOP!!
UM... ER...
THAT'S TRUE, BUT...
HEARING SOMEONE ELSE SAY IT OUT LOUD MAKES IT SOUND LIKE... WELL... LIKE I'M JEALOUS OF HIS HOSTAGE...
...OR SOMETHING...

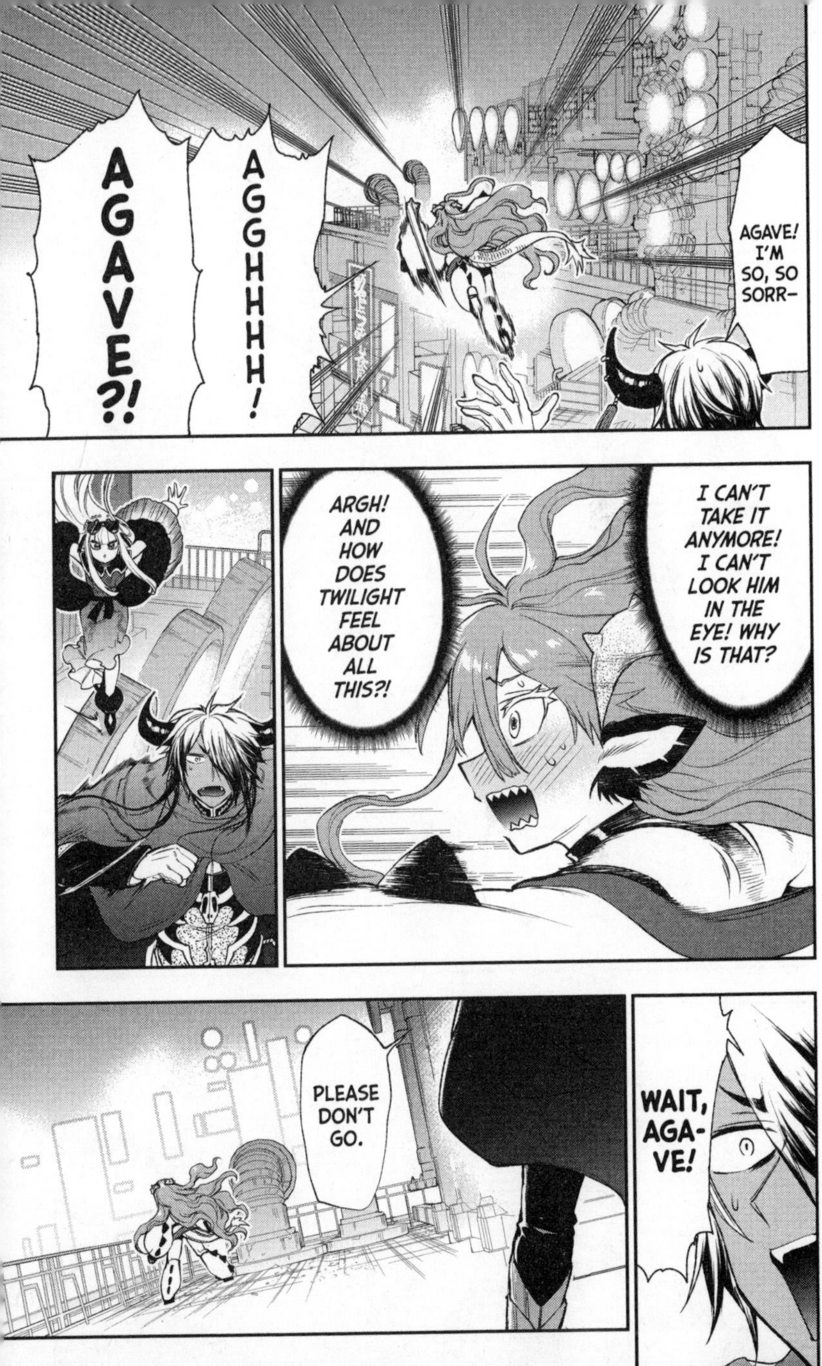
AGAVE! I'M SO, SO SORR–
AGGHHHH!
AGAVE?!
I CAN'T TAKE IT ANYMORE! I CAN'T LOOK HIM IN THE EYE! WHY IS THAT?
ARGH! AND HOW DOES TWILIGHT FEEL ABOUT ALL THIS?!
WAIT, AGA-VE!
PLEASE DON'T GO.

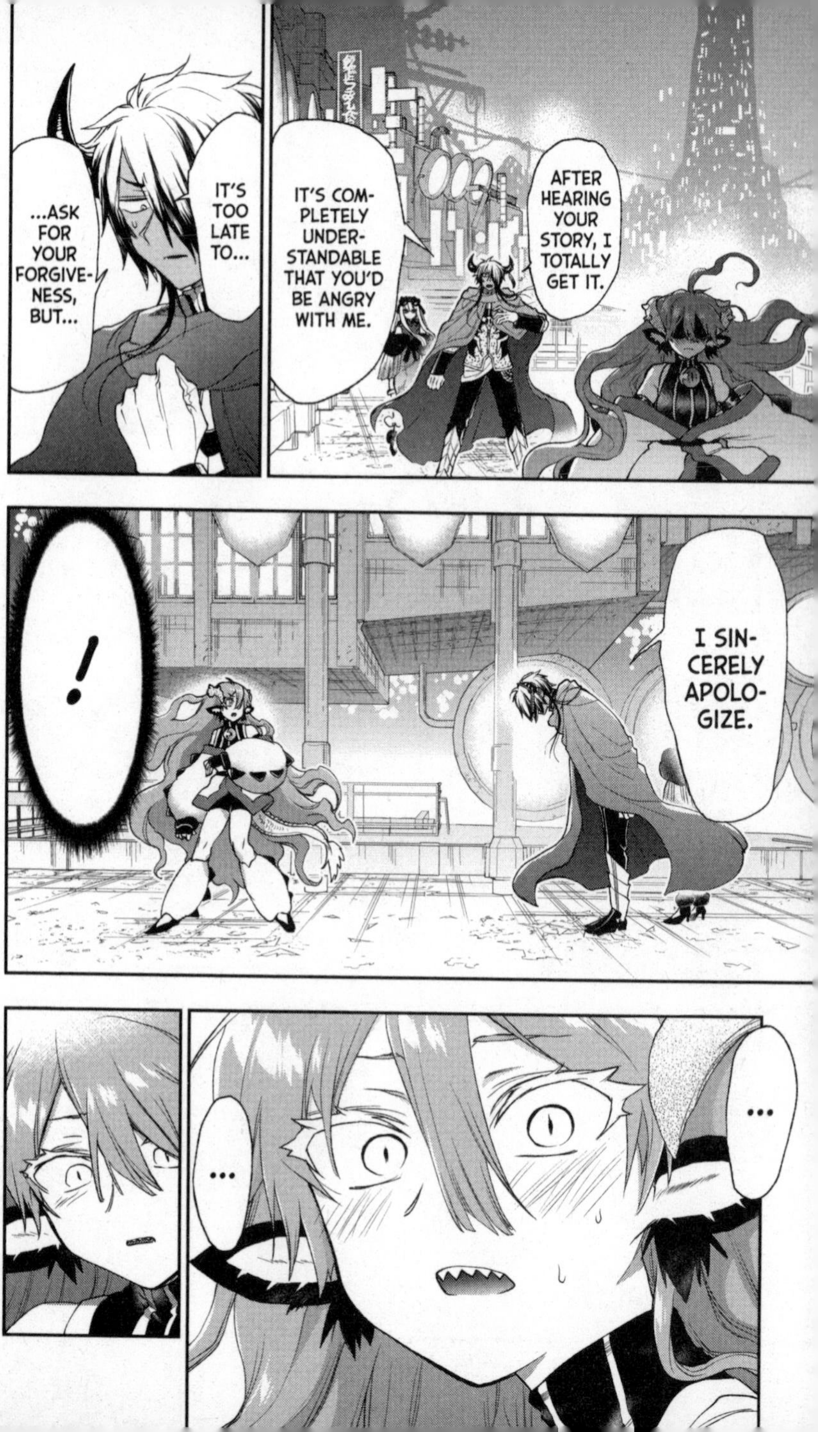
AFTER HEARING YOUR STORY, I TOTALLY GET IT.
IT'S COM-PLETELY UNDER-STANDABLE THAT YOU'D BE ANGRY WITH ME.
IT'S TOO LATE TO...
...ASK FOR YOUR FORGIVE-NESS, BUT...
I SIN-CERELY APOLO-GIZE.
!
...
...

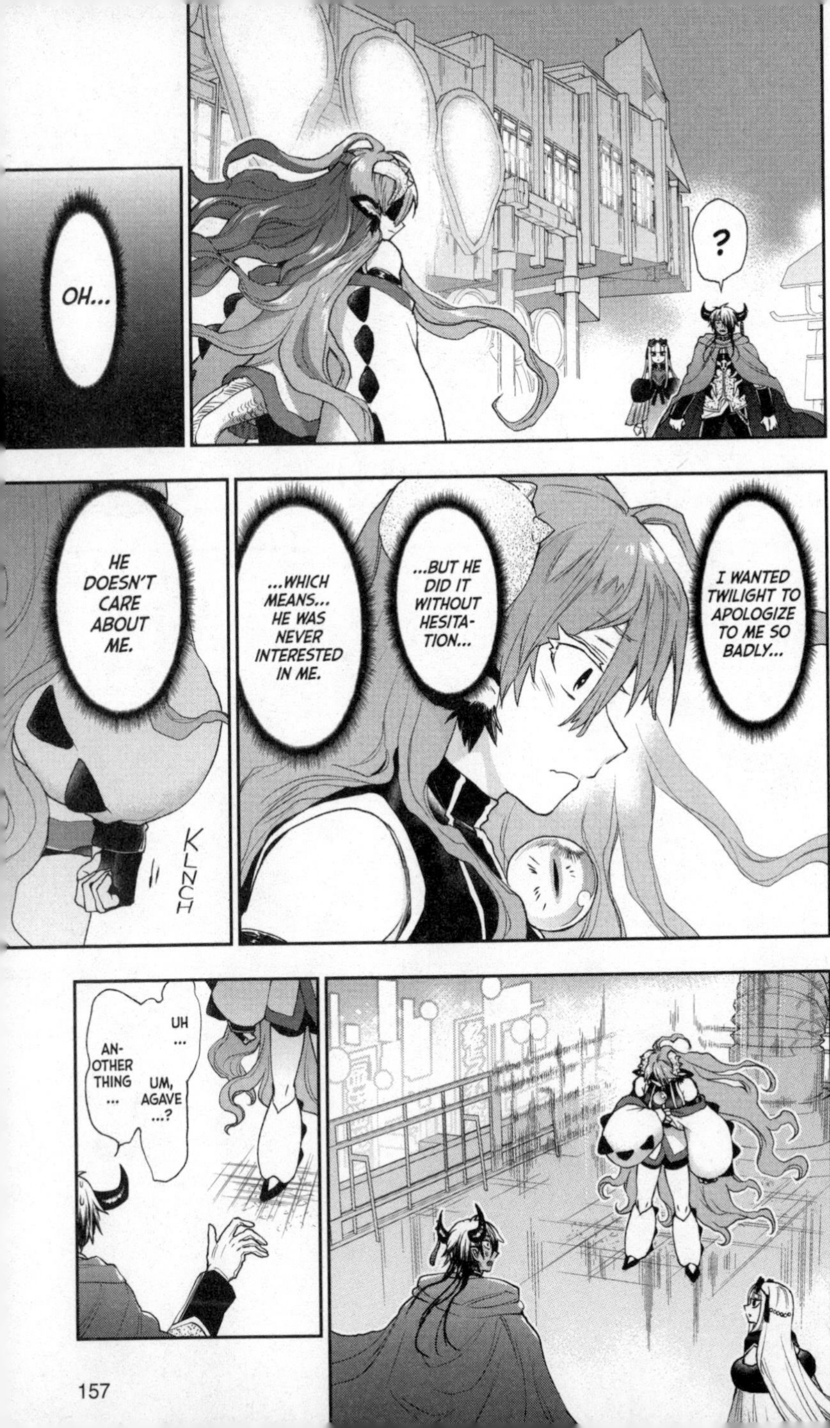
?
OH...
I WANTED TWILIGHT TO APOLOGIZE TO ME SO BADLY...
...BUT HE DID IT WITHOUT HESITATION...
...WHICH MEANS... HE WAS NEVER INTERESTED IN ME.
HE DOESN'T CARE ABOUT ME.
KLNCH
UH ... UM, AGAVE ...?
AN-OTHER THING ...

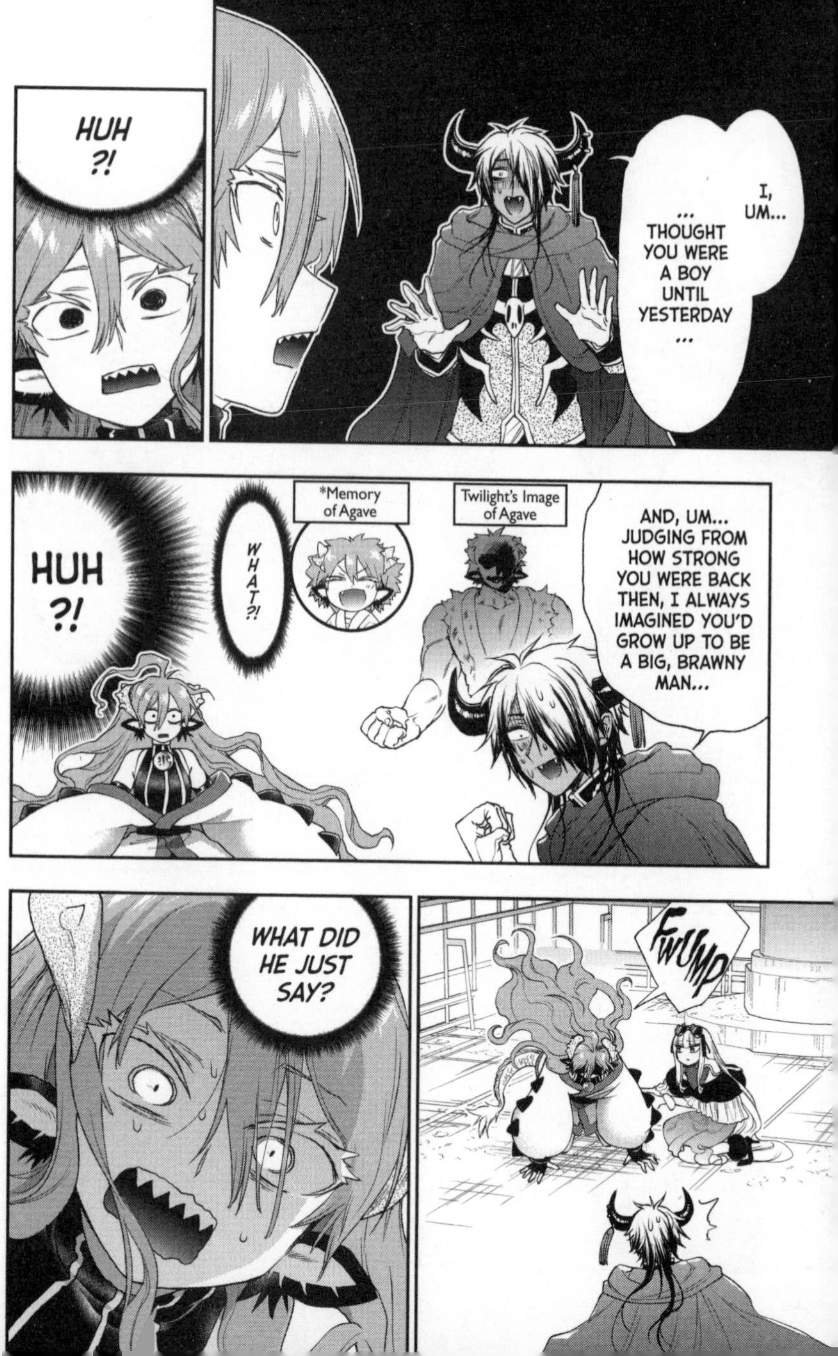
I, UM...
...THOUGHT YOU WERE A BOY UNTIL YESTERDAY...
HUH ?!
AND, UM... JUDGING FROM HOW STRONG YOU WERE BACK THEN, I ALWAYS IMAGINED YOU'D GROW UP TO BE A BIG, BRAWNY MAN...
Twilight's Image of Agave
*Memory of Agave
WHAT ?!
HUH ?!
FWUMP
WHAT DID HE JUST SAY?

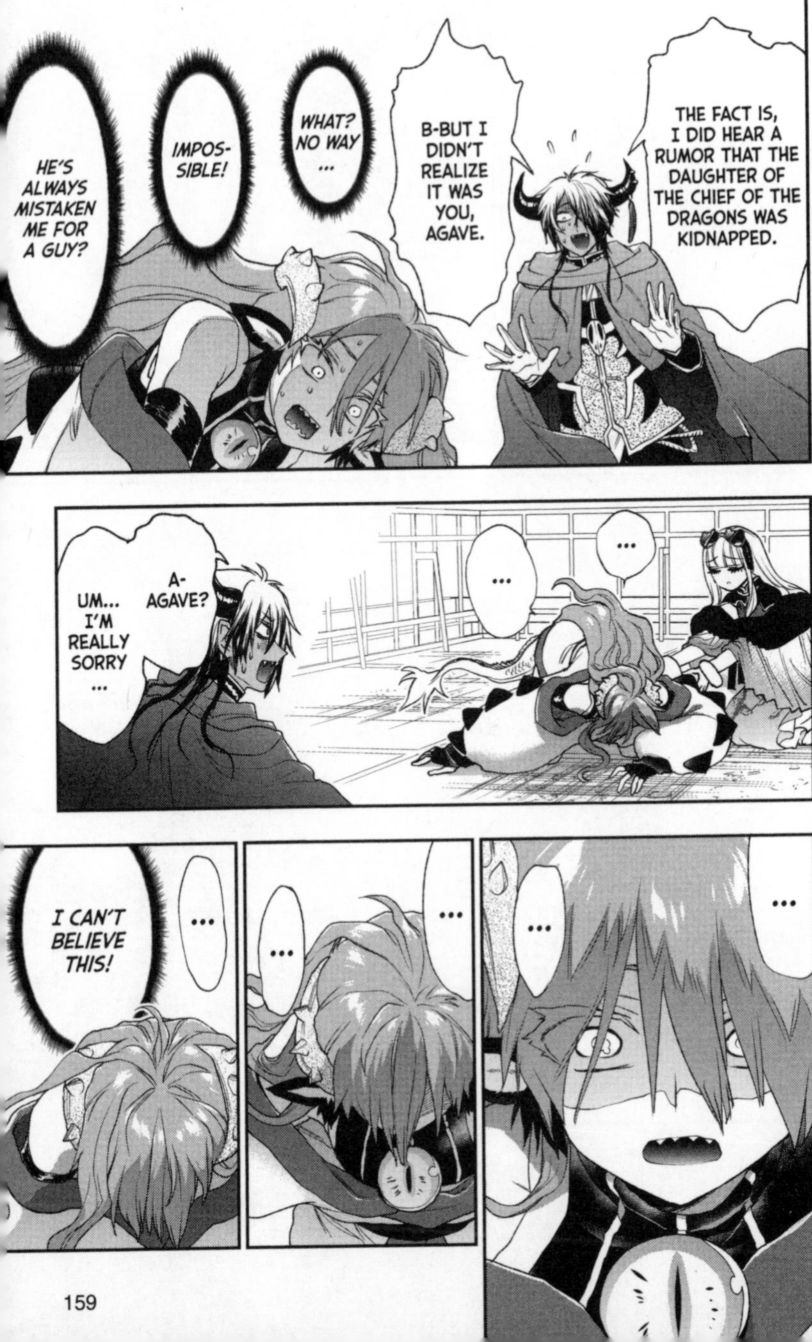
THE FACT IS, I DID HEAR A RUMOR THAT THE DAUGHTER OF THE CHIEF OF THE DRAGONS WAS KIDNAPPED.
B-BUT I DIDN'T REALIZE IT WAS YOU, AGAVE.
WHAT? NO WAY ...
IMPOS-SIBLE!
HE'S ALWAYS MISTAKEN ME FOR A GUY?
...
...
A- AGAVE?
UM... I'M REALLY SORRY ...
...
...
...
...
...
I CAN'T BELIEVE THIS!

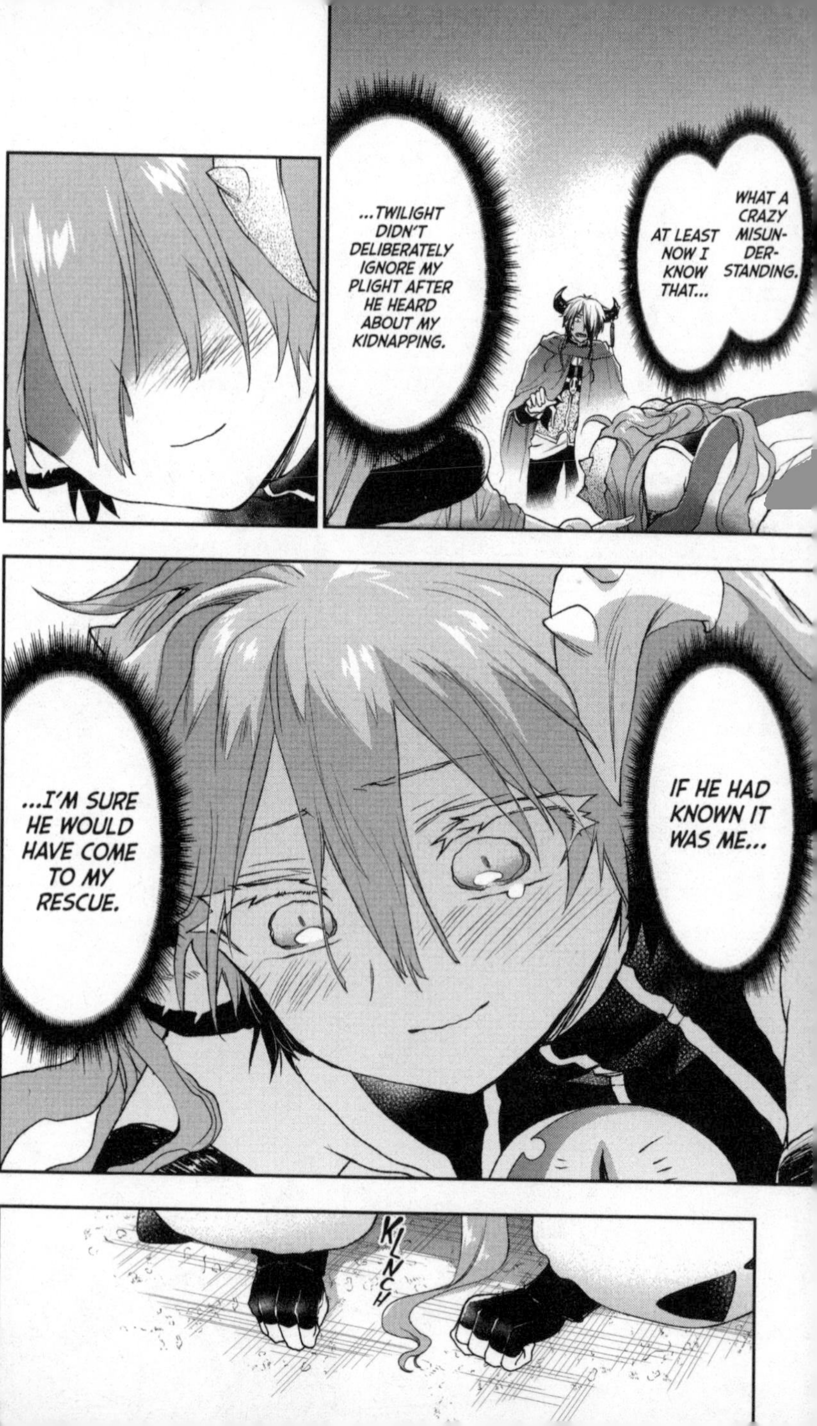
WHAT A CRAZY MISUN-DER-STANDING.
AT LEAST NOW I KNOW THAT...
...TWILIGHT DIDN'T DELIBERATELY IGNORE MY PLIGHT AFTER HE HEARD ABOUT MY KIDNAPPING.
IF HE HAD KNOWN IT WAS ME...
...I'M SURE HE WOULD HAVE COME TO MY RESCUE.
KLINCH

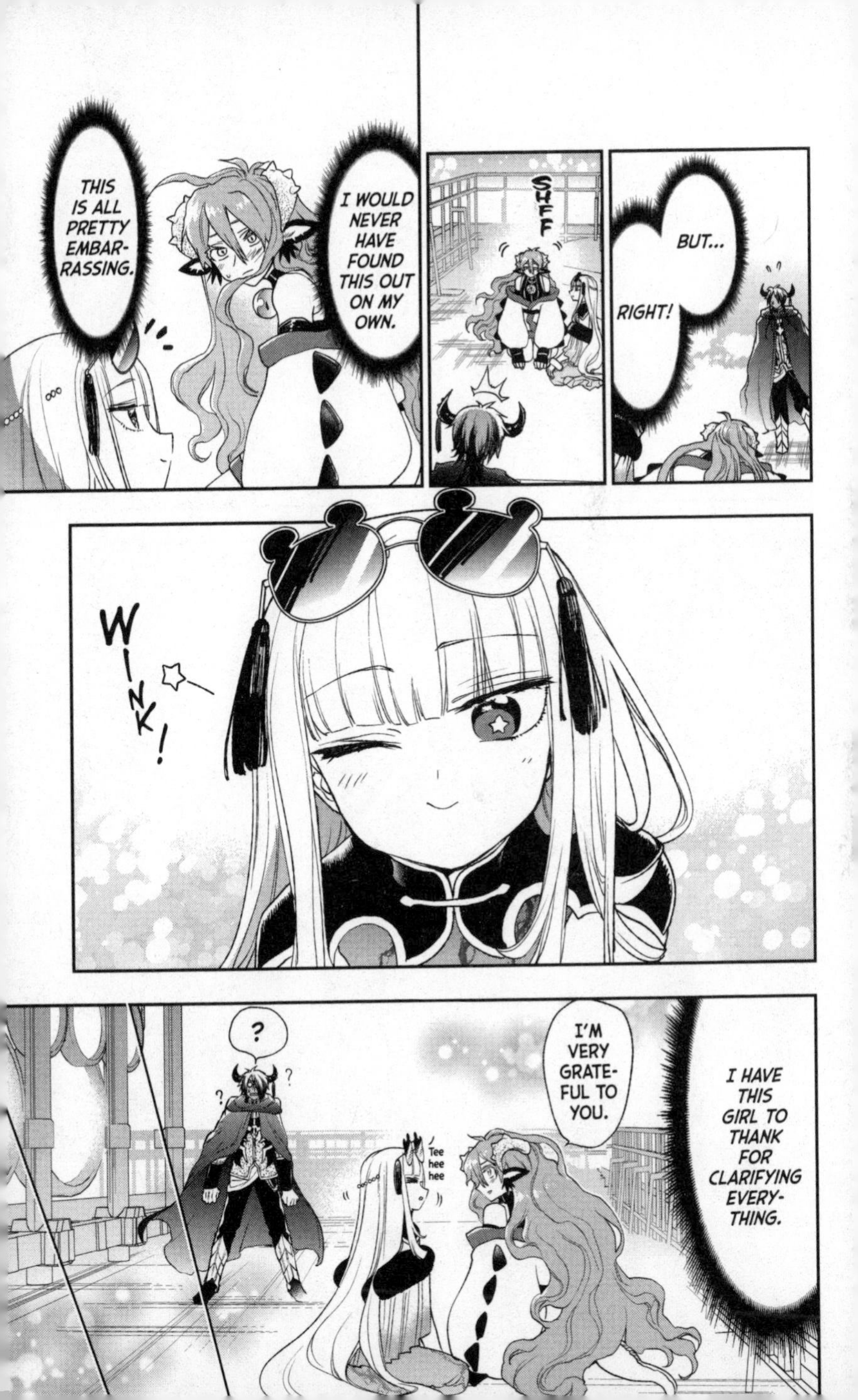
BUT...
RIGHT!
SHFF
I WOULD NEVER HAVE FOUND THIS OUT ON MY OWN.
THIS IS ALL PRETTY EMBARRASSING.
WINK!
I HAVE THIS GIRL TO THANK FOR CLARIFYING EVERYTHING.
I'M VERY GRATEFUL TO YOU.
Tee hee hee
?

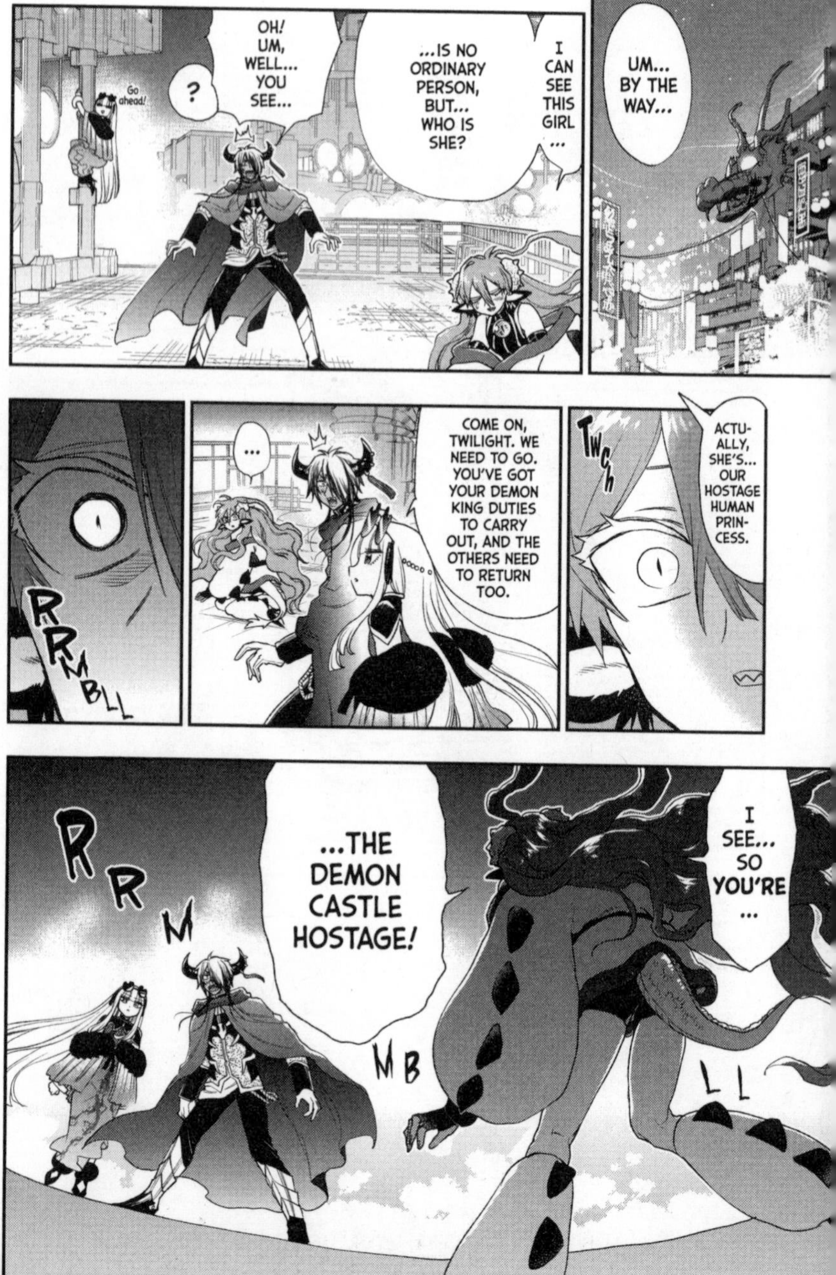
UM... BY THE WAY...
I CAN SEE THIS GIRL...
...IS NO ORDINARY PERSON, BUT... WHO IS SHE?
OH! UM, WELL... YOU SEE...
?
Go ahead!
ACTU-ALLY, SHE'S... OUR HOSTAGE HUMAN PRIN-CESS.
TWCh
COME ON, TWILIGHT. WE NEED TO GO. YOU'VE GOT YOUR DEMON KING DUTIES TO CARRY OUT, AND THE OTHERS NEED TO RETURN TOO.
...
RRRMBLL
I SEE... SO YOU'RE...
...THE DEMON CASTLE HOSTAGE!
RRRMMBLL

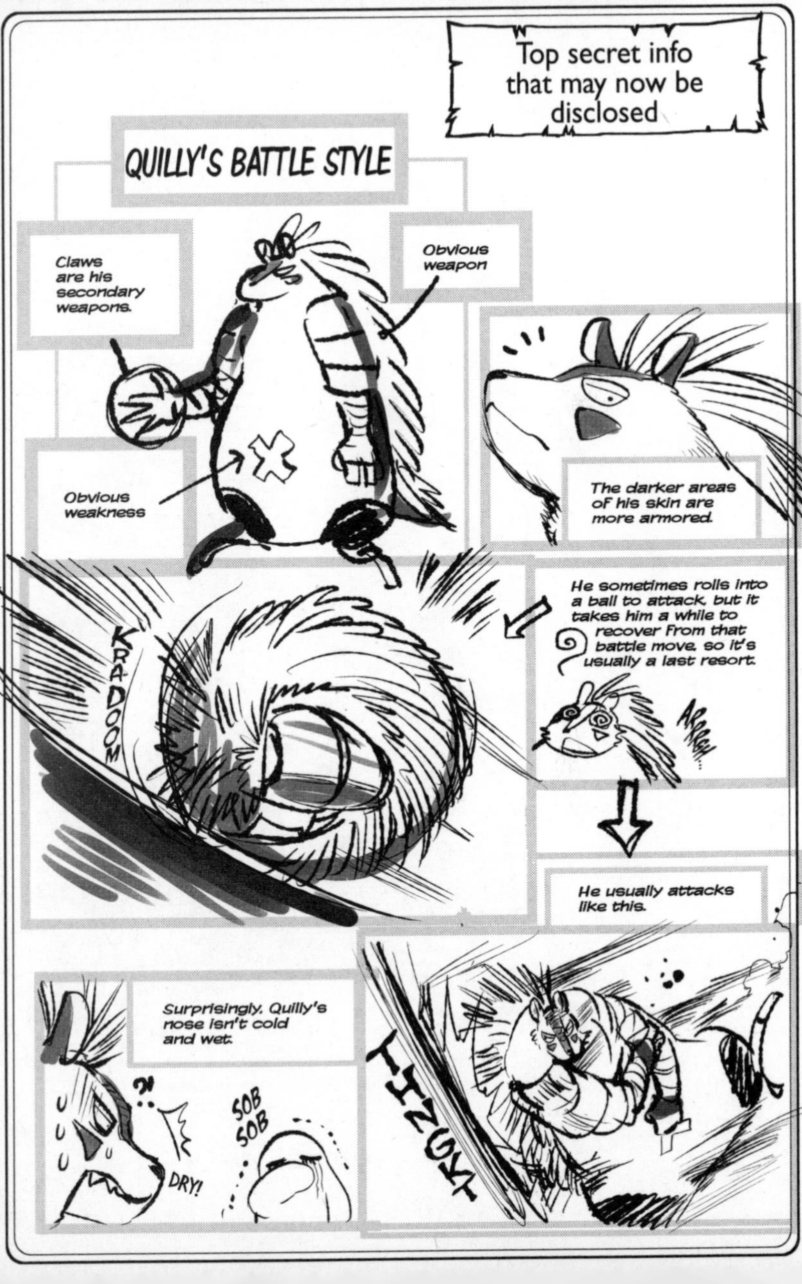

Top secret info that may now be disclosed
QUILLY'S BATTLE STYLE
Obvious weapon
Claws are his secondary weapons.
Obvious weakness
The darker areas of his skin are more armored.
He sometimes rolls into a ball to attack, but it takes him a while to recover from that battle move, so it's usually a last resort.
ARRGH...
He usually attacks like this.
KRADOOM
THNGK
Surprisingly, Quilly's nose isn't cold and wet.
?!
UUU
DRY!
SOB SOB

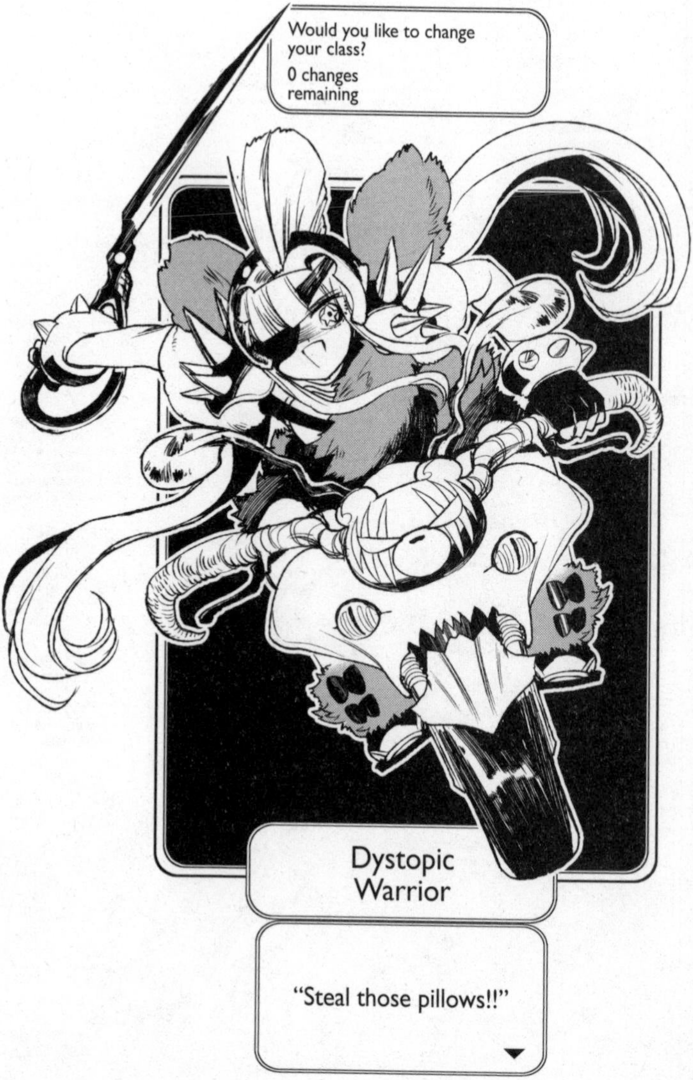
Would you like to change your class?
0 changes remaining
Dystopic Warrior
"Steal those pillows!!"

195th Night: Do I Hear a Lullaby?

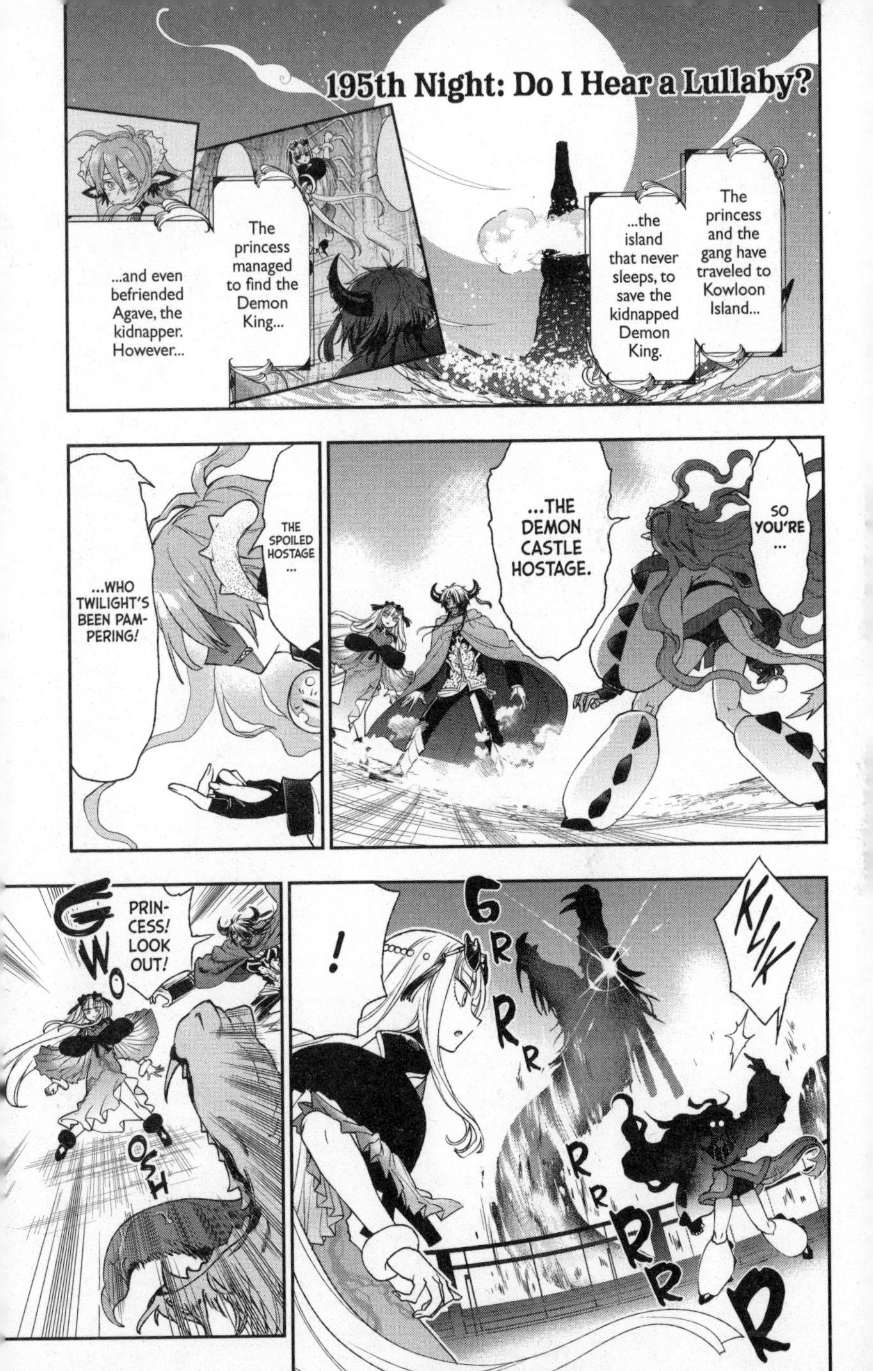
The princess and the gang have traveled to Kowloon Island...
...the island that never sleeps, to save the kidnapped Demon King.
The princess managed to find the Demon King...
...and even befriended Agave, the kidnapper. However...
SO YOU'RE...
...THE DEMON CASTLE HOSTAGE.
THE SPOILED HOSTAGE...
...WHO TWILIGHT'S BEEN PAMPERING!
KLIK
!
GRRRRRRRRRR
PRINCESS! LOOK OUT!
GWO
WOSH

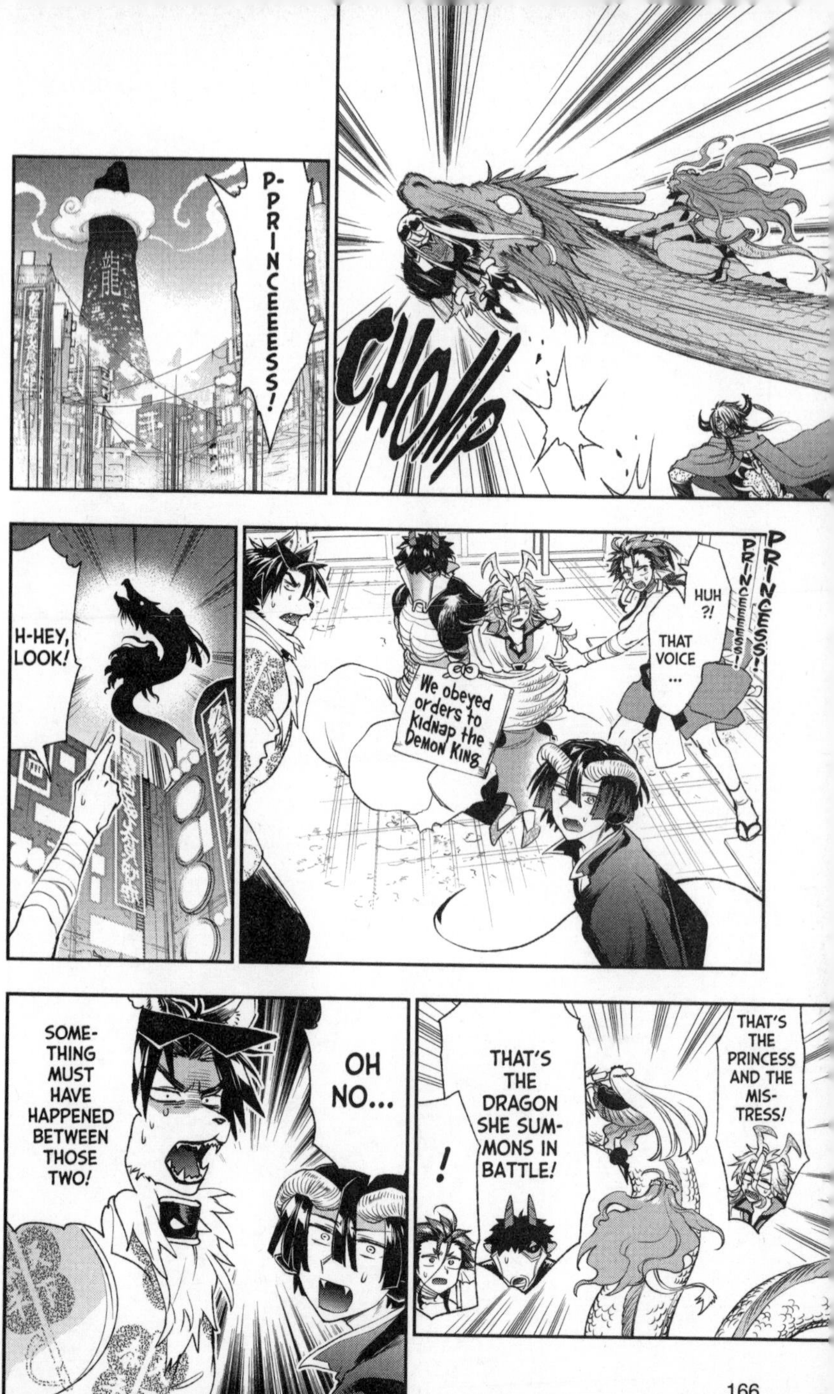
CHOMP
P-PRINCEEEESS!
PRINCESS!
PRINCEEEESS!
HUH?!
THAT VOICE...
We obeyed orders to kidnap the Demon King
H-HEY, LOOK!
THAT'S THE PRINCESS AND THE MISTRESS!
THAT'S THE DRAGON SHE SUMMONS IN BATTLE!
!
OH NO...
SOMETHING MUST HAVE HAPPENED BETWEEN THOSE TWO!

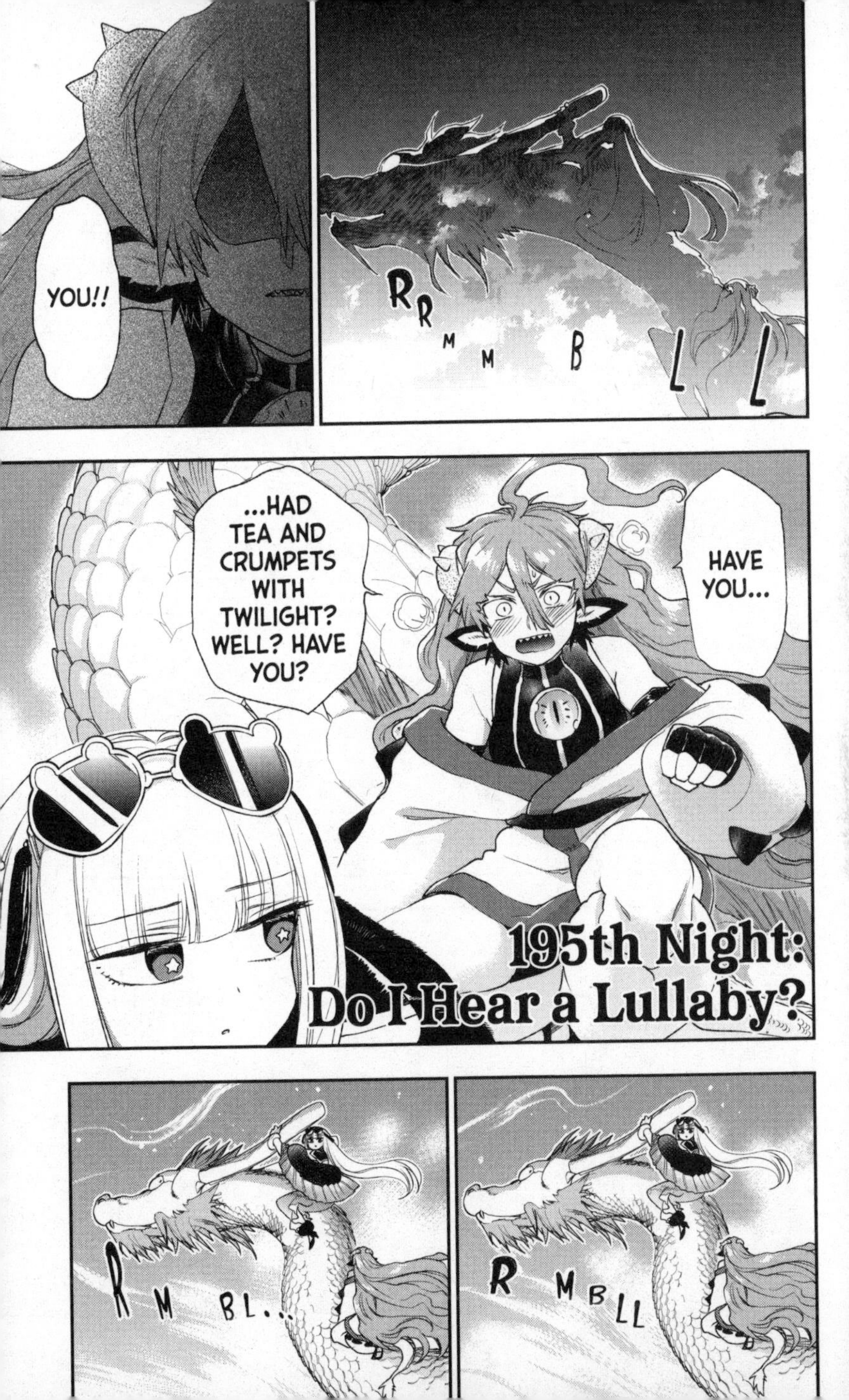
RRMMBLL
YOU!!
HAVE YOU...
...HAD TEA AND CRUMPETS WITH TWILIGHT? WELL? HAVE YOU?
195th Night: Do I Hear a Lullaby?
RMBLL
RMBL...

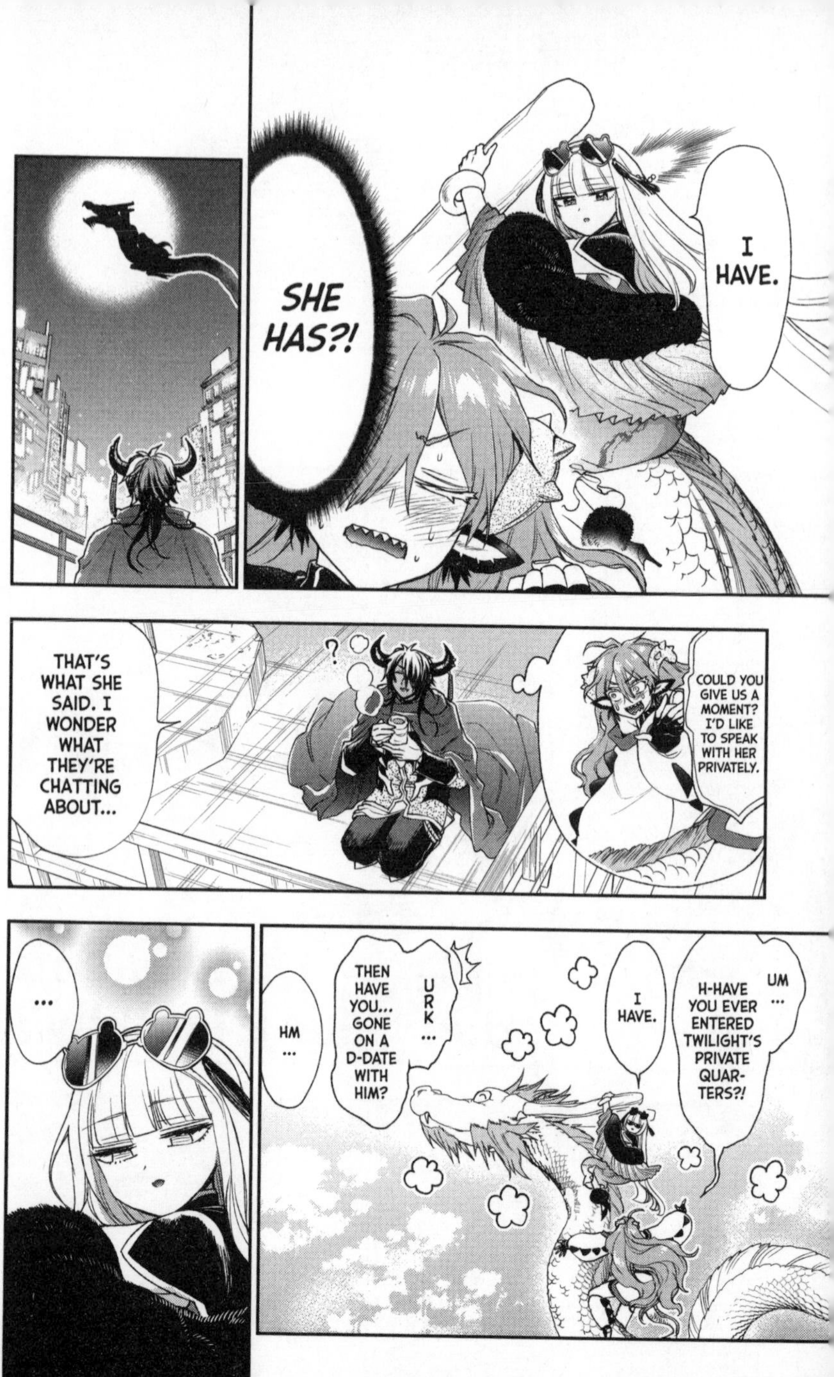
I HAVE.
SHE HAS?!
COULD YOU GIVE US A MOMENT? I'D LIKE TO SPEAK WITH HER PRIVATELY.
THAT'S WHAT SHE SAID. I WONDER WHAT THEY'RE CHATTING ABOUT...
UM...
H-HAVE YOU EVER ENTERED TWILIGHT'S PRIVATE QUAR-TERS?!
I HAVE.
URK...
THEN HAVE YOU... GONE ON A D-DATE WITH HIM?
HM...
...

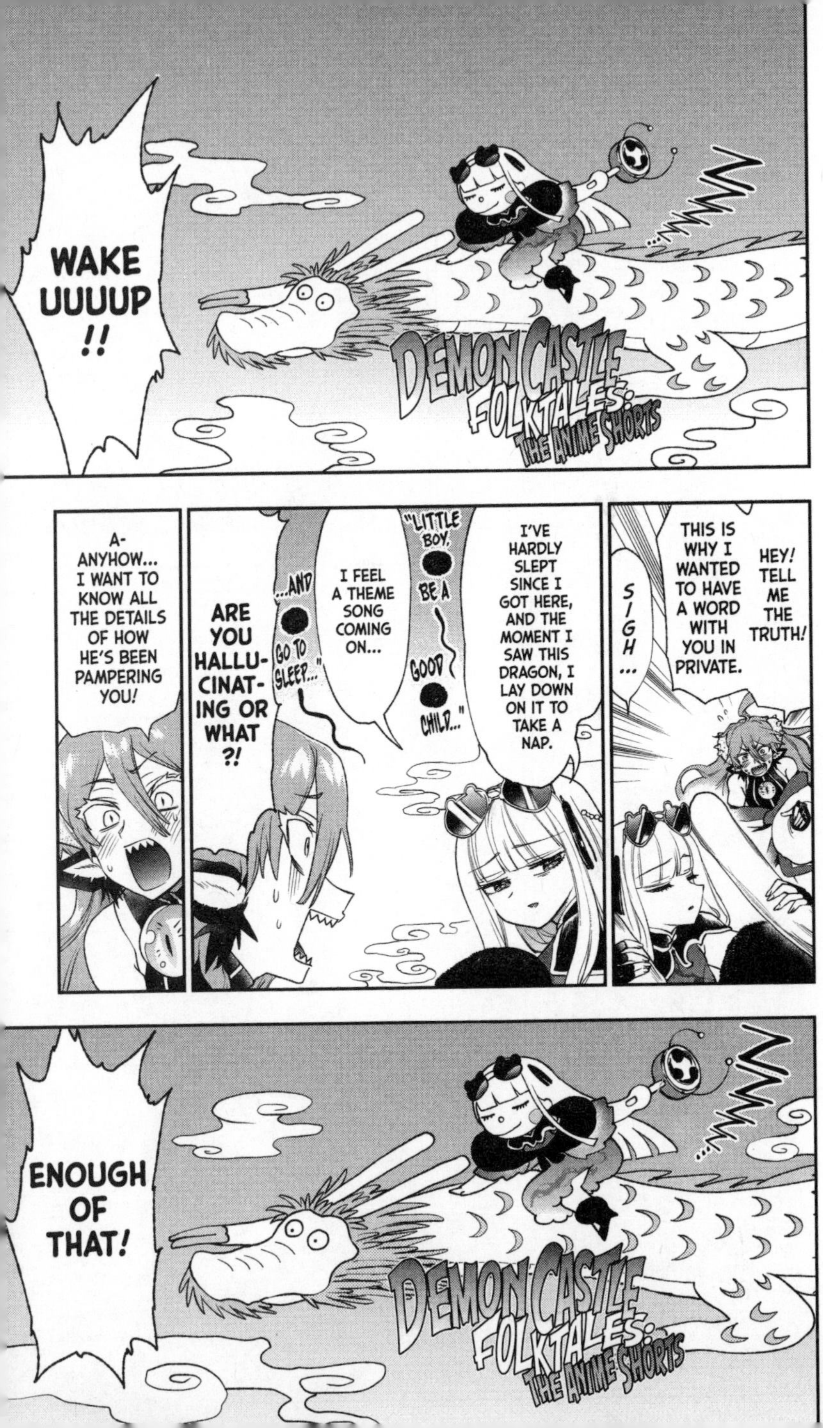
WAKE UUUUP!!
DEMON CASTLE FOLKTALES: THE ANIME SHORTS
HEY! TELL ME THE TRUTH!
THIS IS WHY I WANTED TO HAVE A WORD WITH YOU IN PRIVATE.
SIGH...
I'VE HARDLY SLEPT SINCE I GOT HERE, AND THE MOMENT I SAW THIS DRAGON, I LAY DOWN ON IT TO TAKE A NAP.
"LITTLE BOY, BE A GOOD CHILD..."
I FEEL A THEME SONG COMING ON...
...AND GO TO SLEEP..."
ARE YOU HALLUCINATING OR WHAT?!
A- ANYHOW... I WANT TO KNOW ALL THE DETAILS OF HOW HE'S BEEN PAMPERING YOU!
ENOUGH OF THAT!
DEMON CASTLE FOLKTALES: THE ANIME SHORTS

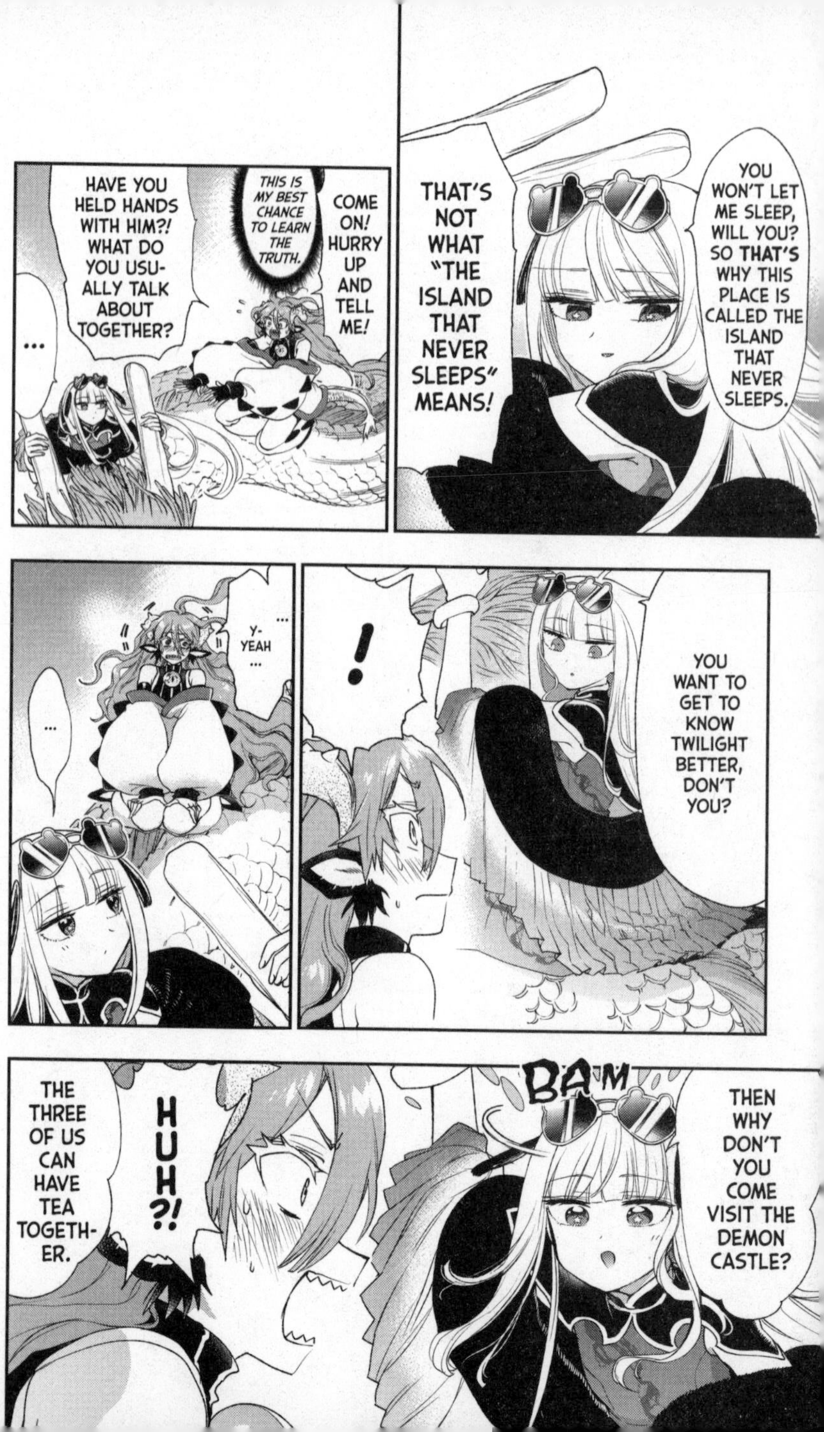
YOU WON'T LET ME SLEEP, WILL YOU? SO THAT'S WHY THIS PLACE IS CALLED THE ISLAND THAT NEVER SLEEPS.
THAT'S NOT WHAT "THE ISLAND THAT NEVER SLEEPS" MEANS!
COME ON! HURRY UP AND TELL ME!
THIS IS MY BEST CHANCE TO LEARN THE TRUTH.
HAVE YOU HELD HANDS WITH HIM?! WHAT DO YOU USU-ALLY TALK ABOUT TOGETHER?
...
!
YOU WANT TO GET TO KNOW TWILIGHT BETTER, DON'T YOU?
... Y-YEAH ...
...
BAM
THEN WHY DON'T YOU COME VISIT THE DEMON CASTLE?
HUH?!
THE THREE OF US CAN HAVE TEA TOGETH-ER.

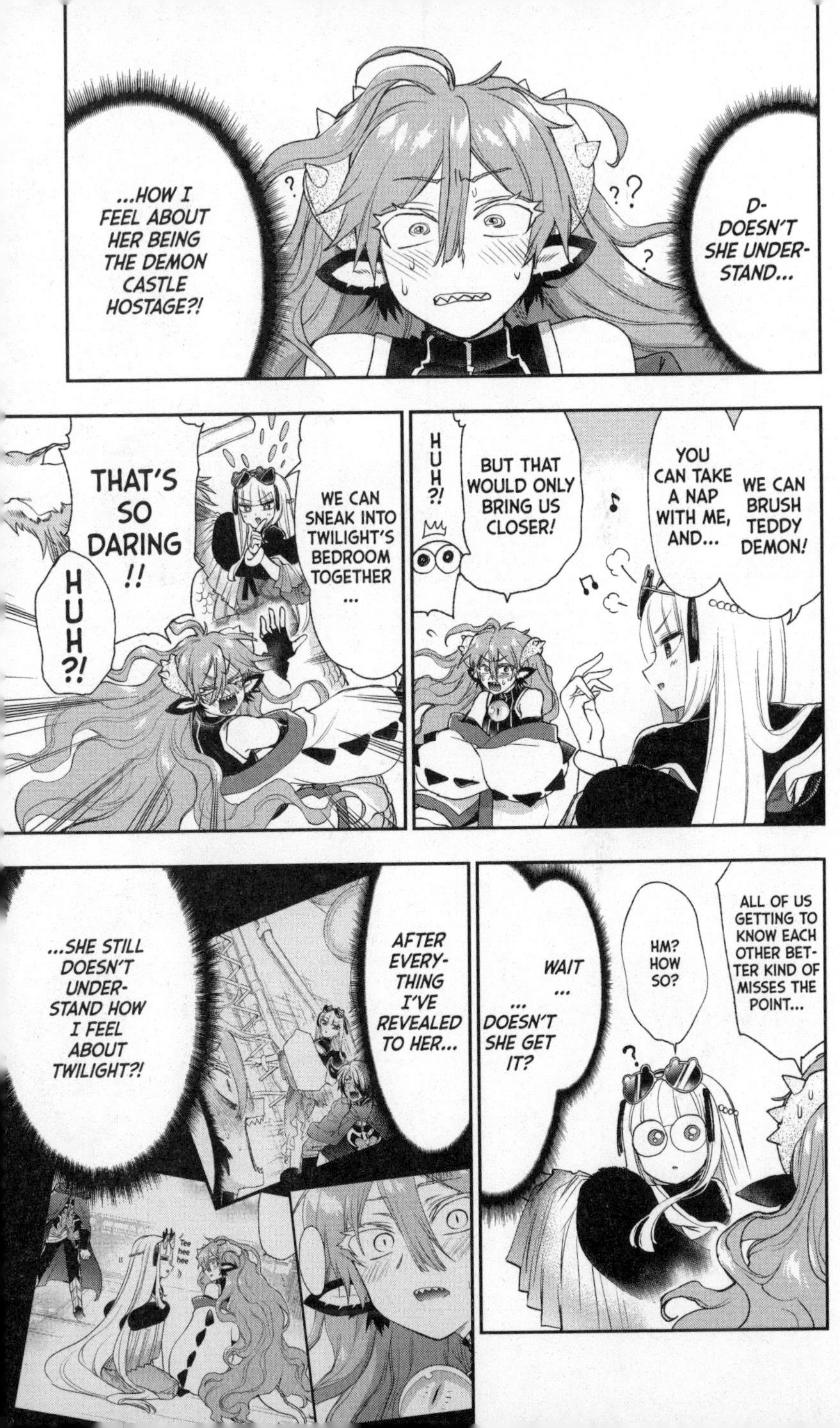
D-DOESN'T SHE UNDERSTAND...
...HOW I FEEL ABOUT HER BEING THE DEMON CASTLE HOSTAGE?!
WE CAN BRUSH TEDDY DEMON!
YOU CAN TAKE A NAP WITH ME, AND...
BUT THAT WOULD ONLY BRING US CLOSER!
HUH?!
WE CAN SNEAK INTO TWILIGHT'S BEDROOM TOGETHER...
THAT'S SO DARING!!
HUH?!
ALL OF US GETTING TO KNOW EACH OTHER BETTER KIND OF MISSES THE POINT...
HM? HOW SO?
WAIT... ...DOESN'T SHE GET IT?
AFTER EVERYTHING I'VE REVEALED TO HER...
...SHE STILL DOESN'T UNDERSTAND HOW I FEEL ABOUT TWILIGHT?!
Tee hee hee

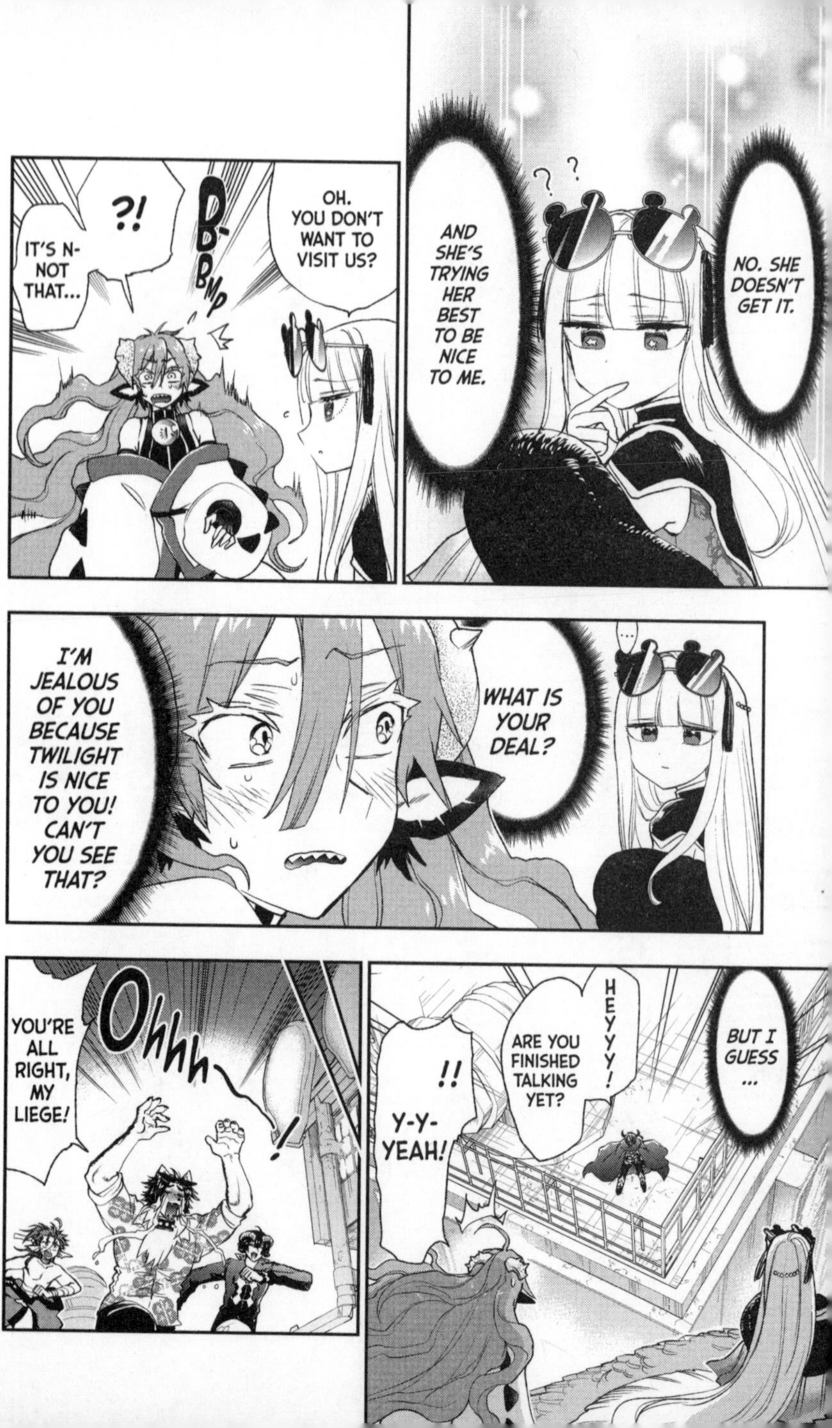
? ?
NO. SHE DOESN'T GET IT.
AND SHE'S TRYING HER BEST TO BE NICE TO ME.
OH. YOU DON'T WANT TO VISIT US?
B-BMP
?!
IT'S N-NOT THAT...
...
WHAT IS YOUR DEAL?
I'M JEALOUS OF YOU BECAUSE TWILIGHT IS NICE TO YOU! CAN'T YOU SEE THAT?
BUT I GUESS ...
HEYYY!
ARE YOU FINISHED TALKING YET?
!!
Y-Y-YEAH!
Ohhh~!
YOU'RE ALL RIGHT, MY LIEGE!

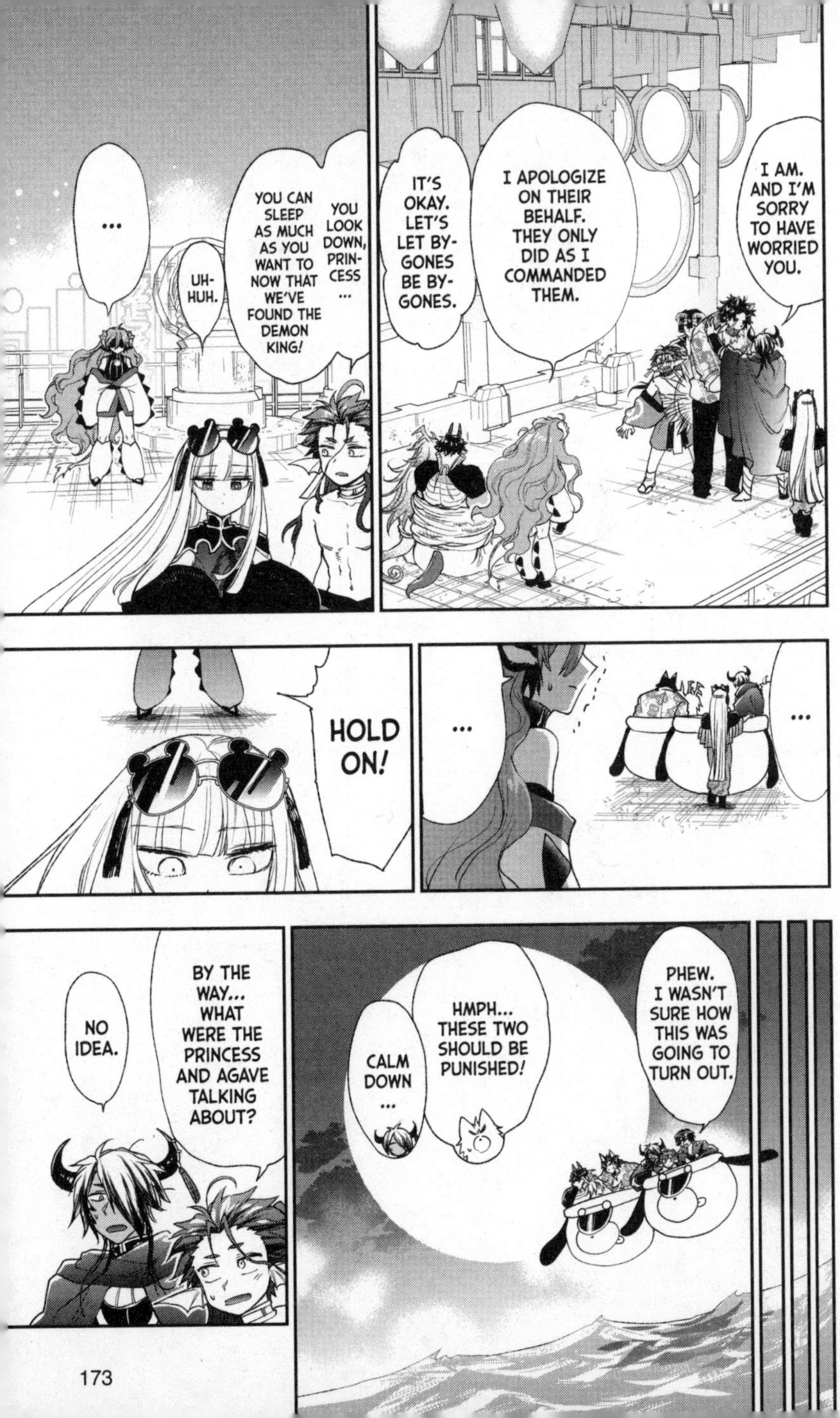
I AM. AND I'M SORRY TO HAVE WORRIED YOU.
I APOLOGIZE ON THEIR BEHALF. THEY ONLY DID AS I COMMANDED THEM.
IT'S OKAY. LET'S LET BYGONES BE BYGONES.
YOU LOOK DOWN, PRINCESS...
YOU CAN SLEEP AS MUCH AS YOU WANT TO NOW THAT WE'VE FOUND THE DEMON KING!
UH-HUH.
...
...
...
HOLD ON!
PHEW. I WASN'T SURE HOW THIS WAS GOING TO TURN OUT.
HMPH... THESE TWO SHOULD BE PUNISHED!
CALM DOWN...
BY THE WAY... WHAT WERE THE PRINCESS AND AGAVE TALKING ABOUT?
NO IDEA.

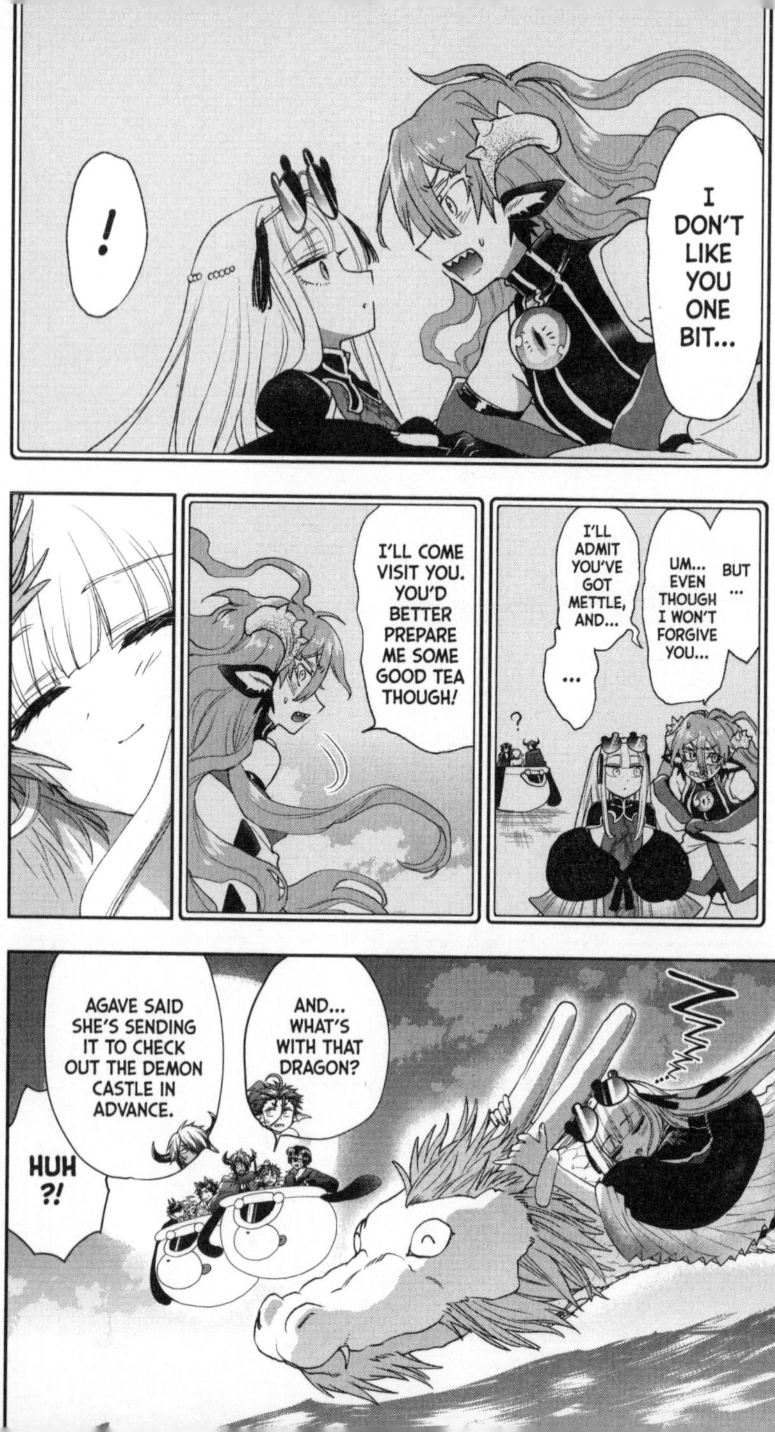
I DON'T LIKE YOU ONE BIT...
!
UM... EVEN THOUGH I WON'T FORGIVE YOU...
BUT ...
I'LL ADMIT YOU'VE GOT METTLE, AND...
...
?
I'LL COME VISIT YOU. YOU'D BETTER PREPARE ME SOME GOOD TEA THOUGH!
AND... WHAT'S WITH THAT DRAGON?
AGAVE SAID SHE'S SENDING IT TO CHECK OUT THE DEMON CASTLE IN ADVANCE.
HUH ?!

How to Kidnap the Demon King

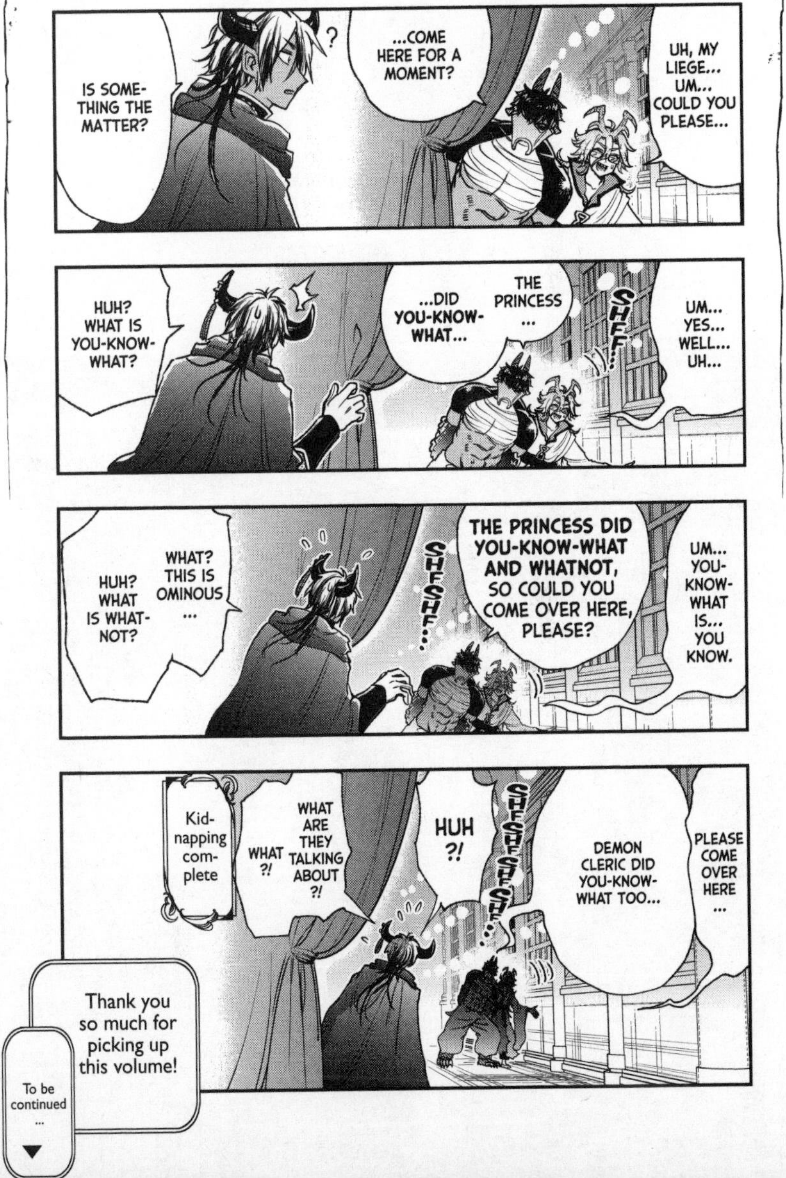
UH, MY LIEGE... UM... COULD YOU PLEASE...
...COME HERE FOR A MOMENT?
?
IS SOME-THING THE MATTER?
UM... YES... WELL... UH...
SHFF...
THE PRINCESS ...
...DID YOU-KNOW-WHAT...
HUH? WHAT IS YOU-KNOW-WHAT?
UM... YOU-KNOW-WHAT IS... YOU KNOW.
THE PRINCESS DID YOU-KNOW-WHAT AND WHATNOT, SO COULD YOU COME OVER HERE, PLEASE?
SHFSHF...
WHAT? THIS IS OMINOUS ...
HUH? WHAT IS WHAT-NOT?
PLEASE COME OVER HERE ...
DEMON CLERIC DID YOU-KNOW-WHAT TOO...
SHFSHFSHFSHF...
HUH ?!
WHAT ARE THEY TALKING ABOUT ?!
WHAT ?!
Kid-napping com-plete
Thank you so much for picking up this volume!
To be continued ...

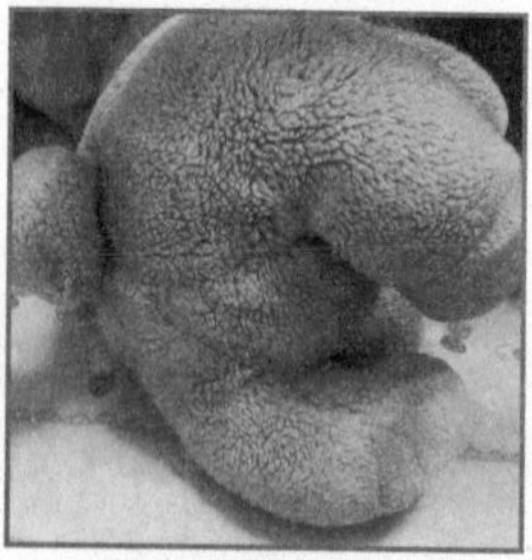

It's starting to take me a lot longer to complete my final drafts!!

– KAGIJI KUMANOMATA

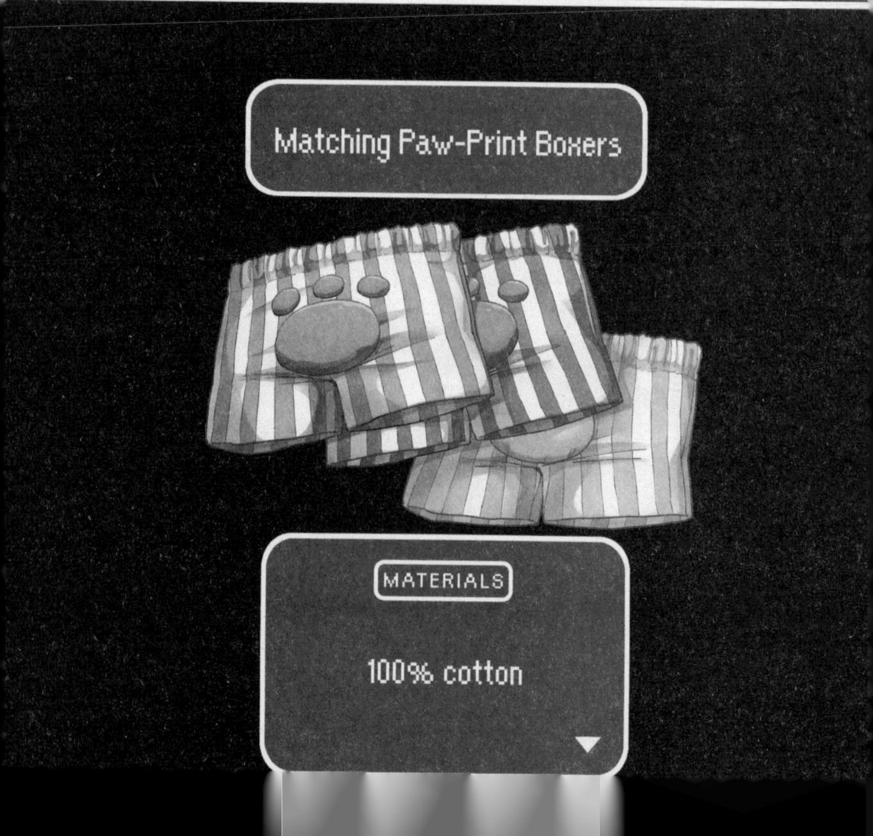
Matching Paw-Print Boxers
MATERIALS
100% cotton

Those who lurk beneath the cover...

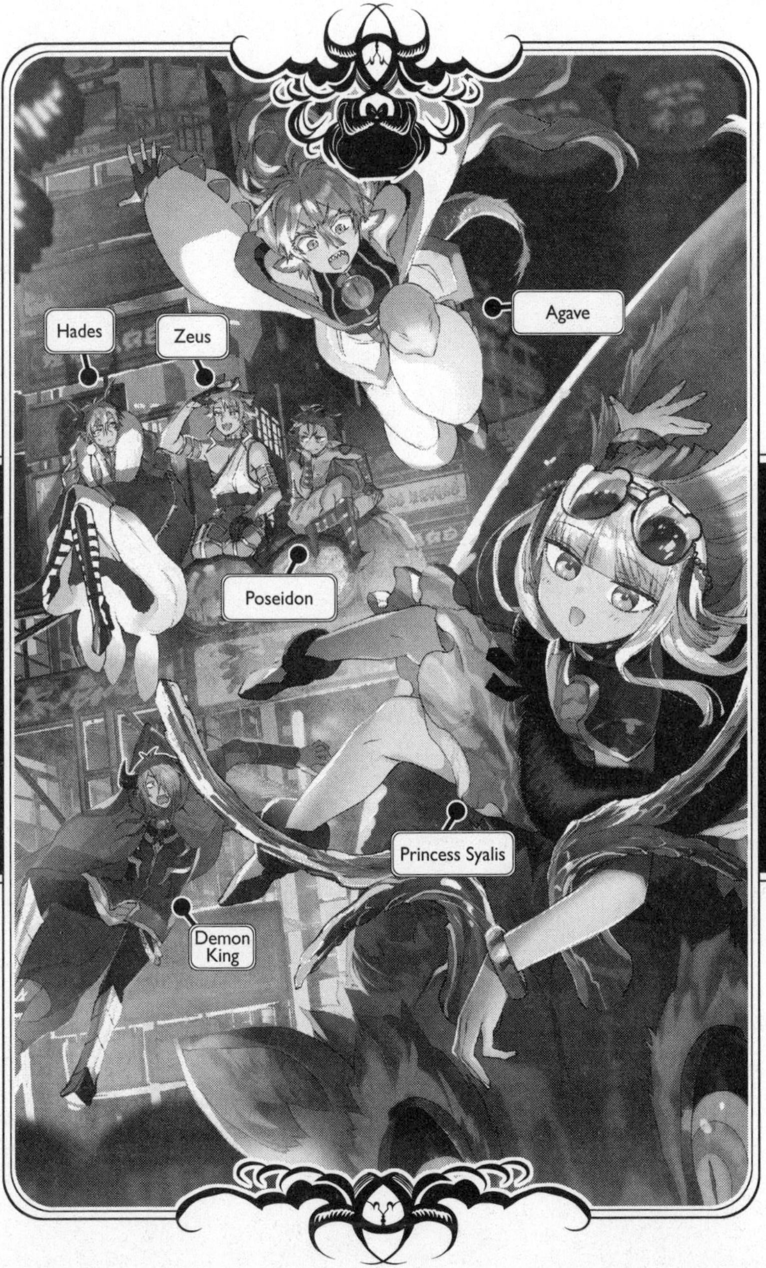

Agave
Hades
Zeus
Poseidon
Princess Syalis
Demon King

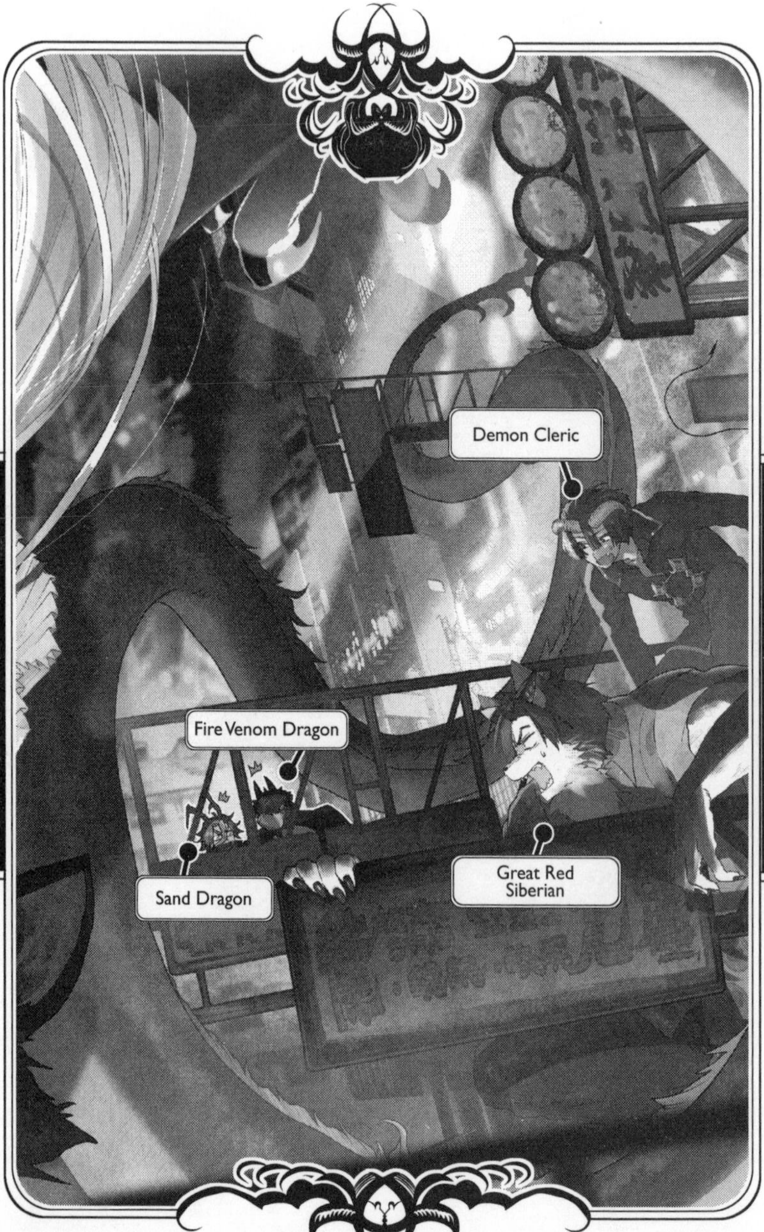
Demon Cleric
Fire Venom Dragon
Sand Dragon
Great Red Siberian

SLEEPY PRINCESS IN THE DEMON CASTLE

15

Shonen Sunday Edition

STORY AND ART BY

KAGIJI KUMANOMATA

MAOUJO DE OYASUMI Vol. 15
by Kagiji KUMANOMATA
© 2016 Kagiji KUMANOMATA
All rights reserved.
Original Japanese edition published by SHOGAKUKAN.
English translation rights in the United States of America, Canada,
the United Kingdom, Ireland, Australia and New Zealand arranged
with SHOGAKUKAN.

TRANSLATION **TETSUICHIRO MIYAKI**

ENGLISH ADAPTATION **ANNETTE ROMAN**

TOUCH-UP ART & LETTERING **JAMES GAUBATZ**

COVER & INTERIOR DESIGN **ALICE LEWIS**

EDITOR **ANNETTE ROMAN**

The stories, characters and incidents mentioned in this publication
are entirely fictional.

Printed in the U.S.A.

Published by VIZ Media, LLC
P.O. Box 77010
San Francisco, CA 94107

10 9 8 7 6 5 4 3 2 1
First printing, August 2021

 MEDIA

viz.com

shonensunday.com

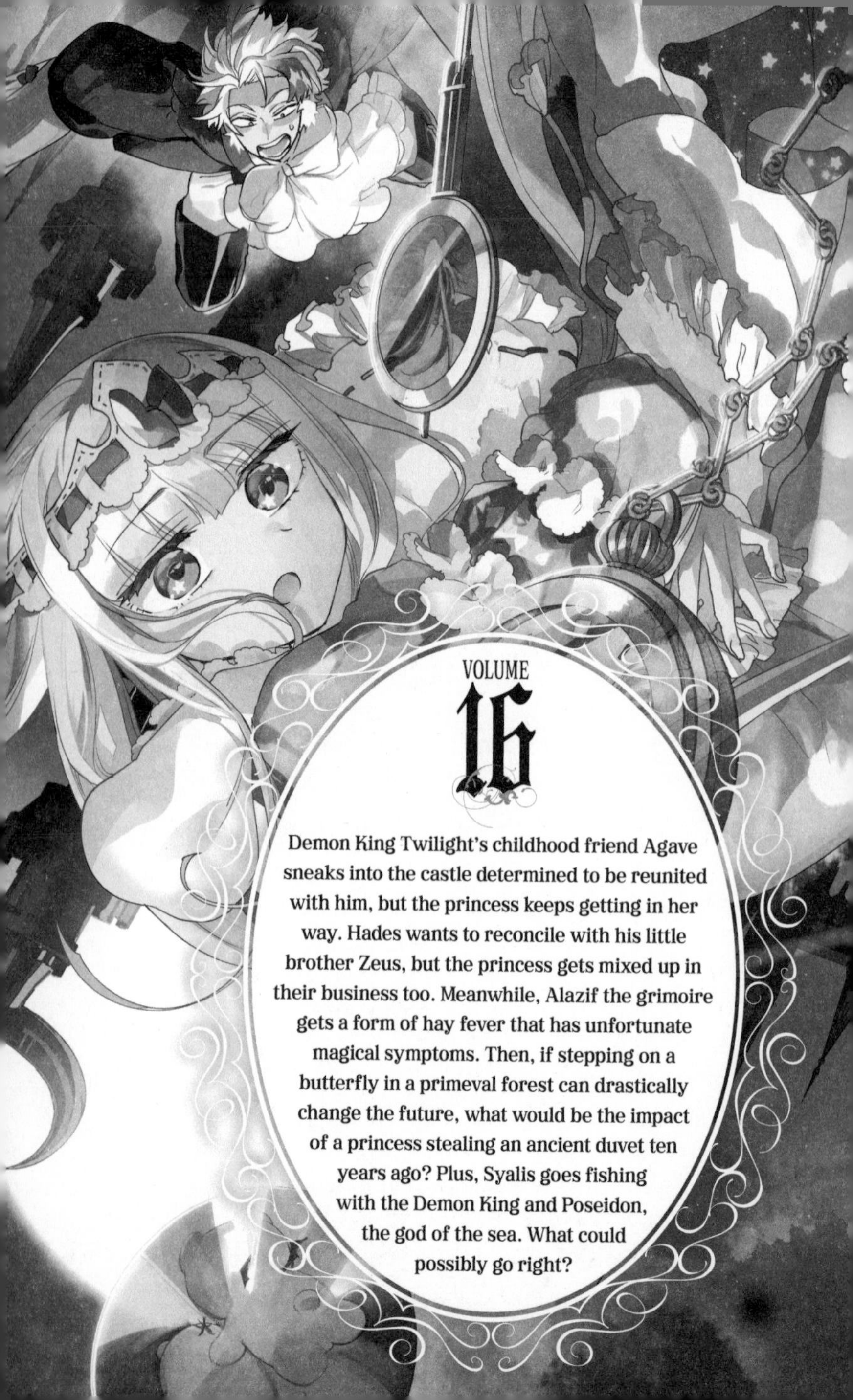

VOLUME

16

Demon King Twilight's childhood friend Agave sneaks into the castle determined to be reunited with him, but the princess keeps getting in her way. Hades wants to reconcile with his little brother Zeus, but the princess gets mixed up in their business too. Meanwhile, Alazif the grimoire gets a form of hay fever that has unfortunate magical symptoms. Then, if stepping on a butterfly in a primeval forest can drastically change the future, what would be the impact of a princess stealing an ancient duvet ten years ago? Plus, Syalis goes fishing with the Demon King and Poseidon, the god of the sea. What could possibly go right?

Komi Can't Communicate

Story & Art by Tomohito Oda

The journey to a hundred friends begins with a single conversation.

Socially anxious high school student Shoko Komi's greatest dream is to make some friends, but everyone at school mistakes her crippling social anxiety for cool reserve. With the whole student body keeping its distance and Komi unable to utter a single word, friendship might be forever beyond her reach.

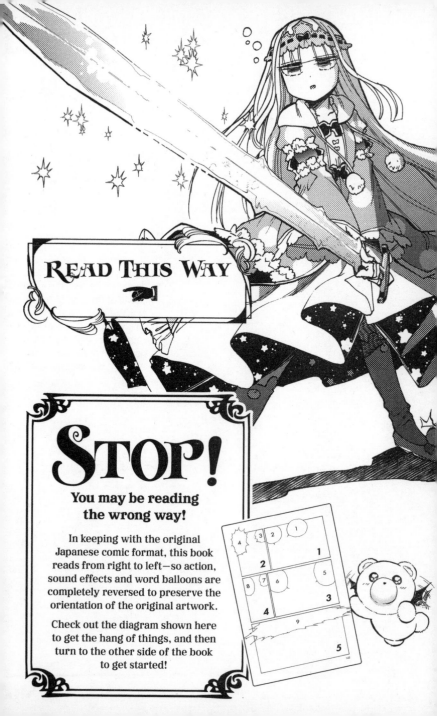

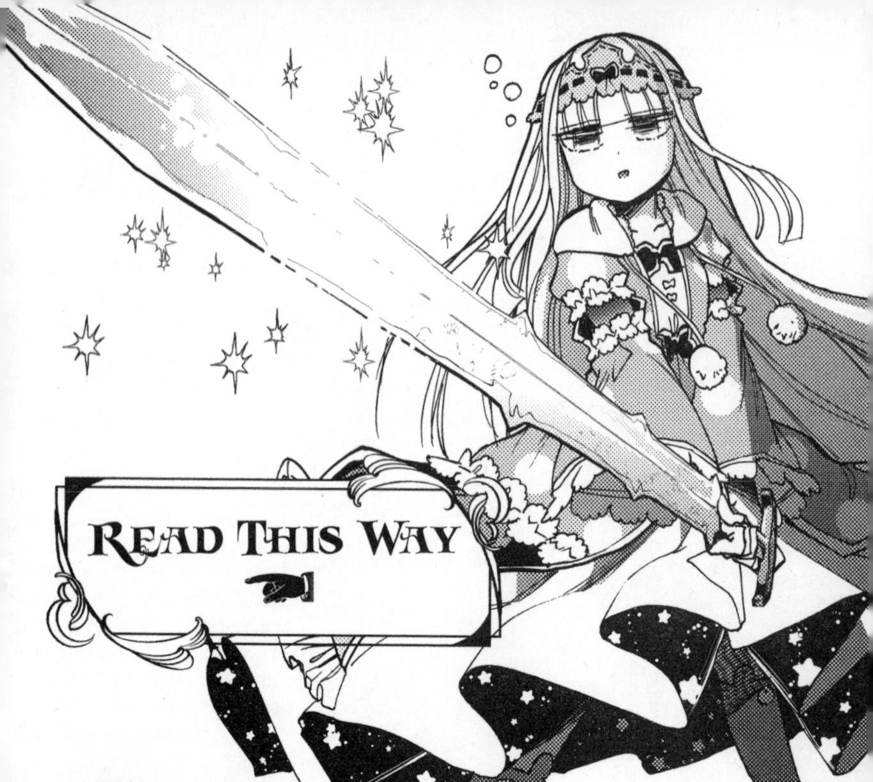
READ THIS WAY

STOP!

You may be reading the wrong way!

In keeping with the original Japanese comic format, this book reads from right to left—so action, sound effects and word balloons are completely reversed to preserve the orientation of the original artwork.

Check out the diagram shown here to get the hang of things, and then turn to the other side of the book to get started!

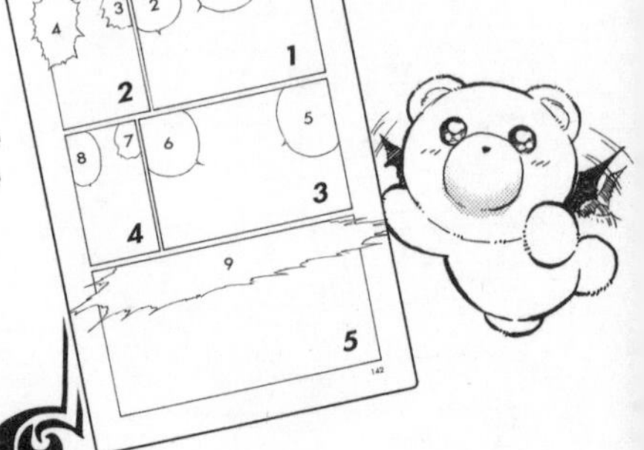